BEYOND THE PRISON GATES

Studies in Legal History

Published by the
University of North Carolina Press
in association with the American Society
for Legal History

Thomas A. Green, Hendrik Hartog, and
Daniel Ernst, *editors*

The University of

North Carolina Press

Chapel Hill

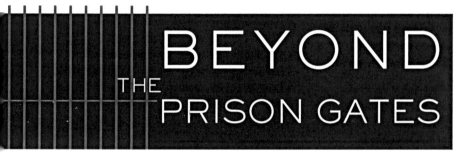

BEYOND THE PRISON GATES

*Punishment & Welfare
in Germany, 1850–1933*

WARREN ROSENBLUM

© 2008 The University of
North Carolina Press
All rights reserved

Designed by Jacquline Johnson
Set in Minion
by Keystone Typesetting, Inc.
Manufactured in the
United States of America

The paper in this book
meets the guidelines for
permanence and durability
of the Committee on
Production Guidelines for
Book Longevity of the
Council on Library
Resources.

The University of North
Carolina Press has been a
member of the Green Press
Initiative since 2003.

THIS BOOK WAS DIGITALLY PRINTED.

Library of Congress Cataloging-in-Publication Data
Rosenblum, Warren.
Beyond the prison gates : punishment and welfare in
Germany, 1850–1933 / Warren Rosenblum.
p. cm. — (Studies in legal history)
Includes bibliographical references and index.
ISBN 978-0-8078-3204-2 (cloth : alk. paper)
1. Punishment—Germany—History. 2. Criminals—
Rehabilitation—Germany—History. 3. Criminal justice,
Administration of—Social aspects—Germany—History.
I. Title.
HV9358.R67 2008
364.60943'09034—dc22

2008027196

12 11 10 09 08   5 4 3 2 1

For *Mom,*
Nicole, Eve,
and Vera

CONTENTS

ILLUSTRATIONS

ACKNOWLEDGMENTS

At various stages of this project, friends, colleagues, and mentors provided support and assistance. I owe a special debt to Kathleen Canning and Geoff Eley for insights, inspiration, and a few doses of tough love. Tom Green read multiple versions of this work and offered invaluable advice and encouragement.

Wolf Gruner, Sandra Gruner-Domic, Julia Bellabarba, and Bodo Pisarsky made Berlin into a warm and wonderful place and tried their best to make a geeky midwesterner into an *echt* Berliner. Mindy Roseman, Jean Quataert, Richard Wetzell, Drew Bergerson, Gaby Finder, Kathy Pence, Henry Pickford, Brian Kennelly, Peter Rosenblum, Jon Rosenblum, and Nicole Blumner offered skeptical questions and critical comments here and there over the years.

My colleagues at Webster University have made St. Louis into an intellectually stimulating environment. I especially want to thank Dan Hellinger for setting an example as scholar-teacher and universal gadfly and Dean David Wilson, who provided me with a course release and significant cheerleading at a crucial stage in this work.

Professor Andrew Lees and an anonymous reader for University of North Carolina Press offered many helpful suggestions.

A fellowship from the German Academic Exchange Service allowed me to complete the initial research for this book, while a Charlotte Newcombe Fellowship gave me time to write. A faculty research grant from Webster University allowed me to return to Germany for follow-up investigations.

The staff of Webster University's Emerson Library provided enormous assistance. I would especially like to thank Sara Fitzpatrick, Will Soll, Christine Dugan, and Erik Palmore. I also want to thank librarians and archivists at the Archiv des diakonischen Werkes, Geheimes Staatsarchiv preussischer Kulturbesitz, Staatsbibliothek Berlin, Bielefeld Stadtsarchiv, and the archive at Bethel.

Special thanks go to the perpetual seminar of Rosenblums: Susan, Ellen, Laura, Keith, Jon, Peter, and Josh, and all the (relative) newcomers whose name (as Grama Vera would say) is legion. My father, Victor Rosenblum, inspired my initial interest in law—as a "Political Instrument," a source of (his)stories, a collection of puzzles. He would have been the most eager and attentive of readers, and I miss him.

My mother, Louise Rosenblum, whom I sometimes suspected of clandestine work for the editors at UNC Press, has been a first-class *noodge* and an inexhaustible source of love and enthusiasm. My daughters, Eve and Vera, kept me young, alert, and preternaturally happy. My only regret is not having done more research on princesses (maybe in the next book). Nicole Blumner lived with this project—even when it was a rude, uninvited guest on Saturday nights and family vacations. It would take a whole other book at least to acknowledge what I owe her for the past six years.

BEYOND THE PRISON GATES

INTRODUCTION

One could have reasonably expected Germans after World War I to support harsh measures against criminal offenders. In the immediate postwar years, rates of burglary, theft, and violent assault increased precipitously. The press, enjoying a now limitless freedom, produced lurid accounts of murders and armed criminal gangs terrorizing the citizenry. Even otherwise sober analysts of crime were caught up in this social panic. A leading criminologist claimed that degenerate soldiers had abandoned their units and, along with escaped prison and workhouse inmates (many of them liberated by the revolutionary mobs of 1919), were preying on the domestic population. A prominent liberal judge and reformer pointed his finger at foreign criminals who were exploiting the collapse of border controls and Germany's overall state of weakness.[1] With popular fear and anger brewing, this seemed an unlikely time for experiments in criminal policy.

Yet the early Weimar Republic saw far-reaching reforms aimed at ameliorating the treatment of criminal offenders. A Prussian state decree of 1919 abolished corporal punishment and the rule of silence in prisons and allowed prisoners greater correspondence with the outside world. A law of 1920 protected the privacy of ex-offenders by restricting official access to criminal records and actually erasing these records following a certain period of law-abiding behavior. The 1923 Juvenile Court law profoundly altered the treatment of youth offenders. Other decrees streamlined the processing of pardons and encouraged judges and administrators to be merciful in cases with mitigating circumstances. In the midst of a massive crime wave, a dramatic increase in pardons—from 23,000 in 1919 to 125,000 two years later—easily outpaced the rise in convictions.[2] The most far-reaching reform was the establishment of *Soziale Gerichtshilfe*, welfare advisers who investigated the personal and social backgrounds of adult offenders, provided "social diagnoses" to judges and penal officials, and arranged for protective supervision for those deemed worthy of a conditional pardon.[3]

Many Weimar commentators believed they were witnessing a fundamental transformation in the nature of criminal justice. Prussian official (and future Supreme Court president) Erwin Bumke wrote that reforms were unfolding as if "driven by an irresistible natural law." Legal scholar Wolfgang Mittermaier enthused that Gerichtshilfe was destined to bring judges down from their elevated positions and place them at a "roundtable" with social experts and welfare volunteers to decide on the most practical and just treatment for offenders. At a landmark conference on "the asocial question," Pastor Paul Troschke declared that Germany was at a juncture in criminal reform similar to the era in psychiatric care when the no-restraint system "competed with the straitjacket" and concern for healing the insane challenged the tradition of "merely protecting the public." In spite of the chronic social and political crises of the Weimar era, it was possible to believe that—at least in the area of criminal justice—progress and enlightenment were on the march.[4]

This book describes the origins and the consequences of this "irresistible" reform wave. Recent histories of German criminal policy have focused largely on the triumph of biomedical theories of crime that embodied the darker, exclusionary aspects of modern criminal reform. Such works have traced a clear, if tortuous, path from the "medicalization" of crime in the 1880s to the authoritarian, racial hygienic measures against criminals under the Nazis.[5] The present account differs in its focus on modern criminal reform as a subset of the social question. As Jacques Donzelot argues, the social question was not simply about poverty but concerned the problem of "general solidarity and the production of a life-style." Nineteenth-century social reformers sought to understand and affect family relations, education, and work, in order to provide even the most marginal citizens with the security to withstand the stresses of economic and political and personal dislocation.[6] A social approach to criminal policy required protective supervision for criminally at-risk individuals, something fundamentally different (or so it was claimed) from the repressive police supervision and retributive justice of the classical penal system.

The protagonists of this story are thus not the great criminologists and legal theorists who dominate recent accounts, but the practical reformers who created institutions and organizations that defined and facilitated a social approach to crime. Prisoner benevolence associations made the ex-offender into an object of social intervention. Worker colonies and women's asylums created models for the supervision of weak-willed, unsteady persons who were at risk of becoming criminal. Anti-prostitution groups carved out spaces for women charitable workers as advisers to the courts and the police. Utopian projects, like the effort to create colonies for ex-offenders in Africa and the South Seas, stretched the imaginative boundaries of criminal policy even when they were not realized in practice. By century's end, the concept of criminal policy encompassed a whole range of nonpunitive, extra-juridical welfare measures. During World War I, an alliance of Christian charities, reform-minded jurists, and state officials sought to institutionalize the nexus between welfare and justice, giving private associations a formal voice within criminal justice. While reform on a grand scale continually stalled, the local efforts of myriad reform associations set the stage for the remarkable transformation of criminal policy during the Weimar Republic.

The impact of criminal policy reforms before, during, and after World War I was complex and paradoxical. There is no doubt that punishment became milder in the fifty years between 1880 and 1930. One need only point to the increase in pardons (one critic called it the "pardon plague"), lighter sentences, improved prison conditions, and the decline of police supervision and other restrictions on ex-offenders. The overwhelming trend in criminal policy—illustrated by the rise of Gerichtshilfe in the Weimar years—was to bring a therapeutic discourse into all areas of the criminal justice system. The welfarization of criminal policy was only partially halted during the Third Reich and then only temporarily. It climaxed in the German criminal reforms of the 1950s and 1960s.

The history of social approaches to criminal policy points to interesting continuities between the Wilhelmine era and our own that most historians, focused on the paths from progressivism to Nazism, have ignored.[7] Today rates of incarceration in Germany are among the lowest in the world, while prison conditions are among the best. Social welfare principles play an essential role at all levels of the German criminal justice system.[8] Franz von Liszt's declaration that the "best criminal policy is social policy" and the Weimar reformers' cry that "true punishment is welfare work" have both found their realization in contemporary German criminal justice.[9] This study tries to give these "German peculiarities" their due.

There are, however, important connections between the struggle to make justice social in Wilhelmine and Weimar Germany and the harsh, dehumanizing criminal policy measures introduced under the Nazis. First, the reformers' infatuation with welfare as a tool of criminal policy gave new legitimacy to extra-juridical surveillance and control of former offenders and even at-risk persons who had never committed a crime. After a decades-long struggle to tame police power and bolster judicial authority, many liberals and Socialists in the Weimar era embraced the concept of a new police state. Their faith in welfare institutions overshadowed their historical misgivings about administrative power. Even if they opposed the Nazi seizure of power (and most did), the reformers' distrust of the judiciary, ambivalence about individual rights, and optimism about enlightened administration undermined the liberal Rechtsstaat and softened resistance to authoritarian innovations.[10]

Second, the National Socialists' criminal policies were defined largely as a response to the crisis in criminal reform during the Weimar Republic. The origins of this crisis were in the distinctively German competition over the control of welfare between private, mostly Christian charities and public welfare offices affiliated with Socialist and left-liberal city governments.[11] The progressive vision of criminal policy reform assumed that state governments must establish bureaucracies for the social diagnosis and supervision of offenders.[12] This is what happened in most American states and in England in the years prior to World War I. German law scholar Franz von Liszt, the leader of the "Modern School" in criminal reform, praised American reformers for building a probation system that granted broad powers to trained welfare advisers.[13] In the Weimar Republic, however, Saxony was the only state to create its own agencies for the diagnosis and supervision of offenders. In the super-state of Prussia, an alliance of "robe and frock"—clergy and judges—blocked the progressive agenda by preventing state agencies from controlling welfare's engagement with criminal justice. Judges and clergy feared that state welfare offices would seize control of criminal policy and destroy the moral economy of punishment, pardoning, and assistance for released offenders.

The failure to develop a viable, broadly accepted state model for the social diagnosis and supervision of offenders resulted in widespread accusations that reform meant simply the "softening" (*Verweichlichung*) of justice. Four and a half times as many persons were conditionally pardoned between 1921 and 1924 as in the four years leading up to World War I, and the rates of pardons stayed high throughout the Weimar era. Fines and supervision in lieu of incarceration became the norm for many lesser crimes. Yet the social turn in Weimar justice was not accompanied by the anticipated growth in the mechanisms of social assistance or social control. Offenders increasingly avoided incarceration but were not subject to the kinds of guidance and oversight supposed necessary to making them social.

It is in this context that this book explores the growing importance of scientific criminology and its impact upon policy. There is no doubt, as recent historians have shown, that support for medical-hygienic approaches to crime grew in the 1890s and accelerated after World War I. This does not mean, however, as Richard Evans asserts, that German society adopted a "darker view of the criminal as . . . fundamentally incorrigible." In spite of a cultural fascination with Lombroso's "born criminal" and other criminological bogeymen, social approaches to crime flourished in Germany, with remarkably broad support, even into the Great Depression. For reformers, "criminal biology" provided not a manual or blueprint for criminal policy, but a set of tools for refining and improving ongoing projects. Criminology provided scientific legitimacy for reformers in a period of growing contradictions and crisis. It rescued the plausibility of a social approach to criminal policy.

This book thus questions the privileged place of science or the "rise of a scientific worldview" in the historiography of German social policy. As Edward Dickinson notes, recent work in the history of "biopolitics" has created a new master narrative in German history from the Kaiserreich to the Nazis. Historians depict the reform of welfare, health, and reproduction as an essentially undemocratic, elite-driven process.[14] Typical is Paul Weindling's assertion that "scientifically-educated experts" after 1880 "acquired a directing role as prescribers of social polices and personal lifestyle." Weindling argues that the state assumed increasing control over medical and welfare policy particularly during the First World War and forced social practice to conform to scientific principles.[15] Historians Christoph Sachße and Florian Tennstedt likewise summarize the transformation of social policy as a single integrated process of "scientification, nationalization, and professionalization."[16] The new faith in science, they argue, reconstituted the very goals and purpose of government.[17]

Historians of German criminal policy have especially emphasized the role of bio-medical research in promoting harsh exclusionary policies toward legal offenders. Christian Müller argues that psychiatric paradigms increasingly dominated criminal policy starting in the 1870s. According to Richard Evans, the emergence of criminology undermined the "previous liberal faith" in rehabilitative ideals and practice. In the 1920s, Evans claims, criminal biology "push[ed] . . . the social theory of crime out to the margins." Peter Becker argues similarly that criminology shifted the concerns of criminal policy away from social practices and lived experience and toward abstract categories of deviance. The rise of criminologists, he suggests, meant the decline of the "practitioner," that is, the practical men and women who sought to morally transform criminal offenders by attending to their education and environment. The "medicalization" of crime, historians assert, stripped the criminal from his social context.[18]

The master narrative of criminal policy in the age of criminology, however, frequently ignores the strong sociological currents, the nuances, and ambiguities in German criminology.[19] Richard Wetzell's detailed study of criminology demonstrates that researchers in the Kaiserreich and the Weimar Republic never lost their appreciation for the social origins of crime. Even the leading proponents of a eugenic approach to criminology, he observes, rarely believed in a "rigid biological determinism that dismissed environmental factors." If German criminologists increasingly focused on racial hygiene in the 1920s and 1930s, he argues, this was "because they had convinced themselves that the social causes of crime were intractable."[20]

Most important, the focus on the repressive aspects of biopolitics fails to take full account of the emancipatory impulses behind social policy reforms from the 1880s through the Weimar Republic. As Andrew Lees's work on "cities and sin" in the Imperial era demonstrates, policies toward felons, prostitutes, and the homeless were inspired in good part by empathy with the downtrodden and dismay with the cruelty and inefficiencies of Imperial governance.[21] Legal historian James Whitman notes that Christian ideals of mercy and compassion produced a concern for the dignity of "honorable" offenders. Starting in the 1850s and continuing well into the twentieth century, Whitman argues, preoccupations with the "morally worthy" offender led to milder punishments and increased granting of pardons.[22] Kevin Repp's study of the "generation of 1890" and Young-Sun Hong's work on welfare in the Weimar era each document how the concept of social citizenship animated the reform milieus.[23]

The historical literature has not adequately addressed the impact of the many ambitious, at some points utopian, projects to rescue and transform criminals. How did the success or failure of social reform efforts shape the image of the criminal and the goals of criminal policy? Why did criminologists, in Wetzell's words, increasingly come to see the social roots of crime as "intractable"? Why did proponents of a social criminal policy increasingly turn to biomedical models? Recent studies of criminology and criminal justice leave us with a pair of tautologies: first, that criminologists were limited by the "biases and assumptions" inherent to their professional identity; second, that secular, scientific belief systems after 1890 increasingly dominated reformers' perceptions of the social.[24] The present work tries to move beyond these tautologies by analyzing the politics of criminal policy reform in the contexts of cultural and economic change, war, and revolution. As Young Sun Hong has shown, welfare in modern Germany was always a highly contested arena. As welfare became part of criminal policy, individuals and organizations struggled fiercely for authority over the institutions and practices that would constitute this social terrain of justice. Understanding this struggle is vital to retracing the strange evolution of a social criminal policy in Germany.

This study moves between intellectual, institutional, and sociopolitical history. Chapter 1 explores the relationship between prison reform discourse in the nineteenth century and classical liberal ideals of citizenship and the rule of law. The chapter challenges the claim that a modern discourse of welfare control emerged only with the disintegration of liberal assumptions about the limits of state power. Even the purest forms of classical liberal jurisprudence, I argue, authorized extra-juridical administrative exclusions against subjects who were labeled outcasts. In this sense, the concepts of justice and police (*Rechtsstaat* and *Polizeistaat*) did not exist in a chronological relationship, nor were they binary opposites, but coexisted as different modes of regulation for different types of legal subjects. Social responses to crime, which had their roots in the Pietist movements of the Vormärz, flourished so long as they stayed within the domain of police control and did not affect the realm of justice. Johann Hinrich Wichern's effort to transform Prussian prisons according to Christian ideals produced a fierce liberal backlash with lasting effects.

In chapter 2, I describe how Christian social approaches to crime were reconstituted during the Imperial era. Protective supervision began as a voluntary welfare measure for released prisoners, wanderers, and in particular sexually endangered women and girls. Over time, however, protective supervision became increasingly entangled with criminal justice. This chapter explores this process by focusing in particular upon the history of worker colonies. The institution, which Friedrich von Bodelschwingh conceived as a sanctuary for willing and able workers who were victims of social circumstances, soon evolved into an asylum for weak-willed, "damaged" individuals who were otherwise a burden to society.

In chapter 3, I discuss the efforts to introduce the deportation or resettlement of criminals to German colonies overseas. While this utopian movement failed, it nevertheless marked an important step forward in imagining a comprehensive solution to the crime question in modern Germany. Penal colonies were inspired by the dream that every criminal could be made usable to the nation, and that many more could be resocialized if only they found their proper place. Chapter 4 examines the intensification of popular interest in the fate of ex-offenders in German society by focusing on one particular cultural event: the story of the "Captain from Köpenick," a life-long "prison bird" and vagabond, who became a national hero during the first decade of the new century. In the ten years before the war, while interest in deportation and resettlement persisted, practical steps were taken toward screening and adapting ex-criminals for a place in German society. With the continued growth of prison associations in the years leading up to the war, the concept of welfare for released criminals as a vital element within a comprehensive criminal policy gained significant ground.

Chapter 5 turns to the question of penal policy during the First World War, and the role of a "peace within the fortress" (*Burgfrieden*) in furthering interest in protective supervision and the integration of ex-offenders into the national economy. Chapter 6 traces the development of one particular institution, the Bielefeld System, which linked private associations for protective supervision directly with the criminal courts. Henceforth, criminal justice guaranteed the authority of social interventions against prostitutes, vagabonds, and former prisoners, while welfare provided a new flexibility for the courts both in defining the criminal and in addressing the causes of crime.

After World War I, there was a fragile consensus in favor of making welfare knowledge and technologies into a fundamental aspect of criminal policy more broadly. The social diagnosis of criminal offenders was to shape not merely the supervision that followed the punishment, but the punishment itself, and, at least in some minds, the determination of guilt or innocence. At this point, some of the most intractable and sensitive questions around the relationship of punishment and welfare reemerged. Who should initiate and who should control the social investigation of the criminal? How should social knowledge be used within the context of criminal procedure? How could public security be guaranteed even as the resocialization of offenders became the principal goal of criminal policy?

Chapter 7 traces the emergence of *Soziale Gerichtshilfe*, or "social court-assistance," an elaboration of the Bielefeld System which made social investigations a part of potentially all criminal trials. Fearing the triumph of administrative welfare and police ideologies, judges and prosecutors sought to appropriate this new institution and reassert the courts' control over punishment, pardoning, and protective supervision. At the same time, as part of their revolt against ossified legal traditions, the proponents of public welfare sought to use Gerichtshilfe as a vehicle for a more radical transformation of criminal policy, essentially absorbing justice into social policy. The ensuing debate over this institution became an important symbol of the crisis of modern criminal policy during the Weimar Republic.

Chapter 8 looks at the crisis of the criminal reform movement during the Weimar Republic in relationship to broader conflicts in public culture and politics. I look at three episodes in particular that revealed the growing clash of *Weltanschauungen* as left-leaning organizations appropriated the "traditional" themes of Christian social reformers. At the end of the Weimar Republic, reformers increasingly turned to racial hygienic tools as a way out of this crisis in the reform movement. The comprehensive screening of offenders according to biological, scientific criteria was supposed to render criminal policy safe for the continued use of liberal pardon policies and welfare interventions in lieu of incarceration. The triumph of criminal biology, I argue, was thus not a reaction against the project of making justice social, but was rather an effort to rescue its legitimacy.

THE "INTERNAL BORDERS"
Strategies of Exclusion in the Nineteenth Century

In his *Addresses to the German Nation*, Johann Gottlieb Fichte argued that "the first, original and truly natural borders of states are beyond doubt their internal borders." The people of one nation, he declared, "are joined to each other by a multitude of invisible bonds by nature herself, long before any human art begins." Fichte, a philosopher and erstwhile revolutionary, sought to rally his fellow Germans together at a time when the country's external borders were overrun by Napoleon's armies. The reinforcement of internal dividing lines, in his view, was essential to reviving the Fatherland. A true nation, he warned, cannot "absorb and mingle with itself any other people of different descent and language without itself becoming confused . . . and violently disturbing the even progress of its culture." Fichte's call for unity was thus predicated upon the idea of national purification: the recognition and the nurturing of "invisible bonds" required the recognition of the invisible sources of difference between citizen and Other, and the expulsion of the latter from the *Volk*.[1]

Decades ago, Hannah Arendt called Fichte "the favorite modern scapegoat for German race-thinking."[2] For more recent historians as well, Fichte's indulgence of romantic nationalism has been portrayed as the original sin in the German political imagination.[3] According to Leonard Krieger, "Fichte represented the liberal intellectual who was politicized, under the auspices of nationalism, in a conservative direction."[4] James Sheehan sees Fichte as typical of a generation, "propelled along a path from Enlightenment cosmopolitanism to intense national enthusiasm by the experiences of war and upheaval."[5] In these interpretations, a sober and universalist form of liberalism, based solidly upon principles of inclusion, was derailed by an impassioned, poetic mysticism driven by an obsession with eternal contaminations.[6]

This chapter challenges such an essential opposition between juridical liberalism and romantic nationalism by exploring the role of "hidden bonds" and "internal borders" within a classic enlightenment project, the creation of the modern *Rechtsstaat*. The so-called "classical-liberal" jurists in Germany understood the law as a tool not only for protecting the rights of citizens against arbitrary state power, but for defining and enforcing meaningful borders between the loyal and productive citizen and his other. Though liberal jurisprudence defined the criminal (*Verbrecher*) as the agent of a specific criminal act, liberal writings on police and penal practice operated with a more complex and flexible concept of criminality. In administrative theory and practice, the criminal connoted any person with a will or predisposition to illegal behavior. As a problem of policy, the criminal was not an isolated phenomenon but part of a larger "sociopolitical" challenge: the criminal class or subculture known as "*Verbrechertum*." Criminals were therefore presumed to constitute a distinct category of persons, united by conscious or unconscious bonds of affinity. In scholarly and popular writings of the nineteenth century, *Verbrechertum* could be compared to a hostile army occupying German territory or a virus living upon the body of the *Volk*. Like the Jew and the Gypsy, the criminal was marked off not only as a threat to the security of civil society, but to the integrity and the health of the nation. These were races of men who stubbornly refused to adapt to the norms of productive labor and civic life.[7] As long as they remained essentially rootless and alien, they were destined to be economically parasitic and politically disloyal.

An underlying tenet of classical liberal doctrine was the belief in equality and man's capacity for self-improvement, but this optimistic theory begged the question of how, in practice, genuine individual advancement was to be distinguished from a mere superficial or external adaptation.[8] The notion of "invisible bonds" provided a hermeneutic of suspicion concerning anyone once marked as "other." Criminals, like Jews, were presumed to possess a hidden language, secret rituals, and codes that were indecipherable to the uninitiated. Indeed, the criminal dialect (*Gaunersprache*) was supposed to be closely related to Yiddish, Hebrew, and certain Gypsy dialects.[9] Criminals, likewise, could mimic bourgeois norms and infiltrate cultural codes. They could disguise their appearance, speak (seemingly) perfect German, and effortlessly imitate the outward forms of respectability. This preoccupation with hidden difference qualified and restricted any attempts by German liberals to use law as a tool of universal social integration.

This chapter considers the place of exclusionary mechanisms, that is, efforts to label, segregate, and contain "*Verbrechertum*," within nineteenth century criminal justice. For classical-liberal jurists, the security of civil society could be ensured by denying full juridical rights and privileges to previously convicted persons and individuals branded as threats to public welfare. Dangerous individuals were the objects of police-administrative regulation, while citizens were shielded from such controls within the ever-expanding domain of the *Rechtsstaat*. The two forms of regulation complemented, indeed helped to constitute each other. Starting at mid-century, however, Christian social reformers challenged the stark dualities inherent to this juridical model of regulation. Against the dichotomy of citizens and criminals, they stressed the image of a fallen man: deprived of spiritual knowledge and community, corrupted and entrapped by criminal societies. As an alternative to police and juridical power, they proposed that Christian associations "missionize" among the outcasts, guiding the internal, moral transformation of former offenders within and then beyond the penitentiary walls. For many jurists, this Pietist-inflected intervention in criminal justice threatened the very notion of individual freedom as a foundation for citizenship. Bismarckian jurists reasserted the importance of classical measures of exclusion and a classical threshold of independent virtue, competence, and respectability as a qualification for inclusion. Free labor, in their view, was the only legitimate touchstone of moral worth and the only conceivable lever of moral transformation.

Feuerbach and the Classical Liberal Tradition

According to standard accounts of German legal history, classical liberal jurisprudence emerged in the early nineteenth century as the logical and necessary ideology of a historically emergent class, the "productive middle strata" or *Bürgertum*.[10] Eberhard Schmidt argues that the development of middle-class trade and industry in the post-Napoleonic era required the standardization and regularity afforded by a strong legal system. Moreover, the burghers' practical and political ambitions during the first quarter of the nineteenth century were consistently blocked by the administrative police state, which was essentially under the control of the aristocracy. "The burghers' emergent moral self-awareness," writes Schmidt, "could not bear the shabby police spirit" of the times. Police science (*Polizeiwissenschaft*), the dominant theory of government in these times, held that the state was responsible for all aspects of the citizens' lives and welfare. Against this ideal, the burghers defended the concept of civil society as autonomous and self-constituting. According to historians, Paul Johann Anselm von Feuerbach best represented the aspirations of the *Bürgertum* when he imagined a German state whose role was limited to that of a "*Schutzanstalt*," an institution of protection.[11] The state's task, according to Feuerbach, was to ensure "the mutual freedom of all Burghers . . . the condition in which each can fully exercise his rights free from attacks against his sphere of personality."[12]

A professor in Jena and an early follower of Kant, Feuerbach was a prolific scholar, a judge, and the author of one of the most influential penal codes ever written, the 1813 code for Bavaria. According to Schmidt, Feuerbach's jurisprudence influenced the character of German criminal law theory and practice for the next one hundred years. A pair of aphorisms from Feuerbach became slogans for generations of liberal reformers: *"nulla pene sine crimen"*—no punishment without crime, and *"nulla crimen sine lege"*—no crime without law. Punishment, in other words, must represent a response by the state to an actual crime, and crime must be understood as representing the violation of some existing, commonly recognized statute. Feuerbach's writings challenged both the police principle of "special prevention," which held that citizens who posed a threat to order and safety might be detained indefinitely, as well as the traditional practice of justice through which judges defined certain behaviors as criminal simply by "analogizing" to existing laws or customs. According to Schmidt, Feuerbach's political sensibility drove his effort "to eliminate all arbitrariness through legal binds."[13] He reasoned that the state must not attempt to influence the personality of the criminal through punishment, but that it should concern itself only with the sanction specified in the laws. Thus punishment, in his view, served the limited purpose of "general deterrence." The clear and specific threat of a sanction for any and all violators of the law provided the citizenry with a framework for moral education.

In effect, Feuerbach's jurisprudence established the idea of the criminal as a purely juridic entity. Stripped of all social or psychological characteristics, the criminal became, by definition, merely the agent of a specific, legally proscribed act. Assuming that the criminal was found legally responsible for his crime, the punishment was set by the specific language of the law. This promise of legal certainty provided the foundation for political equality and for the exercise of freedom. It was essential to the larger classical liberal project of "containing" monarchic absolutism and any other form of arbitrary government.

In Feuerbach's ideal justice system, judges exercised their power with an almost mechanical formality. The task of the judge, according to his textbook, was to "compare a given case with the letters" of the law, without consideration of the law's "sense and spirit."[14] The purpose of the trial was not to protect society, to improve the lawbreaker, or even to enact justice; rather, it was to protect "the body" of the law. This anthropomorphizing of law was not accidental but reflected an association of law with sovereignty. The law had a "majesty" and an "aura" that constituted preconditions for orderly and good government.[15] Law needed to be autonomous from politics and social preoccupations and the concerns of a particular situation. Law should not be "penetrated" or "violated" (as later commentators expressed it) by ideas and methodologies that were essentially foreign.[16]

As historian Pasquale Pasquino notes, Feuerbach's jurisprudence was predicated upon denying any significance to variations among individual offenders, let alone the supposition of "human types." In place of the criminal, Pasquino argues, is the postulate of a "free will" as establishing the subjective basis of the power to punish.

> By its very nature this free will is precisely the faculty which is common to all (i.e. to every juridical subject). As such, it is not the object of a special form of knowledge. Anyone can commit a crime: *homo penalis* is not a separate species, but a function. What serves to explain the actions of *homo penalis* is not criminology but rather a "general anthropology."[17]

Feuerbach's "general anthropology" presumed that people's actions were based on the rational calculation of pleasure and pain. Desire drove them to commit crimes; fear (of punishment), on the other hand, could "annul" their "sensible impulsion" toward the breach of the law.[18] This image of the criminal offender corresponded to what Eberhard Schmidt called the "ideal of the middle-class human-type" (*bürgerlich Menschen-typus*). Feuerbach's legal subject was the autonomous, rational, and responsible individual, one who recognized both the benefits and the obligations imposed by the legal system and was therefore truly free to choose whether to abide by the law.

Even as Feuerbach's jurisprudence presented a clear and unequivocal image of the responsible and free legal subject, a different image of the criminal emerged in his two-volume book, *Narratives of Remarkable Criminals*.[19] The *Narratives* never received the same attention from later jurists, or from historians, as Feuerbach's writings on law.[20] Clearly looking past the idealized "juridic entity" invoked by his jurisprudence, this work was an exploration of criminal behavior based upon dossiers from recent criminal cases. Here Feuerbach searched for the "seeds of crime in the secret crevices of the [criminal's] soul."[21] The work suggested that in the details of the criminal's life and person one would find the essential nature of the criminal, "the ultimate cause" of a crime or even "the higher, governing principle of necessity."[22] *Narratives* described criminals as hemmed in by overwhelming desires, mental disturbance and social needs. What is more, the work explored the circumstantial complexities surrounding particular crimes with elaborate care and sensitivity, a notable contrast with Feuerbach's rejection of such information in his jurisprudence.

Feuerbach's criminal biographies mobilized popular and literary prejudices about "homo criminalis" as essentially different but treated the commission of crimes as complicated events rooted in a confluence of diverse psychological, social, and historical circumstances. The work was admired by a later generation of criminologists because of its treatment of human psychology as multilayered and contingent within different contexts.[23] Criminal drives and urges, he asserted, did not always or necessarily lead to criminal behavior. "On the tragic stage of crime," wrote Feuerbach, "the exact same driving forces [*Triebfedern*] are at play which intervene . . . in many heroic world occurrences . . . [and also] daily in the narrow circle of bourgeois life and common social [*gesellige*] relations." Criminal urges were "hidden behind the display of pomp or other deceptive externalities, here veiled in excellent forms, there moderated or restricted through cleverness or skill." The banality of criminal inclinations, according to Feuerbach, made them easy to miss. It required one with "knowledge of people" (*der Menschenkenner*) to uncover the individual's true, evil inner core.[24]

Feuerbach's *Narratives* may have been reconcilable with his jurisprudence, but they clearly operated in a different universe of political concerns.[25] In his own words, he was drawn to present these cases by a "curiosity" concerning matters "beyond the borders of strict judicial judgment."[26] The information upon which his narratives were drawn came not from criminal court proceedings, but from the dossiers presented to higher authorities who, in the name of the monarch, decided whether to grant some degree of clemency or even a complete pardon. Pardons were a crucial aspect of government policy under a classical liberal penal regime precisely because legal positivist assumptions prevented judges from tailoring punishments to match individual circumstances or using their discretion to decide when a punishment was politically inopportune. The granting of pardons did not contradict classical liberal principles, because pardons were not part of the juridical process.[27] By pardoning, the sovereign tempered justice with mercy and moderated the impractical, impolitic, or morally dubious effects of an inflexible legal system.[28] Feuerbach's engagement with the physical, mental, and social circumstances thus operated in a post-juridical space.

For Feuerbach, then, there was an inherent, irresolvable tension between the domains of justice and administration. Feuerbach's jurisprudence rested upon a rigid distinction between those who must be convicted by the courts because they were morally autonomous and thus legally responsible for their crimes versus those who could not be legally condemned because their acts were caused by an overwhelming, uncontrollable passion. Feuerbach's police writings, however, recognized the complex shades of moral responsibility and seemed to acknowledge the state's need to regulate criminal conduct with an eye toward pragmatic considerations. The *Narratives* allowed that some criminals were pardoned, even though they acted deliberately and out of free will, while other criminals faced the naked letter of the law, even though they were most likely driven by forces beyond their control.[29]

While Feuerbach's *Narratives* were in tension with the concept of juridical responsibility in his jurisprudence, other *Vormärz* literature on "criminal types" blatantly contradicted the concepts of moral freedom and a universal norm of subjectivity. Police literature in particular essentialized the criminal through its depiction of "internal enemies": marauding robber bands in the countryside, deviant and dangerous individuals in the cities.[30] Much of this literature directly identified the criminal with the Jew and the Gypsy. More commonplace, especially among the representatives of an enlightened, liberal police practice, was to describe a vague set of social, cultural, and biological attributes "natural" to criminals, which corresponded to stereotypes of Jews, Gypsies, and other outsiders. These criminal qualities were said to be spawned among the rootless and vagrant populations that plagued the high roads and the cities, living parasitically upon the productive classes through an underground economy of second-hand commerce, black marketeering, and organized begging. The criminal class was marked as fundamentally peripatetic, driven to avoid honest labor, uncomfortable with rational and open discourse. "*Gaunersprache*"—the dialect of thieves, vagrants, and prostitutes—was presumed the natural language of this nation within a nation. It was a language of deceit and secrecy, reflecting the criminals' basic aversion to clarity and directness. Not coincidentally, as noted, *Gaunersprache* was widely believed to have its roots in Yiddish, Hebrew, and dialects of the Gypsies. It was both the sign of the dangerous other and a source of social infection. It was the "syntax of criminality."[31]

In the "Police Machine"

The tensions between Feuerbach's jurisprudence and his portraits of criminal offenders illustrated how liberal ideals of the autonomous, rational individual and the classical liberal investment in juridical rights and political equality coexisted with a discourse of the criminal as dangerous other. Jurisprudence was, for liberals, an endeavor essentially concerned with the adjudication of conflict among fellow burghers, that is, among equals. It was thus a right of citizenship, a testament to one's position as a free subject, to be granted a trial, to be prosecuted as a responsible individual before a magistrate. The court's refusal to psychologize, or to define the defendant as anything but a free, willing subject, was a political necessity, part of the symbolic guarantee that all subjects were equal before the law. Once the defendant was convicted of a crime, however, he became an object of study, analysis, and evaluation according to different rules. In short, after conviction, the legal subject became "the criminal" (*der Verbrecher*). As such, his body, psyche, personal history, and affiliations were not only legitimate but necessary matters of state concern.

Feuerbach was unusual among classical liberal jurists in having shown an intense interest in criminal culture and in the practical meaning of punishment.[32] Most of the leading theorists in nineteenth-century criminal jurisprudence explored the intricacies of criminal behavior only in passing and treated penal practice (*Strafvollzug*) and policing as peripheral to their disciplinary concerns and expertise.[33] This marginalization of discourses about criminality within liberal jurisprudence facilitated the marginalization of criminals within the liberal polity. "Criminals" and other subjects of a special police authority had few privileges or rights because their subject position was so poorly defined within the dominant discourse of law.[34]

The exclusion of pardon policy and the practice of incarceration from the concerns of jurisprudence was undergirded by a distinction between punishment as a juridical formality (*die Strafe*), which was really the "threat" or the promise of punishment (sometimes called *die Strafdrohung*), and the execution of punishment (*der Strafvollzug*), which represented the actual measures taken against prisoners. *Strafe* existed firmly in the realm of jurisprudence. The Penal Code's promise of legal certainty included the promise that every punishment would constitute a legally defined sanction corresponding to a legally defined crime. Classical liberalism defined the actual mechanics of punishment, however, as a police-administrative matter.[35] The penal codes of 1851 and 1870 mentioned *Strafvollzug* only in the broadest of terms. It was left to government ministries to determine how incarceration would be structured. The ministries, in turn, authorized provincial and local governments to create specific standards. Many crucial decisions about prison life were finally left to the administrators of individual institutions.[36]

Judges, lawyers, and legislators thus had inherently limited roles in penal practice, especially as it concerned the penitentiaries. The special autonomy of Prussian penitentiaries from juridical authorities was underscored by the fact that they were administered not by the Ministry of Justice but by the Ministry of the Interior, the same department that oversaw police, health, and welfare matters. In theory, this was because the penitentiary (*Zuchthaus*), unlike the ordinary prison (*Gefängnis*), was a "total institution," designed for the moral transformation of criminals through labor, education, and spiritual guidance. By contrast, the prisons were designed with a narrower and more modest function in mind: enacting retribution and deterrence against legal subjects who had committed relatively minor offenses.[37] The prisons were simple, harsh reminders to every citizen of his duties and responsibilities to the law and to the nation. Penitentiaries, on the other hand, were designed to create better, more manageable subjects, to transform those persons who had been stripped of legal rights and privileges and marked as outcasts from civil society. Jurists often referred to prisons as direct arms of the law and the courts, while penitentiaries performed the "police function" of promoting the general welfare and defending public security.[38] This so-called "dualism" in Prussian penal administration persisted until 1918, an era when the distinction between normal or rational "offenders" versus socially deviant "criminals" had become especially problematic.[39] After 1918, prison and penitentiary administration were unified, with both institutions placed under the Ministry of the Interior.[40]

The guiding principles for Prussian penitentiaries throughout most of the nineteenth century were modeled on a set of regulations first formulated at the prison in Rawicz, in Posen, in the 1830s. The Rawiczer regulations were based upon military concepts of organization and discipline.[41] The system constructed a perfect counterpart to the liberal ideal of civil life by negating each inmate's sense of a distinct, individual identity. The prisoners were forced to wear the same ill-fitting, striped uniforms. They lived together in cramped quarters, marched in the "lock-step," and were addressed by prison personnel not with the customary and respectful "*Sie*," but with the informal "*du*," a form of address that Mr. Settembrini, the classical liberal character in *The Magic Mountain*, described as "directed—shamelessly and obnoxiously— against civilization and cultivated humanity."[42] There was very little direct contact between inmates and overseers, but the relationship was principally one of surveillance and the construction of limits. "Like a dead police machine," wrote Johann Hinrich Wichern in 1862, "the watchman works among 30, 50, often up to 100 prisoners, for whom he is made responsible."[43]

The Rawiczer system institutionalized the idea that controlling the "army of criminals" in Prussia was a duty logically entrusted to the military class.

Starting in the 1850s, the Interior Ministry decreed that Prussian penal institutions, like police forces in Prussia, must give priority in hiring to retiring
Prussian Army officers and soldiers.[44] The military-police aspect of the penitentiaries demarcated them as zones of state action beyond the purview of
normal juridical oversight.[45] As the primary guarantor of German independence, sovereignty, and public order, the military was constitutionally ensured of autonomy from the scrutiny of political or judicial authorities. The
carceral system had no such formal guarantee of independence, but it was
similarly insulated through laws, traditions, and administrative decrees. The
state's only obligations to prison inmates were in the category of "bureaucratic duties" (*Amtspflichte*), which meant that prisoners had no recourse to
the courts if they were mistreated but were forced to file complaints from
"within the administrative organism." This system was consciously modeled
on the army's complaint system, imposing upon complainants a waiting
period in which they were supposed to reconsider their grievance.[46]

After the release from prison, the process of branding the criminal as
juridical other continued, albeit in different form. In certain cases, the Prussian state could impose "supplementary penal measures," including correctional custody, police surveillance, and the denial of civil rights (*Ehrenrechte*).[47] Correctional custody generally meant confinement in a "house of
corrections," or workhouse. Jurists considered correctional custody to be a
peculiar institution because it was defined in the legal codes as a penal sanction, yet imposed by the state more like an administrative-police measure.
The Prussian penal code of 1794 empowered the police to intern prostitutes
and thieves in the workhouse for an unlimited period of time, subject only to
approval every six months by provincial administrators. The Penal Code of
1851 changed this law substantially, but preserved the unique role of the
workhouse as a place for criminals with a certain special status. Henceforth
the police could incarcerate former prisoners convicted of prostitution, begging, vagrancy, or work-shyness for a period of "only" two years. The famously liberal penal code of 1871 changed matters only in that it required
judges to authorize each offender's "transfer" to the police following his or
her release from prison. Even after 1871, the police had discretion concerning
whether and how long to detain these petty offenders—many of whom had
been punished with just a few days in jail.[48] The persistence of correctional
custody allowed the police's special concern with controlling prostitution
and vagrancy to take precedence over juridical-liberal principles of legal
certainty and fairness.[49]

In spite of its name, the house of corrections had few pretensions of improving the character or behavior of its inmates. The "most distinctive element of the workhouse," legal scholar Robert Hippel wrote in 1895, "is that—untouched by the widespread individualized tendency [of] our modern penal system—it pursues success in punishment simply in the disciplining of work shy masses by dint of the iron severity of forced labor." Most workhouses hardly bothered to separate older inmates with multiple felonies from younger inmates guilty of a single misdemeanor. Moreover, many workhouse inmates were not guilty of any crime, but had been committed through civil procedures, often involving a case brought to the civil courts by parents, the clergy, or some local authority. The so-called police courts, which exercised summary justice against persons who had violated police ordinances, also used the workhouses for "special detention."[50] In his survey of workhouses, Hippel found that they were collection points for all kinds of social outsiders, including the elderly and the mentally and physically disabled. The true purpose of the workhouse, it seemed, was to provide the state with special authority over persons considered individually perhaps a mere nuisance, but collectively a threat to social welfare.[51]

Another means by which the state branded ex-offenders was the police supervision of released convicts. Like custody in the workhouse, police supervision was authorized by the court, but administered as a matter of "welfare and security." The Prussian penal code of 1851 empowered the police to ban persons under supervision from particular establishments, neighborhoods, towns, or even regions for up to ten years (this was later shortened). Foreign offenders could be banished from the country. The code also allowed the police to impose a nighttime curfew upon persons previously convicted of theft, robbery, or the receipt of stolen goods.[52] The police was authorized to maintain oversight of ex-offenders through house searches, visits to the workplace, and interviews with associates. In this way, police supervision fed social prejudices against released prisoners and helped ensure their exclusion from bourgeois society.[53]

Correctional custody and police supervision, even more so than the penitentiary, had an ambiguous place in liberal jurisprudence. The origins of these measures went back to the time when the nature of evidentiary requirements made it possible for hardened and experienced criminals to avoid convictions simply by withstanding torture and refusing to confess or by intimidating witnesses. Extra-judicial detention and surveillance was a way of ensuring that dangerous individuals acquitted of crimes did not pose a continual threat to the public welfare. Feuerbach himself, supposedly the great opponent of arbitrary police practice, noted dryly that "in a well-ordered state, criminals should not be left to their fate at the end of the pun-ishment without the state carefully considering the question, what should become of this person?" His solution was as follows:

> The criminal, upon his release, must be required to indicate the mode of living through which he intends to feed himself in the future and the location of his future residence. If he does not want to do this, then he will be given some occupation in a very particular place—the work-house—and will remain under continuous surveillance by the police, who will be charged with seeing to it that he does not give himself over to idleness or dissoluteness and that he does not leave his place of domicile without permission. If he nevertheless does one or the other, then he should be held in that particular place until he shows definite proof of his improvement.[54]

Although this investment in police authority and improvement through the workhouse sat uneasily with Feuerbach's commitment to *"nulla poena sine lege,"* he made little effort to justify or to spell out the implications of this argument. Rather, he treated it as self-evident that respectable, law-abiding persons must be rooted in one place and engaged in industrious labor and orderly living. These were the necessary, and presumed, signi-fiers of a released prisoner's transformation from the category of dangerous individual.

Perhaps because of the relative silence of canonical liberal texts concerning police supervision and post-penal custody, reformers between 1848 and 1870 showed a certain ambivalence and confusion about the place of these mea-sures within a liberal order. At certain points, their suspicion (if not antipa-thy) toward the police and other administrative authorities in Prussia led them to press for greater juridical regulation and limits upon these measures. The liberal Reich Penal Code of 1871, for example, essentially gave judges authority to prevent the police from detaining released petty offenders. The new code also removed the police's right to impose curfews. Nevertheless, the principle of special police authority over certain categories of people, pros-titutes, vagabonds, and ex-felons in particular continued. Persons caught in the net of police supervision could be made into permanent social outcasts. The liberals' refusal to overturn what recent scholars have seen as a peculiar vestige of the pre-modern police state was not a retreat in the face of reaction-ary forces or a concession to "illiberal" thinking.[55] Special police powers were recognized as vital to the liberal polity, the ultimate protection of sovereignty and of the legal foundations of the liberal Rechtsstaat.[56]

Punishment and the Protestant Utopia

Perhaps the most formidable challenge to traditional exclusionary practices in German criminal justice until the last decades of the nineteenth century came not from liberal constitutional reformers but from conservative Christian social reformers. Pietist writers on criminality at mid-century shared the commonly held perception of criminals as "savage," but they also subscribed to an optimistic faith in the ability of Christian communities to colonize and transform the savage subject. Protestant penal reformers stressed the vulnerable and childlike qualities of the criminal. Like the pagans in Africa and Asia, the criminals within the Christian world were to be "liberated" through education and spiritual guidance. Wichern founded the Central Committee of the Inner Mission in 1848 in order to organize great "networks of mercy" that would draw the unruly underclass into the German nation. The Inner Mission prepared clergy, deacons and deaconnesses, and lay volunteers to work in rescue homes for wayward and delinquent children, prisons, and workhouses. The Central Committee sought to coordinate the work of hundreds of cells and create standards for Christian care. It also sought to expand the authority of the Church in social policy by advocating legislative and administrative reforms in Berlin.[57]

The founder and leader of the Central Committee of the Inner Mission, Pastor Johann Hinrich Wichern, was the towering figure in nineteenth-century Protestant social reform more generally.[58] Wichern preached and wrote energetically between 1845 and 1875, attacking free-market capitalism, revolutionary socialism, liberalism, democracy, and materialism. Deeply influenced by the nationalist-inflected pietism of the Vormärz, Wichern aimed to reconstruct the moral relationship between the respectable class and its others.[59] On behalf of the Church and for the Prussian government, he carried out investigations into the lives of factory workers and the urban underclass and conditions in penitentiaries, jails, and workhouses. He started numerous organizations for welfare and penal reform that were later integrated under the Inner Mission umbrella.[60] Wichern and the Inner Mission became controversial both among theological conservatives suspicious of a Christian volunteerism based on the "priesthood of all believers" and among liberal bureaucrats and politicians concerned that the Church had moved from organizing charitable works to intervening in the very structure of state power.[61] Nevertheless, Wichern became a powerful and influential force in Prussian politics, serving as a close adviser in penal affairs to King Friedrich Wilhelm IV of Prussia, and, from 1857 to 1874, as head of the Department of

Prison Affairs in the Prussian Ministry of the Interior. In spite of liberal opposition, the Inner Mission became an important part of the criminal justice landscape, in some regions of Prussia spurring the building or the transformation of penitentiaries based on their prison reform principles.[62]

For Wichern, penal reform was a pivotal issue in his overall strategy of social transformation. In the programmatic speeches that launched the Inner Mission, texts that historian William Shanahan refers to as a "Protestant Manifesto," Wichern described the "army of criminals" as a principal threat to political and social stability and a major obstacle to moral outreach among the poor.[63] Criminality was intimately connected to Communism, in Wichern's view, and both were closely related to paganism. It was no coincidence that the founding of the Inner Mission took place in the revolutionary year of 1848. In his famous address to the Wittenberger Kirchentag, Wichern argued that the urban poor's antagonism toward the social order was a product of its "complete isolation" from the middle and upper classes. The speech described an urban subculture barricaded against all positive spiritual and patriotic forces. In many areas of the cities, Wichern declared, "it was physically impossible for the clergy to perform their functions."[64]

It was Wichern's view that the prisons were a key location in which this radical sensibility and poisonous hatred of authority was bred among the underclasses (*die unterste Pöbel*). "Every year," he argued, "hundreds of criminals are released [from prison] who are worse off than when they entered." The Wittenberg speech recounted the story of two prisoners praying to God, getting no response and turning to "supernatural forces." It also referred to a recent and notorious double-murderer who, Wichern asserted, had learned to pray to the devil while in prison. It was in this fashion, he declared, that "pure pagan worship originates in the center of Christianity."[65] In the large cities, the ex-prisoners constituted an "ever more compact and dangerous mass in which the spirit that repeatedly produces crime and endangers the public security of persons and things is strengthened in its breadth and its depth."[66]

Wichern's analogy between the criminal subculture in the German metropole and the pagan nations beyond "*Christentum*" provided the rhetorical foundation for his strategies of criminal justice reform.[67] "Just as Christian civilization carries the message and the blessing of grace to the heathen world . . . through the *external mission*," Wichern wrote, "so the love in the *Inner Mission* will prove itself for the baptized Christians and, through Christian breeding and morals, will actuate the belief in love among alienated branches within the Christian nation."[68] Like Fichte, Wichern was preoccupied with "internal borders."[69] Unlike Fichte, however, who adopted the metaphor of the border to support a rhetoric of social exclusion, Wichern called for effacing these borders through "Christian love." The "heathen mission" had established the principle of popular, lay participation in the work of the Church, channeled through private, predominantly bourgeois associations. The Inner Mission sought to harness this popular energy and enthusiasm, redirecting it inward. The volunteer army of Protestant lay people would "penetrate the prison world" and the world of the urban *Lumpenproletariat* and fight back the "emergent anti-Christian forces within the territory of the Christian folk."[70]

Wichern promised to reestablish Christian hegemony in the cities and, by promoting "inner colonization," to halt the "catastrophic" scattering and dilution of German civilization caused by the massive waves of emigration. The Inner Mission was supposed to demarcate new domains for the practice of "Christian love," a force for spiritual conditioning and discipline carried by one person to another. "Love," according to Wichern,

> allows itself to be concentrated and gathered together in its work, because it understands proportion, and this ability to measure is one of its beautiful virtues. But love will not therefore allow itself to be kept provincial, as if it were captured in a thread. Still less would love allow itself to be blocked by doors and borders.

In one of his early programmatic essays, Wichern mused that he should like to produce a "geognostic map": a drawing that would "geographically" trace the distribution of charitable energies (*Liebestätigkeit*), "the relative richness or poverty in the fatherland's supply of precious and less-precious metals." Through such a map, he believed, the Inner Mission could plot a comprehensive strategy of social transformation.[71]

Wichern's ideal of "concentrated love" reached its ultimate form in his efforts to introduce solitary confinement into German penitentiaries. The system of shared cells and collective eating and work spaces, he argued, had turned German penitentiaries into recruitment centers and "schools of criminality." Younger and more impressionable inmates were constantly subjected to the influence (and the brutalities) of other, more hardened criminals. Wichern believed that individualized incarceration would break the criminals' internal bonds of solidarity and allow for their moral transformation through penance, education, and spiritual guidance. Under solitary confinement, the prisoners' only human contact would be with overseers, teachers, and prison chaplains. The arrangement of space thus allowed for a more direct and purposeful application of "moral power" and, as Michel Foucault has noted, solitary confinement was "accompanied—both as a condition and a consequence—by the development of a knowledge of the individual [prisoners]."[72] For German Protestant reformers, as for the Anglo-American reformers discussed by Foucault, the isolation of the prisoner had the benefit of allowing for calibrated and continuous observation and analysis.[73] Largely as a result of Wichern's agitation, Prussia built its first penitentiary according to the single-cell, panopticon model (made famous by London's Pentonville prison) in 1849.[74] Later, the Inner Mission fought for the introduction of solitary confinement in penitentiaries across Germany, first through administrative means and, when that failed, through legislation.

The second element in the Inner Mission's vision of penal reform was to create an "evangelical corps" of overseers for the prisons specially trained for work with inmates. Wichern created a model for such overseers when he founded the "brethren of the Rauhen-Haus" in Hamburg and the Johannes Foundation in Berlin.[75] The Johannes-brethren were unmarried men between the ages of twenty and twenty-nine "from all ranks and circles," who were skilled in some profession to which they could return when their tour with the brethren was finished.[76] Under Wichern's tutelage, they served in prisons and penitentiaries around Germany and, to some extent, the world. In 1856, Wichern turned the famous Berlin penitentiary in Moabit into a model institution by employing the Johannes Brethren in all levels of the operation. Wichern's effort to make similar inroads at other institutions failed—like many of his initiatives—in the face of liberal parliamentary opposition. He had succeeded, however, in focusing the attention of Christian activists upon the challenge of directly reaching and influencing criminal offenders.[77]

Wichern's ideal of the penal overseer was a person who could both minister to the "spiritual needs" of the prisoners and lay the groundwork for their eventual reintegration in civil society. The Inner Mission was not averse to the violence caught up with Prussian prison practice—occasional thrashings, Wichern believed, might be necessary to break the "obstinate spirit" of recalcitrant inmates—but the Protestant reformers opposed the "factory-like" and "mechanical" aspects of military discipline. The Rawicz system focused on formal, external obedience, upon the control of bodies beyond all else. It neglected the question of "internal loyalty" or the cultivation of the criminal's soul.[78]

The third pillar of the Protestant reform strategy was the effort to transform policies toward released prisoners, especially police surveillance and the revocation of civil rights. Wichern argued that police surveillance did little to prevent unrepentant, habitual criminals from wreaking havoc upon society. The new density of cities, the increased mobility and ease of travel, and the limits in communication between distant parts of Germany meant that criminals could no longer be tracked and controlled as in previous eras. In Wichern's view, police surveillance in a modern society was doomed to be ineffectual. At the same time, he argued, the practice caused immense social damage. First, police surveillance placed a devastating psychological burden upon any prison inmate who hoped after serving his sentence "to re-enter orderly civil circumstances [*geordnete bürgerliche Verhältnisse*] as a free man."[79] The punishment itself became the lesser misfortune compared to the prospect of facing "civil death" (*bürgerlich vernichtet zu sein*) under the yoke of police surveillance. In such a context, it was impossible for the prison experience to exercise a positive effect upon the criminal's soul or psyche.

The most persistent criticism of police surveillance was that it unraveled the slow and methodical work of moral reformation, of "rebuilding souls," because it forced released convicts to live among the underworld and, in all likelihood, return to the underground economy.[80] The police's limits on residence, the imposition of curfews, and the insistent inquiries among landlords and employers allegedly prevented released convicts from rejoining respectable society. Faced with the prospect of homelessness, they were forced to live in disreputable houses with "unscrupulous landlords." There, according to Wichern, they typically fell prey to the lure of prostitution and other morally corrupting pursuits. Often, he asserted, "the same criminals had already come to know each other as comrades in the penal institutions." In this way, Wichern argued, police surveillance caused the "continued existence of that criminal society initiated through collective incarceration."[81]

Police surveillance, in the view of Protestant reformers, reinforced the "insurmountable dividing-walls" that civil society naturally constructed between the bourgeoisie and the proletariat. The loss of civil rights (*Ehrenrechte*) literally meant the loss of honor. Former prisoners stripped of their *Ehrenrechte* were banned from the armed forces, which cut them off from one potential path toward rehabilitation. As second-class citizens, they had diminished legal standing in the courts and administrative proceedings and were forbidden to work in the civil service (a broad category of employment in Prussia) and many other public offices. If ex-convicts were fortunate enough to find employment in the private sector, police investigations and interviews of employers and coworkers frequently led to their prompt dismissal. The practice of police curfews and banishment likewise forced many former prisoners into unemployment. Surveying the results of such policies, Wichern concluded that police surveillance "essentially made all former convicts into a special social class, that is a criminal class, which, especially in the large cities, will prove extremely dangerous to public security and morality."[82]

Wichern's objections to police surveillance, like his criticism of the military model of prison discipline, concerned the undiscriminating manner in which the institution excluded lawbreakers from the community and the nation. Punishment, in his view, "once it is suffered . . . must come to an end." No less than the great liberal jurists, Wichern was for juridical and police barriers guarding the true (Christian) nation against its internal enemies, but he opposed relying upon secular legal codes to mechanically and categorically define the criminal as "other." Wichern's Pietist view of human nature stressed the essential weakness of all persons and the importance of temptation as a causal element in the genesis of evil behavior. The commission of a crime, he claimed, was not a definitive sign of human difference but the symptom of spiritual crisis and a breakdown in communal solidarity. Penal reformers therefore must aim to reknit the shredded bonds of community, constructing institutions of discipline and surveillance in the fabric of everyday life, a task that naturally devolved upon the army of volunteers within the Protestant bourgeoisie.[83] "Love," Wichern declared, "has the sharp eye which sees everything."[84]

Wichern's critique and the Inner Mission's efforts against liberal strategies of exclusion resonated not only among Protestant clergy and lay-people active in charitable associations, but also among some criminal justice professionals in Prussia.[85] The best example of a reformer working within the criminal justice system inspired by Pietist reform ideals was Friedrich Christian Benedikt Avé-Lallemant, a police administrator in Lübeck and a prolific author on crime and public security. Avé-Lallemant's four-volume study of "German Criminality" (*Gaunerthum*) was a comprehensive attack on the dominant police and juridical discourse of the criminal as other. It provided a scholarly underpinning to Wichern's reform movement through its analysis of the "*Gauner*," and it reimagined the role of the police in a manner consistent with Wichern's ideals of community, solidarity, and social discipline.

Using historical and ethnographic tools, Avé-Lallemant attacked the concept that criminals constituted a "distinct ethnic or racial [*volksthümlichen*] group" that could be extirpated or excluded from civil society. Criminal inclinations, in his view, were not innate to people but were produced through environmental influences. He called crime a "socio-political" phenomenon, by which he meant that it came from socially and politically alienated sectors of the population that had developed into deviant and parasitical subcultures. Criminals received an "education" in a particular set of "values and skills": Crime was a "profession."[86] Thus, in his view, a latent potential for criminality existed across the human spectrum and throughout modern German society. Since the origins of criminal behavior were culturally conditioned and different in each case, it was impossible to categorize criminals through a science of human typology. The criminal, he concluded, "remains unknowable to the anthropologist."

The key to Avé-Lallemant's theory of crime and his critique of traditional police practice was his analysis of *Gaunersprache*, the underworld dialect. He rejected the traditional claim that *Gaunersprache* was a mere amalgamation of Yiddish and Hebrew, or that it otherwise represented a "true national dialect."[87] In his view, the language represented a kind of moral infection: It was the medium through which evil inclinations, thoughts, and desires were transferred among souls. Like a virus, it could invade and spread among any host. Elsewhere Avé-Lallemant compared the criminal dialect to the web of a spider. "*Gaunersprache* is not just the expression of the criminal's power," he asserted, "it is in itself the criminal's strongest intellectual or spiritual force. It is the web of a thousand taut threads by means of which the Gauner holds the customs and the language of the people ensnared."[88]

Like Wichern, Avé-Lallemant perceived the cultural coherence of the criminal underworld as largely a product of social, legal, and administrative exclusions. Understanding and treating criminal behavior, in his view, were part of the same process. Society was an organism, crime was an illness (*Siechthum*), and criminal justice should ideally be engaged in a task analogous to medicine. The criminal expert, like the doctor, must "penetrate" the "living-scientific individuality" of the criminal. A police investigation (*Untersuchung*) was ideally a kind of clinical examination, an opportunity to view the distinct "art" and "skill" that developed through a long, indeterminate process of evolution and adaptation. The police experts' success rested upon his intimacy and familiarity with the subjects of study and his investment in their "moral transformation." This intimate "ethnography," Avé-Lallemant believed, was fundamentally different from the objective, detached methods of classification that undergirded the emergent field of anthropology.[89]

Like Wichern, Avé-Lallemant was especially critical of the traditional police regulation of petty offenders and released prisoners, and he looked to private, bourgeois, Christian associations as the vital component in the transformation of social order. For Avé-Lallemant, however, the police was to remain at the center of this regulatory nexus. The key to reform, in his view, was a "reconciliation" and "alliance between the police and the bourgeois associations," a rallying of forces against criminality, through which both the police and the *Bürgertum* would ultimately be transformed. Avé-Lallemant's vision of a "*Volkspolizei*," not unlike Wichern's ideals in penal reform, only gained widespread institutional support and acceptance after the turn of the century. Nevertheless, again like Wichern, his ideas helped to crystallize a new impulse in criminal justice reform at the point of German unification. Avé-Lallemant's writings gave added weight to the assertion that classical liberalism's legally defined and legally enforced exclusions were producing, rather than containing, "socio-political" dangers.[90]

Both Wichern and Avé-Lallemant sought in particular to revitalize and expand the role of charitable associations for prisoners, released prisoners, and the families of convicted offenders. These so-called prison associations first rose to prominence in the 1820s. Usually they were founded by a consortium of local clergy, justice and prison officials, and civic leaders. Their original focus was getting pious and respected members of the community to visit inmates in their cells. They also provided spiritual and financial support to the wives and children of incarcerated men and assistance to released prisoners. In the 1820s, the Rhenish-Westphalian Prison Society and the Berlin Association for the Improvement of Prisoners were founded in order to coordinate the efforts of local associations and promote their expansion. The Rhenish-Westphalian Society helped spawn over forty new associations in less than ten years.[91] The Prussian royal family played a key role in supporting this work by putting both societies under their protection. The king of Prussia's 1837 cabinet order required government administrators to encourage the spread of the associations and to help fund them where necessary. The king's involvement also encouraged upper-class and bourgeois notables across the nation to volunteer for the societies.[92]

It was the broad popular participation in the associations that particularly appealed to reformers like Wichern and Avé-Lallemant. The associations generated interest and involvement in the prison question. The reformers saw them as vital both for enlightening the broader public and for bringing Christian ideals into the dark corners of the prisons. The associations, they believed, dealt with criminals not as juridical abstractions but as flesh and blood persons with a specific history and specific failings. They reforged the broken links between criminals and society.

While the prison societies evoked great popular enthusiasm in the 1830s, by the 1850s they were commonly perceived as stagnant and largely ineffectual. The efforts by Wichern and Avé-Lallemant to mobilize the societies on behalf of reform were partly about resuscitating dying institutions. But the Protestant thinkers of the fifties and sixties dreamed of new departures as well. Wichern in particular saw the prison societies as vanguards for the transformation of criminal justice. He disdained liberal pleas for boundaries between the state's punishing power and the charities' outreach and good works. Wichern wanted Christian activism to penetrate all levels of government: his own decision to enter government service and to place the Johannes Brethren at the state's disposal was the clearest indication of this will. By envisioning Protestant associations that straddled the worlds of private charity and public punishment, Wichern and Avé-Lallemant questioned both the accepted role of the Church and the responsibility of the state in the definition and execution of policy.

Beyond Love and Surveillance: Liberal Critiques of Christian Social Reform

The Inner Mission's agenda for criminal justice reform faced its most powerful opposition from liberal jurists. Two of the sharpest critics were C. J. A. Mittermaier, Feuerbach's most prominent student and a professor in Heidelberg, and Franz von Holtzendorff, holder of the prestigious chair in criminal law in Berlin.[93] Like most liberals of the 1850s and 1860s, they were advocates of reform, which for them meant principally more parliamentary power, rule of law, and independence for the judiciary. They were critics of "Prussian absolutism," the persistence of aristocratic privileges, and police power. Mittermaier, furthermore, was a leading opponent of the death penalty, while Holtzendorff supported the Irish system of "progressive punishment" and wrote one of the earliest essays in German arguing that juvenile offenders should have special status in the courts and the prisons.[94]

The law professors' interest in reform, however, was carefully delimited by a set of classical juridical preoccupations. Mittermaier continued in the Feuerbachean tradition of legal positivism, opposing the death penalty because it was ineffective as a deterrent measure and freighted with "metaphysical" baggage inconsistent with the goal of making punishment fair and proportional to the crime. Holtzendorff was more invested than Mittermaier in the use of punishment to improve certain categories of criminal offenders, but he was truly Feuerbachean in his indifference to the "souls" of prisoners, and, most important, in his insistence on individual freedom as a precondition for moral development. Improvement, in Holtzendorff's view, was a

"Help us." Fund-raising and publicity card for the Prison Association in Baden. (Bundesarchiv, Berlin)

process through which the criminal offender moderated his external behavior out of enlightened self-interest. He embraced the reforms in Ireland because they structured punishment according to a standardized system of "progressive" rewards and sanctions, as opposed to the British system of "individualizing" punishment so admired by Wichern. The implication of Holtzendorff's perspective was that improvement would be possible only for offenders who were capable of recognizing and acting upon rational self-interest. These were the offenders who could be reconciled with civil society and "resocialized." His embrace of juvenile reform similarly operated within this rational-individualist perspective. Since underage offenders did not fully possess free will and facility for rational judgment, he reasoned, the entire panoply of questions regarding the punishment or the resocialization of youth offenders properly belonged outside the domain of the justice system.[95]

While Wichern adapted metaphors of colonialism to the task of surveilling and "civilizing" pockets of criminal subversion at home, Holtzendorff advocated the expulsion of undisciplined, drifting, and potentially dangerous populations of criminals to overseas colonies. "Settlement matters [*Ansiedlungswesen*]," he wrote, "were a necessary factor in modern criminal law."[96] Solitary confinement, in his view, was an insufficient lever of moral transformation, because it did nothing to ensure the prisoner's adjustment to life in a free society. Criminals, he argued, needed to develop practical skills for survival, and they needed to go through a "transitional stage" (*Übergangsstufe*) after the pain of incarceration in order to learn independence and self-reliance. Moreover, Holtzendorff believed, criminals, upon their release from prison, needed to be segregated from their former prison mates, and they needed to be assured of employment.[97] Deportation, for these reasons, was "ideally, and more than any other punishment, to be utilized for the purpose of [individual] improvement." Within the colonies, the former prisoner could "remain within a uniformly distributed population, without the pernicious contact points of a large urban proletariat . . . especially so long as he is not taken into a certain economic class."[98] Thus, even as Holtzendorff shared Wichern's interest in transcending traditional measures of social exclusion, he insisted upon the necessity of segregating former prisoners as a sanitary measure at least in the initial stages.

Holtzendorff and Mittermaier feared that the Inner Mission's reform efforts presaged the "infiltration" of the "confessional moment" into penality. The mixture of governmental and religious modes of authority led Holtzendorff to compare Wichern's Johannes Brethren to the Jesuits (a severe and heavily laden insult) and to decry the Inner Mission as an essentially un-

German institution. Holtzendorff rejected the charities' interpretation of the soul as an object of criminal justice and therefore rejected their claim to special authority in punishment. There was simply no reason, in his view, for charities to play a mediating role between the state and the individual.[99]

During the era of German national unification, liberal jurists like Holtzendorff led the way in a series of fragile compromises with Prussian police traditions. As Albrecht Funk has shown, the constitutional arrangements of 1866 to 1871 legitimized the principle of special police powers in "emergency conditions" without carefully delimiting the concept of emergency.[100] It was "no longer controversial" among liberals to argue that political rights must be suspended when sovereignty was threatened. This logic culminated in the liberals' acquiescence, eight years after German reunification, in the Anti-Socialist Laws. After a period of difficult soul-searching and marked discontent among left-liberal jurists in particular, the "special measures" introduced by *Justiz* and *Polizei* against suspected Socialists soon became "a normal part of order under the rule of law."[101]

At the crux of what many deemed (and many historians have since regarded) as "the great capitulation" of German liberalism, there appeared a wave of writings on crime and punishment, calling with unusual clarity and aggressiveness for the rejection of "welfare" approaches to punishment and the resuscitation of a traditional project of punishment as social exclusion. The leading light in this movement was Otto Mittelstädt, whose thoroughgoing and virulent critique of the penal reform movement was first published in 1877. Mittelstädt, the chief prosecutor in Hamburg, originally published his polemic as an article in the right-wing National-Liberal journal, *Die Preussische Jahrbücher*.[102] The essay became famous in its revised form two years later as a pamphlet with the provocative title *Against Incarceration*.[103] The author was a self-styled opponent of the status quo who believed that "humanitarian reformers" had become the dominant force in German criminal justice since national unification. While Mittelstädt condemned Protestant prison reformers for "humanitarian quackery" and "simple-minded sentimentality," he was especially contemptuous of his fellow jurists for their infatuation with ideologies of improvement and reformist currents in French, British, and American criminal justice. His tirade "against incarceration" was thus, in some sense, a ritual self-cleansing for the German classical tradition. The spread of the modern penitentiary, he argued, with its attendant discourses of individualization, penance, and rehabilitation, reflected the "penetration" of foreign ideas into German law. Against such "popular conceptions of humanity and earthly justice circulating in present-day liberalism," Mittelstädt appealed to a purist, almost extremist version of liberal penal doctrine reminiscent of Feuerbach and the era before social welfare.[104]

Punishment and Nation-Building

The starting place for Mittelstädt's critique was his rejection of metaphysical justifications of punishment and religious assumptions of community and solidarity underlying prison welfare. In these modern times, he argued, German society was no longer held together by shared moral values. The Protestant Church, in his view, constantly revising its doctrine and riveted by internal divisions, was not equipped to generate a broad consensus on ethics and social norms. The Catholic Church could not be trusted, because it was too infected by internationalist ideals. In any case, with industrialization and the rapid growth of cities, the dissolution of traditional bonds of community was an accomplished fact. It was therefore absurd, in Mittelstädt's view, to invest punishment with a moral purpose. With no shared framework for the consideration of justice, there could be no consensus on the parameters of retribution, and there could be no sturdy, reliable position from which to engage in the "improvement" of criminally inclined individuals.[105]

In a "post-metaphysical" world, Mittelstädt argued, the logic behind solitary confinement was naive and outdated. Few criminals could be convinced that they should fear eternal damnation. As a result, he reasoned, only those who voluntarily embraced their solitude would feel any urge to repent. Rehabilitating criminals through prison labor was likewise impossible, because work only had a "moral effect" on the individual when it was productive and fulfilling. Forced labor would always be ineffectual precisely because it was forced. The penitentiary in the modern world, Mittelstädt argued, was thus faced by irresolvable contradictions. Punishment could educate and improve criminals only when it was no longer fundamentally structured by coercion, but if it ceased to be coercive, then it would no longer be punishment. Mittelstädt's liberal presuppositions led him to the conclusion that man cannot be "educated for freedom through compulsion."[106] The goal of rehabilitation, therefore, had no place within the penal regime.

In Mittelstädt's view, the only coherent purpose for punishment was deterrence, and that required sanctions marked by the "severe, merciless rule of deprivation, hardship and pain."[107] He argued for the reinstatement of corporal punishment, deportation, and an end to the "amenities" of modern prison life. In his view, serious criminals had placed themselves outside the bounds of the civilized community. They had sacrificed their honor and rights and therefore could be subject to whatever forms of police regulation might be in the interests of public safety and well-being. Mittelstädt argued for the expanded and intensified use of special police powers against criminal offenders:

> The criminal courts want to be unburdened in favor of police power and authority. One can try to delimit police action through juridical controls and structures. . . . Ultimately it will be necessary to proceed even without such limits. The times are not favorable for the expansion of civil freedoms. Society has to prepare itself for long-term conditions of war against its internal enemies. As long as we remain hemmed in by the spirit of our earlier humanitarianism, . . . then the overall level of freedom in our society will continue to decrease.[108]

It made little sense to Mittelstädt that petty offenders, like prostitutes, vagrants, and beggars, were subject to police detention after their release from prison, but serious criminals were not. Just as German liberals had "grown accustomed. . . . to granting the state almost unlimited authority" to confront issues of public health, a similar attitude was necessary "to fight the social epidemics which threaten the national condition and the roots of all civilization."[109]

Mittelstädt's pamphlet provoked an extraordinary response, winning widespread applause in the bourgeois press, but also many outraged rebuttals, especially from prison officials.[110] Though the author himself worried that his essay would be dismissed as part of the reactionary current of the late 1870s, it had a remarkable effect on the reform movement. Franz von Liszt, the founder of the Modern School of jurisprudence and a left-liberal Reichstag deputy, credited Mittelstädt's essay with single-handedly forcing jurists to reopen "the question of why we punish."[111] Classical law scholar Richard Sontag praised Mittelstädt for convincing the government not to keep building upon the existing foundation in criminal law but to plan for a fundamental revision of the penal code.[112] The liberal city-state of Hamburg rewarded Mittelstädt with an appointment to the Reich Supreme Court in 1881.[113] Even many clergy active in the Inner Mission and the prison associations embraced Mittelstädt's argument that punishment and welfare should operate on separate tracks. In 1900, Heinrich Seyfarth, later a national leader of the prison societies, declared that "the entire modern reform movement against incarceration essentially rests upon his shoulders."[114]

Understanding the appeal of Mittelstädt's work to criminal justice reformers is difficult given the seemingly reactionary character of his message. In his politics, as well as in his jurisprudence, Mittelstädt condemned the democratic tides of his day in the most extreme language. He lamented the growing authority of the Reichstag and other challenges to monarchical power. He had no objections in principle to abolishing the Reichstag in order to save the Empire. Nevertheless, Mittelstädt was not looking backward but forward. He continued to support parliamentarism, because he could see no viable way to rule without some element of popular sovereignty in modern societies. Germany's most pressing problem, in his view, was not the threat of democracy but the nation's fractured culture. He envied the French and the Italians because of their "common national sense" and the gift for politics that existed among the people.[115] Compared to other nations, Germany faced "the most numerous, most powerful, most dangerous forces of disintegration from within its own organism." Nowhere else in the modern world, Mittelstädt argued, was there such an anti-patriotic democracy, an anti-national church, an irreconcilable split among internal cultures.[116]

Mittelstädt believed the classical liberal distinction between *Rechtsstaat* and *Polizei* was vital for "completing Bismarck's work" of nation-building. The constitutional crises of the unification era, in his view, should have taught liberals that matters essential to the survival of the state and society could not be subject to ordinary legal checks and balances.[117] He believed the police must have the authority to isolate and control dangerous elements, including both political opponents and common criminals. Mittelstädt was certainly not a liberal in our conventional understanding of the term. He supported the legal order only conditionally and from purely pragmatic grounds. On the other hand, like his friend the historian Heinrich Treitschke, Mittelstädt's dream of inventing a nation that was orderly, loyal, and patriotic was predicated upon certain classical liberal assumptions about the contrasting purposes of constitutional and administrative powers, and the indispensable role of individual freedom—and especially free labor—to the process of creating citizens.

Otto Mittelstädt and the Origins of Modern Criminal Reform

Historians of German social reform in the Kaiserreich have tended to focus upon the role of progressive, left-liberals thinkers like Franz von Liszt, Eduard Lasker, and Friedrich Naumann in articulating a reform agenda. Under their leadership, the argument goes, German ideology was liberated from both the Manchesterite models imported from England and the moralizing rhetoric of an earlier generation of social thinkers. Right-wing liberals like Treitschke and Mittelstädt are often seen as obstacles to change, spoilers, or, in the romantic tradition of Fichte, figures pointing down a different path: toward the racist distopia realized under the Nazis.[118] In his standard work on German liberalism, James Sheehan only briefly discusses the right-wing liberals, describing them simply as opponents of reform, out to protect "social and economic freedom . . . [and] the essentially hierarchical nature of the social order." Over the course of the Imperial period, Sheehan states, such attitudes hardened, with right-wing and left-wing liberals moving into increasingly irreconcilable camps.[119]

In the case of criminal policy, however, Mittelstädt's ideas had a galvanizing effect on both progressive and conservative reformers. His arguments crystallized widespread discomfort with the penitentiary. Of course the prison persisted in Germany (as it did throughout the industrialized world), but it would never again draw the same kind of utopian hopes and energies.[120] The dream of a total institution was dead: not simply because it failed to rehabilitate criminals, but because, as Mittelstädt demonstrated, its operating assumptions were out of step with the dominant ideologies of freedom and citizenship in the new German Reich.

Mittelstädt's arguments against rehabilitation as a goal of punishment pushed reformers to focus on other arenas, outside criminal justice, in which to influence the social adaptation of criminals and potential criminals. Many Christian reformers embraced Mittelstädt's implicit dichotomies between the state and society, deterrence and rehabilitation. If the state had exclusive authority to punish, and punishment was solely about deterrence, then welfare was the responsibility of society and rehabilitation was principally the responsibility of welfare. The great, seemingly eternal battle between advocates of deterrence and rehabilitation could be resolved in a division of responsibility that was complementary and also largely sequential. The state deterred serious crime by punishing offenders. Private welfare then turned these ex-offenders into productive and law-abiding citizens. In the case of petty offenders or "endangered persons," reformers envisioned a sequence that was reversed. Welfare would give these potential criminals the opportunity to conform to social norms. The state would bolster the authority of the welfare realm by punishing those who rejected this offer of grace.

Mittelstädt's work was undoubtedly "reactionary" in its effort to reinscribe impermeable borders between the criminal class and respectable society. Yet there was also something distinctly modern in his critique of Wichern's total institution. Even as he mocked the "humanist" concerns of prison reformers, Mittelstädt declared it was "inhumane" to subject all criminal offenders to the inevitable dishonor and distress inflicted by prisons. The logic of Mittelstädt's analysis pointed toward what historian Monika Frommel calls a "polarized" approach to criminal policy: harsh and degrading punishments for the bad offenders, but less punishment for everyone else. After Mittelstädt, a new generation of reformers focused on rehabilitative measures that occurred beyond the prison gates. They dreamed of noncoercive institutions that could somehow make ex-offenders into free, productive, orderly citizens while never endangering the general public or undermining the deterrent aims of criminal justice.

Mittelstädt's relationship with penal reformers was complicated. He was "honored" that his polemic against the penitentiary was considered one of the inspirations behind the founding in 1889 of the International Penal Union (IKV), Germany's most important criminal justice reform organization.[121] Though he joined the IKV and remained a member for years, Mittelstädt bitterly criticized the organization for its advocacy of making pedagogical, social, and police goals a part of punishment. Mittelstädt's dogmatic insistence upon an absolute distinction between justice and administration could not fit within the open, experimental atmosphere of the IKV. In the 1890s, he engaged von Liszt in a furious polemic about the goals of criminal reform. Yet Liszt generously credited Mittelstädt with "reopening the question of why we punish"—and not without reason. Mittelstädt's polemics delegitimized the moral ideology of the penitentiary. As legal scholar Reinhard Frank argued, Mittelstädt carried the reform movement "from doctrinaire humanitarianism to practical severity, from academic abstraction to sober judgment."[122] He distilled the idea that there were limits to what criminal justice could and should accomplish. There were numerous aspects of a good "criminal policy"—including both protecting public safety and resocializing offenders—that, in his mind, had nothing to do with punishment. In this way, Mittelstädt forcefully directed the attention of criminal policy reformers toward social measures outside the realm of criminal justice.

PROTECTIVE SUPERVISION

Die Liebe hat das scharfe Auge, alles zu sehen.
(Love has the sharp eye, which sees everything.)
—Johann Hinrich Wichern, 1848

In the last decades of the nineteenth century, private welfare organizations transformed the landscape of criminal policy. Prisoner benevolent associations grew in number and scale. Worker colonies for indigent wanderers, first created in 1882, became de facto asylums for ex-offenders. A range of new and existing asylums sheltered "unsupervised" women and girls considered at risk of engaging in venal sex. From a strict juridical standpoint, none of these institutions dealt with criminals. From the perspective of welfare, however, strict juridical definitions were increasingly irrelevant. The charities of the Wilhelmine era saw released prisoners, chronically unemployed men, and deracinated men and women as "endangered" persons who, without welfare intervention, were destined to turn (or return) to crime. Their solution was "protective supervision." Its aim was to shield at-risk persons from social poisons, render them productive and "useful" in the short term, and educate and strengthen their wills over the long term to resist the morally destructive temptations of modern society. Protective supervision was, in essence, the first large-scale experiment in a preventative, social approach to criminal policy.

The historiography of German criminal policy has generally ignored private welfare associations or treated them as traditionalists fighting a rearguard action against modernist, science-oriented reformers. Peter Becker argues that the rise of criminology transformed the focus of criminal discourse from morally "fallen men" to mentally and physically "impaired men." The "medicalization" of the criminal, according to Richard Wetzell, was the key step in the modernization of criminal policy at the fin de siècle. Liberal law scholars enthralled by the latest criminological advances are the heroes (or villains) in this story, arguing for the transformation of the penal code, the courts, and the prisons in order to treat offenders based on the scientific assessment of their dangerousness and prognosis for resocialization.[1]

This chapter demonstrates how private charities contributed to the breakthrough of modernist criminal policy by creating spaces beyond criminal justice in which to evaluate and treat at-risk persons. If we can say that the architecture and organization of the early penitentiary created a discourse around the criminal, then institutions like the worker colony, the women's asylums, and the prison associations made the endangered individual into a coherent object of social intervention.[2] Protective supervision in one form or another was an essential element in every major criminal policy reform proposal after 1880. Whatever their claims to scientific authority, the criminologists and legal reformers of the fin de siècle relied upon the infrastructure and practice of private charity in their visions of modernism.

The Renaissance of the Prison Associations

Starting in the 1870s, there was a surge of popular interest in the prison associations. Over the next two decades, reformers established hundreds of new associations which took a prominent role in the practice of criminal supervision and helped set the agenda in criminal policy reform. Prominent legal scholars, judges, psychiatrists, and government officials joined their local associations in order to develop direct knowledge of criminal milieus and help address the social pathologies that produced crime. The meetings and publications of prison societies became increasingly important forums for proposing and debating new directions in criminal policy.

As in the early nineteenth century, the initial push for the associations' growth came from above. Wichern and the Inner Mission had been trying to revive the associations since the 1850s.[3] In the newly founded German Reich of 1871, the royal family renewed its interest in the public grant of pardons, particularly when bestowed upon pious and repentant criminals.[4] In 1879 a decree by the Prussian Ministry of the Interior expressed official regret that the associations were not doing more to help former offenders return to society. The decree called upon prison directors and clergy to warmly support efforts to establish more associations, and, perhaps most important, made funds available to defray costs.[5]

The Inner Mission and the Protestant clergy helped create momentum for the associations in the wake of the ministry's decree. In 1882, the Royal Consortium made welfare for released prisoners into an official topic for all of the district church councils across Prussia. Over the next two decades, the number of associations in the Rhineland and Westphalia leaped from twenty-seven to sixty-six. Overall membership, revenues, and expenditures more than doubled. In regions which never had prison associations, the growth was even more dramatic. In the provinces of Saxony and Anhalt, only one prison association existed before 1870 (in Merseburg). By 1886, there were twenty-four local associations with hundreds of members. In Hessen and Nassau, five of the seven largest prison associations were founded in the decade after 1885. Many of the new associations, particularly in the Rhineland and Westphalia, were Catholic. After 1897, the Catholic welfare organization Caritas played an organizing role comparable to the Protestants' Inner Mission. Jewish prison societies were also established in Berlin, Frankfurt, and Hamburg. By the outbreak of World War I, there were a total of 600 local associations in Germany organized into twenty-five major prison societies.[6]

Membership in the associations was made up mostly of notables. Clergy often constituted the largest group, followed by prison and justice officials, and then a contingent of businessmen, local aristocrats, and middle-class professionals. Factory owners, master artisans, and teachers were especially well represented. While the official policy of the associations was to recruit members from all classes of the people, there seem to have been few or no members from the working class prior to World War I.[7] Among women members, the class bias was even more apparent. Aristocratic women, wealthy benefactresses, and widows of prominent citizens were, for a long time, the only women in the societies. In the local associations, only "ladies" could practice welfare for former prisoners and primarily worked either with women offenders or with the families of incarcerated men.[8]

The growth of the prison associations after 1870 was marked by a redefinition of their role vis-à-vis the criminal justice system. The associations' leaders embraced the principle that charity and justice had fundamentally different functions. In the spirit of Mittelstädt's polemic against the prisons, the associations stressed the deterrent function of punishment. They were distrustful, if not disdainful, of the penitentiary's rehabilitative promises. The task of repairing human souls and the severed bonds of community, in their view, belonged essentially to private welfare. It was a mantra of the prison associations after 1871 that welfare for ex-prisoners was by its nature a role for society, not the state.[9] Any effort by the state to influence or, in the worst-case scenario, control prisoner welfare would destroy it. The flipside of this expectation of state restraint was an implied promise by the prison associations to pull back from the actual arenas of punishment. Gone were the days when prison association members poured into the penitentiaries to visit inmates in their cells and urge wardens to uphold Christian principles of a well-ordered prison. When volunteers did enter the prisons, it was now mainly to lay the groundwork for the supervision that would commence upon the offenders' release, or to mediate between inmates and their families. The focus of "prison welfare" had shifted from education and spiritual guidance in the confines of the cell to advice and assistance in meeting the challenges of work and community in the broader world.[10]

The prison associations were more than ever an integral part of the social question. Adolf Fuchs, a national leader of the associations, described their work as intimately linked to various forms of welfare. His list included job-training and assistance, asylums for alcoholics and endangered women and girls, and welfare for vagrants and panhandlers. Released prisoners in German society faced unique challenges in finding stable employment and a supportive community, but ultimately the "social poisons" that threatened them were the same ones that threatened other vulnerable elements in German society. In a time of social awakening, these poisons were increasingly the focus of specialized welfare institutions.[11]

The mostly conservative members of the prison associations were sharply attuned to the failures of modern capitalism and urban cultures in accommodating former offenders. Pastor Heinrich Seyfarth, the head of the German Help-Association in Hamburg, revealed the harsh lot of the ex-offender by sending a survey to 500 employers to ask if they would consider hiring former prisoners whose character and skills were tested through six months in a welfare-run "transition-station." Numerous employers wrote back with contributions. Only one employer, however, stated that he might be willing to hire an ex-convict. Seyfarth also sent letters to salesmen's employment offices in all the major German cities, requesting their help in finding "modest posts" for former prisoners whose abilities and worthiness would likewise be screened in advance. Numerous offices responded that either their statutes forbade mediation on behalf of ex-prisoners, that they were overwhelmed with ordinary, noncriminal applicants, or that protecting their reputations prevented them from taking ex-offenders as clients.[12] Seyfarth tried placing employment ads in 300 German newspapers, but only netted responses from people looking to exploit the former prisoners' desperate situation.[13]

Seyfarth believed that such prejudices were not unreasonable under present circumstances. Many former prisoners were bad people who had no intention of living honest and productive lives. Prison often wrecked inmates physically, mentally, and morally, and sent them forth with little or no prospect of succeeding in the "struggle for existence." The biggest problem, in his view, was that employers had no way of distinguishing the genuinely penitent ex-offenders who were ready and willing to live orderly, productive lives. He believed that the associations' goal should be to find or produce such good human material and provide a recognized and trustworthy imprimatur. Seyfarth thus sought to reinvent the ideal of patronage and adapt it to the context of big cities, large-scale employers, and an atomized liberal society without guilds. The associations were to create dedicated paths along which "fallen" men and women could find their way to full citizenship.

The key to the associations' mission was protective supervision. In contrast to police supervision, which the reformers derided as "control," protective supervision aimed to strengthen the individual will, promote self-sufficiency, and nurture the instinct for community. Work was the sine qua non of this policy. The prison association in Halle started a "writing shop" in which released prisoners copied manuscripts and addressed mailing labels for a modest wage. The ex-convicts were supposed to rebuild their strength and discover "joy in work." Those who succeeded gained the imprimatur of Halle's notables and assistance in finding future employment. In Hamburg, the German Help-Association tested the moral fitness of released prisoners from all over the empire and helped those of good character resettle somewhere in Germany, find work on a ship, or relocate to a German community overseas. The Hamburg association used an urban halfway house and writing shop to evaluate and prepare ex-offenders from the educated classes and an agricultural worker colony for working class ex-cons. Other prison associations established their own labor exchanges for ex-offenders or developed close ties with local independent exchanges.[14]

Supervision and the Vagabond Question

The rhetoric of mercy and noblesse oblige that undergirded the work of the prison associations also marked the efforts of charities to combat vagrancy and begging. The charities established closed institutions of "welfare for wanderers" as a means of assisting persons with the will and the ability to work who were forced by circumstances to wander from town to town.[15] The oldest and most numerous of these institutions were the workers' hostels (*Herberge zur Heimat*). They offered an overnight stay for a small fee. The second institution, known as natural provision stations, provided a room to indigent persons for at most a few nights, in return for work, usually chopping wood. Finally, and most important, the worker colony was a longer-term residential facility in which unemployed persons contracted to stay in exchange for work, food, and shelter. All these institutions were supposed to provide protection from "vagabond pubs" and the moral dangers of life on the road. Pastor Friedrich von Bodelschwingh, the leader of the famous Bethel Asylum, envisioned the institutions as an ensemble: supervising a mass population at risk of spiritual and physical decline.

The backdrop to the development of these welfare measures was a massive increase in internal migration, especially after the 1871 Franco-Prussian War.[16] Observers were shocked by the chaotic demobilization at war's end that put tens of thousands of young men on the road in search of work or adventure. In reality, the "army of wanderers" had deeper and complex social roots. Years of agriculture crises, particularly in East Prussia, combined with booming industrial production in the west, had driven many peasants to try their luck in new lands and especially in the emerging factory towns.[17] The worldwide economic crisis of 1873 accelerated this process. Young, single men were the largest group of migrants, but unmarried women, hoping for work as domestic servants, were on the roads as well.[18] People not only migrated more often than their parents or grandparents, but migrated much greater distances on average. During most of the nineteenth century, the vast majority of migrants to the Ruhr came from a few neighboring districts. After 1875, migrants routinely arrived from far-flung Prussian provinces with vastly different cultures, dialects, and traditions.[19] Such factors made the newcomers more conspicuous and thus made the jump in migration seem even greater. Many German cities, moreover, introduced new registration systems in the 1870s, making it easier to track the arrival of new residents and the loss of old.[20]

The line between legitimate wandering and illegal vagrancy was notoriously difficult to fix. A rich romantic tradition of poetry, songs, and literature in German conflated the vagabond's instinctual rootlessness with the wanderlust of artists and journeymen.[21] The American investigator Josiah Flynt found that the German public was "even more inanely generous than its counterpart in the United States" when it came to handouts to strangers. German vagrants could reportedly earn more from door-to-door begging than they could possibly make from typical manual labor. Reports by writers who traveled among the tramps describe a remarkably vibrant subculture with its own language and rituals and a strong sense of fellowship.[22]

The wanderers were, nevertheless, clearly an unsettling element in Imperial German politics and society. In the 1870s, authorities ranging from small-town mayors to Reich-Chancellor Bismarck spoke of a "plague of vagabondage." The flipside of the wayfarer's romantic image was the fear provoked by rootless, unsteady, and sometimes rambunctious outsiders.[23] Flynt described how a sudden "storm" of vagrants could frighten villagers into providing bread and meat.[24] With the decline of artisan guilds and handicraft traditions, even Christian journeymen became objects of suspicion.[25] Wichern, in spite of his intense support for guild traditions, worried that artisan culture encouraged rootlessness and subjected young men to the temptations of moral corruption. The journeyman has "deceived himself about the precious possession of 'freedom,' " Wichern declared at the founding of the Hamburg home-hostel in 1872. "It will soon become a burden to him, a mother of all needs." Under the current system the journeymen were "self-alienated," because they were not bound to other men by love but only by their own material needs. On their tours, the artisans-in-training became habituated to living off the largesse of others—a form of dependence that was only a short step away from begging.[26]

Just as popular traditions blurred the boundaries between migration and vagabondage, criminal justice was exceedingly vague about the crime of vagrancy.[27] Paragraph 361 of the Reich Criminal Code described vagrancy as moving from place to place with the intention of seeking alms from strangers. Commentators on German law noted that under this law almost any propertyless wayfarer could be charged with vagrancy.[28] Scholars even debated whether the paragraph effectively outlawed hallowed traditions like the journeymen's tours or the "*Terminieren*" of Catholic monks, in which they walked from town to town, subsisting upon the gifts of the righteous. One jurist argued that the monks' ritual wandering clearly violated Paragraph 361, and that the courts were therefore obliged to prosecute them. The author concluded, however, that the police should use its discretion not to arrest the monks, who were practicing "charitable activities of the noblest kind."[29] The author's readiness to abandon the principle of legality in regard to administrative (police) practice—even while upholding it as a principle of judicial authority—exasperated at least one later commentator, but it was typical of juridical strategies for regulating the underclass, while avoiding the harassment of respectable persons.[30]

In essence the law gave the state authority to prosecute any man who failed to demonstrate that he was economically independent or at least belonged in a given place. It was left to the police to make substantive determinations between the legitimate guest and the unwelcome alien, between necessary journeys and "purposeless wandering."[31] In some German states, local laws allowed the police to prosecute suspected vagrants without even referring the matter to a judge. Through this "summary process," vagrants were sentenced for up to fourteen days in a police jail. Ultimately, criminal justice practice in the regulation of vagrancy differed from place to place, shifted over time, and was frequently obtuse.[32]

Though the distinction between legitimate wayfarers and illegitimate vagrants was often arbitrary and unclear, it was nevertheless an organizing principle in welfare for wanderers. In theory, there was a division of responsibility between the state and the charities. The police handled vagabonds. Charitable organizations offered aid and assistance to persons migrating in search of honest work.

Prior to the 1880s, charity for wanderers was largely synonymous with giving alms and sponsoring overnight shelters like the great City Mission in Berlin or Wichern's "Midnight Mission" in Hamburg. Whatever their good intentions, the overburdened clergy and volunteer staff at these asylums ultimately provided little to visitors beyond a bed and a warm meal.[33] Any pedagogic or therapeutic function was largely symbolic. An exception to this was the workers' hostel movement (*Herberge zur Heimat*), which Wichern helped start in 1854. The hostels were created specifically to protect the moral welfare of journeymen. They promised a secure refuge from the corrupting atmosphere of the "wild shelters" and "vagabond pubs," a safe haven where craft solidarity and artisan pride could reassert itself. House rules typically forbade brandy, gambling, and sexual intermingling. The directors of the homes, known as "house fathers," were supposed to be firm but caring men of great piety. Frequently the hostels also served as labor exchanges for the local guilds.

Over time, however, the moral and pedagogic function of the hostels became less clear. By the time of German unification, the hostels were open to any male guest at any hour who was "legitimate and sober." Henceforth the only condition for admission was the nominal charge for room and board and the promise to abide by house rules. Inevitably the clientele changed. The official aim of the institution was still to quarantine young craftsmen against the "sickness" of vagabondage, but the reality was that most hostels were simply places to stay, distinguished only by degrees from the homeless shelters.[34] Critics of the hostels claimed that they not only failed to protect honest travelers but actually facilitated the spread of vagrancy.[35] Chronic drinkers and professional vagabonds, it was argued, exploited the charities to maintain their lifestyles. While the housefathers might prevent drinking and gambling inside the hostels, the guests developed an "organic relationship" with neighboring pubs. Drunkenness was the rule rather than the exception.[36] Far from preserving a "poor but respectable" environment, the hostels had become "schools for the education of indolence and turpitude."[37]

The criticism of the hostels became part of a powerful movement to re-form charitable giving by stopping "indiscriminate" assistance to indigent persons. Historians have noted how secular, liberal thinkers in organizations like the German Association for Poor Relief contributed to this backlash against traditional Christian charity.[38] Many of the attacks on such charity, however, were still phrased in Christian idioms. The writings of Wilhelm Riehl in particular helped give intellectual cache to what Friedrich Nietzsche derided as the "tireless talk of the 'blessings of labor.' " In his analysis of the German national character, Riehl argued that labor was the key to moral development—including forced labor if necessary.[39] As Paul Lafargue asserted, "priests, economists, and moralists" elevated work into something "holy."[40]

Certainly Lafargue's description fit the sermons of Pastor von Bodel-schwingh of Bethel. Bodelschwingh condemned the giving of alms to way-farers as "uncharitable charity" because of how it corrupted the recipients.[41] In almost lurid terms, he described how diligent workers descended into indolence after "strong hands reach[ed] out for handouts." According to Bodelschwingh, there was a direct line of descent from idleness to alcohol-ism, to despair and finally to a hatred of society:

> As the hands become slack toward work, so also the heart becomes gradu-ally lame and every cheerful hope for God and Man is extinguished in his breast, and is turned into bitterness, yes fury and hatred, when he realizes that in an earthly reckoning it is wisest to howl with the wolves. Yes, when even a taste develops for the moral void of the misery of brandy and for the dirt and mocking songs of the vagabond hostels, and when from week to week the bog in which one sinks becomes deeper, until finally not even a sigh is left for one to utter forth.[42]

Inspired by Bodelschwingh and others, "Associations Against House-Begging" sprang up across Germany in the 1870s and 1880s. Members of the associations pledged not to give alms to beggars and posted signs on their homes and notices in their neighborhoods to warn away supplicants. In case the beggars were illiterate, signs were also posted in the "secret" language of symbols used by German vagrants.[43]

It was in the spirit of this backlash against traditional charity that Dekan Kemmler in the city of Würtemburg created the first "natural provisions stations" in 1880. The stations offered short-term lodging, meals, and clothes for indigent travelers in exchange for work, usually chopping wood. As in Wichern's conception of the home-hostels, the stations were supposed to protect well-intentioned travelers from the dangers of moral corruption. The work requirement, however, was a crucial difference. Labor was to be the means to test the character of every newcomer. The true vagabonds, it was said, would refuse even a couple of hours of good physical work. The stations, if they became universal, would establish the principle that assistance was forthcoming only in return for labor. Kind-hearted burghers, reformers argued, could refuse to give alms to beggars, secure in the knowledge that Christian charities would provide shelter to those (and only to those) who truly deserved it.[44]

The most important new institution in the emerging system of welfare for wanderers was the worker colony. This was a residential facility, usually, but not necessarily in a rural area. The colony required its clients to engage in hard, physical labor each day in exchange for room and board. The founder of the first worker colony, Pastor von Bodelschwingh, was also the institution's greatest propagandist. It was Bodelschwingh who envisioned a comprehensive system of welfare for wanderers that encompassed the provision stations and the home-hostels, as well as the worker colonies. As head of the German Hostel Association, a leader in the Inner Mission, and a member of the Prussian parliament, Bodelschwingh propagated the dream of a giant network of institutions to protect vulnerable persons from the risks of mobility, alcohol, and indolence.

A leading church historian describes Bodelschwingh as "one of the most revered figures of modern German Protestantism."[45] He was from a prominent family that had figured largely in Prussian history, impeccably Junker and fervently devoted to noblesse oblige. Friedrich's father, Ernst, was the chief Prussian administrator in the Rhineland in the 1830s and later served as Prussian Interior Minister. Deeply influenced by the Pietist movement and the Inner Mission, his father was instrumental in creating Prussia's first law to regulate factory labor. Wichern was a frequent guest in the family home.[46] Friedrich von Bodelschwingh gained national prominence in the 1860s as the editor of a Christian-Conservative weekly in which "public dancing and sectarian liberalism were denounced with equal vehemence." In 1872 he was appointed Director of Bethel, near Bielefeld. Bethel had been founded at Wichern's initiative as a home for epileptics.[47] Bodelschwingh expanded the asylum into a chain of institutions that soon constituted the largest and most prestigious medical-welfare complex in Germany. Bethel eventually included a hospital, homes for epileptics, the mentally and physically disabled, and chronic drinkers, and a school for training female charity workers.[48] Bodelschwingh's success at Bethel propelled him into the national hierarchy of the Inner Mission and into the Prussian Landtag, where he represented the Conservative Party and was especially active on issues related to vagrancy and begging.

Bodelschwingh founded the first worker colony, Wilhelmsdorf, in 1882 near Bethel.[49] He envisioned it as a refuge for ordinary persons who were willing and able to work, but weakened and disillusioned by long-term unemployment. Such wanderers were often physically exhausted, harassed by the police, alienated from their families, and badly in need of clothes, shoes, and nourishment. Many were especially vulnerable to the lure of brandy. Bodelschwingh called Wilhelmsdorf a "port of security for all the crafts damaged on the high seas in storms or still winds, who needed long and basic repairs."[50] Its aim was to rescue wanderers from the vicious circle of begging, arrest, conviction, prison, workhouse, and a return to begging, with its attendant spiral of physical and moral degeneration.

Time in the worker colony was highly structured and controlled. As originally conceived, colonists stayed for up to six weeks, worked seven to ten hours every day except Sunday, and followed a regimen of prayer, sobriety, and abstinence. The rules forbade gambling, card-playing, loud conversations, political speech, lying and gossip. It was also forbidden for the colonists to loan each other money or possessions. Attendance at meals was required, while attendance at prayer services was "strongly encouraged." Colonists were not allowed to leave the institution without permission. The punishment in the case of multiple infractions was expulsion.[51]

Labor was the key element in the colony's educational experience, though little effort was made to impart useful training or skills. Instead, the colonies assigned mainly hard, physical work. Many of the colonies focused on turning arid wastelands into productive farming operations, with the hope that such grueling but rewarding challenges would teach colonists the virtues of self-help. The leaders of Bethel thus established Wilhelmsdorf on a dreary, sandy plateau that had long been considered non-arable. They assigned colonists to prepare the soil by removing the meter-thick layer of sand, breaking the hard but fertile marl, and digging irrigation wells and ditches.[52] The founders of the Kästorf Colony near Berlin believed their spot was "exceptionally favorable" because of the iron-saturated, hard rock boulders that needed to be removed from the earth before they could plant.[53] Bodelschwingh's son later recommended moving colonies constantly, in order to keep the work focused on "inner colonization" and the reclamation of new lands.[54] The remuneration, meanwhile, was minimal. For the first two weeks, in fact, the colonists' entire earnings went toward offsetting the cost of room, board, and new clothing.[55]

Alongside this educational purpose, work in the colonies was supposed to test the individual's moral fitness. According to Bodelschwingh, hard physical labor was an "almost foolproof" way of distinguishing the deserving poor from chronic idlers.[56] Work was the "ancient touchstone" that revealed a man's inner self. Wihelmsdorf's house father forwarded the names of diligent and well-mannered colonists to the labor exchange in nearby Bielefeld and frequently found work for ex-colonists with other charitable associations, including asylums for wayward youth.[57] Those who refused to work in the colonies were expelled, blacklisted from other institutions, and, at least in theory, transferred to the police. Bodelschwingh's empathy for the innocent unemployed was matched by an equally powerful malice toward those who had revealed themselves to be "true vagabonds." He had no qualms about the workhouse as a destination for those who were demonstrably work-shy.[58]

Nevertheless, Bodelschwingh and his followers were fierce critics of the indiscriminate prosecution of indigent wanderers by the police and the tendency of the workhouses to throw the victims of social circumstances together with hardened vagabonds. Under German law, convicted vagrants were sentenced to short prison terms but then transferred to the police, who were empowered to confine them in a "house of correction" for up to two years. Moreover, an exceptions clause in the 1867 Law of Free Mobility gave states the right to forbid the right of settlement to anyone who had been convicted of recidivist begging or vagrancy during the past twelve months.[59] Bodelschwingh argued that many of these convicted offenders were impoverished men who begged only out of desperation. He recommended the prosecution of city officials who chased away indigent persons knowing that they would have no alternative other than to beg for handouts on the road. He condemned the police for hastening the destruction of people's lives by "addressing the unfortunate poor and the professional tramps with the same words."[60]

The charities, however, reserved their sharpest criticism for the workhouse. "To be sentenced once to the house of correction," Bodelschwingh declared, "is in many cases worse than a death sentence." Levin Freiherr von Wintzingeroda-Knorr in 1884 argued that the workhouse could force inmates to work, but could not instill the "well-ordered way of life" that would keep them from falling back into bad habits once outside. A former workhouse director, now the director of a worker colony, wrote Bodelschwingh that the workhouse "murders" individual dignity and "has a destructive effect" upon morals. The director of the worker colony in Lühlerheim asserted that the workhouse failed to "stimulate the power of the will" and thus inevitably failed to rehabilitate ex-offenders. In 1893, Bodelschwingh surveyed directors and clergy on whether they believed that the worker colony was more likely than the workhouse to have a positive effect upon corrigible individuals who were convicted under Paragraph 361. A majority responded in the affirmative.[61] Bodelschwingh later declared of the workhouse simply, "Everyone comes out worse than they came in."[62]

Was the worker colony, however, an improvement over the workhouse? Leftists in particular expressed doubts. The radical writer Hans Ostwald ridiculed Bodelschwingh for expecting workers to freely subject themselves to a work-regime that was more strenuous and possibly even less remunerative. Socialist leader Karl Kautsky dismissed the colony as a "voluntary penitentiary."[63] Historians of the colonies, including those writing in publications sponsored by the colonies' successor institutions, describe them as bleak places with an authoritarian cast and a reactionary, paternalistic social agenda.[64]

For Bodelschwingh, however, the colony and the workhouse were as different "as morning from evening and heaven from earth."[65] He stressed that no colonist was held against his will. There were no walls, no guards, and no corporal punishment: the only sanction was expulsion.[66] The colony offered each resident a contract. Success or failure rested upon the colonist's willingness to fulfill his own promises. Proponents of the worker colony also believed it was distinguished by the nature of the labor routine and the organization of daily life. They saw the clearing of rocky fields and the draining of swamps for agriculture as both spiritually gratifying and physically invigorating. The residents of mature colonies, meanwhile, were supposed to find meaning in growing crops, feeding animals, and performing other tasks that supported the actual operation of the institution. Colony labor was thus valued for the practical and demonstrable results that were said to be missing in the case of forced labor in state institutions.

Finally, Bodelschwingh and his disciples believed that the uniqueness of the worker colonies, along with the provision stations and the worker hostels, lay in the meticulous observation of the visitors and the individualized treatment.[67] Bodelschwingh was famously obsessed with the details of the wanderers' lives. He recalled moving among them in his youth, dressed as a tramp, in order to study their ways.[68] Later he pushed the young pastoral candidates and deacons at Bethel to engage in similar participant observation. He advised his assistants to record the minutiae of wanderers' habits, attitudes, and behavior, including "the differences . . . between paying guests and charity cases? Which are more orderly? Which are least bothered by prayer services?"[69] Dress, grooming, and physique were especially important signs for assessing the individual's level of moral endangerment.[70] The leaders of the Worker Colonies were constantly defining and redefining systems for the classification of colonists. For a time, they spoke of five types of colonists. Later it was three. The essential task, in any case, was to know the colonist's true personality and to use this classification to determine the right measures.[71]

In spite of its critics, the worker colony movement grew quickly under the auspices of Protestant and Catholic charities and with help from noble patrons in particular. Crown Prince Friedrich Wilhelm took Wilhelmsdorf under his patronage in 1883 and provided 10,000 marks to each of the other colonies as well. The prince enabled Bodelschwingh to create the nearby Friedrichshuette colony for alcoholics. The Empress Victoria helped Bodelschwingh create the first worker colony for women, Hoffnungsthal, near Berlin in 1905. In many regions, local volunteer organizations, including local chapters of the Inner Mission, the prison societies, and the chambers of commerce, formed new associations to administer the colonies, often with strong representation from jurists.[72] By 1890, there were twenty-two worker colonies in Prussia admitting up to 15,500 colonists per year, while there were 362 home hostels and 951 provision stations. Germany was still a long way from the seamless net of institutions that Bodelschwingh envisioned, but these institutions of "enclosed welfare" had already created new options and new principles for the supervision of wayward, unsteady persons.

Rescuing Women and Girls

Like the vagabond question, the preoccupation with prostitution in the Imperial era came out of a perception of acute crisis. Once again, the objective basis of this crisis is open to dispute. Most statistics on prostitution concerned women who were registered with the police, but the vast majority of prostitutes avoided such controls and were thus difficult to count. Estimates regarding the number of unlicensed prostitutes were also marred by the researchers' changing definitions of venal sex.[73] Nevertheless, reformers after 1900 frequently cited a Reichstag committee report claiming that in Berlin alone there were 3,000 licensed prostitutes and between 40,000 and 50,000 unlicensed sex workers. Such figures represented a fourfold increase over the estimates from the 1870s.[74]

Concerns with prostitution were fueled as well by the growing population of unmarried, independent women who migrated to the cities after 1890. Even more so than male migrants, women migrants were seen as morally uprooted and vulnerable to social poisons. While the men turned to alcohol, begging, and life on the road, unsupervised young women, it was said, were lured into prostitution by the temptations of easy money and unscrupulous seducers. The guidelines for a Brandenburg welfare organization stated that "migrant girls in a certain sense are almost always at-risk and must have assistance to gain a footing in the life of the community." Popular wisdom held that servant girls, nurses, and clerks were particularly susceptible to these dangers, whereas many welfare organizations often railed against the moral threat of factory work.[75]

Undoubtedly, medical fears about the spread of venereal disease also played a role in placing the prostitution question on the public agenda. Scholars have shown that the image of the commercial woman in nineteenth-century Europe was a metonym for a whole set of fears of contagion and disease.[76] In Alain Corbin's words, "The virus incubated by the prostitutes sets in motion a process of degeneration that threatens to annihilate the bourgeoisie."[77] Organizations like the Society to Combat Venereal Diseases founded in 1902 promoted a reform movement that focused on using state and medical expertise to address the dire and immediate public health threat.[78] Most German cities saw an intensification in the highly intrusive forms of forced medical examination imposed upon prostitutes around the turn of the century.[79] Police regulations sought to "construct a clear dividing wall" between the prostitutes and respectable society. In Berlin, registered prostitutes were "not permitted to lounge about" and were prohibited from whole areas of the city. The American investigator Abraham Flexner claimed that the regulation system also helped police to force prostitutes to cooperate in their investigations into more serious crimes. A few cities sought to isolate and control prostitutes even further by restricting them to state-licensed brothels or red-light districts.[80]

At the same time, women's organizations in the 1890s mobilized against this exclusionary and repressive approach to the prostitution question. Women activists opposed forced medical examinations and the confinement of sex workers in officially sanctioned red-light districts and brothels. The entire logic of registration, in their view, was based upon a double standard. Registration guaranteed male access to venal sex, while stigmatizing the women who met this demand.[81] Women's organizations were increasingly critical of the police, the courts, and the medical professionals who worked with them.[82]

Such activism on the prostitution question came from both the right and the left. It is not surprising perhaps that abolitionists—women who supported the legalization of prostitution—attacked the state's degrading policies. According to Ursula Nienhaus, the abolitionist movement was based upon a critique of patriarchal authority that posed "organized motherliness" as an alternative to punitive and strictly regulatory power.[83] Conservative religious women's organizations, however, were hardly less strident than their feminist counterparts in criticizing police practice. The leading Protestant women's organization, the German Evangelical Women's Union (DEF), condemned the police's clumsy one-size-fits-all approach to regulating prostitution. Even the Conference of Morality Associations, which was explicitly anti-feminist and favored an outright ban on prostitution, attacked the police for heavy-handed policies that pushed salvageable women deeper into the sump of immorality.[84]

Conservative anti-prostitution organizations pursued a strategy of lay activism that was similar to the prison associations. The women and men of the DEF and the Morality Associations argued that state-run bureaucracies inevitably failed, while popular participation was essential to saving morally endangered women. For these activists, the participation of bourgeois women was key.[85] The arch-conservative court preacher Adolph Stoecker, who helped found the DEF, was among those who vigorously promoted women's social activism. Stoecker produced guidelines for women's associations, which became the official views of the Inner Mission's Central Committee. In his guidelines, Stoecker rejected the idea that women charitable workers must be subservient to men and declared it woman's "essential duty" to engage "the service of love both inside and outside the home." Although the DEF was founded as a conservative counterweight to liberal feminists, it vigorously promoted women's participation in anti-prostitution measures. The predominantly urban and upper-class members of the DEF used their clout with municipal authorities to open up opportunities for women.[86]

Conservative Christian organizations rarely opposed punitive approaches to prostitution per se.[87] Pastors in the Prison Society of Saxony and Anhalt were appalled at the mere suggestion of decriminalizing prostitution. Punishment in this case, one pastor argued, was healthy. General deterrence was necessary both for individual moral development and for upholding moral standards across society.[88] But while conservative groups believed that prostitution must be punished, they were also committed to the concept of rehabilitation and shared the feminists' conviction that the prisons and workhouses were unsuitable as sites of rehabilitation. Here again was an echo of

Mittelstädt's critique of the penitentiary, that one cannot prepare men for freedom through unfreedom. Punishment per se, they believed, would never make people moral. As historian Young Sun Hong writes, the associations saw "state coercion and regulation . . . as an unnatural force that violated the quintessentially religious nature of voluntary charitable activity."[89] Only private charity, they argued, could provide the ersatz family, meaningful work, and moral guidance that was necessary to transform these souls.[90]

Like Bodelschwingh and other proponents of the worker colonies, moral reformers were sharply critical of state institutions for undermining their efforts at moral reclamation. They condemned the prisons and workhouses for failing to differentiate among the various categories of endangered or fallen women. The workhouses, in particular, routinely put first-time women offenders together with hardened prostitutes. The charities also criticized police regulation. While clearly approving of efforts to keep prostitutes away from "respectable society," they lamented overzealous medical and police measures that dishonored and marginalized girls and young women who might otherwise be saved.

The principal site of protective supervision for women and girls was the asylum. Institutions for "fallen women" had existed in Germany since the Middle Ages. Prior to the 1880s, the so-called "Magdalene homes" took a largely punitive approach to the unmarried pregnant women and former prostitutes who were their main clients. The nuns and priests who typically administered these homes demanded demonstrations of penitence and a willingness to work hard and follow stringent house rules. Obedient women could hope to eventually find employment as domestic servants with a good Christian family. Over the course of the Imperial era, the character of the Magdalene homes changed drastically, particularly after 1900 when the Prussian Welfare Education Law forced a mass influx of younger women and girls who had not necessarily engaged in overt sexual misconduct but whom judges deemed to be at-risk of such behavior. Starting in the 1880s, reformers also established hundreds of specialized asylums to serve diverse categories of fallen or endangered women and girls, each supposedly based upon distinct principles of treatment and care.

Though still frequently referred to as Magdalene homes, the new homes for "endangered women and girls" were less rigid, less religious, and more oriented toward worldly education and training. The goal of the asylums was not penitence per se, but strengthening the will and preparing women for the challenges and temptations of modern life. Many of the homes followed the "open-door" principles of the Dutch reformer Otto Gerhard Heldring. The

Inner Mission asylums accepted women whom the traditional Magdalene would have rejected as hopeless cases, including those who had multiple out-of-wedlock births. With certain limitations, the residents could come and go as they wished. The Sisters of the Inner Mission were thereby forced to provide incentives for the women to stay. They taught gardening, housework, and craft skills and sought to provide the "motherly attention" that their charges had presumably missed.[91]

The interest in homes for endangered women and girls spread along with fears about women who migrated to urban areas and about wayward girls. Feminist organizations, the Jewish Women's Association, and the Salvation Army all established their own asylums to serve this population. In some communities, liberal feminists worked closely with arch-conservative moral reformers to build institutions. In industrial towns, companies sponsored dormitories for women factory workers modeled on the Protestant homes. Many of the dormitories employed Catholic or Protestant sisters as supervisors and provided training and organized activities intended to shield the girls from moral corruption and prepare them to eventually become good housewives or domestic servants.[92] An important Catholic movement in welfare for endangered women and girls emerged after 1899 through the efforts of Agnes Neuhaus. Under Neuhaus's vigorous leadership, Catholic Welfare Association founded forty-three homes between 1900 and 1920. Neuhaus's asylums depended upon a close relationship with local police forces to identify and bring in at-risk women and girls, but she was a strong proponent of the educational and spiritual mission of welfare. Like the leaders of the worker colonies, Neuhaus refused to allow formal juridical categories or simplistic moral judgments to preempt her own organization's responsibility to assess the will and the abilities of individual clients.[93]

Critics have frequently derided the women's asylums, Protestant and Catholic, as voluntary prisons.[94] Certainly there is evidence to suggest that many German women loathed the charitable houses and did everything possible to avoid them. Nancy Reagin estimates that fewer than one-tenth of the unmarried pregnant women in Hannover turned to the home for unwed mothers. Richard Evans notes the "numerical insignificance of 'rescue work' as far as registered prostitutes were concerned."[95] No doubt, the asylums were often cold, oppressive places that stripped women of their dignity. The Vinzenz-heim in Dortmund restricted the residents' dress and hairstyles, monitored their correspondence, and required "absolute silence" during much of the ordinary day and night routine. The director of the Bernbug asylum boasted that he assigned his residents only the kind of work that would limit their opportunities for thinking about the past. Knitting and sewing were out of the question. Washing and ironing were better because they required total focus.[96]

Reformers of this era, however, focused not upon the "repressive atmosphere" of the women's asylum but upon the essential differences between the charitable homes and the principal alternative, the workhouse. In matters of diet, hygiene, and the character of work, the workhouses revealed their punitive purpose. The workhouses' regulations on behavior were also more restrictive than the harshest asylums, and the punishments for infractions were far more draconian. Workhouse administrators punished inmates with bread and water diets and solitary confinement for even relatively minor infractions.[97] Most important, the workhouse removed young women from any semblance of a normal community or family, which was a particular hardship for young mothers. By contrast, a key goal of protective supervision was to repair the bonds between endangered girls and women, their offspring, and their families.[98]

Noting the differences between workhouse and women's asylum is essential for understanding the consensus in fin-de-siècle Germany behind protective supervision. Feminists and moral reformers differed vehemently over a host of issues, but they agreed that private welfare in almost any form was vastly more able than the police, the courts, or the medical authorities to prevent sexual immorality and rescue fallen women. To a remarkable extent, reformers with wildly varying agendas collaborated in creating options for protective supervision. Their shared faith in the asylum was the flipside of a deep skepticism about the state's ability to assess the social and moral condition of women and to help endangered women and girls develop their faculties as autonomous moral agents. The march of "organized motherliness" was in many ways a direct challenge to state power.[99]

Welfare as Ideology

Starting in 1887, the German Worker Colony Association commissioned a series of studies from Georg Berthold, a sociologist affiliated with the German Association for Poor Relief. Berthold's six annual studies became progressively more critical in tone. He found that the colonies did not adequately prepare colonists for the labor market, that a majority of colonists left without having found work, and that a growing number of colonists (46 percent in 1891) were repeat visitors. Berthold argued that the colonies were failing to achieve their goals and that the reason had mostly to do with the inadequate screening of people upon their arrival. According to Berthold, over three-quarters of the colonists were former offenders and the percentage was rising. While many of these ex-offenders had only committed misdemeanors, a significant number were habitual criminals with multiple felonies to their names. The colonies, Berthold concluded, were not serving the respectable unemployed, but had become "a hideout for vagrants and other degenerate persons seeking refuge from the police."[100] His solution was simple: they should ban recidivist offenders and serious felons and penalize repeat visitors.[101]

The leaders of the colonies rejected Berthold's recommendations and maintained their open-door policy even in the face of criticism from the German Association of Poor Relief, prominent law scholars, and representatives of the working class. Bodelschwingh refused to accept that a man could be judged unworthy of assistance simply because of his criminal past. He held fast to the idea that every man who came in search of alms should have the opportunity to reveal his true character through hard work and obedience to authority. Other leaders of the worker colony movement similarly argued against any kind of formal, juridical constraints upon the practice of charity. The only criteria with which to screen persons from a charitable institution, they believed, were welfare criteria. They insisted upon the duty of the colonies themselves to diagnose each person according to how he lived up to the demands of the institution.[102]

The colonies' defense of open door policies illustrated their growing confidence in welfare as an autonomous practice with its own methods, logic, and authority. The prison associations and the homes for endangered women and girls similarly resisted outside efforts at imposing formal restrictions on aid. Most local associations claimed to provide assistance to released prisoners without regard to their criminal record. A prison pastor's observations about an offender were more important to the associations than the police file—which, in any case, they never saw. The asylums for women and girls were eager to keep hardened prostitutes away from young and impressionable girls, but they too refused to rely upon juridical formulas to screen their clientele. Welfare judged the whole person, meaning the individual as a social being, and was therefore not reducible to a tally of crimes in a police blotter.

The charities' self-confidence led to an ambivalent and complex relationship to criminal justice. On the one hand, the charities continued to see protective supervision as separate and complementary to criminal justice. Punishment provided moral retribution, deterrence against future crimes, and protection for society against dangerous individuals. Welfare repaired bodies and souls and prepared the way for a worthy individual's reintegration into community. Most of the charities supported vigorous law enforcement, including swift and severe punishment for criminal offenders, most of the time. In contrast to Wichern, they believed that the borders of the kingdom of charity (like the kingdom of mercy) started where the kingdom of justice stopped. On the other hand, it was impossible, in practice, for the charities to stand up for the increasingly important category of endangered persons without challenging criminal justice norms. In essentially all areas of protective supervision, the charities' members became to a greater or lesser degree critics of judicial, prison, and police practice.

After 1890, the charities increasingly sought to replace the state in the supervision of criminal offenders: the worker colony in place of the workhouse, welfare supervision in place of police supervision and police regulation. While the charities justified such measures in terms of protecting vulnerable persons from the destructive influence of state institutions, they also sought to bolster their own authority and ability to pressure clients into accepting protective supervision. Indeed, the two goals—protection and authority—were deeply intertwined. Many of the people most in need of supervision, it was argued, did not recognize or could not act upon their own self-interest. The charities' turn to coercive levers of power was driven by a changing image of the subject of welfare.

The Invention of the Asocial

Bodelschwingh envisioned the worker colony as a refuge for ordinary, respectable workers who were forced by circumstances to wander in search of work. In practice, the colonies' leaders found that their clientele was very different. Georg Berthold's statistical studies of the colonies confirmed the widespread impression that a majority of the colonists were ex-convicts, chronic wanderers, or persons with marked, if moderate, physical and mental disabilities. It became increasingly common after 1890 to speak of the colonists as peculiarly vulnerable persons who would not be able to live stable, orderly, and productive lives without special supervision. The colonists, in other words, were becoming a distinct "human type."

For Berthold and others, the preponderance of criminals and disabled persons in the colonies discredited the overall project. Berthold, as we have seen, called upon the colonies to screen out the morally questionable elements. Socialist Karl Kautsky condemned the colonies as extensions of the criminal justice system. In a review of Berthold, he mocked the idea that respectable workers would ever be drawn to the colonies. Those who strived for "orderly conditions in their lives," he wrote, stayed "far away" from the colony.[103] Progressive speakers at the conference for the German Association for Poor Relief also criticized the worker colonies for admitting the dregs of the working class (*Halbkräfte*).[104]

Bodelschwingh's associate Konrad von Massow acknowledged that over 50 percent of the colonists had some form of disability. These were the unhappiest people in the world, he told the German Association for Poor Relief. In hard times, they were unemployed. In good times, they earned barely enough for survival. The worker colonies, von Massow declared, offered them "a sanctuary from the battle between capital and labor" and restored their "sense of self worth."[105] The colonies, in short, were no longer an emergency shelter for battered and exhausted but otherwise normal people. They served a particular "type" of person who had an inherently problematic relationship with the dominant culture.[106]

In a seminal essay, Bodelschwingh's successor at Bethel, his son Fritz, coined the term "adult children" (*Grosse Kinder*) to describe this marginal, highly vulnerable population, which fell between the cracks of medical and legal regulation. The adult children were mentally slow but not mentally incompetent. They were therefore unlikely to be subject to guardianship proceedings. They lacked any "sense of honor," but were not (yet) true criminals. The police and the courts therefore could not detain them. According to Bodelschwingh, adult children often thrived within the controlled, comfortable setting of the worker colony. In the outside world, however, they stumbled. "They overestimate their own abilities and underestimate the tasks and the challenges of life," Bodelschwingh writes. "For this reason, they are unable to resist momentary desires and moods . . . and become victims of the lowest passions." In an earlier time, when relations between workers and employers were on a more "patriarchal foundation," the adult children could find decent and appropriate opportunities for work. However, the modern economy had no place for them—thanks largely, Bodelschwingh claimed, to the unions' success in creating a system of fixed wages. Under modern conditions, the adult children were condemned to homelessness and wandering.[107]

In the early Weimar Republic, the notion of the adult child was subsumed into the concept of the "asocial." In the most rigorous definitions, welfare theorists differentiated the inherently passive and reactive asocial from the aggressive "anti-social." Whereas the latter was the "enemy of society," the former was principally society's "burden." Whereas anti-socials were the ideal subjects of criminal justice, asocials were more appropriately objects of welfare intervention. In practice, these terms were fluid and the borders were uncertain. Gustav Aschaffenburg used asociality as an umbrella term for essentially all categories of deviant behavior, including serious criminality, and the Nazis—twelve years later—followed suit. The original purpose of the term, however, was to identify a distinct class of marginal social beings, the ideal type for the institutions of protective supervision. Its primary reference point was not science at all, but the experience of welfare for endangered persons.[108]

The colonies' recognition of the adult child/asocial emerged in conjunction with ever more stringent regulations. Starting in 1892, the colonies required guests to stay for significantly longer periods of time: a minimum of three months, rather than the previous maximum of six weeks. To leave early, colonists had to prove they had secured outside employment. The punishment for unauthorized departures was threefold: Blacklisting from other welfare institutions, denial of a wanderer's pass, and loss of all wages accumulated over the period of work in the colony.[109]

Increasingly, the colonies defined welfare as a counterpoint, an alternative to criminal justice. In 1894 The Central Association of German Worker Colonies recommended that the colonies assume probationary supervision over persons convicted of vagrancy and begging whom the police would conditionally excuse from the workhouse. The colonies themselves would screen the candidates for probation by evaluating "their previous lives and personalities" and assessing the prognosis for their improvement. If they failed to live out their full term as good colonists, they would be transferred to the police, who would then send them to the workhouse. The leaders of the Central Association rejected the idea that taking in vagrants and beggars on criminal justice probation would violate the colonies' voluntarist principles. "Like all colonists," the association declared, a bit disingenuously, those on probation "will be free to leave whenever they choose. The choice must be theirs."[110]

The colonies' efforts to save convicted offenders from the workhouse failed in the face of resistance from local police officials. Nevertheless the colonies' effort to play a role in the supervision of offenders marked a turning point in the relationship between welfare and criminal justice. Was the proposed nexus between the worker colony and the police a humanitarian measure to rescue impressionable, young offenders from the workhouse, or a repressive measure to give the worker colonies power over the colonists? This either/or question would have baffled the charities' proponents. For them, the only hope of making weak-willed, rootless, and mentally deficient vagrants and beggars into autonomous, productive members of society was to force them into long-term protective supervision in a welfare institution. They were not "free men" so long as they were driven by a self-destructive urge to wander. Welfare, and welfare alone, could set them free. In his struggle for a welfare detention law in the Prussian parliament, Father Bodelschwingh steered clear of both humanitarian and law-and-order justifications.[111] He insisted that welfare was—no less than medicine—essential to protecting the health of the individual and society. It was ironic, he argued, that the worker colony was the only institution at Bethel in which the overseers had no formal, legal authority over their charges. It was time to change that anomaly.[112]

Interestingly, many liberal reformers objected to Bodelschwingh's proposal as an unwholesome combination of welfare and police functions. The German Association for Poor Relief opposed the plan outright.[113] Legal scholar Robert von Hippel, a student of Franz von Liszt and the Modern School's leading authority on the vagabond question, argued that welfare organizations were not equipped to handle a criminal population or to guarantee public security. In any case, he asserted, taking custody over persons who were still under a juridical sentence (as opposed to the ordinary released prisoners) distorted the organizations' basic purpose. "The colonies are not there to protect convicted offenders from repressive state measures," Hippel argued, "but rather to offer asylum to those worthy individuals who voluntarily and passionately seek it."[114] In short, Hippel, the modernist, defended a traditional interpretation of the charities' mission, while Bodelschwingh, the archconservative, sought to redefine the charities' role within a modern nexus of disciplinary institutions. This was not the last time that the conservatives would be at the vanguard of reform.[115]

Supervising Youth: The Welfare Education Law of 1900

The introduction of a new Reich Civil Code and the passage of the Prussian Welfare Education Law in 1900 marked another important watershed in protective supervision. Taken together, the new laws empowered guardianship courts to forcibly place youths ages eighteen and under in a welfare institution when parental neglect endangered their mental or physical well-being. The law also applied to minors who had committed a crime, but were not prosecuted due to their age or other mitigating factors. In practice, there were two areas of behavior in particular that made youth "conspicuous": vagrancy in the case of boys and sexual misconduct in the case of girls.[116]

The chairman of the Central Committee of German Worker Colonies declared the Welfare Education Law to be "one of the greatest, if not *the* greatest social acts . . . in the history of states and nations." His enthusiasm rested upon the fact that the law brought the principle of preventing moral degeneration through protective supervision to its highest fulfillment. If the worker colony made sense for shipwrecked adults, then how much more logical to reach the youth, who due to the lack of adult guidance were in manifest peril. Here, moreover, the issue of consent was irrelevant. The welfare institution that assumed guardianship over a youth was not compromising his or her freedom, but was merely taking the natural authority that previously belonged to the parents.[117]

Most of the boys who were committed to institutions under the Welfare Education Law ended up in special institutions, separated from the adult vagrants and beggars in the worker colonies. There was no equivalent concern, at least at first, with segregating endangered girls from adult prostitutes. The guardianship courts readily sent girls to the existing asylums for fallen women, and the institutions accepted. This influx of guardianship cases changed the make-up and the character of the asylums, with many homes forced to modify their "open-door" policies. A number of asylums stopped accepting older experienced prostitutes altogether, partly for fear of corrupting the girls and partly due to lack of space. In subsequent years, reformers, when possible, established new homes specifically for unmarried mothers, former prostitutes, and released women prisoners.[118]

Charity, Policing, and the Question of Consent

Even before the worker colonies proposed to supervise vagrants and beggars in lieu of the police, the prison associations were actively seeking ways to gain some measure of coercive authority over released prisoners. Prison societies were especially frustrated with the difficulties of getting released prisoners to register with their local prison associations. One by one, the associations began asking local police authorities to let them hold and distribute the accumulated wages that offenders had earned while in prison. Historically this money had been paid out by the police upon the released prisoners' arrival in their hometowns. A common complaint was that ex-convicts spent their earnings quickly and frivolously and only approached the prison associations after they were desperate for welfare assistance. By holding their back wages, the prison associations hoped to force offenders to register with them immediately and to follow their moral guidelines on spending.[119]

Liberals objected that the police had no right to place the prisoners' legitimate earnings into the hands of private associations. The state, however, sided with the charities, asserting that the money actually represented a "gift" that only belonged to released prisoners once it was handed to them. The Prison Society of Sachsen-Anhalt encouraged local associations to seize this opportunity to gain leverage over ex-offenders and to set conditions for the individual's receipt of back-wages.[120] It was an important step in routinizing the practice of protective supervision over released prisoners.

The prison associations also pressed for the authority to supervise released prisoners in lieu of police supervision. The Prussian Interior Ministry granted the associations this authority in the pivotal reform year of 1900. A ministerial decree authorized local officials to suspend police supervision for as long as a released offender "placed himself under the care" of a prison association. If at any point the offender failed to follow the association's directives, the privilege was revoked and police supervision would follow.[121] The measure was predicated upon the usual doubts about the effectiveness of police supervision and optimism about the ability of private charities to transform individual behavior. The prison associations promised to provide "oversight, welfare, and moral social support" to former prisoners and their families. A charitable leader from Kassel stated that the prison associations were pushing the traditional emphasis of criminal policy, protecting society, into the background. The press applauded, declaring that the new policy breathed "the true spirit of humanity." Did not the coercive aspects of the policy destroy the essentially voluntary character of protective supervision? For most Germans, and certainly for the associations themselves, the answer was no, since offenders still decided for themselves whether to accept this charitable benefit.[122]

Protective supervision for endangered women and girls, likewise, became increasingly intertwined with state power around the turn of the century. A major justification for keeping prostitution illegal and maintaining the despised and ineffectual system of police regulation was that these repressive measures drove endangered young women into the arms of protective associations. The Catholic welfare pioneer Agnes Neuhaus was particularly adept at using her ties with local police officials to keep a steady supply of women and girls entering her asylums. The police routinely delivered women and girls to the Catholic Welfare Association's homes whom they deemed to be at risk of serious moral decline. Many of these women were feeble-minded, physically disabled, or chronically unemployed (or all of the above). Others the police had simply picked up in the wrong place at the wrong time. The

Catholic Welfare Association frequently sent back to the police those clients who would not or could not adapt to the regimen at the homes.[123]

Protestant and Catholic charities inserted themselves further into criminal policy by sponsoring positions for "women police assistants" in many towns and cities, starting around the turn of the century. The title "police assistant" was a misnomer in as much as the job was essentially a welfare position. Many of the police assistants were employees of private charities or clubs like the local morality associations, DEF chapters, or feminist organizations. They had no actual police training or powers of arrest, at least up until World War I.[124] The DEF chapter in Hanover described the police assistant in terms that worked equally well for many charitable activities. She was to bring aid and comfort to "those unhappy, seduced young women, who lacked a parent's love and care."[125]

The title of the "police assistant," however, underscored the changing relationship between private charities and the state. The police assistants mediated between the police, the asylums, and the women and girls who, for various reasons, became objects of police suspicion or concern. They gave "organized motherliness" a footing within the masculine world of criminal justice. With the passage of the Juvenile Welfare Act in 1900, the charities had an important role to play in the disposition of unruly and endangered youth of both sexes. With the Prussian ministerial pronouncements on police supervision in the same year, charities had a growing opportunity to act as proxies for police authority in those cases where extenuating circumstances warranted some measure of mercy.[126] But the police assistants also carried the repressive power of the state into the world of the charities. Even if she was not empowered to make arrests herself, she usually played a role in determining whether a woman or girl was to be treated as an object of criminal justice or welfare intervention.[127]

In Bielefeld, where the position was created in 1907, the woman police assistant had an office at police headquarters while also administering the DEF's asylum for girls. She worked closely with police officials in all cases of women and girls arrested for the first time on suspicion of sexually immoral behavior.[128] She accompanied the detainees during their physical examinations and often during any interrogations. Frequently she visited their homes, investigated their "personal conditions," and explored the influence of the milieu upon their behaviors. If the detainees were sent to the prison, hospital, or workhouse, then she visited them there, met them upon their release, and brought them to the DEF asylum. At this point, she, or the association, became the primary supervisor.[129] She was responsible for any and all "appropriate steps" toward helping the women "turn themselves around." This might mean returning to her parents' home or entering into "orderly employment," or it might mean an extended stay in the asylum.[130]

Did women and girls accused of immoral behaviors have the option to refuse protective supervision? Reformers were mostly unconcerned about this question. They assumed that a woman or girl who was arrested—regardless of whether she was charged with a crime—would prefer to deal with the woman police assistant than with the regular officers. A girl inevitably "chose" protective supervision because it constituted probably her only chance at humane and sympathetic treatment, as well opportunities for gainful employment.

Speaking before an audience of women activists in 1907, the first Bielefeld police assistant, Clara Hermelbrecht, emphasized her role as an emissary of mercy and compassion. The parents of endangered girls, she argued, had failed them, because they did not "steel" their daughters against temptations and allowed them to become sick "through a life in sin." Male police officials were incapable of assessing the girls' condition and therefore could not direct them toward the appropriate help.[131] The only hope for these damaged and vulnerable souls was for Christian ladies and their pastors to step in and offer the "mercy of Jesus."[132] For police assistant Hermelbrecht, it was inconceivable that the objects of this mercy could have reasonable and legitimate grounds for rejecting the gift of protective supervision and therefore the question of consent was essentially moot. Throughout this long address to her colleagues, she never mentioned the Damocles sword of police regulation that hung over the entire project of charitable assistance.[133]

Protective Supervision and the Progressive Reform Movement

What was the relationship of the charities to the progressive jurists, psychiatrists, and social policy thinkers who led the famous "Modern School" of criminal reform at the fin de siècle? It should not be surprising that historians downplay the role of private welfare associations in the development of a modern reform agenda, since the leading modernists frequently distanced themselves from the "prison reform" tradition. Legal scholar Franz von Liszt, whose lucid essays and charismatic leadership inspired a generation of reformers, at times even disparaged unnamed Christian reformers for "dizzy humanitarianism," "fanatic moralism," and "zealotry" (*Schwärmerei*). Liszt and his students believed that the state must become *more* involved in regulating criminals, ex-criminals, and potential criminals. Only the state could legitimately and effectively exercise power over the entire spectrum of at-risk persons. The Modern School reformers, moreover, made a constant appeal to "science" as the guiding force behind their movement. These were two good reasons for Liszt and others to emphasize their differences with the charities.

There is a danger, however, in confusing the Modern School's brilliant self-representation with authoritative history. Its very label was tendentious. Liszt and his followers called themselves "modern" in an effort to outmaneuver the positivist jurists whom they dubbed the "classical school."[134] Both schools were trying to open up German criminal policy to the new sciences. The modernists wanted to address crime by integrating psychology, medicine, and sociology into jurisprudence; the classicists sought to ensure the autonomy and the flexibility of police authority by keeping administrative, medical, and social matters separate from justice.[135] Both schools claimed to be tough on crime: strengthening the authority of the state while attacking the "metaphysical" presuppositions of the traditionalists. Attacking unnamed Christian reformers for the sin of sentimental moralism was a convenient way of establishing their bona fides as tough on crime and loyal to science.[136]

In practice, the Modern School borrowed copiously from the charities' rhetoric and institutional models. Liszt defined his entire reform project as an effort to address crime as a "social phenomenon." He saw the modern school as part of a broader awakening in social reform which encompassed the efforts of prison societies, morality associations, and private welfare in general.[137] While he sought to marshal the authority of the state, he shared the charities' belief in the necessity of private volunteers as the foot soldiers of protective supervision.

In spite of the Modern School's incessant appeals to scientific authority, their interpretations of crime and criminality were remarkably consonant with the Christian reformers'. The Italian criminologist Cesare Lombroso undoubtedly had a following among German men of letters, but the influence of his "born criminal" hypothesis upon German criminal reformers and practitioners in the Wilhelmine era has been exaggerated. For Liszt, "hereditary defects" played a role mainly in how they weakened the individual's "power of resistance."[138] His view was that people were conditioned to criminal behavior in the course of striving and failing in the "struggle for existence." The celebrated German criminal psychiatrist Gustav Aschaffenburg similarly argued that weakness of will, the failure of social adaptation, and the corrupting temptations of modern society were the chief sources of criminal behavior.[139] The typical criminal, he wrote, was a person whose "intellectual and ethical powers have rendered him incapable of surviving the struggle for existence without overstepping the borders created by the law."[140] The pool of potential criminals came from a larger class of "inferior persons" (*Minder-wertige*) whom he defined as "socially incompetent" or "unequal to the social relations in which they are forced to live." Ultimately, they "succumb to the temptations and difficulties" of modern society.[141]

As a supposed proponent of the medicalization of criminal policy, it is striking how much Aschaffenburg's arguments focused on nonscientific evidence and used morally laden terminology—starting with "inferiority" and "weakness of will"—that was plucked from everyday usage.[142] He had surprisingly little faith in clinical assessment and rejected all of the human typologies developed by his fellow psychiatrists, including his *Doktorvater* Emil Kraepelin. "We have no canon of the normal man by which to measure all deviations," he wrote in his influential textbook.[143] Aschaffenburg argued that the degenerative effects of drinking, prostitution, gambling, bad housing, and bad diet were gradual and fluid. "At present," he declared, "we are not able to describe the psychology of the criminal." Generalizations could be constructed through statistics, but the criminal's "passions, moral perceptions, degree of altruistic thought, and remorse" had to be examined on a case-by-case basis. Effective knowledge was local knowledge, based upon intimate, close, and sustained observation in a relevant social context. The decisive point in diagnosing a potential criminal was not whether the individual showed signs of pathology, but whether he demonstrated a need for supervision. In essence, the scientist deferred to the welfare expert.[144]

For Modern School thinkers, the decisive moment in the development of the criminal personality was an exogenous one: the demands and pressures of modern society, which pulled forth the criminal act. Like their conservative counterparts, the progressive reformers pointed to the strenuous, debilitating forms of urban life and to the inherently destructive effects of mobility. "Thousands and tens of thousands have been ripped from the protective earth of their home [*Heimat*]," Liszt wrote, "and thrown into the gears of the metropolis, in which the weak ones simply sink, forming the fertile soil for the infectious germ of criminality."[145] Much of Liszt's explanation for criminal behavior also lined up with the more narrowly moral concerns of the associations. He claimed that the religious and ethical values among the lower classes were "deeply shaken." The schools neglected to "strengthen their character" and dealt only with matters of "understanding." The army, on the other, "the best of all the national educational institutions," could not remedy the situation because it was closed precisely to those who were weak in body and mind, and because many of the people most in need of such moral discipline had "already made themselves unworthy to wear the King's dress by committing felonies."[146] Finally, Liszt mourned the breakdown of familial structures among the working classes—mothers working outside the home, children growing up "too intimately" with each other, the "aberration" of male and female boarders in the home—as another factor in the litany of causes that produced criminal behavior.[147]

What was to be done? Modern School thinkers echoed the charities' critique of incarceration. Liszt attacked the prisons for their failure to supervise offenders, suggesting that the very term "supervision" had taken on the particular connotations given to it by the charities. Liszt and his followers especially condemned the short prison sentences given to petty offenders that needlessly disrupted social and familial bonds, stigmatized offenders and their families, and drove criminals together into a community of outlaws. Research by the psychiatrist Karl Wilmanns gave a scientific foundation to longstanding claims that the prisons were more likely to cause pathologies than to cure them.[148] The psychiatrist Karl Bonhoeffer recapitulated decades-old grievances against the workhouse for its punitive approach to mentally deficient, weak-willed vagrants and beggars. Bonhoeffer estimated that three-quarters of the vagabonds and prostitutes in the workhouses fundamentally lacked self-control and were thus not fully responsible for their actions in a legal sense. Punishment, he argued, particularly for those with an inborn predilection for alcohol, was useless. The only solution was "supervision." The psychiatrist Otto Mönkemöller, who made a career of research into vagrancy, begging, and prostitution, endorsed Fritz Bodelschwingh's concept of the "adult child" and praised the worker colonies as the most promising remedy for this population of morally endangered men and women.[149]

Liszt, the great "impresario" of criminological research, argued that the most important goal of reformers was to create a range of alternatives for the improvement of offenders. "Our most dangerous opponents," he proclaimed, "are the radical naturalists who deny the possibility of education."[150] A major cause for Liszt and his followers was to introduce conditional sentencing into a revised German penal code. This would give judges the power to suspend prison sentences in cases where they saw mitigating circumstances or simply believed that it was in society's best interest to grant conditional freedom. Liszt wanted to see conditionally released offenders put under the supervision of private welfare volunteers, but with the state providing oversight and direction. More generally, Liszt believed the prison associations must play an important role in the criminal policy of the future

"Father will be happy when he comes out of prison and sees how many we are!"
(Heinrich Zille, "Five Siblings," 1904, Heinrich Zille Museum, Berlin)

and was himself an active member of the Prison Society of Saxony and Anhalt.[151] Clergy and other leaders of the charities were, in turn, drawn to Liszt's movement, with many members of the leading prison societies also becoming members of Liszt's International Penal Union.

The tensions between the Modern School and the charities—and these were significant—mostly concerned the role of the state in welfare supervision. Many of Liszt's students went farther than their professor in seeing the state as the ideal agent of protective supervision. Robert von Hippel, the leading legal expert on vagabonds and prostitutes, criticized Bodelschwingh's efforts to use the worker colonies as a substitute for the workhouse. Ernst Rosenfeld, who focused his research on the prison associations, argued that welfare for released prisoners should ultimately become the responsibility of the state. Karl Fuhr, an expert on police supervision, rejected the idea that private welfare could displace the police in the oversight of ex-felons. The Modern School's statist tendencies worried many members of the charities, who wanted to protect the autonomy of private welfare, as well as the principle that welfare was a benefit reserved ultimately for "worthy" persons, not a tool of social control and certainly not an entitlement.[152]

While the charities increasingly sought to steer endangered persons from state institutions to private welfare, Liszt and his circle sought to transform state institutions, including the workhouse and the police in order to eventually augment their role in criminal policy. In fact, the IKV's proposed changes to the Penal Code would have created longer workhouse sentences for vagabonds and prostitutes and would have broadened the pool of petty offenders who could be committed to state custody. On the face of it, here is an issue that seemed to mark the modernists abandonment of the "traditional" prison reformers.

Yet even this seemingly stark difference between the modernists and the charities dissolves upon closer observation. The Modern School wanted to resuscitate the workhouse and revitalize police supervision, but only while transforming these institutions in line with welfare principles. Organizations like the IKV and the German Association for Poor Relief sought to strip the workhouse of its punitive character and to make it an institution that had more in common with the private charities. They sought to rethink the concept of police supervision in line with the practice of welfare supervision. However much they gestured to "medical" and "scientific" ideals, the content of reform was a step toward and not away from the private charity model.[153]

Conclusion

Protective supervision was created under the assumption that welfare and justice performed separate and complementary functions. "It is a fundamental experience," worker colony director Paul Troschke wrote, "that the will can only be educated voluntarily."[154] Welfare operated in a zone of freedom. Punishment, by contrast, was essentially coercive. The slogan of one prison society illustrated the modest, limited goals of protective supervision in the nineteenth century: *Caritas et justitia osculantur* (charity and justice kiss).

Over time, however, charity and justice became promiscuously intertwined. This process began in the Wilhelmine era. During the First World War, an institutional nexus between these ideological worlds was forged. At the center of the new discourse was the endangered individual, now frequently known as the "asocial." At a landmark meeting in 1918 (only months before the war's end), the leading figures in prostitution reform met in Frankfurt to discuss postwar reform strategies. The Bielefeld judge Alfred Bozi set the tone of the meeting by recapitulating a by-now familiar litany of complaints about the workhouse. The progressive welfare leader Hans Maier delineated the common ground between the Christian charities and progressive reformers. Their shared goal, he said, was to replace the police as much as possible with welfare.[155]

Four years later, many of the same figures met in Bielefeld with an even broader agenda: to strategize a policy for "asocials." At this meeting, Gustav Aschaffenburg defined asocials as "persons who limit or damage the existence and the development of society." This almost absurdly broad definition included persons with various forms of disabilities, unruly youth, beggars, vagrants, and prostitutes, all the way up to habitual and professional criminals. From the "standpoint of the personality," asocials included the mentally disabled, the mentally ill, drinkers, sexual perverts, sociopaths, and brutal impulsives. The only possible use-value for such a catch-all term was that it pulled the entire question of crime into the realm of welfare discourse. In fact, crime was now just one point on a continuum of social disorders.

At the Bielefeld meeting, representatives of the charities considered what sort of confinement measures could be imposed upon "asocials." The conference officially launched an effort to create a "custodial law" that would mandate protective supervision in many cases. The charities now proposed to occupy an even broader swath of criminal justice's traditional territory. The effort is only comprehensible when we realize the stunning optimism on the part of the charities behind protective supervision. "In welfare for the asocial," Pastor Troschke declared, "we are standing at a similar juncture, as in the care of the mentally ill in the era when . . . the strait-jacket and the spinning chair competed with the No-Restraint system."[156] Reformers believed so strongly in their role as emancipators, they had grown blind to the repressive potential of their own institutions.

PENAL UTOPIAS

The Deportation Movement
in the Wilhelmine Era

In 1896, law professor Felix Bruck published a proposal to create vast penal colonies for German criminals in Southwest Africa. The plan called for the eventual deportation of hundreds of thousands of vagrants and prostitutes, along with serious offenders. Bruck's proposal inspired heated debates in the popular press and at the meetings of reform societies and professional organizations before becoming the basis for Reichstag legislation. Opposition by the Imperial government killed the initiative, but new plans and new reform coalitions quickly emerged to keep the dream of penal colonies alive. In 1908, the *Berliner Morgenpost* asserted that an "overwhelming majority" of criminal justice professionals "declared deportation to be the penal measure of the future." Reform societies continued to debate the deportation question right up to the outbreak of the First World War, and the policy even had its proponents during the Weimar Republic.[1]

How do we understand the persistent interest in penal colonies after 1890? It is tempting to see deportation as an atavistic form of punishment: a return to rituals of exile and expulsion—what Foucault calls the "leper-model" of regulation—in place of modern technologies of discipline.[2] Indeed, some proponents of German penal colonies wrote of cleansing the national community of its criminal elements, and many welfare advocates accused the penal colony movement as a whole of abandoning modern ideals of a humane criminal policy. Some historians suggest that the penal colony movement was a manifestation of the "dark side of modernity." Richard Evans argues that the movement was inspired by Cesare Lombroso's theory of the "born criminal." German opinion in the 1890s, he claims, "move[d] away from its previous liberal faith in the ameliorative mission of imprisonment towards a darker view of the criminal as hereditarily tainted, a eugenic threat to the racial community and fundamentally incorrigible." Deportation, Evans claims, was consistent with other proposals aimed at "eliminating" infectious elements from the social organism.[3]

This chapter argues that the penal colony movement represented a more complex version of criminal policy than these interpretations allow. Wilhelmine proponents of deportation envisioned penal colonies as utopian sites in which to evaluate and classify criminal offenders according to social criteria, guide deportees toward productive lives, and permit ex-offenders to work their way toward full civic rehabilitation. Like the worker colonies, the penal colonies were to provide a sanctuary for morally "endangered persons" and a testing ground in which to discover their "true personalities." Driving the movement was tremendous optimism concerning the potential for ex-offenders, under the right conditions, to contribute to the fatherland and to work toward self-renewal. Far from being a dumping ground for society's refuse, the German penal colony was to be an important laboratory of modernity.

This chapter explores the debates over penal colonies during the late Wilhelmine era. There were, in fact, two separate movements. Both movements were shaped by the popular nationalism and imperialist longings that were intensifying at the turn of the century. Germany in this moment seemed poised to develop a massive colonial empire, including colonial settlements, trading stations, and satellite nations across Africa and the South Seas. The dream of a perfect site for ex-offenders was based on expectations of a distinct, vital, and hierarchical relationship between colonial settlements and the German motherland. Placed at the peripheries of the Empire, the deportees would be given an opportunity to lead meaningful lives even as they were prevented from causing immediate harm to German society. They could contribute to the Empire (*Reich*) without threatening the nation (*Volk*), and continue to be German (*deutsch*) without diminishing Germanness (*Deutschtum*). The colonies, in other words, offered a liminal space for the growth and development of liminal populations, many of whom—depending upon the extent of one's "optimism"—were destined to reclimb the ladder of civilization.

While advocates of deportation embraced a social interpretation of crime, it was their opponents who focused most relentlessly upon the inherent and immutable qualities of dangerousness. Colonial officials, settlers, and their proxies insisted that classificatory and disciplinary schemes could not be sustained within the territories available to Germany, and that horrible disorders, including cultural and biological miscegenation and the moral degeneration of European and native populations, would ensue. Not only would the deportees corrupt the natives and reduce the quality of the white population, it was charged, but they would undermine the hegemony of colonial governments vis-à-vis the natives.[4] The implication was that degenerate Europeans must be banned from the colonies. The opponents of deportation thus invoked a "leper-model" of criminal policy as exclusion. The fortunes of the penal colony movement, on the other hand, depended upon its ability to persuade a German public that a "resettlement" program was a logical culmination and fulfillment of modern ideals in criminal policy.

The deportation movement posed an answer to the twin paradoxes of liberal criminal reform: how to force weak-willed, morally damaged individuals to live as free and productive persons, and how to give criminals the chance to practice freedom without threatening society or being threatened in turn by social positions. Deportation proponents thus helped recast the discussion of crime and resocialization as a problem of space. As an imaginative possibility in criminal justice, the utopian ideal of deportation could therefore outlive all the debates over its practical implementation, continuing to inspire other projects in criminal policy well beyond the collapse of the Kaiserreich.

Deportation and the Modern Criminal Reform Movement

The image of deportation as a strategy of exile and banishment makes sense in reference to the discourse of the early to mid-nineteenth century. A number of German states actually practiced deportation, and there were periodic debates about its legitimacy and usefulness as a penal measure. The fault lines on this issue frequently marked a split between self-styled modernizers and traditionalists. Modernizers supported the building of penitentiaries and condemned deportation as wasteful, uncertain, and unpredictable in its effects. The notorious images of English convict ships and hot, disease-ridden French colonies offered a powerful foil to the Benthamite ideal of a carefully planned institution, in which the state's power to punish was perfectly economized and distributed through architecture and organization.

The German states that practiced deportation were often those that resisted the pressure to build penitentiaries. They saw deportation as an inexpensive means of ridding themselves of burdensome and dangerous populations. Prussia in the early nineteenth century deported offenders to Siberia—before Wichern's ascendance and the building of the model prison in Moabit. Hamburg, Mecklenburg, and Saxe-Coburg-Gotha in the 1830s and 1840s sent criminals to the Americas. Hanover used large scale deportations in order to save itself the cost and the trouble of housing "incorrigible" offenders.[5]

After German unification in 1871, support for deportation initially involved a self-conscious evocation of "teutonic" practices of banishment and exile.[6] Deportation, like the death penalty, was supposed to purify the tribe, fulfilling the natural, instinctive revulsion of the *Volk* against morally sick and contagious individuals.[7] The particular destination for the deportees was treated as an afterthought: they were dumping grounds for the excrescence of European civilization. In his 1879 polemic against incarceration, Justice Mittelstädt advocated deportation as a "casting forth" of the criminal from the protection of laws, civilization, and the fellowship of men. In this way, Mittelstädt argued, the criminal was "thrown back on his own egoism in a battle with nature" and forced to see the true value of "peaceful coexistence, law and property, work and production, ethics and law." Such a punishment, he claimed, was consistent with the teutonic ideal of exile, while also affirming liberal society's belief in moral autonomy and individual responsibility.[8] Instead of "rotting away within prison walls," the criminal would at least have the dignity of dying as a free man—what the Romantic School of legal studies called a "wolf"—*outside* the law and in the realm of nature.

Such arguments for deportation resonated among certain sectors of the German bourgeoisie in the period of liberal retrenchment and anti-Socialist agitation immediately after 1879.[9] Friedrich Fabri, the great colonial agitator, supported deportation as a measure for the "intractable" Social Democrats with whom the Conservative German state would soon have its violent "reckoning." According to historian Klaus Bade, Fabri saw penal colonies as the repressive counterpart to the positive strategy of luring German workers away from Socialism through "social imperialism."[10] Penal colonies were for those who had shown themselves to be hopelessly alienated from the civilized nation or moral community.

Such arguments appalled Left-liberal social reformers and Social Democrats in the Bismarckian era, as well as the prison reformers who had dedicated their lives to building effective institutions for resocialization at home. In 1879, the members of the Rhenish-Westphalian Prison Society rejected the draconian logic of expulsion and reasserted their commitment to moral improvement and resocialization.[11] Karl Krohne, Wichern's successor at the Prussian Ministry of Prisons, condemned deportation as "cowardice" and "social laziness." Society, he argued, must be willing "to heal with earnest moral labor the social damages from which crime emerges [and] direct its attention to welfare for the class out of which criminality expands."[12]

Penal Modernism and the Recasting of the Deportation Ideal

The Wilhelmine advocates of deportation departed from their predecessors by advocating resettlement as one component of a modern, humane, and rational criminal policy. Mittelstädt's critique of the prison and Bodelschwingh's ideal of protective supervision inspired them in equal measure. Like the worker colonies, Bruck's penal colonies were supposed to provide a refuge for Germans who failed in the Metropole's "struggle for existence." There was to be no overt coercion. Prisoners would learn to live as free men and women by confronting what worker colony advocates referred to as "cold hard need." The penal colony was life stripped to its essentials, a testing ground in which outcasts could demonstrate whether they were made of worthy stuff. The new advocates of deportation, moreover, envisioned deportees as a vanguard for German colonialism. Settled in forbidding marshlands and deserts, these colonists would be responsible for the difficult preparatory labors necessary to making these regions habitable for free whites. The task of colony-building complemented the criminological goals: Inspiring criminals with a sense of national purpose and justifying the enormous costs of relocation.[13]

The father of the new movement, Felix Bruck, fully expected to be embraced by Franz von Liszt and his legal reform movement.[14] A professor of law in Breslau, Bruck had previously authored books on criminal negligence and free will. These works codified and interpreted the trend in legal practice away from holding individuals criminally responsible for negligence.[15] His first intervention on the subject of deportation, *Away with the Penitentiaries!* was an all-out attack upon the penal system, principally for its failure to resocialize offenders. The title clearly evoked Mittelstädt's polemic against the prison reformers, while the contents revealed a great debt to both Christian social thinkers and left-liberals like von Liszt. Bruck argued that long-term incarceration sapped human labor power and destroyed human souls and advocated that prisons only be used for sentences of one year or less. Incarceration, he asserted, worked best as a quick deterrent, to impress the majesty of the law upon those offenders who were still subject to rational persuasion. Resocialization, however, required other, more sustained measures.[16]

Away with the Penitentiaries! proposed creating penal colonies for all classes of recidivist offenders. According to his plan, deportees would engage in forced labor for a limited period of time, after which they would be settled in special territories. If they succeeded as independent producers and accumulated enough resources to support themselves back in Germany, then they might return to the mainland after eight years.[17]

Bruck's proposal placed the initial decision-making power in judges' hands. They could authorize the deportation of any individual convicted of a major felony or repeatedly convicted of minor or petty offenses. The judges would determine the duration of forced labor, as well as the minimum period of exile. Administrative authorities would then make a final determination about whether the individual was healthy enough to be deported and whether conditions in the colony presently allowed the intake of new offenders.[18] Both men and women could be deported, but no one under the age of sixteen or over the age of sixty. Recidivist vagrancy, begging, and prostitution were included on the list of applicable offenses.[19] Figuring that there were 200,000 vagabonds alone in Germany, Bruck expected such petty offenders would constitute the majority of the deportees.[20] The judges were supposed to base their decision not on the seriousness of the offense but upon their assessment of the criminal's personality and the likelihood of moral improvement if he remained in the motherland. Bruck also envisioned changes to the Code of Criminal Procedure, which would specify legal conditions for determining when precisely the criminal fit this category.[21]

In the colonies, the deportees would be divided among various penal farms and housed in barracks. The farms were to be located apart from each other, on territories that could eventually support self-sufficient communities and which, in the meantime, could be supplied through the delivery of outside foodstuffs. The colonial governor was to determine where to send particular offenders based upon individual reports forwarded by the state's attorney or the criminal court. It was Bruck's expectation that

> because of the size of the available land, it would be possible to institute the principle of individualization to a far greater extent than was the case in domestic penality. It could be possible to make modifications in discipline and punishment in the various penal farms corresponding to the different categories of criminals, under consideration of their previous life-experience, the seriousness of their crimes, and the manner and form of their commission.

The deportees could also be assigned to farms with an eye to their particular skills, though it had to be assumed that different jobs would become available as the communities developed.[22]

While the offenders would be handled according to "type," unremitting labor would be an essential component of all punishments. Male offenders would be given labor assignments corresponding to their future profession as settlers and to the needs of the colony. In the first stages of their punishment, they were to engage in physically strenuous outdoor work. Bruck's proposed legislation mentioned road and railway building, water management, and the construction of ports in particular. Their principal employment, however, was to be agricultural work.[23] After the period of forced labor, which was set at a minimum of seven years, the deportees would be assisted in "achieving economic independence" in special settlements reserved for ex-offenders. The families of the deportees would be permitted to join them at this point, and educated deportees would be able to practice their trained professions, to the extent this was possible. Still, the deportees would remain under the observation of a special "disciplinary authority" for another ten years. If they passed this test-period (*Probezeit*), then they would be granted citizenship rights (*Bürgerrecht*), at which point they would be allowed to settle where they pleased within the colonial territory.[24] A male deportee who was not condemned to life-long exile would be allowed to return to the continent on the condition that he "prove he was in a position to support himself and his family."[25]

Female deportees were to be brought directly into the settlement regions for released prisoners. The women would be required to serve as domestic servants in the households of settlers, colonial officials, and officers and were expected to engage in vegetable gardening, the raising of livestock, and other appropriate "female labors." After completing their period of forced labor, they were expected to either marry a settler or to assume a profession such as washing, tailoring, or working in trade. Unmarried women would have to show continual proof that they were living from "honest" means.[26]

Bruck's proposal brought the issue of deportation back into the newspapers, the prison societies, and the legal associations, but the terms of debate had altered since Mittelstädt and Fabri raised the issue more than a decade before.[27] The new proponents of deportation consisted of a far more diverse array of jurists, welfare activists, journalists, and colonialists. They included numerous scholars with experience in penal welfare and impeccable credentials as progressive reform advocates. Each of Germany's major prison societies revisited the deportation question in 1894 and 1895. The august Rhenish-Westphalian and the Sachsen-Anhalt Societies each voted to support some kind of deportation policy after hearing enthusiastic presentations from members. At the Sachsen-Anhalt meeting, law professor Reinhard von Frank argued that a well-ordered deportation policy would represent a logical extension of other trends in modern justice reform.[28] The Rhenish-Westphalian Society commissioned its presentation from Friedrich Freund, an official in Koblenz, who was active in welfare for released prisoners. In his paper, later republished in the *Preussische Jahrbücher*, Freund vigorously supported the essentials of Bruck's proposal, though with the insistence that some form of closed institution must be created in the colonies to provide adequate surveillance over some classes of deportees.[29] Freund was invited to make a similar presentation at the German Bar Association meetings in 1897, and Bruck prepared a paper for the 1897 meeting of the International Penal Union (IKV). Also in 1897, the Holtzendorff Foundation announced a prize for the best essay on the deportation question, to be judged by Franz von Liszt and Adolph Prins, the co-founders of the IKV, as well as Paul Aschrott, a specialist on law and welfare issues.[30] While Liszt remained skeptical about the rehabilitative promise of deportation, a number of his closest followers announced their support, including Robert von Hippel, the IKV's expert on vagabondage and prostitution.[31]

Reactions to the deportation proposal cut across political and ideological divides. Numerous journals, organizations, and individuals with ties to the Conservative Party declared their enthusiasm for establishing penal colonies.[32] Conservative missionary groups, on the other hand, were almost uniformly and stridently opposed.[33] Meanwhile, support for Bruck's plan appeared in the publications of the Christian social Inner Mission and in Martin Rade's Liberal-Protestant standard-bearer, *Die Christliche Welt*.[34] While it was not unusual for proponents of deportation to identify themselves with Mittelstädt's effort to break down the walls of "doctrinaire humanitarianism," most of them actively sought the mantel of progressive and modern idealism.[35] Like Mittelstädt, they questioned the idea that man could be "trained for freedom through coercion" and rejected the "metaphysical presuppositions" of the old penality. Unlike Mittelstädt, they were committed to using criminal justice to promote social reform goals.[36] It was in the framework of a new humanitarianism, one Berlin law professor asserted in 1898, that "a wave of public opinion increasingly demanded" deportation.[37]

The Wilhelmine deportation movement's debt to Modern School criminology was clearest in its diagnosis of the failures of nineteenth-century penality. The case for deportation was based in large part upon a critique of penitentiaries as tools of individual improvement. For Bruck, it was self-evident that "the preponderance of inmates in our penal institutions consist not of evil but rather of weak-willed individuals" who had "failed in the struggle for existence."[38] The "complete bankruptcy of the prisons," Bruck argued, rested upon their failure to prepare such persons for competition in the outside world. Instead, the carceral experience "dulled" offenders' mental faculties and weakened them physically and spiritually.[39] Frank called prisons the "treadmills of eternal monotony."[40] They drained the offenders' "energy" and weakened their "ability to resist criminal temptations." Even if the prisons were restructured along the most modern and progressive principles, Frank argued, they would still be unable to recreate the "real" conditions of life, which provided the only possible training for a normal existence. Such prisons could offer "at best a doll's house."[41]

The single biggest failing of the penitentiary, in the view of deportation proponents, was its inability to provide a meaningful work experience. Until the 1880s, German prisoners had been conscripted by private industry or else organized for production under the auspices of state governments. These practices were phased out, however, as unions became more powerful and as businessmen increasingly accepted the liberal idea that prison manufacturing was a threat to the principles of free labor.[42] According to one newspaper, the percentage of prison inmates engaged in manufacturing dropped from 73 to 49 percent in the final decades of the century. After the abolition of work programs, Bruck asserted, prisoners were frequently idle or forced to engage in "useless work," such as chopping wood, picking tow, or hauling rocks. The reliance upon such pointless, symbolic labors underscored the impracticality (*Weltfremdheit*) of the prison experience for its detractors. Make-work, unlike productive labor, had no lasting moral or educative effect.[43]

While the penitentiaries were accused of producing individuals sapped of mental and physical energy, German society, it was claimed, was increasingly unable to absorb even the most healthy and willing ex-offenders. According to Bruck, the sheer number of former offenders in Germany made a systematic policy of resocialization in the motherland unmanageable. He cited Reich statistics showing that the number of ex-offenders had increased from 82,000 in 1882 to 193,000 in 1900, or from 277 to 341 per 100,000 adults. According to Frank, a member of the Sachsen-Anhalt Prison Society, welfare associations could guide some of these individuals into the work force, but they would always be hampered by the fundamental "mistrust" of respectable Germans toward anyone who had spent time in prison.[44] Invoking a familiar Christian-Social critique of administrative regulation, Bruck asserted that police supervision and restrictive regulations upon the former prisoners inevitably drove them to seek refuge in the large cities, where it was only a matter of time before they fell into their "earlier life-styles."[45]

Contrary to Evans's assertions, none of the major proposals for deportation in the Wilhelmine era aimed to purge "hereditarily tainted" material from the national community. Even as they argued for the physical segregation of criminals by category, the reformers were attempting to transcend the traditional barriers separating bourgeois society from its outcasts. "In judging our fallen brothers," Bruck declared,

we should guard ourselves against hypocrisy. The criminals are usually people like us. They have very often become what they are simply as a result of the milieu. If we could create better life conditions for these unhappy individuals, they would often quite quickly become useful members of society again, and society would have no grounds to fear for their morality and security.[46]

Others argued that social maladies, including poor housing, urban overcrowding, and low wages, drove released prisoners "back into the arms" of the underworld.[47] Bruck criticized the IKV's proposal of life-long security detention for incorrigibles because of its loose and poorly defined notion of incorrigibility.[48] The ex-offender's capacity to improve, he argued, was always relative, never absolute. Judges could use the fact of multiple recidivism as at most a sign (*Erkenntnismittel*) of incurable inclinations to criminal behavior.[49] Frank, on the other hand, asserted that "absolute incorrigibility" did exist, but that it needed to be carefully determined through scrupulous investigations. The courts must distinguish between those who could benefit from a certain treatment and prosper within a new and different environment, versus those who were already subjected to "all available punitive influences . . . and nevertheless committed another crime without abnormal instigation." The new deportation policy, in Frank's view, should only apply to "*relatively* incorrigible" persons. Bruck and Frank shared the conviction that most recidivists who were "useless" under ordinary conditions could become valuable members of a community under the conditions of carefully structured colonial settlement. Deportation was ideally suited for such a category of offenders, because it did not foreclose the possibility of their improvement, success, and rehabilitation, even while it ensured that they posed no immediate threat to the welfare of mainstream German society.[50]

Deportation as an Imperialist Project

The reformers' ideal of a progressive deportation policy was also rooted in hopes of furthering the expansion of the German colonial realm. Starting in 1884, Germany acquired vast territories in Africa and the South Pacific, but the Imperial government did little to promote German settlement abroad. During the 1890s migrationist colonialism emerged as a popular cause. Journalists, politicians, and extra-parliamentary pressure groups mobilized around the argument that massive settlement was necessary to regenerate the German race and German culture and to guarantee Germany's relative position on the world stage. Prominent colonialists lent rhetorical support to the idea of deportation at various junctures, even when they vigorously opposed particular initiatives on practical grounds. A few colonialists, among them Joachim Graf Pfeil and Karl Wettstein, eventually became leaders in the deportation movement. More important than this direct influence, however, was the more general, cultural impact of the idea that agricultural labor and "living space" (*Lebensraum*), Germany's "place in the sun," would provide new opportunities for repairing damaged racial material, defusing social conflicts and bolstering the sense of national community.

Though German proponents of deportation prior to the Wilhelmine era hardly bothered to discuss specific destinations for the deportees, the Wilhelmine debates frequently centered upon geographic particulars. Bruck insisted upon Southwest Africa (SWA), to the point of being unwilling even to discuss other alternatives. Members of the German Deportation League after 1905 were equally adamant in their support of certain South Sea Islands. The most influential opponents of deportation proposals, meanwhile, focused upon the practical limits and potential problems of penal discipline within a given colonial space. Geography was, thus, never incidental to an argument but constituted the essential terrain of criminal- and colonial-policy debate. Among the most important questions about a territory were the climate, the availability of land, the proximity of native populations, the types of labor needed to make the lands "habitable" (i.e., for free whites), and the ultimate significance of any such development for German colonial policy and German imperialism more generally.

All the leading deportation proposals claimed to promote the settlement of territories that had been unjustly neglected or "underestimated" until recently.[51] According to Bruck, Richard Hindorf's 1894 "Memorandum" on SWA was the first German work to offer a detailed and objective analysis of the region's suitability for farming. Hindorf had supposedly refuted the commonly accepted wisdom that SWA was a "sandbox" that would never support intensive cultivation.[52] This report and other studies published over the next five years made the case that by draining swamps and channeling water through irrigation canals, the Germans could create vast swathes of fertile land in SWA.[53] This wave of publications, often on the border between scholarly research and promotional propaganda, also addressed the contested issue of the African environment's effects upon the European temperament. Hindorf insisted that, though individual Europeans would suffer a slight "climate fever," the "purity and dryness of the air . . . intense sunshine [and] fresh wind" was essentially healthy and especially beneficial to Europeans with weakened respiratory organs.[54] The supporters of the Admiralty Islands made similar claims a few years later.

Bruck and his followers saw Southwest Africa as ideal for a penal colony because of the territory's desperate shortage of laborers to build an infrastructure for capitalist development. Deportation advocates drew upon a familiar argument in colonial circles that Africa's tremendous economic potential would never be realized by free white settlers or the free enterprise system alone. The tasks of draining swamps, clearing fields, and laying railroad track, it was argued, were simply too physically taxing and too unpleasant for the ordinary system of punishments and rewards.[55] "The natives don't like to work," the governor of SWA, Theodor Leutwein, complained to Pastor Heinrich Seyfarth in 1897, "while the whites in Africa are not easily persuaded to engage in hard labor."[56] In 1898 a shortage of railroad workers forced colonists to halt the building of a new line from Swakopmund to Windhoek. Settler organizations soon grew increasingly interested in the idea of importing convict labor. Graf Pfeil insisted that native workers could not be relied upon for such projects, due to their inferior skills and work habits.[57] At the same time, Carl Peters argued that the colonial context required a work force that was pliable and submissive. "The German colonial official," he noted dryly, "generally gets along better with people over whom he has the power to give orders [Befehlsgewalt], than he does with free colonists."[58]

Bruck argued that conditions in SWA would allow deportees to play a special role in colonial policy in the vanguard of national expansion and development. This was obviously desirable from a standpoint of mobilizing national resources and conserving and allocating national energies: no longer would "labor-power" be "pointlessly squandered" in the prisons.[59] But exploiting criminals for the cause of imperial expansion was also valued in terms of its expected moral and psychological effects upon the individual. The penal colony could promise the ex-offender something that modern German society could not: meaningful, practical, honest work.[60] Such service to the empire was supposed to instill into the deportees a sense of solidarity and pride.[61] In Carl Peters's words, "useful labor" on behalf of imperialism would "free the individual from the horrifying degeneration, which is a result of long incarceration."[62] This was the reference point for Bruck's repeated assertion that criminal policy, social policy, and colonial policy were all intertwined in his deportation proposal. According to prison clergyman Heinrich Seyfarth, giving inmates the opportunity to serve their nation was an important tool in restoring their sense of purpose and hope and therefore their will to self-transformation.

The other important question in determining the suitability of particular territories as penal colonies concerned the location and type of natives and free white settlers in the vicinity. Deportation advocates generally agreed that the ex-offenders must be segregated from the natives as much as possible and restricted in their intercourse with free white settler communities. Bruck favored SWA in part because of its sheer vastness: the penal colonies would be established in regions that were almost free of natives, and they could be continually relocated after deportees had prepared an area for white settlement. The Deportation League argued for the island of Neu-Pommern because its native population was "in decline" and possessed a "low level of civilization," both of which were deemed "indispensable conditions" for a successful penal colony.[63]

The reasons for the failure of deportation proposals will be discussed in greater detail below, but it is important to note that opponents never challenged the principle of removing former offenders from German towns and cities as a step toward resocialization. Some of the opposition to deportation was simply embedded in a more general resistance on the part of the prison bureaucracy and the Ministries of Justice and the Interior to proposals emanating from the academies and religious societies. Even the International Penal Union, which steadily gained in prominence and prestige around the turn of the century, was only moderately successful in carrying through its agenda for criminal justice reform. The most important objections to deportation proposals, however, like the proposals themselves, were addressed to the specifics of place. Bruck's proposal for penal colonies in Africa failed due to the opposition of colonial spokesmen, many of whom had announced their support for deportation in the abstract and some of whom went on to promote their own deportation schemes for other regions. The Deportation League's proposals in 1905, 1906, and 1908 failed as well, after the Justice Ministry again deferred to the judgment of those deemed most familiar with the geography of the territory under question, in this case the Admiralty Islands. The proponents of deportation were continually stymied by their failure to find a "suitable place" for the German ex-offender: the ideal of organized, systematic resettlement persisted.

Categorization as a Form of Charitable Assistance

One of the early supporters of Bruck's proposal was Heinrich Seyfarth, an obscure prison pastor in Thuringia and chair of the local prison society, who would soon become a leading figure in welfare for released offenders. Born in 1867 to a family of clergy, Seyfarth completed his doctorate in theology in 1887 and apprenticed himself to Friedrich von Bodelschwingh at Bethel. Mittelstädt's critique of the penitentiary affected him profoundly. Bruck's work on deportation inspired him to pursue new directions in criminal policy. In 1897, Seyfarth wrote two icons of the German colonial movement, Major Theodor Leutwein, the governor of SWA, and Carl Peters, the founder of the German colony in East Africa, in order to solicit their support for Bruck's proposal.[64] A year later, Seyfarth published a book on punishment, which included a comprehensive discussion of Bruck's proposal. On the strength of this published work, Seyfarth was called to Hamburg in 1901 to become the pastor of Germany's largest penitentiary.[65] He gained national prominence in 1903 when he founded the Deutsche Hilfsverein für entlassene Gefangene, an association principally devoted to resettling former criminals in German communities overseas. In the next few years, he spearheaded an effort to transport released prisoners to the Admiralty Islands, a German colony in the South Seas. Seyfarth eventually became chairman of the German Deportation League.

Seyfarth's efforts in the Deutsche Hilfsverein—an organization that helped shape penal-welfare practice down to the Nazi era—illustrated the links between the discourse of deportation and domestic criminal justice reform. The Hilfsverein addressed the dilemma of released prisoners who were ready and eager to become productive members of society but likely to have trouble finding a secure place in German society.[66] Seyfarth's idea was to resettle these former offenders in German communities around the world, with employment and other vital assistance arranged by contact persons, especially German clergy, abroad.[67] The success of this system, in Seyfarth's view, depended upon treating such welfare assistance as a privilege for carefully screened worthy and able individuals.

Candidates for the Deutsche Hilfsverein's resettlement program were recommended by prison associations across Germany. Former prisoners traveled to Hamburg, where they underwent a six-month testing and transition period, living and working in a so-called "transition-station." Clients from the educated professions resided in a supervised group home in a suburb of Hamburg, attached to which was a "writing shop" that employed them copying manuscripts. Multiple recidivists and those hoping to settle in less-developed regions of the world were sent for their probationary period to the worker colony in Freistaat, known as the "marsh colony."[68] Passing the test meant working diligently and obeying house rules for six months. Those who failed to meet the most exacting standards were ineligible for transportation but might still be resettled somewhere in Germany. Those who completely failed to meet the demands of their transition period were stripped of all assistance.

Seyfarth's project was animated by many of the same concerns as Bruck's. Like Bruck, he believed that the penitentiaries corrupted first-time offenders by exposing them to hardened criminals and destroyed the mental and physical health of all inmates subjected to solitary confinement. Incarceration had become all the more damaging in recent times, in Seyfarth's view, because the inmates were "hermetically closed off" from the profound and rapid changes taking place in the social and industrial life of the people. They emerged into the outside world with little or no knowledge and preparation for the times.[69]

Seyfarth noted ruefully that even great outpourings of generosity and concern regarding the fate of ex-prisoners rarely translated into a willingness to offer direct assistance. Extraordinary numbers of businessmen, he reported, "sacrificed their time and their money" on behalf of the prison societies, but still refused to assume the risk of employing former offenders. Seven hundred freemason societies eventually became supporting members of the Deutsche Hilfsverein, but would not offer anything beyond financial aid. The new association was established in June 1903 with the support of 440 prison and welfare societies, the Reich, and local governments, and with a membership board that included Pastor von Bodelschwingh, Franz von Liszt, and jurist Wilhelm Kahl. Almost 40 percent of its funding came through individual contributions and membership dues. By the end of its first year, it had an endowment of 23,000 marks, an amount that grew steadily over the next five years, in spite of rising outlays.[70] For Seyfarth, the rapid and overwhelming response to this experiment in penal welfare was further proof of the former prisoners' desperate situation: even the most enlightened of German reformers apparently saw fundamental limits in the ability of German society to absorb ex-offenders.

Like Bruck's proposal, Seyfarth's resettlement project was based upon the presumption that individuals deemed incorrigible under some conditions could be made social under different circumstances.[71] The educated ex-offenders of middle-class origins seemed, on the face of it, best equipped to succeed in modern society and to break free of their outcast status. Certainly they were the ex-prisoners with whom middle- and upper-class Germans found it easiest to empathize.[72] Yet, according to Seyfarth, this group actually faced the most extreme and entrenched prejudices from their former communities and typically had more difficulties than ex-offenders from the working class in finding some measure of acceptance. Locked out of respectable society, they constituted a "world of their own, a state within a state."[73] Frequently they found their ultimate refuge in the urban underworld. If the truly deserving and capable subset of this population could be placed in German communities abroad, Seyfarth reasoned, they would spare themselves and German society from becoming a permanent burden and social risk.

Seyfarth's project was certainly not the first organized effort to resettle

German ex-convicts abroad on a voluntary basis. What was unprecedented, however, was the emphasis upon screening the candidates, preparing them for their future, and carefully matching them with suitable communities overseas. The Hilfsverein assigned itself the task of guaranteeing the quality of this "human material." If burdensome (*lästige*) or antisocial individuals were sent abroad, then the entire program would be endangered, since few of the German contact communities would be willing to risk taking former prisoners in the future.[74] The transition stations were supposed to impose a rigorous and demanding work routine upon each released prisoner, in order to make a "reliable determination of his character, his abilities, and his physical condition." Both the worker colony and the writing shop ostensibly gave the residents real, productive labors to perform, as well as some measure of training. The colonists drained marshland for agricultural purposes; the writing shop copied manuscripts for local businesses. In the latter enterprise, the former prisoners learned office skills like typing and stenography.[75] In each case the work was modestly remunerated, although wages could be withheld in the case of unacceptable behavior. Both facilities were to avoid seeming "institutional" (*anstalts-mässig*). While shielding the residents from alcohol, prostitution, and other outside temptations, they were supposed to "strengthen them internally, so they became reaccustomed to freedom."[76] In the first two years of the Verein's existence, only one-third of the cases referred to them were actually taken on. Some of these persons were rejected by the Verein because of doubts about their physical health or their moral character, but a much larger number simply refused to undergo the testing period, especially if this was to take place in the colony.[77]

While Seyfarth's resettlement project would not necessarily preserve the labor power of ex-prisoners for the German Empire, it did attempt to help the transportees maintain their German identity by directing them toward culturally and economically viable German communities, whether in industrial or non-industrial regions of the globe. In 1905, the stations' "absolvees" were taken in by German communities in Egypt, Peru, Brazil, Chile, and Argentina. It was assumed that many of these former prisoners would eventually return to the German motherland after popular resentments had been forgotten and they had regained a measure of respectability.[78] In a large number of cases, the Verein was able to find suitable work and communities for its charges, in spite of local prejudice, within Germany. Starting in 1905, the Verein also placed young offenders as sailors and fishermen on the German coasts, after putting them through "serious testing and observation [*Prüfung und Sichtung*] of whether they seemed appropriate for this profession."[79]

The Verein's preoccupation with the categorization of ex-offenders placed an additional burden upon local charities. One of Seyfarth's greatest fears was that prison associations would forward ex-offenders to the Hilfsverein without properly screening their character and capabilities. The only way to avoid this was for all local welfare organizations to participate in testing and observing ex-offenders. Hopelessly antisocial elements, in his view, must be stripped of all welfare assistance. Persons who were prepared for unsupervised living must be distinguished from those who still needed guidance and strengthening. Seyfarth believed that the enforcement of such distinctions was essential to combatting the social prejudices that were a constant burden to ex-offenders, especially to those who were worthy of help and ready for rehabilitation.

From Penal Welfare (Back) to Penal Deportation

From 1903 to 1908, the question of the ex-offender in German society took on new contours. Two works arguing for a welfare approach to penal reform grabbed popular attention well beyond the usual narrow circles of jurists and prison officials.[80] Both works were by journalists, who fiercely attacked the penitentiaries for producing "useless" and "bestial" individuals, while also seeking to generate sympathy for the plight of the ex-prisoner in German society. Both works argued for deportation as a more rational and humane alternative, because the penal colonies would give former criminals the chance to acclimate themselves to responsible, productive lives. The first book, Hans Leuß's *From the Penitentiary*, was ostensibly a memoir of prison life. Convicted of perjury while trying to "protect a woman's honor," Leuß spent three years at a penitentiary in Sachsen-Anhalt.[81] Prior to his conviction, he was the editor of Adolph Stoecker's *Volkswacht* in the late 1880s and, later, a contributor to Maximilian Harden's *Die Zukunft*.[82] As a journalist Leuß had occasionally written on criminal justice, criticizing the "excessive mildness" of most punishments. Leuß's memoir of his own experience was thus, in some ways, a drama of discovery and ideological transformation. In prison, Leuß learned that solitary confinement was "the most refined invention ever discovered for the torture of human beings."[83] He also developed empathy for his fellow inmates, including the most degenerate criminals, seeing them all as victims of a fundamentally inhumane, crushing system.

The other work to cause a particular stir in the broader public sphere in these years was by the journalist Max Treu.[84] Treu's open letter to the Justice

Ministry, entitled *The Bankruptcy of Modern Penality and Its Reform*, reiterated the argument that penitentiaries and solitary confinement in particular destroyed human material. Invoking the argument that Mittelstädt had used to condemn the idea of resocialization as such, Treu asserted that only "free persons were capable of being educated and improved." Ultimately, they have to "do right because it is right" and "avoid wrong because it is wrong," rather than modifying their behavior simply as a result of "supervision, punishment, and deprivation."[85] Deportation, in Treu's view, presented a way out of this paradox. "He who would learn to swim must be surrounded by water," Treu declared.[86] In the penal colony, the ex-offenders would have such an opportunity to learn, without being allowed either to drown or to pull German society down with them.[87]

While a new wave of publications evoked a broader, progressive, public interest in deportation, the attentions of deportation proponents shifted from Africa to the South Seas as the site of a future penal colony. The most important proposal came from a subsection of the German Kolonialbund, under the leadership of jurists, penal welfare proponents, and colonialists. Two of the leading figures in the new organization were Joachim Graf Pfeil and Heinrich Seyfarth.[88] In 1905, the group incorporated itself as the German Deportation League and presented a plan for penal colonies in the Admiralty Islands, part of the German-controlled Bismarck Archipelago, near Papua New Guinea. The largest of the Admiralty Islands, Manus, was to be reserved for offenders still serving out their sentences. A different island, Neu-Pommern, would be the site for the permanent settlement of former offenders. The islands' attractions included a temperate climate, a solid potential for agricultural development, and extremely modest population density. In 1906, according to the League's figures, there were fewer than 400 natives per ten square kilometers on the two islands. The natives, it was argued, were also unusually passive and pliant and would, of course, be deprived of all firearms. As a further guarantee of the colony's integrity, the League suggested "resettling" the natives on a "special reservation." Free white settlers, while allowed on Neu-Pommern, could be sufficiently segregated from the deportees "to avoid any tensions."[89]

Unlike Bruck and Frank, the members of the League did not propose to reform the German penal code. Deportation in their plan would not constitute a principal sanction (*Hauptstrafe*) imposed by the judge at sentencing, but instead would be a "voluntary" measure introduced administratively. Selected inmates from German penitentiaries, prisons, and workhouses would be presented with a form of early conditional release, predicated on their willingness to be resettled and to comply with a series of conditions.[90]

In its letters and petitions to the Reich Government, the Deportation League drew upon an eclectic mix of alarmist social, hygienic, moral, political, and national economic arguments. The penitentiaries, they argued ominously, had become breeding grounds of infection. Prisoners were "irreparably" damaged by "immobile decay" in a "narrow cell." Citing unnamed health experts, the League claimed tuberculosis developed and spread from within the penitentiaries, "and from there it is carried into the population." Such risks to health, they concluded, "are the most decisive argument for the choice of a punitive process in the free air."[91] In a still more provocative step, the League quoted Socialist George Gradnauer's recent assertion that the essential nature of the German penal system contradicted "the humanist strivings of the time."[92] While the League members could not have shared Gradnauer's views on "class justice" in Imperial Germany, they did share his sense that a sub-proletariat class was created through juridical exclusions, and they perhaps invoked Gradnauer's views in order to remind the ministers that official injustice could exacerbate the spread of radical politics. As always, however, the most prominent argument against the current penal system and in favor of deportation focused upon the risk of a spreading criminal infection: former offenders, hounded from place to place, and bereft of hope, were left with nothing to fear and nothing to lose in committing further crimes.[93]

The League's proposal invoked the spirit of Bodelschwingh and the worker colony movement in its insistence that deportation should be based upon a voluntary, conscious choice by the prisoners themselves. The prisoners were expected to recognize not only the opportunity to escape the horrors of the penitentiary, but the opportunity for "becoming whole" and breaking free of the cycle of degeneration, more crime, and more punishment. This voluntarist element was deemed necessary to give a "powerful and lasting impulse toward unyielding labor" (*ausgiebige Arbeitsbetätigung*) on the part of the deportees. Seyfarth's influence was perhaps most marked in the League's petitions after 1907, when he assumed the chairmanship of the group and made the Deutsche Hilfsverein into a major partner in their work. For Seyfarth, deportation was not a substitute for domestic penal welfare but was rather its logical extension and complement. Penal colonies, he believed, were a necessary option in criminal policy, one suited to those individuals who were especially vulnerable to the negative effects of prison and the social poisons of modern society.

In its petitions to the German government in 1905 and 1906, the League argued for choosing 500 volunteers for the penal colony based upon a careful analysis of the prisoners' physical and mental characteristics and the likelihood that they would benefit from and contribute to colonial life. The prisoners would be required to commit to at least five years hard labor in the colony. If they fared well, they would be settled on another island, deemed transitional. After five years of good behavior, the ex-offenders would be granted "full legal and public rights."[94]

After the failure of these petitions, the Deportation League modified its proposal by focusing still more directly upon the task of reintegrating former prison inmates into a viable and productive social context. A 1908 petition called for the experimental colonization of 300 persons who had completed their prison sentences, or were pardoned or offered conditional release. The group was to include 100 single men and 100 married men, plus their wives and children. Again, the volunteers would be carefully screened to ensure that they were appropriate material for work in the tropics. They would also be selected with the long-term goal of creating a viable, self-supporting community. The group would have to include a range of skilled workers, including a carpenter, shoemaker, bricklayer, and baker. Before their travels to the South Seas, the former prisoners would be sent to an "agricultural preparation-station" administered by the Deutsche Hilfsverein. Using existing institutions and a minimum of state subvention, the Verein, over three months, would teach the former prisoners basic agricultural skills and "acclimatize" them to country work. Although they would be technically "free," the participants would still be watched over by gendarmes, segregated according to "type," and disciplined according to "severe" and "rigid" orders.

Once in the penal colony, the privileges and rights of the deportees were to be determined by their ability to prosper and to pay back their debts to the state. Besides arranging their transportation, the state was to offer them plots of land, tools, equipment, and possibly livestock on credit. Until these debts were paid off, the colonists were considered "vassals" (*Lehnsleute*), subject to the "disciplinary power" of the state, required to pay a yearly head tax, and required to serve six days of compulsory labor each year. When they paid off their debts, they became known as "independents." Along the way, they were expected to help build civilization on the island, contributing to a pooled health-care system and furthering religious and educational institutions. The constant challenge of "practical labor," it was argued, "would soon reveal the true nature" of the deportees. Those who showed themselves to be "useless and incorrigible" would be held in positions of relative bondage through the requirement that they perform "public labor for the colony" until their debts were paid. Those who succeeded through all the stages of transition, from parasite to producer, would be elevated back into the ranks of full citizens.

In all, the Deportation League's 1908 proposal imagined a world stripped of the complications of modernity and therefore suitable to a population that had failed to find its "proper place" in the German motherland. Freed from the temptation of alcohol or the luxury of laziness, the ex-offenders would succeed or fail based only upon their readiness to work and their commitment to the community. As in Bentham's panopticon, the deportees were rendered completely subject to the seeing eye of the state: there was nowhere to hide, no way to "dissimulate" or disguise their "true natures," and there was no way to obfuscate the causes of their failure or misbehavior. As a world of perfect transparency, the penal colony was to represent the purest modern utopia. Here damaged subjects would be offered the freedom to become citizens, but with the restraints necessary for the security and the safety of both themselves and the societies they left (however temporarily) behind.

Racial Uplift

The Wilhelmine deportation projects envisioned liminal spaces for liminal subjects at the peripheries of the Empire. The deportees would be lower in status than free white settlers, but superior to the native populations they displaced. They were exiles from the German nation and yet spiritually, economically, and politically bound to the German Empire. On the one hand, penal colonies would spatially delineate and inscribe racial hierarchies: to every race its "proper place," from the most primitive to the most advanced. Each population would be expected to make a distinct, if limited, contribution to imperial welfare. At the same time, penal colonies were to allow for the graduated movement of individuals up through the stages of racial betterment. Just as the natives would be civilized through work, education, and moral tutelage, so Europe's own unruly, undisciplined elements, the asocials, would recapitulate the process of evolution and advance toward the levels of their productive and morally responsible brethren.[95]

The Wilhelmine deportation movement thus, in some sense, literalized the metaphor that historically associated refractory and deviant populations in Europe with the "primitive" and "savage" races of Africa and Asia. Wichern, the mid-century reformer, helped to forge this association within a religious idiom when he condemned the prisons as "breeding grounds for paganism" within the heart of Europe.[96] He founded the "Inner Mission" as a domestic counterpart to the "external mission": a project for civilizing the lost, dark races at home. Some charities, including Bethel, functioned in both worlds, creating African stations modeled on their projects in Germany and often borrowing some of the personnel.[97] Lombroso, the Italian criminal-anthropologist, provided a scientific basis to the argument that criminals constituted a separate "atavistic" race, whose level of evolutionary advancement corresponded to certain primitive races outside of Europe.[98] German criminal reformers at the fin de siècle, as noted above, rejected the determinist assumptions of Lombroso's argument and insisted upon exploring and treating the causes of criminal behavior with reference to *cultural* and *social* attributes and contexts. The essential conceptual links, however, between primitivism at home and abroad remained intact. Even Hans Leuß's memoir of his own experience as a penitentiary inmate begins with this analogy, promising to describe an "unknown land," new "tribes," and the "life and the pursuits of savages."[99] Fin-de-siècle reformers were encouraged by the dynamic assumptions inherent in the biological theory of recapitulation—the idea that every healthy individual organism, during its growth to maturity, retraced the steps of evolutionary development for the species as a whole. The goal of modernist reformers was to promote the evolution of primitive peoples through active intervention: the penal colony projects boldly envisioned an overarching concentration and coordination of the "internal" and "external" dimensions of this project.

Against Deportation: The Theater of Horrors

The leading opponents of the deportation movement included colonial administrators, settlers' organizations, and missionary societies. Their perspectives were especially valued by the German government, which often solicited their input.[100] Their fundamental concern was that the presence of deportees would somehow corrupt the colonial mission. "Land speculators," according to the conservative *Kreuzzeitung*, organized against Bruck's proposal in 1897, because they feared it would produce a drop in property values.[101] Missionaries questioned the proposal on the grounds that criminals would undermine the effort to civilize the natives and present a positive moral image of the white man.[102] "We have taken the natives' land," wrote E. A. Fabarius,

> and promised, in exchange for this theft, to place them under our protection. Where is the German loyalty, when we now burden them with our criminals, under whose destructive influence . . . they will be ruined in body and soul! Not to speak of our own naked self-interest, which should prevent us from subjecting the natives to so great an evil, since no colony can flourish with ruined natives.[103]

Similarly, colonial administrators in Africa referred to the deportees as a morally infectious element.[104] General Eduard Liebert feared that the natives might learn criminal traits from the deportees. "White criminals must not be permitted to serve as models to the black natives," the general declared to widespread applause at a Pan-German League meeting.[105]

Anthropologist Ann Stoler has pointed out how the "anxieties of empire" drove French and Dutch colonizers to prevent the development of a white underclass in the colonies. The presence of deviant, weak, or impoverished settlers, it was believed, would undermine the authority of the colonizers and could lead to dangerous forms of cultural or physical miscegenation.[106] Similarly, in the German colonial context, Fabarius argued that "the European will only maintain his influence and his respected position among the natives to the extent that he shows himself as representative of a higher, more noble civilization." Even the "savages despise the bad white elements," he wrote.[107] Graf Pfeil, who vigorously supported the aims of deportation, helped to derail Bruck's proposal, in part because of concerns about the fragile relations between African natives and the scattered white settler population in SWA. Ensuring the security of the free whites, he argued, would require empowering natives to help in the recapture of escaped deportees, a step that would fundamentally alter the power balance in the colony.[108] Henceforth, Pfeil argued, every native would have the power to investigate and control every white man.[109]

According to Pfeil, SWA was unsuited for penal colonies because there was not enough habitable land to create "penal farms" sufficiently separated from the free white and native populations.[110] It was ultimately impossible, in his view, to create an effective system for supervising the deportees, without turning all of SWA into "a police state."[111] Other opponents challenged Bruck's important contention that the northern regions of SWA could support the settlement of farmers on small plots. Josef von Bülow was one among many experienced colonialists who believed that Southwest Africa would only be economically viable if parceled into "giant farms," engaged principally in cattle production.[112]

The arguments for establishing a penal colony in SWA were especially shaky after 1904, with the outbreak of the so-called "Herero Uprising." According to Lora Wildenthal, this conflict upset the Germans' "confidence in their 'cultural achievements' as colonizers."[113] Without such a faith in their ability to civilize (and control) the natives, the plausibility of a project to educate and uplift the refractory and dangerous classes of Europe through transportation to the colonies seemed dubious indeed.[114] As early as 1896, one colonialist had expressed the fear about the "inevitable 'entanglement' of uncertain elements among the deportees with the 'uncertain' portion of the natives." Leaving aside the destructive influence of the degenerate whites upon the natives, Fabarius argued, the "discontented deportees would always attempt to make common cause with the natives against the colonial government; they will be an 'element of decomposition,' constantly delivering the combustible material for disturbances, revolts, lootings and pillaging minor wars."[115] When rumors spread that the penal colony project for SWA had been resuscitated in 1908, Afrikaner settlers in SWA responded with panicked and furious letters to a Pretoria daily and sought the intervention of the British regime. The Pretoria *Volkstem* defended them, asserting that experiences in Australia proved that deportation was a disastrous policy and that "whenever a particularly raw crime is committed" in South Africa, the public assumes that the criminal was either from Australia or America. On behalf of the settlers in SWA, the newspaper begged the German government not to allow this "discarded refuse from a rotten element into their midst."[116]

Opponents of the Deportation League's proposal employed similar arguments to attack the idea of penal colonies in the South Sea Islands. In his report to the German Colonial Office, the governor of Neu-Guinea challenged many of the League's basic presuppositions about the climatic and geographic suitability of the Admiralty Islands for use as a penal colony.[117] In 1905, the general assembly of settlers across the Bismarck Archipelago met in Herbertshöhe to protest the Deportation League's proposal. The Assembly's official declaration, sent to the German Colonial Office, and then forwarded to the Justice Ministry, rehearsed familiar anxieties about the potentially disruptive and corruptive effects of introducing former offenders into the region. Faced again by unequivocal and seemingly unanimous objections by the German citizens most familiar with the geography and most affected by the government's decisions, the legislators postponed a decision, asking the German Foreign Office to gather more detailed information on the experience of other nations with deportation and penal colonies.[118]

A final blow to the prewar deportation movement came with the publication of Robert Heindl's remarkable 1912 book, *My Travels to the Penal Colonies*.[119] With financial support from the Bavarian government, Heindl, a police criminologist, visited many of the world's existing and former penal colonies and wrote about his experience in a 470-page memoir/scholarly report. The work was to represent the definitive account of deportation's successes and failures in recent history, and its value as a policy for the German Empire.[120] Written in the voice of the urbane, educated traveler, it reads like a bizarre mixture of Cesare Lombroso and Paul Theroux. Heindl presented the details of conversations, not only with colony administrators but with the deportees, the natives, and various incidental characters, including the wives of local officials. His description of life in the colonies was always mediated by his own role as observer and the drama of his investigation and discovery of the facts.

Heindl's book sought to delegitimize the concept of deportation through the relentless accumulation of detail, illustrating archaic systems of power, marked by chaos, brutality, and utter irrationality. Heindl's portrait offered the perfect counterpoint to the classical image of the well-ordered penitentiary. Alluding repeatedly to Dante's *Inferno*, he described shadow zones of quiet suffering and unholy copulations, interrupted by public theaters of cruelty and pain and absurd, almost gratuitous displays of domination. Juxtaposed with the horrors of life among the deportees, however, were images of French and Dutch gentlemen wearing "outrageous" white pants and "embarrassingly" short jackets in nearby hotels, with their wives spending entire days in their "negligees," something the author found "occasionally quite charming, but usually quite horrid."[121] The natives appeared in a range of guises, including comically unprepared policemen, prostitutes, and incidental laborers—basically well-meaning people forced into inappropriate or even ridiculous roles in an unwholesome situation. Overall, Heindl drew a portrait of the colonies as places with endless rules and the unceasing exercise of power, and yet no legitimate or consistent hierarchies and principles of order.

The book opened with the author's arrival in the French colony in New Caledonia. Heindl playfully described the occupational roles of the convicted felons on the island. A notorious poisoner worked in the kitchen. A convicted knife-murderer worked as a barber. A serial killer was responsible for the ropes that pulled a car of people across a steep ravine. The striking aspect of these images—other than their macabre humor—was in how they illustrated the failure to organize the prisoners' labor according to principles of criminological classification.[122] Allowing poisoners to work in the kitchen was only the most obvious example of indifference to cardinal rules of disciplinary power: the need to regiment bodies and personalities by type.[123]

Heindl went on to describe New Caledonia as a world in which violence was random; crime and escapes were common; and executions were routine. His description of a public execution, performed by guillotine before the assembled deportees on a square by the jailhouse, was especially evocative of a premodern power regime. After first describing "the scenery," Heindl offered the "drama" in minute detail, including the various sounds on the

Der Mörder als Raseur

Der Mörder als Kindermädchen

Against the penal colony. Photos from Robert Heindl's visit to a British colony. Left: The murderer as barber. Right: The murderer as nanny. (From Robert Heindl, Meine Reise nach den Strafkolonien*)*

square and the droplets of sweat on the condemned man's forehead.[124] The condemned offered a homily, "words of resignation, encouragement and good advice to this crowd of sufferers who kneel before him," and then he was thrown forward into the apparatus "like bread into the oven." His severed head was briefly shown to the crowd before the deportees were sent off to begin their "day's work."[125]

In direct contrast to the visions of Wilhelmine deportation advocates, Heindl described the colonies as zones of promiscuous mixing on all levels: among the different types of criminals, among the criminals and the free settlers, and among both of these groups and the native populations. Images of miscegenation abound. Reporting on his conversations with "half-breeds," Heindl mused about the criminological threats posed by the "mulatto personality." The natives of New Caledonia, meanwhile, reported to the author about whole classes of degenerate offspring populating the region, while the author himself periodically discovered local women "in the arms" of European criminals.

Heindl's book challenged the deportation movement's most important assertion: that penal colonies could be humane and efficient alternatives to domestic incarceration. A member of the Reichstag praised Heindl for de-

bunking the mythology of a "metamorphosis of thieves into property owners, of vagrants into settled farmers, of pimps into bourgeois paters fami-
lias."[126] It hardly mattered that many of the colonies investigated by Heindl
had made little or no claim to being "progressive." The book's shocking
vignettes reasserted the association of deportation with chaos, expulsion, and
the disintegration of modern structures of power. It probably also provided
the inspiration for Franz Kafka's story *In the Penal Colony*, which was written
in 1914.[127] Describing the visit of a foreign investigator to an unnamed European colony, Kafka presented the image of a perfect hell, in which the Europeans' desperate efforts to impose law and order were both terrifying and
comic. The colonial administrator in Kafka's story built an extremely complex, technologically advanced "apparatus," which was used to gouge the text
of the law into the flesh of any person caught committing a crime. There were
no efforts to educate or enlighten the accused. In fact, the criminal was not
even informed of his offense. ("There would be no point in telling him," an
officer tells the investigator blandly. "He'll learn it on his body.") Kafka undoubtedly chose the setting of a penal colony in order to address issues well
beyond contemporary debates among penal reform societies, but the satire in
his story was based essentially upon the stark juxtaposition of a pious and
bureaucratic discourse of legal modernism alongside the outrageously brutal
and inhumane practice within a domain "beyond civilization." In that sense,
Kafka's story was a perfect satire of the Wilhelmine deportation movement
and its fantasies of a penal utopia.

One might have expected discussions of deportation to come to an end
during World War I, when the blockade of Germany and the eventual seizure
of German colonies seemed to have decided the question. Remarkably, however, prison society meetings and publications on welfare and punishment
continued to weigh the benefits and drawbacks of penal deportation during
the war and even during the Weimar Republic.[128] In an impassioned brochure, written in the heady days of 1919, the left-wing journalist Hans Hyan
outlined a plan for radical criminal justice reform, which included penal
colonies—organized upon Christian principles of "love and supervision"—
for the most persistently refractory and inassimilable criminal populations.
If Germany had really lost its colonies for good, Hyan argued, then at least it
should be possible to borrow some lonely island in the Pacific.[129] Hyan's
advocacy of deportation in the context of other progressive proposals on
criminal justice policy underscored the fact that the goals and assumptions
behind deportation maintained their legitimacy—even if the practical nature

of the project was in doubt.[130] Hyan later modified his proposal to stress the "penal colonization" of marshlands and "desert" within Germany.[131]

Heinrich Seyfarth and other veterans of the fin-de-siècle deportation movement were less inclined to speak in terms of colonizing the ex-offender during the Weimar Republic, but they continued to pay homage to their erstwhile passion.[132] Even those who dismissed the progressive ideal of penal colonies as utopian acknowledged that this was a vision pieced together out of the hopes and the principles of mainstream modernist thinking. Like many utopias, the penal colony ideal inspired and informed subsequent movements and projects for social reform. If a true terra nova could not be found for this purpose, then reformers would just have to find a substitute.

THE EX-CONVICT AS NATIONAL HERO
The Captain from Köpenick
and the Discourse of Reform

On the sixteenth of October, 1906, an ex-prisoner, shoemaker-turned-vagabond named Wilhelm Voigt donned the uniform of a Prussian army captain, commandeered a small troupe of soldiers, and occupied the Town Hall of Köpenick, a village on the outskirts of Metropolitan Berlin. Imitating the imperious tone and gestures of a Prussian officer, Voigt informed Köpenick's officials that irregularities had been found in their bookkeeping, and that he had been ordered by the authorities in Berlin to arrest the mayor and confiscate the municipal cashbox. Neither the soldiers nor the townspeople offered any resistance but dutifully followed the "captain's" orders. While the soldiers escorted the mayor into Berlin by coach, Voigt fled with the cashbox by train: back to the city and into the realm of historical mythology.[1]

The escapade in Köpenick was an international news event even before Voigt's identity was known. After his arrest and imprisonment, the former prisoner and vagabond became a public sensation. Voigt's shameful past and the years spent in prisons, workhouses, hostels, and asylums only added to the dense mystique around the "genius swindler." He was a product of Rawicz, the penitentiary that had given its name to the militarist style of prison discipline, and had somehow managed to use this "training" to turn the tables against the system. The popular press published interviews with Voigt and regular reports on his life in prison. Cabarets and street-singers recounted his exploits. "Perhaps never before," wrote the journalist Maximilian Harden, "has the *vox populi, populorum* so unanimously crowned a person, whom the state legally persecuted as a robber and swindler." Voigt's trial was covered as a major national event. After being pardoned by the Kaiser, he went on a triumphant speaking tour, in which his popularity reached a pitch of intensity seeming almost to presage the Lindbergh phenomenon some fifteen years later.[2]

This chapter will consider Voigt's celebrity in the context of criminal policy reform discourse in the decade before the war. The Köpenick affair is often recalled as an exposé of the subservient mentality in Germany and a critique of Prussian militarism. However, Voigt's contemporaries also discussed his "strike" as an illustration of the ex-offender's desperate search for a place in German society. Voigt's imitation of a Prussian officer, in that sense, was not just a parody of Germans' deference for authority but of their demand that vagrants and ex-offenders rejoin society through the performance of citizenship. Marginalized, declassé persons were somehow supposed to become respectable through dress, comportment, hard work, and initiative. Voigt accomplished this task in what seemed the only way available to him.

The serious side of Voigt's story—which resonated long after the laughter died down—was the image of the ex-offender as a victim of the police machine. The captain from Köpenick quickly became an archetype of the fundamentally decent and talented but socially maladjusted individual, who, after one bad mistake, was perpetually marginalized. The heroization of Voigt represented a carnivalesque celebration of resourcefulness and justice at the expense of ossified bureaucratic authority. The principal demon in Voigt's saga was thus not simply militarism but legalism, not simply the Junker elites but the craven and hypocritical police officials who blocked his efforts to become a respectable citizen. Like the fantasy of deportation, Voigt's tale became a parable of the outcast's struggle to be "made social."

Köpenick and the Authoritarian Mentality

The creation of the Voigt phenomenon owed a great deal to the new role of the press in the construction of big-city events. As Peter Fritzsche has noted, with the phenomenal growth of the mass-circulation "boulevard press" around the turn of the century, the newspapers became responsible for maintaining the imaginative coherence of the city as a single organic unit.[3] Crime reporting played an especially important role in "staging" the city, and manhunts for real or imagined criminals were important occasions for the press to boost circulation, while generating a kind of popular frenzy.[4] The manhunt for Voigt, meanwhile, was unprecedented in its scope and in the excitement it generated. Over 1,000 people submitted denunciations to the police, all of which turned out to be wrong.[5] Wilhelm Voigt stepped into this whirlwind of publicity after he was betrayed by an old acquaintance who sought the 2,000 mark reward.[6] There was widespread amazement when it became known that the perpetrator had never served in the armed forces and was an "old prison bird," a man who had spent twenty-seven years of his life behind bars.[7]

From the earliest stages of the Voigt phenomenon, many commentators saw him as a heroic figure for having stripped bare the authoritarian mentality beneath Imperial Germany. The *New York Times* first reported on the affair alongside the notice that Alfred Dreyfus had resumed his duties as a major in the French artillery.[8] While the juxtaposition may have been accidental, it highlighted an image of reactionary militarism run amok. The tale of Prussian civil servants cringing obsequiously before a common swindler in a second-hand uniform fit well alongside that of pompous French officers breaking Dreyfus's sword. In both cases, caste prejudices supposedly obscured the Europeans' ability to make reasoned distinctions between true officers and their counterfeits. The Köpenick affair made for especially good comic relief when counterpoised to this and other tragedies.[9] For French papers, the Köpenick affair manifested the peculiarly German phenomenon of the "sub-altern spirit." It underscored the Prussians' reverence for authority and inability to exercise independent judgment.[10] The German Social Democratic newspaper *Vorwärts* declared solemnly that foreigners' respect for Germany, based largely on science and industry, "suffocates in this mocking laughter." The liberal papers *Die Tageblatt* and *Die Nationalzeitung* lamented the Prussians' "fetish for uniforms" and overwrought regard for authority.[11]

The great liberal thinker Friedrich Naumann congratulated Voigt for accomplishing an "intellectual success" worthy of Machiavelli. Voigt's "picture should be placed at the front of the textbooks on public law," Naumann wrote, "because he is an enlightener." He demonstrated "how easy it is to rule people, when one understands how to observe them without illusions." As the ultimate outsider, Naumann asserted, Voigt was able to recognize the deceptively simple truth that soldiers controlled the cashboxes, while uniforms and letters controlled the soldiers. The lesson from the Köpenick affair, according to Naumann, was for people to follow the Constitution and not to believe every alleged administrative decree and every person in uniform who showed up at their door.[12]

During the late Weimar Republic, Voigt's story became a kind of semi-official Republican mythology.[13] The vagabond-ex-convict-shoemaker who exposed the authoritarian undercurrents of Prussian society was a perfect symbol for the new social state. Voigt and the affair had been initially forgotten after World War I. In 1926, however, the Social Democratic state government of Prussia organized an immensely popular "International Police Exhibition" in Berlin, which included an exhibit on the Köpenick affair, featuring a wax replica of Voigt in uniform, borrowed from the Panopticon wax museum in Berlin. The point of the display, like the exhibition overall, was to highlight the change in German governmental institutions since the fall of the Kaiser in 1918. Against the protests of the Reich government, the organizers invoked the Köpenick affair to remind viewers of a time when an authoritarian *Rechtsstaat* operated through a fetish for rules, hierarchies, and symbols. The exhibition used Voigt's oppressors as a foil for the new Prussian state with its focus on social considerations. The great embodiment of the new Prussian authority was the new Prussian police officer, whose simple, unadorned uniform and approachable manner were the exact opposite of the ceremoniously overdressed, militarized constables of the old regime.[14]

A wave of imaginative retellings of the Köpenick affair followed the exhibit in Berlin, starting with the first film version of the story in 1926. A novelized version of Voigt's life was published in 1930. In 1931, Carl Zuckmayer wrote his classic stage version of the story, which premiered in Berlin on the twenty-fifth anniversary of the affair. Responding to the rise of paramilitary violence in Germany, Zuckmayer highlighted the theme of the uniform and its fetishistic power, offering a warning to his fellow citizens about the vestiges of a "Prussian mentality" in German culture. For this reason, the play was denounced in the right-wing press, picketed and disrupted by agitators. Noting that the mayor of Köpenick had been a prominent member of the Progressive Party, Zuckmayer's version also presented the affair as a metaphor for the capitulation of prewar liberals. The town officials appear as well-meaning men seduced by Junker culture and the ideals of a well-regulated police state. In the months following the play's opening, Zuckmayer wrote the screenplay for a sound version of the film, produced by UFA, which opened in December of 1931. Interestingly, the director of the film, Richard Oswald, had done a popular dramatization of the Dreyfus affair one year earlier.[15]

Subsequent histories of the Köpenick story have focused upon the affair as a political parable with an anti-militarist message—possibly because of the lasting impact of Zuckmayer's play.[16] Winfried Löschburg describes the affair as exposing the "faith in authority" and "submissive mentality" of the German bourgeoisie.[17] The literary scholar Anthony Greenville links the affair to Hans-Ulrich Wehler's notion of "social militarism." According to Greenville, the story shows "the contamination of the democratic values of liberal politics in civil society by militarized attitudes and authoritarian, hierarchical values."[18] In Zuckmayer's play, as in Imperial Germany, according to Greenville, "the Prussian-German *Rechtsstaat* . . . stands revealed as a sham."[19]

This reduction of the story to a moral saga of "authoritarian mentalities" obscures the specific, distinctly social reading of the Voigt affair that existed at the time and during its aftermath. Voigt never attempted to embarrass the

Prussian authorities, and his popular memoir offered little in the way of critical reflections on militarism or the culture of what Interior Minister Theodor Bethmann-Hollweg later defended as "a people under arms."[20] Instead, Voigt emphasized his own life saga as an ex-offender and vagabond. The memoir described him as the product of a legal system that branded him as outcast and then relentlessly reinforced his subaltern position. In his appearances around Germany and as a symbol within late Wilhelmine discourse, Voigt stood for the travails of those who had the will and the ability to come back from the margins of bourgeois society, but were held back by traditional exclusionary mechanisms.

Not long after Voigt's arrest, the popular boulevard dailies began to describe him as a victim of overzealous police supervision. Even the pro-military, pro-monarchical Scherl papers and the Catholic Center Party's organ, *Germania*, provided sympathetic interpretations of Voigt's life story. The papers reported that Voigt tried everything possible to live honestly after his last release from prison. He found work in Wismar, Mecklenburg, but without warning or explanation received notice that he was banished from the region under the terms of the police supervision laws. He then moved to Berlin with "good intentions," hoping to find an environment in which to live and work more or less anonymously. Relatives offered to help find work, an apartment. In spite of this network of assistance, when Voigt tried to register with the local authorities, he was banished from Berlin as well.[21] Scherl's *Der Tag* summarized Voigt's life in a poem entitled, with only a little irony, "the Hero." (In these "small times," the author joked, we celebrate "small personalities.")

Wäre gern ein Eigentümer
Heirat. Spätes Glück. Frau Riemer.
Zuchthaus wiederholte Male
Altershoffnung: Schuhfiliale.

Schöner Plan. Es störte diesen
Polizei. Raus! Ausgewiesen.
Rumgestossen, westlich, östlich.
Rechtssystem bewährt sich köstlich.[22]

The swindle in Köpenick, the papers claimed, was a last-ditch effort by a desperate man.[23]

Voigt and his lawyer, Walter Bahn, built upon popular sympathy during his trial, a complete transcript of which was printed in the generally sober and unsensational liberal daily *Die Vossische Zeitung*.[24] Bahn told the court that "the case should be judged *not* primarily from a juridical standpoint, but rather from the heart." This extraordinary assertion (what was a court of law without a juridical perspective?) suggested that lawyer and client were speaking to an audience beyond the courtroom in hopes of a royal pardon. Bahn declared that Voigt deserved empathy, like almost no other defendant he had known. He called Voigt's earlier sentences "horribly" unfair: fifteen years in the penitentiary had "poisoned the seed of goodness that was in him."[25] The presiding judge built support for this line of argument with his own questions to the defendant.[26] Voigt described his life as a constant struggle for respectability against the stigma of punishment. Society forced him together with "bad elements," he claimed, which exploited and debased him at every turn. Voigt's "modest appearance" and his simple demeanor amazed the German press. By the end of the trial, popular sentiment seemed more clearly than ever to be weighted in his favor.[27]

His sentence of four years in prison was below what the judge could have imposed for recidivist fraud. In an extraordinary moment, the judge approached Voigt after the sentence and shook his hand—an image the publishers of the court transcript chose for their cover. In the drawing, the judge looks up at Voigt with an admiring, almost adoring gaze as their hands clasp. In spite of this unusual show of sympathy, the daily papers condemned the verdict as harsh and unfair. Reporters covered Voigt's days in prison with the meticulous attention worthy of a martyr preparing for the death pyre.[28]

Not surprisingly, Voigt and his lawyer immediately sought a full pardon from the Kaiser. Letters in support of Voigt poured in from across Germany and from overseas. Readers of the *Berlin Morgenpost* called upon the paper to gather signatures for a petition to the Kaiser. Eventually, Reich Chancellor Prince von Bülow intervened to declare that this "victim of our police regulations" should be granted a pardon soon. The matter filtered down to the local state's attorney, who, true to his legal principles, refused to see any extenuating circumstances in Voigt's case. Prussian leaders persisted, however, in finding the means to justify Voigt's pardon to the Kaiser.[29] According to historian Benjamin Hett, the Prussian Minister of Justice argued that Voigt's fifteen-year prison sentence in 1891 for aggravated theft may have been fair at the time, but was too harsh by the standards of the present day.[30] The accommodation to changing standards of proper and just treatment, in other words, should trump formal correctness. Ultimately, the Reich leadership prevailed. The Kaiser issued a formal pardon, and Voigt was released on 16 August 1908. Within days a storm of excitement broke out across Berlin and then Germany.

The crowd that welcomed Voigt at the prison gates marked the beginning of a new stage of celebrity for the career offender. Swarms of people surrounded his sister's apartment and other buildings where he was sighted. According to the *Abendblatt*, "a great portion of the capital's population was seized by a fever-paroxysm. . . . The man is on the verge of becoming a national icon."[31] An entrepreneur from Bremen offered him the astounding sum of 5000 marks for a series of eight lectures. The International Kinematographic Society filmed him for the Wochenschau, and a gramophone recording was pressed and sold of Voigt giving a long, carefully crafted speech of thanks to all his supporters. Seventy letters per day were delivered to his home.[32] The *Berliner Tageblatt* reported that well-to-do women sent Voigt numerous offers of marriage, a few of which were under consideration. The *Lokal Anzeiger* soon reported that a wealthy benefactress was already supporting him with a stipend of 100 marks per month.[33]

Voigt was happy to seize the opportunities offered by fame. He charged taverns for hosting his public appearances. He gave short speeches, frequently dressed in an officer's uniform, signed autographs, and eventually sold postcards with pictures of himself as "the Captain." His growing popularity produced consternation and concern among the Prussian police. The Berlin authorities went so far as to remind Voigt that the expulsion orders against him were still in effect, although they suspended any enforcement in the face of a public outcry. Hoping to defuse the excitement around Voigt, the Interior Ministry called upon local police forces to exercise the mildest possible application of police supervision laws against him.[34] Nevertheless, when Voigt began to make whistle-stop tours across Prussia, the affront to the local authorities was too much for them to bear. Frequently the visits were organized like the appearance of a dignified celebrity, complete with marching bands and railway-station speeches. Voigt's penchant for planning events was such that he was able to get inns and taverns to pay in advance for sponsoring his appearances. On a number of occasions, two different establishments paid for the same honor. A few local police forces intervened not only to cancel his appearances, but arrested him for impersonating a Prussian officer or for violating regulations forbidding public appearances by persons under police supervision. The most bizarre and perhaps ironic encounter Voigt suffered was when he was arrested by the French for wearing a German military uniform at an event in Nancy.[35]

In the months after his liberation, Voigt found an ideal literary collaborator in Hans Hyan, a journalist who had learned to use the new press for a variety of humanist crusades.[36] In his reportage, essays, and poems, Hyan offered vivid, often sensational accounts of criminal careers, describing offenders as products of both social forces and irrepressible biological laws. In the spirit of

Zola, Hyan created compelling melodramatic narratives, tracing the fate of men and women struggling against their own degenerate urges and the cruelty and indifference of an ossified liberal order.[37] Hyan helped Voigt to shape his memoirs into a tragedy that likewise drew upon contemporary criminological and social ideas.[38] Hyan's preface hit all the familiar points about offenders as social victims: Voigt was the child of a "passionate, reckless gambler" who was probably alcoholic. He was driven into vagrancy through the combination of his own failures, social prejudices, and the almost mechanical efficiency of the police. Voigt, Hyan writes, "is obviously to be counted among the creatures of impulse [*Triebwesen*], whom the newest research has recognized as lacking in sufficient restraints."[39]

Voigt's own account of his life fleshed out a portrait that mixed biological and environmental explanations of his persistent failures. His first confrontation with the Prussian police came as a child, while staying with relatives in Königsberg in order to get away from his abusive father in far-off Tilsit. A police constable insisted that Wilhelm had come to Königsberg to panhandle, and he beat the poor child until he confessed.[40] This led to Voigt's first overnight incarceration. Later, as a young man, he committed his first crime, fraud, according to his description almost by accident. After a stay in the notorious Moabit prison in Berlin, he was thrown together with a "bad sort," and was lured by his cronies into the commission of more serious crimes. From that point on, the memoir recounted a life spent in and out of penitentiaries, confronting a series of colorful and harrowing figures, like the warden who flogged the inmates shouting, "Here there is no God; here I am both your god and your devil." Outside the prisons, there was the constant reality of police harassment and the constant need for the underworld as the only sanctuary. The penitentiary "destroyed" him, he writes, placing him among the "living dead," an "outcast," a "hunted savage."[41]

Halfway into the memoir came the notorious day in Köpenick. The progression of the work suggested an anti-*Bildungsroman*: a young German's descent from shoemaker to prisoner to vagabond to "criminal," inexorably moving toward the tragic-heroic events of 1906. Biology and upbringing predestined Voigt to struggle for his place in society, but it was the great "*Moloch*," the German police-justice system, that ultimately drove him down the path toward a seemingly necessary crime. The pardon, when it comes, is a complete surprise, a true *deus ex machina*. Finally there is a merciful accounting by the powers above of Voigt's suffering and the absurdity of any continued torment.

Far from criticizing Prussian militarism in his memoir, Voigt underscored his admiration for military values and traditions. Military discipline, he claimed later, was the one worthwhile thing he learned at the penitentiary at

Rawicz. While this comment has been cited as an ironic and embittered statement on prison life, the memoir as a whole suggests it was serious. Throughout the book, there are seemingly gratuitous references to military regiments and men in uniform, with his admiration for the military shown as forming already in childhood. While in Rawicz, there was a crucial scene in which an officer from a nearby regiment visited Voigt's cell and noted his shock at the long and severe sentence he served for a seemingly minor case of fraud. Upon leaving, the officer advised the inmate to "seek the way of justice one more time."[42] There was also very little irony to be found in Voigt's expressions of admiration for the Kaiser and the Junker elites. The most famous manifestation of his loyalty—again something that historians have found hard to take seriously—was the sycophantic letter to the emperor that Voigt passed on to the newspapers after his pardon.

In his memoir, Voigt's entire life experience explains the germination of the great crime. Voigt portrayed himself as the quintessential *asocial*, in the original sense of the word. He was chronically stuck at the margins of society, maladjusted, passive, easily seduced into idiotic adventures. He was not, however, *anti-social*: he was no opponent of the existing order and never an active criminal. Repeated incarceration had a "destructive" effect upon him, but also offered an education in survival. Unlike other, less gifted criminals, he was not rendered completely "useless," but developed a form of self-discipline, a concern for "justice" (as opposed to "law"), and a collection of skills. His act in Köpenick was the fulfillment of this education.

Ultimately, the popular resonance of Voigt's life story was as much a challenge to German legalism as to Prussian militarism. Voigt and his advocates, including Hans Hyan and another popular journalist, Hans Ostwald, used his tale to condemn the rigid juridical structure of the criminal justice system.[43] Judges and police officials, it was argued, had sentenced Voigt to a life outside the bounds of respectable society. The cause of the tragedy was not the exercise of arbitrary power but the overly zealous application of laws and police traditions, without regard to the peculiar "human circumstances" of his case. In this interpretation, the traditional German *Rechtsstaat* was alive and well—and that was precisely the problem.

Policy toward Ex-Convicts in the Wake of the Köpenick Affair

The Köpenick affair made police supervision of ex-offenders, and especially the practice of banishment, into a major topic of public discussion. Defenders of police supervision claimed that between

30,000 and 35,000 ex-offenders moved to Berlin every year. Many came in order to start new lives as productive citizens, but a significant number were lured by the unparalleled opportunities for criminal activity. Keeping tabs on the bad elements, officials argued, was absolutely necessary to protecting respectable society. Police supervision, which could last up to five years, was primarily a matter of interviewing coworkers and community members to make sure that released prisoners were law-abiding and decent. The police frequently forbade ex-offenders from visiting locales they suspected were criminal hangouts. They might also demand that they stay away altogether from pubs, particularly in cases of documented drinking problems. Police officials claimed to be restrained in the use of their power to banish ex-offenders from entire cities or regions. In Berlin, the police expelled "only" 600 ex-offenders in 1905, against 20,000 who were allowed to remain under police supervision.[44]

In the wake of the Köpenick affair, a great tide of criticism focused on the institution of police supervision and especially the practice of banishing ex-offenders from whole cities or regions. Robert von Hippel, the IKV's leading academic expert on asocials, claimed that Voigt would probably have become an upstanding shoemaker in Wismar if not for the wrong-headed order of banishment he received in February 1906.[45] A popular postcard showed the "ex-captain" in a cell in Berlin-Moabit juxtaposed with an image of him diligently repairing shoes. In the latter photo, under the heading "police supervision," a hand intrudes into the picture holding a sign that says "banishment." A larger heading reads, "Who Is Really the Guilty One?"[46] The first published dramatization of the Köpenick affair likewise focused on the bureaucratic idiocy of police supervision and the injustice of banishment.[47]

Stories surfaced about other ex-offenders who were "hunted" and "harassed" by the police even as they tried to gain a footing in respectable society. The *Posener Zeitung* told of a bartender named Richter who served sixteen years in prison and was then banished on five occasions from towns where he hoped to make a new start. He eventually settled in Halle, married a respectable and propertied woman, and, with her help, opened a restaurant. Four months later the police appeared and told him he was banished from Halle as well. They explained that the restaurant offered "too many opportunities for dishonesty."[48] Members of the Berlin Prisoners Association confronted a Prussian official with their own examples similar to Herr Richter. A liberal deputy in the Prussian parliament alluded to cases of overzealous police supervision that he had seen as a defense attorney. Social Democratic Reichstag deputy Wolfgang Heine, also a prominent defense attorney, described cases in which workers guilty of some minor offense in the distant past were suddenly banished from their hometowns after getting involved in socialist politics or union affairs.[49] In short, critics argued that police supervision stripped ex-offenders of their fundamental rights as citizens and destroyed any hope of their reintegration into society.

Criticism of police supervision reflected both growing empathy with ex-offenders and growing anxiety about the rise of a new criminal underclass. Hippel claimed that limits on ex-offenders' right to settle where they wished were "not a means to protect society, but a means for the furtherance of habitual criminality." A satirical paper in Vienna declared:

Heute . . . fühlt sich keiner
So ungeniert und frei,
Als wenn er unter Aufsicht
der Popopolizei.[50]

Police supervision was simply not an effective tool of social control under such modern urban conditions. Two cartoonists pointed out the role of a Jewish second-hand clothing dealer in facilitating Voigt's swindle in Köpenick. It was the Jews—the quintessential symbols of modernity—who allegedly permitted the revered symbols of military authority to become mere commodities, available to everyone. One postcard shows a Jewish peddlar on the road to Köpenick holding an officer's sword and a box full of uniforms. "Buy, buy," he says. "The clothes make the man." A cartoon in the weekly *Die Muskete* shows a Jewish clothier dressing a man in an officer's uniform and saying, "So, now you can conquer Braunschweig on behalf of Prussia."[51] In this modern era, disguises are plentiful and readily available.

The alternative to police supervision, it was widely agreed, was welfare supervision. So-called "sympathy postcards" for Voigt paired a drawing of him as a diligent and humble shoemaker in work smock with a drawing of the "ingenious" captain in full dress uniform. For every 1,000 postcards sold, the publisher promised to give 10 marks to the association of welfare for released prisoners in hopes that Voigt could eventually be allowed the quiet, honest, productive life he deserved.[52] Inspired by Voigt's story, a citizen in Halle became a member of his local prison association and offered 100 marks as a starting gift.[53] No one seemed to notice that in fact Wilhelm Voigt had sought help from a local prison association after his release from Rawicz prison and was refused assistance on the grounds that he was too morally corrupted.[54] More resources and greater authority for prison welfare was the cry of the moment.

Prussian officials could not stand aloof from these passionate calls for the reform of state policies toward ex-offenders. The authorities dispatched Dr. Lindenau, a high Berlin police official, to meetings of the Berlin Prisoners Association and the Prison Society of Sachsen-Anhalt. Lindenau defended police supervision and banishment as elements of a pragmatic and humane social policy. Because the milieu was so important, he argued, it was essential for the police to have authority to forbid the ex-offender's access to problematic areas and establishments. Theodor Bethmann-Hollweg, the Prussian Interior Minister, defended police supervision before the Prussian parliament. Bethmann had enormous credibility as a proponent of social policy. In his inaugural address as minister in 1905, he called social welfare "the most important and the most serious issue of our time." He had close ties to private charities and supported their interests within policy circles. Like Lindenau, Bethmann argued that police supervision was an indispensable element for a modern, socially oriented criminal policy.[55]

The Köpenick affair, however, unleashed an unprecedented wave of criticism of police supervision. Even Reich Chancellor Bülow referred to Voigt as a "victim of our police regulations."[56] On the left, there were growing calls to abolish police supervision or, at the very least, subject it to controls by the courts. Bethmann deflected these criticisms by introducing a decree to enhance the authority of private associations in the regulation of ex-offenders. The Interior Minister's decree called for "an individual handling" of every released prisoner "through examination of the files." While the decree of 1900 had established the principle that ex-prisoners under the care of a welfare organization might be spared the indignities and the harassments of police surveillance, the 1907 decree mandated police contact with welfare associations in all cases where the suspension of police supervision was possible.[57]

As with the deportation issue, Modern School reformers were divided in their responses to the Voigt case and to the impassioned public interest in welfare for offenders. Writing in a popular journal of the arts and politics, Aschaffenburg called for a sober and skeptical look at the Köpenick affair. As a criminal psychologist, Aschaffenburg believed Voigt represented a type of habitual criminal who was inevitably, perhaps inherently, dangerous. Such swindlers were so highly conditioned to their false personas, he stated, that only a trained criminologist could ever penetrate their deceitful facades. Even the most well-meaning volunteers from the realm of private welfare would have been hard pressed to recognize Voigt's pathologies and rescue him from further offenses.[58] Aschaffenburg acknowledged that Voigt's experience with the authorities illustrated irrational and outdated elements in Prussian criminal policy, though he gave only the most hesitant endorsement to the proposals of Christian welfare associations. Writing in the *Deutsche Juristen-zeitung*, however, von Hippel felt that Voigt's case illustrated the pernicious-ness of police regulations that were so extreme as to be an "heavy obstacle to the pursuit of an honest existence."[59]

The Kaiser's pardon offered the ultimate legitimation for claims that Voigt was a victim of the police machine. The Kaiser's intervention essentially repudiated police officials' mechanical conformity to law and regulations in favor of a humane, individualizing approach to damaged human material. The crown, no less than the liberals, denounced any slavish obedience before the "trappings of authority." Signifiers of power—from the officer's cap to the letter of the law—must serve an authentic and rational purpose. They were corrupted if they were "worshipped" and fetishized.[60] For a moment, the emperor and the "old prison bird" were united in the overthrow of sham au-thority, "humbuggery," and the philistines' concern with empty formalities.[61]

The pardon helped bring a qualitative turning point in the efforts of welfare associations to transform their role in criminal justice. In the summer of 1907, a member of the Inner Mission's Central Committee excitedly re-ported that prison associations were multiplying "through the transforma-tion of police-supervision into welfare supervision."[62] In the Rhineland and Westphalia alone, fifteen prison associations were founded in 1907 and 1908. In Brandenburg, 700 inmates turned to the prison associations in hopes of being able to avoid police supervision. From the standpoint of the Inner Mission, the Prussian legal authorities had finally transcended their jealous regard for the prerogatives of state power and attained a more enlightened perspective on the fate of the criminal. Under these circumstances, mused another Inner Mission official, "the first priority is not the preservation of state authority, but rather the development of civilization [*Kulturarbeit*]."[63] Private welfare organizations were to be at the forefront of this effort to rebuild "*Kultur.*"

The growth in the size and scope of private associations of welfare for released prisoners continued rapidly in the years before World War I.[64] In lockstep with this change, popular criticism of the police's role in social control became increasingly bold and emphatic. In 1910, there was public outrage when the police rescinded the conditional pardon granted a young offender because he raised funds for a miners' strike in Bergenhausen. For the police, the man's affiliation with the Social Democrats was a clear viola-tion of the law requiring a demonstration of "good behavior" during the period of police supervision. For critics, the case illustrated the problem with entrusting an agency of security with power over the granting of pardons.[65]

Sympathie-Postkarte für dem Wilh. Voigt **Hauptmann v. Köpenick.**

Jeder Käufer dieser Postkarte

gibt kund,
dass er dem Hauptmann v. Köpenick
Sympathie und Achtung
nicht versagen kann, mit Hinblick auf
die bewiesene Arbeitswilligkeit.

in Anbetracht,
dass Wilh. Voigt sich bessern wollte und
fleissig arbeitete, aber überall ausgewiesen wurde, wird die Verlagsfirma
dieser Postkarte von jeden verkauften
1000 Stück Postkarten

=== **Zehn Mark** ===

für Wilh Voigt an den Verein zur Fürsorge für entlassene Strafgefangene am
Weihnachtsheiligabend 1906 abführen,
damit derselbe nach Verbüssung seiner
jetzigen Strafe sein Brot auf ehrliche
Weise verdienen kann.

Als der **Schuster Voigt** fleissig war!

Als der **Hauptmann Voigt** genial war!

"Sympathy postcard for Wilhelm Voigt." Portions of the sale were to be given on Voigt's behalf to the Berlin Prison Association. (Heimatmuseum Köpenick)

The Köpenick affair highlighted long-running debates over the granting of pardons. The prison associations and classical liberal scholars like Karl Binding believed that pardons were the ideal vehicle for bringing social concerns to bear on sentencing practices. As in the Köpenick case, the power of grace exercised by the sovereign could intervene to prevent the justice system from excessive harshness and uphold the public's sense of fairness. Franz von Liszt and his students in the "Modern School" of criminal reform believed that pardons should be reserved for extraordinary occasions when the justice system failed to achieve a just result. For normal cases, they argued, Germany needed a system of conditional sentencing such as existed in Belgium, France, and the United States. In those lands, judges had the power to suspend sentences, and the process of granting a suspended sentence was clear and transparent and subject to appeal. Most important to the Modern School, conditional sentencing was free of the moral overtones of conditional pardons. Under this system, protective supervision became a formal extension of criminal policy, a tool of discipline and surveillance, rather than an act of mercy bestowed upon (and only upon) "worthy individuals." Liszt especially admired the American probation system, with its core of professional overseers.[66]

In a largely forgotten twist of history, it was the prison associations and "classical school" scholars who won this debate. While there was already

Postcard. Left: The ex-captain in Moabit prison. Right: Voigt as shoemaker under police supervision. "Banished," declared the hand-held sign. "Who is really the guilty one?" (Bildarchiv Preussischer Kulturbesitz)

growing use of the pardon before the Köpenick affair, the granting of pardons accelerated in the years after. As James Whitman notes, punishment in Germany was unusual in the persistent concern with moral categories.[67] The prison associations continued to insist that sentences should be suspended only when the offender had demonstrated a will for moral transformation. At the same time, there were practical reasons for the increasing use of the pardon. In particular, government officials sought to postpone punishments for draft-age offenders in order that they could fulfill their military service—which would otherwise be disallowed. The government also gave some young offenders the option of supervision in the military in lieu of punishment. After the war, pardons became the vehicle with which welfare entered the criminal courts. Even as an object of scientific investigation, the criminal could still be saved by a compelling narrative of victimization.

Conclusion

The 1907 reform of police supervision did not bring closure to the issue of overzealous police surveillance of ex-offenders. On the contrary, the topic was more alive than ever over the next few years. Major incidents in both 1908 and 1910 turned individual cases into causes célèbres.[68]

One lasting effect of the Köpenick affair was cultural. The press had discovered a genre of reportage, a formula for tugging at the heartstrings of readers, and an issue behind which mercifully minded conservatives, liberals, and even socialists could line up. The affair fed the popularity of the prison associations as a vehicle for change. "Welfare" had become a key word of criminal policy reform.

Contrary to the popular impression, the use of police supervision had been in decline since the 1880s. While judges authorized police supervision in well over 8,000 cases in 1882, they authorized only 3,085 cases in 1906. The numbers then dropped again, more than thirty percent, in the year following the Köpenick affair. By 1914, judges were authorizing only around 1,500 cases per year across the empire.[69]

As police supervision declined, welfare supervision—in its various manifestations—expanded. Looking back from the standpoint of 1914, the Sachsen-Anhalt Prison Society declared that welfare for released offenders became a "fashion" in the period following the Köpenick affair. Reporting on the leading Berlin association for prison welfare, the *Berliner Lokalanzeiger* referred to mechanisms of social exclusion for ex-convicts in the past tense:

> Once there were times in which every convicted offender was imprisoned. After that, he was considered no longer fit for anything, lost for this world. Driven from door to door, in his confusion he submitted only too easily to temptation and soon allowed the next, greater crime to follow the first. Until finally the last remnant of humanity in him died out and only a distorted image remained, which evoked discomfort or even fear in society.[70]

The article traced the transformation in social attitudes back to the Köpenick affair. The Interior Ministry's decree opened up space for the exercise of surveillance authority by the private welfare associations, thus allowing factors such as "the influence of the milieu [and] hereditary transmissions . . . to be taken into account" in decisions about post-penal surveillance. Organizations like the Berlin Prison Association were better prepared than the police to "build bridges," helping " 'the lost ones' find their way back to an orderly life." Under the old system, it was claimed, in which the police exercised "unmediated surveillance," the authorities lacked real knowledge about former offenders or the social conditions to which they were returning and were thus forced to rely upon harsh and inflexible legal categories.[71]

One could argue whether the Köpenick affair was really so central to the advance of the prison associations. It is clear, however, that the dominant narrative of Voigt's career helped to legitimize the image of the criminal as a weak-willed, vulnerable, and "*a*social" individual who was driven to "*anti*-social" behavior by the harsh treatment received from society and the state. The public's willingness to invest heroic meaning in such a narrative would have been unthinkable twenty years before and was more controversial twenty years later. For the time being, however, a space had been created in German culture in which to imagine major transformations in the nature of punishment and welfare and their relationship to each other.

CRIMINALS IN THE "FORTRESS"

5

War, Punishment, and Welfare

World War I hastened the assimilation of the penal question into the social question. As total war required "exploiting the energy of every individual," inmates, prostitutes, and vagabonds were increasingly perceived as threats to national welfare and ultimately to German power.[1] The discourse of national cohesion and solidarity fueled popular suspicions toward marginal groups and repressive state measures justified as social protection.[2] At the same time, the *Burgfrieden*—or "peace within the fortress"— facilitated efforts to pardon those who were willing and able to join the national cause. Reformers adapted their visions of moral regeneration to fit wartime circumstances. The demand for soldiers and workers provided a "suitable place" for every man and woman willing to cast off the dirty garments of asociality and dress in the uniforms of national service. The war thus created a setting for new and convincing narratives of criminals transformed into citizens.

This chapter focuses on grassroots reform efforts during the Great War. I argue that the war furthered a social interpretation of crime and an interest in protective supervision as an alternative to punishment and police control. Many reformers saw the decline in adult male crime and the increase in juvenile and female crime as proof of the social origins of deviance. The new sense of national community and the focus on mobilizing all possible labor power undermined the already fragile legitimacy of the prisons and workhouses. Wartime initiatives in criminal policy augmented the power of private "organic" institutions in civil society—frequently at the expense of the police.

Ironically, the triumph of the supervision ideal came at a point when prison associations faced unprecedented crises in manpower and finances. Wartime reformers seeking to build effective and legitimate institutions for managing the new criminal policy reconsidered the role of the state. In the next chapter, I turn to the city of Bielefeld, where in the latter years of the war, reformers built a system for supervising criminals based upon the hand-in-hand cooperation of private welfare associations with the courts and the police. The so-called "Bielefeld System" took the weak-willed, impressionable subject of Christian welfare and generalized it as a model of intervention, first in the regulation of vagrancy and begging, then for prostitution, and, finally, for all classes of criminals.

World War I and the "Rationalization of Social Policy"

Historians of German social policy have portrayed World War I as a time of expanding state power, growing authority for science, and increasing support for technologies of social exclusion. The war, according to Paul Weindling, forged an unprecedented alliance between the scientific establishment and the state. Medical professionals in particular directed policies aimed at protecting and reinvigorating public health. They made doctors and nurses into state servants and clinics into outposts of state power. The war thus laid the groundwork ideologically and institutionally for the eventual triumph of eugenics.

In Ludwig Preller's classic history of social policy, the war was the father of the corporatist *Sozialstaat*, creating a triangular relationship between the bureaucracy, bourgeois associations, and working-class organizations.[3] Reform ultimately came from above, in his view, with the government drawing upon the "well of social-liberal ideas" in order to gain more effective control over labor relations and industrial policy.[4] Presenting an essentially teleological view of social policy, Preller sees the war as the "trendsetter" (*Schrittmacher*) for reform, understood as the state's comprehensive mastery of civil society.[5]

This emphasis upon the centrality of the state during the war has survived in subsequent work, even where historians have illustrated the vigor of reformist energies in civil society. Gerald Feldman and Ursula Ratz each stress the growing importance of liberal reform groups (especially the Society for Social Reform), but it is ultimately by reference to their influence upon government ministries and their ability to construct a model for corporatist decision making among a select group of powerful organizations.[6] The crucial watersheds during the war, according to Feldman, were in reforms like the creation of the War Office, the introduction of the Hindenburg Program, and the passage of the Auxiliary Service Law, which marked the state's intervention to appropriate and rationalize private domains of discipline and control.[7] The paradoxical result of social reform efforts, according to historians, was not to enrich civil discourse but to kill it. With the growing irrelevance of the Reichstag and the end of open, partisan debate, politics itself supposedly disappeared and decision making devolved upon powerful cliques, operating farther than ever from the public eye. As the state became less and less a tool of traditional class interests, according to Jürgen Kocka, it was also less responsive, less beholden to a definite set of constituents. By the middle of the war, he writes, "the *Burgfrieden* did not serve as a promise or even as a vehicle for emancipatory reform, but . . . as a means of suppressing controversial and unpopular views and open discussion." By 1918, he argues, Germany was ripe for a revolution, as people could not find "outlets" for their "tensions and conflicts" within "a regulated, institutionalized and clearly organized debate."[8] The government fell, but even then the great corporatist bodies quietly reasserted their self-appointed roles as guardians of the public interest.[9]

This emphasis upon the rise of a more modern and professional, and thus autonomous, state power is also essential to accounts of welfare and medical practice during the war. As the conflict dragged on, according to Sachße and Tennstedt, private institutions and professions were increasingly subject to public administration, while local traditions of charity and assistance were co-opted by the state and subject to centralized control. "The dominant characteristic of developments in welfare during the War," they argue, "was in the growth of state control [*Verstaatlichung*] and centralization through the Imperial government."[10] Political issues were made into problems of management and negotiation; moral and social issues were made into medical problems calling for the application of professional, objective knowledge. As Paul Weindling and others have argued, the war made doctors into agents of the state and encouraged their efforts to colonize wider areas of social reform.[11] The army's interest in containing disease, increasing the birthrate, and cultivating strong, healthy citizens led to unprecedented state intervention in the cause of social hygiene.[12] National health, Weindling argues, became the dominant trope for thinking about almost all important social issues.[13] This medicalization of the social "supplied a rationale for unifying the diverse initiatives of national welfare associations, municipalities and sickness insurance funds, and for ensuring the cooperation of the medical profession."[14] The state's intensified preoccupation with public health and population policy created at one and the same time a greater investment of power in the medical profession and a greater subordination of doctors to the demands of the state.

Beyond the nationalization of particular organizations and professions, historians argue, the war broke down the very distinction between public and private spheres. The mobilization essentially produced one front, Elisabeth Domansky claims, which was divided into two parts: home front and battle front. "When everyone became part of the 'war machine,'" she argues, "civil society ceased to exist."[15] This meant the "dissolution of the bourgeois family," in her terms, and, according to Sachße, an "ever-clearer governmental orientation" to the feminist ideal of 'service to the *Volk*.'" Activism on behalf of infant and child welfare and the organization of female labor represented the "growing integration of the women's movement into the communal and state administrative apparatus."[16] By the end of the war, Sachße argues, "organized motherliness," a movement that had once possessed an independent spirit, with reformist, if not radical, undertones, had become an agent of the military and political executive.[17]

The nationalization of the women's movement, in this view, was the most vivid sign of a larger trend toward ideological co-optation, a kind of proto-*Gleichschaltung* by a new regime of experts. According to Sachße and Tennstedt, the war abolished the Kaiserreich's division of labor between Christian institutions, charged with "the experimental development of new welfare measures," and the public welfare administration, which was supposed to consolidate, rationalize, and institutionalize good ideas.[18] "The war forged welfare on the communal level into a unified complex," writes Sachße, and it was the *public* principle and model of intervention that took precedence.[19] In Weindling's terms, there was a basic shift in the organizing ideology of intervention, from "Naumann's Christian humanitarianism, suiting a voluntary system of welfare, to biological values that expressed the ethos of scientifically trained professionals."[20]

The master narrative of the nationalization and centralization of social policy during the war has provided a useful framework for the analysis of certain institutions created or recast as a result of the war. But it tells only part of the story. As with any narrative of modernization, it risks reducing conflicting interests and the multiplicity of goals among reformers to a uniform ideal with teleological implications. As Young Sun Hong argues, the creation of the *Sozialstaat* was not a "unilinear process," but was "the result of a multitude of essentially contested social, ideological, and political responses" to social transformations.[21] The emergence of new institutional forms for supervision continued to be a result of experimentation and improvisation in the face of immediate crises.[22] In the regulation of asocials and ex-felons, the most important initiatives during the war came from private organizations, frequently working on local levels. These organizations defined new zones and new methods of social intervention, which were frequently in tension with traditional police and administrative practice. By the end of the war, the proper and legitimate borders between state and private activism on the terrain of criminal policy were more uncertain and more contested than ever.

The Siege Law and the Vagabond Question

Preoccupations with the vagabond question intensified almost immediately upon the outbreak of war. Conventional wisdom was that the war would bring severe unemployment and large movements of population, and the first months of the conflict essentially confirmed these expectations.[23] Thousands of factory workers were thrown out of work in industries deemed unessential to the war effort, at a time when munitions factories were not yet prepared to take on the excess labor. At the same time, the military call-up of many native farmworkers and the loss of foreign workers brought the threat of severe labor shortages in many areas of agriculture.[24] The "vagabond plague" of the 1880s had taught that "purposeless wandering" and begging increased during times of labor mobility. Moreover, the lessons of 1871, according to Protestant welfare leaders, were that war and its aftermath inevitably caused a breakdown of public morals and epidemics of vagrancy, especially during the period of demobilization. At least until the autumn of 1915, Germans expected that this war, like the Franco-Prussian conflict, would be over quickly, and they braced themselves for the coming chaos. Pastor "Fritz" Bodelschwingh, who replaced his father as the director of the Bethel Asylum near Bielefeld in 1910, believed that the worker colonies must anticipate a "flood" of vagrants.[25] Another pastor involved in welfare for vagrants predicted that "after the war there will be a calamity of youth vagrancy for one or two years."[26]

The widespread concern with vagabondage led to unprecedented and sometimes draconian measures by the military authorities on the home front. The General Commando for the Seventh District, which included most of Westphalia, was by far the most energetic and extreme in its use of the Siege Law to pursue vagrants and loafers.[27] In the first half of 1915, the army conducted periodic raids against the so-called "wild asylums," seizing anyone they suspected of work-shyness. In a single night, they rounded up 400 presumed vagrants off the highways. Over the course of a month, they captured 123 criminally indolent persons.[28] In November 1915, the Seventh District Commando promulgated a decree announcing its intent to "abolish the still-existent danger of vagrants as much as possible." The new measure declared that persons "encountered in wayfarer-stations, hostels or homeless shelters who were blatantly work-shy" would be taken into military custody and sent, on order of the Commanding General, to a workhouse or worker colony.[29]

Such measures were widely praised. In the case of Merseburg, even the Social Democratic press expressed support, though it was openly acknowledged that some innocent people had been mistakenly seized during the crackdown.[30] More enthusiastic and sustained support came from the private welfare associations involved with the care of vagabonds and wayfarers. In the fall of 1915, representatives of the German Hostel Association, the Central Committee of Worker Colonies, and the Conference of German Wayfarer-Stations met in the Prussian Parliament (*Landtag*) to formulate a wartime and postwar strategy for addressing the vagabond question. After little debate, and with only one abstention, the meeting passed a resolution calling upon the General Commandos throughout the Reich to carry on the practice of vagabond sweeps.[31]

The associations were undoubtedly eager for the authorities to adopt more vigorous policies against suspected vagrants. Nevertheless, there are reasons to doubt historian Ewald Frie's conclusion that "ideals of control and repression were increasingly replacing welfare."[32] The leaders of the worker colonies and provision stations were confident that the army roundups would ultimately funnel greater numbers of vagrants into private welfare institutions. In Westphalia at least, the raids expressly avoided the institutions of "organized welfare" and focused instead upon the "wild asylums," independent hostels, and "vagabond taverns," which had long been accused of germinating social disorder. The army's goal was to find and detain "blatantly work-shy" individuals, that is, healthy and otherwise "normal" men who should be contributing to the war effort. In practice, the work-shy were transferred to the police for forced labor, while the so-called *Halbkräfte*—laborers with diminished capabilities—were sent to the worker colonies.[33]

Westphalia became a model for vigorous Commando intervention precisely because it was the Prussian province with the most developed private institutional apparatus and financial infrastructure for the care of vagabonds and prostitutes.[34] It happened that the Seventh District Commando was headquartered in Münster, which was also the home of the Westfälische Frauenhülfe, an umbrella organization of 456 associations for women's social activism, whose staunchly anti-feminist and anti-Socialist leadership had close ties to the emperor and empress. The energetic director of the Frauen-hülfe, Wilhelm Zoellner, was both the general superintendent of the Evangelical Church in Westphalia and the chairman of the German Hostel Association. He was also notably anti-liberal and was a strong proponent of an active military role in the upholding of social order.[35]

The associations had no objections to the Commandos' draconian policies toward suspected vagabonds, including the routine violations of civil liberties, but they doubted the military's ultimate ability or willingness to make the crucial distinction between those with diminished abilities and the willfully idle. At the October 1915 Berlin meeting, the Middle German Association of Employment Offices proposed that employers and union officials should participate in identifying indolent individuals. The Hostel Association saw a great opportunity in this historic conjuncture, as Zoellner put it, to finally "prove that we can get at the work-shy." The expectation was that the associations themselves would henceforth identify indolent persons and denounce them to the police and the General Commandos. "One should not always speak about the freedom of the individual," Zoellner argued, "under this freedom much is lost."[36] The Commando's own proclamation in November offered at least the possibility of a more active role for the associations. By targeting individuals who "were confronted" in the wayfarer-stations and hostels, it left open the question of how and by whom suspected "work-shy" individuals were to be identified.[37]

The assumption among the welfare organizations was that military intervention would strengthen their role in the future of regulating vagrancy. The roundups and raids would supposedly illustrate to the German bourgeoisie that colonies, hostels, and way stations were necessary foundations of social discipline. When the Silesian representative at the Berlin meeting complained that his region, unlike Westphalia, had nowhere to place vagrants rounded up by the General Commandos, Zoellner responded that precipitating such a crisis would represent, in itself, a "success." The local middle class would be forced to create such institutions once they were confronted with these individuals.[38]

The ultimate goal of the private associations was to serve the war effort by sheltering weak workers, rendering them productive, and, as much as possible, preparing them for some greater service. The rhetoric of national solidarity during wartime brought passion and urgency to discussions of social integration. The grand wartime slogan of a "peace within the fortress" was a call to unity not only among political parties, but among the various historically divided sectors of German culture and society. Protestant organizations in particular promoted a discourse of reconciliation on a range of fronts, as they sought to position themselves as the vanguard of a new "people's church." A well-known pastor, banished form the church in 1912 for his unorthodox opinions, was ostentatiously reinstated because of his service in the war effort. The predominantly unbaptized, Socialist masses who streamed into the churches after the start of the conflict were greeted with milky warmth and enthusiasm.[39] New levels of cooperation were reached between Protestant and Catholic groups, and even Jewish organizations were given cause to believe that their sacrifices on behalf of the war would be rewarded through the realization of total civic and cultural equality.[40]

The prison associations and the prison clergy revisited the vagabond question within this context of *Burgfrieden*. Through practical work and shared sacrifice, the outcasts would rejoin the national community, and diminished subjects would become whole. This happened to some extent automatically, they believed, but it was also a process that Protestant organizations needed to encourage and to guide with their "special expertise." In spite of the anti-vagrancy measures discussed above, the population of both the workhouses and the worker colonies declined significantly during the war. After only a year of fighting, the number of persons staying in worker colonies had declined from 14,000 to fewer than 7,000. Especially after 1916, when the demand for both industrial workers and soldiers became severe, the number of workhouse inmates dropped precipitously—though the number of women inmates rose throughout the war.[41] The prison societies boasted of rising success rates in job placement for all categories of released inmates.[42]

Pastor Klein of Bethel was one of many clergy who believed the war had a positive "moral effect" on vagabonds. "A great number," Klein declared,

> have ceased to be 'wanderers' . . . and have become field-grey; counted among the 'heroes' before whom the best of the *Volk* gladly bow their heads in respect; and many of them will undoubtedly return, decorated with the Iron Cross, proving the saying: 'out of a tiny blot, will come the beautiful butterfly.' . . . To the extent that they are not sent to the field, then most of them are taken into the rows of heroes on the battlefield of the economic war.

The vagrants who remained in the worker colonies, Klein argued, should be seen in the same light as the "wounded warriors." The goal of the clergy and the Inner Mission must be to rejuvenate these sick people, protecting them in particular from brandy, the "arch-enemy."[43] More than ever, the logic of the associations suggested a dialectical relationship between their own labors on behalf of the vagabond question and the drive for national power and efficiency. Turning vagabonds into productive and responsible subjects was both facilitated and, with increasing urgency, necessitated by the mobilization of society for total war.

Dangerous Women, Dangerous Youth, and the Changing Perception of Crime

While wartime conditions helped legitimate the welfare associations' role in the vagabond question, the marked changes in the nature of crime during the war bolstered the interpretation of criminality per se as a "social phenomenon." First, there was the decrease in offenses by adult men in each of the first two years of the war, an impression that was eventually confirmed by official Reich statistics. Still more striking to observers at the time were the increasingly empty prisons and underused penitentiaries.[44] The most obvious explanation for a change in the crime rate was the military call-up. Contemporary observers, however, also focused upon the positive moral effects of the military experience, the decreased availability of alcohol, and what the leader of the Rhenish Prison Society termed the disappearance of "foreign swindlers" who used "drug-nests, bars, and night-cafes as their spawning grounds."[45] Later in the war, the prison association in Berlin noted how wounded veterans unable to succeed in factory jobs became "lazy" welfare dependents and then came into conflict with the law. A leader of the association recommended that they create "warrior settlements" in order to protect those damaged in the war from the corruptions of life in the urban underclass.[46]

The crucial factor unifying different explanations of wartime behavior was the emphasis upon social context. As criminologist Franz Exner years later wrote, "The war offered the strongest imaginable confirmation for the overwhelming impact of external circumstances, economic conditions, in short, of the milieu upon the development of crime, because criminologically observed, the war was nothing other than a gigantic transformation of the milieu with correspondingly gigantic criminal effects."[47]

Still more striking than the drop in male criminality was the increase in offenses by women and by youth of both sexes.[48] Even as the men's prisons and workhouses fell into relative disuse, women's carceral institutions in some regions filled up with offenders convicted of unlicensed prostitution, petty theft, and the violation of wartime ordinances.[49] Towns and cities across Germany also witnessed a drastic increase in juvenile crime, especially disorderly conduct and property crimes. By 1916 the government, the press, and private organizations were referring to "epidemics" of unruly youth.[50]

This upsurge of new crime offered the clearest support yet for progressive interpretations of criminality. Women and youth were the quintessential at-risk populations. Their inherent vulnerability to "seductive temptations" was supposedly exacerbated by the extraordinary circumstances of wartime. Observers pointed to factors like nervous excitement and overstimulation, economic hardship, overtaxed mental and physical resources, and, most important, the decline of traditional social structures and the corresponding absence of supervision.[51] Moreover, the spiraling increase in police and military ordinances on the domestic front made popular illegalities among these populations almost inevitable. Officials came to refer to crimes like black marketeering or the forging of purchase-vouchers as "wartime-offenses," suggesting that they lacked the objective significance of equivalent offenses outside the special context of wartime.[52]

The apparent rise in unlicensed prostitution became an obsession of government and private organizations early in the conflict.[53] Fearing the uncontrolled spread of venereal disease, the military not only expanded the regulatory powers of state medical personnel, but actually organized and ran its own brothels in order to ensure that the women frequented by soldiers were "safe and clean."[54] At the same time, the General Commandos carried out a series of unprecedentedly wide and vigorous sweeps against illegal prostitution. Private organizations fed the alarm in their own publications and annual reports. Pastor Theodor Just, the head of the Rhenish-Westphalian Prison Society, condemned voracious women who "shamelessly" exploited naive young soldiers for the sake of pleasure and profit.[55] Paula Mueller, the national director of the DEF, called for *stricter* medical controls over any woman suspected of venal sex.[56] Even the feminist and abolitionist Anna Pappritz concurred that rising rates of informal prostitution represented the gravest threat to the welfare of the soldiers and thus to the nation.[57]

While the activist community applauded "vigorous measures" against female crime, it was more insistent than ever that police intervention must be counterbalanced, if not guided, by private welfare.[58] Pastor Just insisted that anti-prostitution policies must distinguish between three types of prostitutes: the beginners, the feeble-minded, and the "persistently depraved."[59] The war only increased the associations' preoccupation with the first two categories. "The characteristic phenomena . . . at this point," the Bielefeld prison society declared, "are girls and women who are driven down the path of immorality through disrupted family life, momentary unemployment or a fortuitous seduction."[60] A committee of the Rhenish-Westphalian Prison Society agreed that disruptions to the family were key, and also blamed the new abundance of work opportunities for luring women away from safe and familiar environments. The associations thus linked prostitution to a range of social issues specific to the wartime context, and saw themselves as uniquely qualified to identify these socio-moral concerns, assess their impact upon individuals, and adopt effective measures of intervention.[61] The Catholic Women's Help Organization in Westphalia developed plans for a women's worker colony, while at the same time calling upon the General Commando to crack down upon women's inappropriate and "un-German clothing styles," including "unnaturally wide skirts and high boots."[62] Other associations took measures to protect soldiers' wives and other young women from the temptations of sexual liaisons with male prisoners of war.[63]

The discourse on youth crime during the war was similarly focused upon the consequences of neglect and a more far-reaching crisis in the structures of social order. Many of the General Commandos announced as early as October 1915 that they would take police and punitive measures against youth crime.[64] As a result, large numbers of boys were imprisoned for offenses that previously would have evoked a mere warning or perhaps a brief committal to an educational-welfare institution. Crime was increasingly seen as a juvenile phenomenon—a problem of moral neglect and the seduction of weak-willed individuals. The growing percentage of youthful offenders among the inmate population fueled public dissatisfaction with the prisons in general and a demand for welfare alternatives. The prison association in Aschersleben noted in its annual report that the entire audience for the pastor's Sunday sermons at the local prison consisted of eighteen- to twenty-year-olds.[65] Others interpreted the rising rates of prostitution and vagrancy as a direct result of increasing numbers of disoriented or displaced minors.[66] As the war dragged on, "wayward youth" became a synecdoche for crime as such.[67] Solving the crime question, by extension, became, in large measure, a matter of abolishing "waywardness."

As with the increase in female crime and the drop in adult male crime, most experienced criminal justice reformers were "completely without doubt" that the increase in juvenile crime was a product of the war.[68] In the initial period of war enthusiasm, it was argued, the excessive mental stimulation and emotions of the time overwhelmed many German youth.[69] They were frequently pulled away from school and from ordinary social roles. As they moved into adult employment prematurely, one prominent expert argued, the youth developed an "exaggerated self-image, which slowly buried all the preconditions of educational influence and undermined their character development."[70] Commentators also noted the damaging effects of early sexual encounters and, later in the war, of undernourishment.[71]

The experience of so many women, girls, and boys under the difficult circumstances of wartime sharpened the popular understanding of crime as a function of social marginalization, a product of what social reformer Julia Dünner later called living "beyond the fringes of community."[72] The war tore women and children from their "natural" social structures and social identities, drawing them into immoral and deviant behavior. At the same time, the conflict presented adult males with new structures of community and possibilities for discipline. In either case, reformers saw the decisive influence of "social and political conditions external to the will of the participant." In further legitimating the social interpretation of crime, the war further undermined the concepts of deterrence and retribution. "What is the point of deterrence under such circumstances?" asked Wolfgang Heine, a Social Democratic Deputy in the Reichstag, at a point when the crime rate had once again surged upward. In place of old formulas, Heine, a future Prussian Minister, called for "mildness, understanding and an assessment of the conditions out of which the criminal act is born."[73] In this case at least, the Social Democratic leader was speaking for a broad range of educated and popular opinion.

From the "Prisoner's Jacket" to the "King's Coat": Mobilizing Criminals for War

Drawing serious male felons into the discourse of *Burgfrieden* was a complicated process. While the Kaiser pardoned large number of prison inmates soon after the outbreak of hostilities, this was largely with an eye toward immediate military needs. Even after pardons were granted to accused felons awaiting trial and sentencing, these actions clearly fit into precedents established in the prewar years.[74] As noted above, conditional pardons and postponements had been increasingly applied to draft-age offenders in the years leading up to the war. At the same time, the government maintained its official policy that service in the armed forces was an honor reserved for honest and upstanding German citizens.[75] With the outbreak of war, Paragraph 44 of the Imperial German Penal Code was still on the books. This section on "shame sanctions" (*Ehrenstrafe*) included military service as one of the "civil rights" (*Ehrenrechte*) to be stripped from male citizens either upon conviction of a felony or as part of the administrative, postcarceral punishment. The *Ehrenstrafe* were supposed to preserve the "ancient ideal of infamy" by placing an irrevocable mark upon the criminal.[76] Since service in the armed forces signified the individual's ultimate fulfillment of his role as a citizen, the deprivation of this "privilege" guaranteed a lasting, symbolic exclusion from the nation.[77]

The contradiction between the principle of *Ehrenstrafe* and the goals of a pragmatic criminal policy made Paragraph 44 subject to criticism before the First World War, but with little vehemence or sustained public attention. In his classic textbook on punishment, Karl Krohne conflated the prohibition against military service with other measures, like police banishment, which prevented the former inmate from finding the guidance, fellowship, and opportunities necessary to his resocialization.[78] Liszt criticized the "naïve moral purpose" of the sanction. Like most retributive measures, Liszt argued, the *Ehrenstrafe* had little psychological impact upon degraded figures, most of whom almost certainly preferred to shirk their national duties in any case. The exclusion of former prisoners from the armed forces, moreover, did nothing to promote public security, while from a eugenic standpoint it exacerbated the problem of "negative selection": the best eugenic material would be sacrificed at war, while the degenerate elements reproduced at home.[79]

The outbreak of war inspired a campaign against Paragraph 44 that confronted head-on the symbolic dimensions of the law. The advocates for abolishing the law were in large measure prison clergy. They described the prisoners as wounded limbs of the nation, desperate to be healed and redeemed through service. They claimed to see a spiritual awakening and a sense of urgency among the prisoners, who were now eager to use their time and energy for a worthwhile cause. One pastor reported that

> as a consequence of the temporary reduction in work provision and the . . . short period of total inactivity, [the prisoners] learned to recognize and value the moral, educative, and natural worth of structured, uninterrupted labor. Even those who were everyday thieves and work-shy in the outside world . . . can no longer comprehend how they could maintain lives of constant loitering and loafing. . . . Today the time becomes too long when they have a half day . . . of nothing to do.[80]

This was part of the "blessing of the war for the prisoner." Serving in the military would be the ultimate step toward becoming useful and injecting life with meaning. The machinery of war, with its promise of "rigid, militaristic discipline" and the demand for personal sacrifice, provided a context for striving.[81] Even refractory or dangerous persons would be safely contained within these environments and given the opportunity to grow and improve through action.[82] The old models of infamy and dishonor in prisons and asylums, they argued, constituted an extravagance that Germany could no longer afford.[83]

For Heinrich Seyfarth, military discipline seemed a natural and vital element in the rehabilitation of former offenders. The Hamburg pastor became especially interested in the question of military service once conditions forced him to put aside his criminal reform projects of the past decade. Up until the outbreak of war, the Deutsche Hilfsverein continued to arrange for the overseas resettlement of selected ex-offenders from the educated classes and to place young working-class offenders as sailors on Hamburg ships.[84] Seyfarth had also refused to abandon hope that Germany would someday adopt a policy of organized deportation. During the war, Seyfarth's efforts to bring current and former inmates into the armed forces were driven by a similar nationalist-cum-criminological fantasy of individual moral development through service to the fatherland.

Like transportation to the colonies, serving in the army was to provide a test of character and inner strength, as well as opportunities for healthy camaraderie under the sign of practical and fulfilling labor. The army and the colony were structured environments—not in the mechanical, physical sense of the prison or the workhouse—but in a more organic, *völkisch* sense.[85] In an article in the leading journal for penal professionals, Seyfarth related the stories of prisoners and ex-felons whom he met as a prison chaplain and through his work with the Deutsche Hilfsverein in Hamburg. Many of these men, he declared, were "burning with desire" to serve the Fatherland. One of the Verein's charges, "S. from Kiel," was a former soldier who had served time in the penitentiary and now "instinctively" sought to "fulfill his duty." "R. from Naumburg" was a would-be volunteer who was unable to join the army merely because he had been in the penitentiary for a short sentence a decade before. Another case related by Seyfarth involved a young man who served time in prison because a woman had "led" him into committing perjury. The law made no allowance for the specific circumstance surrounding such crimes but prevented all such ex-prisoners from serving the war effort.[86] For Seyfarth, proscribing military service for former inmates was a policy based on a mystified, impractical notion of honor. "Wide segments of society," he asserted, "including the educated classes, find it unfair and incomprehensible that the blood of our nation and the most valuable forces thereof . . . must bleed to death outside on enemy land, whereas criminal offenders are protected from danger and from necessity during their stay in penal institutions." Seyfarth believed there was a long-term danger to German society in that the "irreproachable people who served in the field" would return in decimated numbers, and perhaps poor health, while "the numbers of criminal offenders will be reduced only slightly." This meant that the percentage of unpunished versus punished persons in German society would change to the disadvantage of the former. On the other hand, Seyfarth claimed, when granted special pardons, many former prisoners had served the nation heroically.[87]

Other prison clergy argued similarly that the war presented a great opportunity for the moral transformation of prison and penitentiary inmates.[88] One of the most widely noted interventions was by Detloff Klatt, the chaplain at Moabit, the "model penitentiary" in Berlin once under the direction of Wichern. In his book *The Unknown Army*, Klatt described patriotic frustration among the inmates and their longing for military engagement in bombastic rhetoric, saturated with pathos and a frenzied, nationalist passion. In public lectures and articles for the daily press, he brought the performance to a wider audience.[89] "The Kaiser's pardon called [them] to arms," he wrote of the ex-convicts, ". . . and they all went into the field with an enthusiasm that was moving. They are fighting for the Fatherland and for their own honor." According to Klatt, war had the capacity to transform the prisoners' antisocial urges. "It is really so," he quotes one prisoner as saying, "the hate is submerged, the vengeance is silenced, and loyalty stands up with irrepressible force." The soldiers' fixation upon the enemy, Klatt asserted, created that larger sense of belonging, love, and responsibility that was necessary to overcoming the selfish and egotistical urges that led to criminal behavior.[90] Klatt appealed for a reform of Paragraph 44 on the grounds of both sentimental pathos and cool, hard facts. "If we would comprehend the question of the ex-offender one time systematically from the standpoint of national economy," he wrote later, "I believe we soon reach our goal." The economic cost of crime, he argued, presented the ultimate, irrefutable case for a socially oriented criminal policy.[91]

The pastors' campaign against Paragraph 44 helped to keep the question of punishment and the ex-convict before the public eye. The story of former prisoners transformed at the front provided a compelling fable of refashioned citizenship. Even usually skeptical and unsentimental prison officials and criminologists offered moving portrayals of the transformed mood among the inmates.[92] Perhaps the most surprising of these interventions was by Hans Gross, the curmudgeonly editor of the *Archiv der Kriminologie*, who described his conversation with the inmates in Graz in the form of a dialogue published in his journal. The Graz prisoners had contributed their own meager financial resources to the Austrian war-welfare office; now some of them asked to be "let loose" on the Russians, while another suggested that as "criminals and bad people" they were better-suited for cannon fodder than the "respectable people." Gross responded to the prisoners in avuncular fashion, commending their "true Austrian" character and encouraging them to work hard at personal change, all the while addressing them, like children, with the informal second-person "du." The exchange, however, led Gross to reflect on the possibility that extraordinary circumstances could bring out hidden sources of strength in the inmates. He recalled a previous experience in Brioni, when prison inmates had courageously battled a fire that a crowd of civilians had passively allowed to rage out of control and threaten valuable wares. "The only social ones among us," Gross recalled, "were the 'anti-socials.' "[93]

A mass influx of ex-offenders into factory jobs after 1916 also affected the image and the practice of protective supervision. Factory work, of course, had less symbolic valence and emotional potency than military service. Many clergy, moreover, continued to believe that industrial labor furthered the moral corruption of young men and women. Nevertheless, the growing recognition of industry's importance to the war effort and its hunger for workers provided prison associations with a patriotic rationale for steering their clients into factory jobs. Seyfarth's Hilfsverein, which prided itself on placing more than 2000 ex-prisoners in sea-faring positions before the war, shifted its focus to decidedly less romantic jobs in German cities and towns. The prison associations in Halle, Magdeburg, Berlin, and Cologne reported enthusiastically about the abundant labor opportunities for ex-offenders in wartime factories.[94] The Sachsen-Anhalt Prison Society developed ties with industrial employers and unions, and recruited representatives from both sides as members in the society. The society's director argued that they must adapt to the growing industrialization of the region. It was imperative, he said, for welfare and industry to work together.[95]

Paragraph 44 was never in fact repealed, but the heightened concern with rendering criminal offenders useful to the war effort furthered the ongoing trend toward administrative and judicial discretion in criminal policy. On the one hand, the General Commandos were encouraged to take special repressive measures against wartime illegalities. On the other hand, the courts and the state aggressively sought to rescue "salvageable" offenders from incarceration in general and the penitentiary in particular. The most important tool in this effort was the conditional pardon, which, if granted at or before the point of sentencing, could preserve even a major felon's privilege to serve in the military.[96] The state granted an increasing number of pardons in every year of the war, even as the total number of convictions declined. In 1918, the state offered clemency in 39,000 cases, almost twice the number from 1912, the prewar high. Most of those pardoned were youth offenders, but pardons for adult offenders also increased by 37 percent.[97] Though many of these offenders were worthy and repentant individuals according to traditional moral standards for clemency, observers realized that the dramatic increase in pardons was attributable to a new, pragmatic approach on the part of state officials. The state's key concern was no longer whether an offender was morally deserving of a pardon, but whether the nation's interest was most likely to be served through incarceration or supervision or total freedom.[98]

Alongside the increase in pardons, judges and prosecutors conspired to charge accused felons with lesser offenses, so that they could be sentenced to the prison (*Gefängnis*) rather than the penitentiary (*Zuchthaus*), which likewise still allowed them to serve in the armed forces. The Penal Code authorized the court to reduce the charge when there were extenuating circumstances. Prior to World War I, extenuating circumstances referred primarily to specific factors surrounding the actual commission of a crime. As James Whitman notes, however, the major law codes of the nineteenth century also recognized evidence of an "honorable" character or attitude as a justification for reducing the sentence. The origins of this doctrine, according to Whitman, were in the "traditions of status differentiation in punishment." Highborn men were presumed to be honorable and were therefore shielded somewhat from the degrading aspects of punishment.

During the Great War, "extenuating circumstances" increasingly referred to any personal or social factors that limited the offender's rational and independent exercise of will. Judges asked not only whether the offender was an upstanding member of the community, but whether there were reasons to doubt that he possessed full moral responsibility for the crime. Indeed, a history of social marginalization and inferiority could militate *in favor of* extenuating circumstances. In practice, wartime judges found extenuating circumstances in 98 percent of the cases of first-degree theft involving first-time offenders. Most such offenders were thereby sent to the prison rather than the penitentiary, with many of them serving the minimum time of three months.[99]

Criminals Unleashed on Society?

It was perhaps inevitable that the increasingly mild application of justice would produce its own backlash among police officials, criminologists, and journalists. At least one leading criminologist was convinced that an undifferentiated flood of former prisoners was wreaking havoc upon the health and moral character of the German people.[100] A press release by the criminal police in Leipzig declared that "the old jailbirds now have good times. Excluded from military service, they are applying themselves quite professionally at the homefront to burglary. When a burglar is caught, it most often comes out that he is a former penitentiary inmate." Newspapers in Leipzig, Dresden, and Rostock advocated forced labor for all former penitentiary inmates as recompense for the fact that they were not sent to the front. "The objection that people who have already served their sentences cannot simply be interned again without further ado," the Rostock paper argued, "is far too subtle [*feinfühlig*] for our raw times." In a context of mass death and destruction, it was argued, any discourse of rights and obligations was absurd. "The best of the nation are bleeding to death," the paper asserted, "without having been first asked whether they perceived the decision over their death as an interference with their personal freedom."[101]

Criminologist Robert Heindl, who had risen to prominence through his critique of the deportation movement, argued against any clemency for convicted felons.[102] Instead he urged the creation of special army units that would employ criminals at the front while maintaining tight supervision and some measure of the odium of punishment. The felons would thus be prevented from poisoning the image of the army or threatening the "security of the public." Heindl agreed that the war was a tremendous opportunity to enact Modern School criminal justice reforms, but he focused on the modernists' proposals for dealing with incorrigible, "habitual criminals." If properly constituted, he believed, special army units could serve as a form of postpenal security detention for dangerous individuals (*Zwangsverwahrung*), such as Liszt and Heindl's mentor, Hans Gross, had once envisioned.[103]

The only way to offset such fears of criminals unleashed on German society would have been to establish a process for screening and controlling the granting of pardons and create mechanisms for the supervision of ex-offenders as a condition of the suspended sentence. In the next chapter, I discuss the development of such a system in considerable detail. Here, I only note that the Reich government, in the final two years of the war, rebuffed efforts by the Reichstag to rationalize the pardon process by introducing conditional sentencing in lieu of administrative pardons. The Social Democrats supported this measure again from the standpoint that a juridicalization of pardon policy would guarantee the rights of offenders. While praising the government's increased use of pardons, Wolfgang Heine complained that it was still essentially a matter of chance whether an individual offender came into contact with state officials willing to administer his request for a pardon.[104] In 1917, a liberal deputy argued for introducing "conditional sentencing" as a "war measure," so that judges could begin making immediate distinctions between "real criminals" and the large numbers of persons who violated wartime codes because of "error" or "negligence."[105] In opposing such legislation, the Reich Ministry of Justice insisted that it could achieve the same positive social ends through the practice of administrative pardons and that wartime, in any case, was hardly the time to impose new burdens upon the courts. For whatever reason, the state was clearly loath to surrender an element of its traditional authority that still held important practical and symbolic meaning.

Conclusion

Wartime criminal policy was driven by a range of preoccupations. While the mobilization for total war led to unprecedented interventions by the state in German society, it also produced new initiatives from within civil society aimed at displacing or scaling back the state's traditional role in certain domains of regulation. In the case of pardon policy, the state was as much an obstacle to change as an engine of rationalization. Large numbers of pardons were granted in a haphazard, unsystematic manner, and no overarching policy or process was established during the war for the supervision of the many conditionally released offenders. Vagrants, beggars, and prostitutes were more subject to police harassment, but there was no clear, systematic policy for addressing these "social plagues." As discussed in the next chapter, the most important and long-lasting changes were eventually introduced through popular initiatives that drew upon the welfare utopia of a perfect space of discipline and supervision.

CITY OF LOVE
AND SUPERVISION
The Bielefeld System

The efforts by the military authorities to create a *cordon sanitaire* against prostitutes, vagabonds, and delinquents merely highlighted the problem of what to do with these outcasts. Wartime ideologies of national solidarity and obsessions with maximizing popular energies whittled away at the already fragile legitimacy of the workhouse. Welfare associations fretted that these unsteady, morally endangered individuals would ultimately be left to struggle for themselves in German society.

The wartime concern with unsupervised released petty offenders led to an important innovation in criminal policy known as the "Bielefeld System." This was an arrangement whereby judges authorized the transfer of convicted vagrants and panhandlers to the police, but spared them the actual confinement in a workhouse so long as they agreed to enter a worker colony and abide by its regulations for a period of time, possibly lasting up to two years. Local prison associations advised judges on the social and mental condition of the offenders and mediated between the courts and the asylums. In practice, the Bielefeld System was only modestly used during the war. Its larger significance, however, was in formalizing a nexus between welfare and criminal justice. The system was quickly expanded to include women convicted of sex-related offenses. In the Weimar era, the Bielefeld System became the model for a more comprehensive reform of criminal court practice.

It is tempting to interpret the Bielefeld System as an example of the state's appropriation of private domains of supervision.[1] Charitable leaders had founded the worker colonies upon strict voluntarist principles. The Bielefeld System effectively placed colonists under a form of forced supervision that was authorized by the courts and supported by the police. It would be wrong, however, to locate the development of the Bielefeld System within the familiar narrative of rationalization and nationalization of welfare practice. First, in spite of its reliance upon state coercion in the last instance, the Bielefeld System represented a transfer of real power from the police to the private associations. Under the Bielefeld System, private welfare advisers diagnosed the offenders' social pathologies and categorized them as objects of intervention. The charities' "special knowledge" of social matters gave them leverage with the judges. Since the police could not authorize workhouse confinement without the judges' approval, it was the latter who, practically speaking, made the important decisions regarding individual offenders. Increasingly, the police perspective, focused on protecting society from dangerous and burdensome elements, was replaced by the welfare perspective, focused on repairing damaged human material.[2]

Advocates of the Bielefeld model distinguished between social, sanitary, and juridical forms of knowledge and power. The legitimacy of the Bielefeld System rested precisely upon its foundations in social authority. It was a product of collaboration between charitable organizations like the German Evangelical Women's Association, the prison societies, and the Bethel asylum, together with liberal jurists, feminists, and Socialists seeking to transform the "police machine." Even as the state became larger and more bureaucratic, the Bielefeld System marshalled "organic" institutions in the service of a "New Germany."[3]

Citizen Bozi

The key figure in the creation of the Bielefeld System was Alfred Bozi, a judge on the Bielefeld City Court, a widely published legal scholar, and the scion of one of Westphalia's leading textile families. Bozi's interest in legal reform was more catholic than the average criminal justice reformer. He believed that civil, administrative, and criminal law had all become dangerously isolated from other pursuits and other scholarly disciplines. In contrast to the great theoreticians of modern criminal policy, Bozi was only marginally interested in criminology. His understanding of the criminal was based upon his practical experience as a judge and in his family's business. He was a social thinker: interested at least as much in industrial-labor relations, adult education, and women's welfare work as in criminal jurisprudence and the reform of the criminal code. His primary goal as a reformer was to reconfigure the relationship between the courts, the people, and the institutions of civil society.[4]

Bozi's earliest writings addressed a crisis in public legitimacy for the justice system as a whole and the judiciary in particular.[5] The essays, originally published in the *Gegenwart* and the *Preußischer Jahrbücher*, argued that judges were alienated from society (*lebensfremd*) because of their narrow, formalist education and the limits upon their ability to travel, do research, and keep pace with social change. Bozi called upon judges to move beyond juridical frames of reference and, "like natural scientists," to become more oriented toward empirical investigation and the verification of facts. He argued that judges-in-training should not be forced to jump over academic hurdles, but should broaden their exposure to people and professions "in a manner appropriate to the time." In particular, he believed judges should have experience with industry and industrial relations in order to understand "social reality" and to have the necessary contacts beyond the legal realm. One of his most influential recommendations was that judicial trainees carry out at least one of their internships with nonjuridical institutions.[6] "The judge," he argued, "should not stand outside the *Volk*."[7]

The emphasis in Bozi's early writings upon business and trade as segues to social reality reflected his own experience coming of age in a milieu that celebrated the myth of self-made men and the role of industry in the constitution of cities. Bielefeld was only a village of 10,000 in 1852, the year that Alfred Bozi's father, Karl, brought the first mechanized spinning machine from Scotland.[8] Karl Bozi founded the textile concern *Spinnerei Vorwärts* and managed the firm, along with Alfred's four uncles, until 1870.[9] While *Vorwärts* grew into one of the region's most successful companies, other textile concerns and a diverse array of other industries sprouted up in and around the town.[10] From 1850 to 1905, Bielefeld experienced a sevenfold increase in population. By 1914, the former village had a bustling commercial district, tram lines, an opera, a large theater, and a public library. At the edge of the town, the Bethel asylum, which had been founded in part through the efforts of C. A. Delius, another Bielefeld textile manufacturer, expanded to become the largest charitable institution in Germany.[11] Through much of the 1880s and early 1890s, Bielefeld's sense of community was marred by violent strikes, police repression against working class organizations, and tensions between the town and the asylum. Nevertheless, there was a marked trend toward peaceful coexistence on all fronts after the turn of the century.[12] While many comparably sized towns underwent a traumatic shift from the rule of local bourgeois notables (*Honoratiorenpolitik*) to a system of genuinely partisan, mass-based politics, Bielefeld seemed to weather this transition with relative ease, guaranteeing the dominance of local businessmen, while creating seats at the table for moderate working-class leaders.[13]

As a member of a leading textile family, Alfred Bozi belonged to a select group "counted among the civic elite, as it were, 'from birth.' "[14] Bozi's understanding of the social question owed a lot to his contact with business leaders in Westphalia and across Prussia. Much of his early scholarship included demands upon his colleagues to overcome their intellectual insularity and their aloofness from industrial milieus. His first important foray into social reform was as co-founder of the Law and Economy Association in 1911.[15] The membership of this group, which was based in Berlin, included prominent figures in new, technology-driven industries like Carl Duisberg of IG Farben and Emil Rathenau of AEG.[16] There were also a number of well-known law professors, most of them experts in civil law. The immediate goal of the association was to bridge the ideological divide between jurists and business-men, but their rhetoric was even more ambitious.[17] In a call to action, they declared their concern was "not the narrow specialized pursuits of admin-istration and justice, but rather . . . deep cultural movements in which all areas of society are equally involved." The proclamation condemned ju-rists for "over-valuing the dead letter of form and the abstract definition of terms," causing law to stand still while technology, industry, trade, and agri-culture assumed new forms.[18]

Bozi wanted the Law and Economy Association to be a forum to discuss practical issues and advocate for practical reforms among a wide range of social groups. As the association's first secretary, he argued for admitting Social Democrats and sought to promote projects aimed at influencing ordi-nary people's everyday experience with the courts and the police.[19] With the outbreak of war, however, the industrialists in the association turned their attention to national policy questions and were increasingly oriented toward Berlin. The academics, according to Bozi, fell into abstract, theoretical de-bates.[20] Bozi soon parted ways, complaining about the machinations of a "Berlin clique."[21]

As his relationship with the Law and Economy Association soured, Bozi focused increasingly on local matters and reached out to men and women laboring in the trenches of social reform. When the Great War began, Bozi created an association in Bielefeld for the discussion of social issues with his friend Carl Severing, a Socialist politician, editor, and union leader. Bozi also corresponded with a remarkably diverse group of welfare reformers, ranging from arch-Conservative Pastors like Friedrich Onnasch and Wilhelm Zoell-ner to the feminist Anna Pappritz and Socialist Max Quarck.[22] In 1915 Bozi founded the Society for Social Law (Gesellschaft für Soziales Recht, GSR) under the auspices of the Vienna Sociological Society and with funding from the city of Bielefeld. The society's board included prominent feminists and Socialists, as well as more mainstream experts in welfare, labor, and legal affairs.[23]

Bozi's efforts were part of what historian Ursula Ratz calls the "intellectual bridge of 1915." Buoyed by the wartime spirit, Socialists and liberals shared ideas and explored collaborative solutions to the divisive issues of the day. Among the fruits of these discussions were "sensational" volumes of essays on social policy by a carefully chosen mix of Socialist and liberal authors.[24] The first and most famous such collection was co-edited by the GSR-member Friedrich Thimme and the union leader Carl Legien. Bozi himself edited the second volume with the union lawyer Hugo Heinemann, and with Carl Severing working behind the scenes.[25] The contributors to Bozi's volume included a striking number of persons who went on to figure prominently in the legal culture of the Weimar Republic, including the author of the Weimar Constitution, Hugo Preuß, the criminal law scholar Karl von Lilienthal, the future Chancellor of the Republic, Wilhelm Marx, and future Prussian Justice Minister, Wolfgang Heine. The essays covered topics such as "the social power of coalitions," the education of jurists, the importance of the labor movement to developments in legal culture, civic education, and the battle against prostitution and public immorality. Each of the essays sought to foreground practical issues in legal and administrative reform and to oppose what they perceived as the straitjacket of politics, bureaucracy, and legal formalism by appeals to the common good.

According to Ratz, this collection demonstrated how the rapidly proliferating working groups of Socialist and bourgeois thinkers created an agenda for legislative and administrative reform.[26] But Bozi's aims went beyond the narrow policy objectives discussed by Ratz. His populist vision called for mobilizing *"völkisch"* energies for tasks of administration and governance and thereby transforming the very meaning of state power. Social reform, in his view, must be founded upon the broadest possible base of participation, because "the most refined sources for comprehending 'the social,' other than the actual conditions themselves, are the perceptions of life among all strata of the *Volk*."[27] The goal, Bozi argued, was to create "social institutions of law" by allowing for popular participation in the regulation and education of wayward citizens. His effort to transcend party divisions, to be *"überparteilich,"* was thus rooted in a social integrationist ideology. Conservatives as well as Social Democrats, feminists as well as morality reformers, were necessary participants in creating a new nexus of disciplinary authority.[28]

The wartime "internal truce," by facilitating the participation of political outsiders, made such an effort plausible. The demands of total war made such an effort imperative.[29] In establishing the GSR, Bozi carefully engineered the choice of leadership to ensure political, religious, and gender diversity. This was partially to lay the groundwork for corporatist solutions, but only in part.[30] Bozi's belief in a *Volksstaat* required that the popular will must somehow shape and enforce the system of social order, as he declared in a manifesto for the GSR:

> In the internal life of the *Volk*, there develops: an overcoming of historical status differences, a regrouping of political and economic interests, before all else the revived consciousness of community in every individual. [This] should now be grasped in its fundamental meaning as a return to natural perspectives on the essence of society. The *Volk* is not the object of a state administration that stands apart from it. It is rather the ground out of which this life form grows.[31]

In short, Bozi saw the war itself as a historical event that would efface class difference and fundamentally transform the relationship between the people and the state.

The GSR, in contrast to the Law and Economy Association, avoided theoretical debates and launched directly into local projects, many of which were only marginally related to traditional domains of legal practice.[32] Though its ambitions (and its membership) were still national in scope, the GSR focused on Bielefeld as a field of experimentation. There the society created an innovative alternative arbitration court and an adult education school (*Volkshochschule*) with the first systematic training program in legal issues for social-welfare workers and lay-judges. The significance of this practical, local activism, according to Bozi, transcended its immediate results. Social engagement built up the community's "internal strength." To prevent the country from falling into "internal divisions," he wrote later,

> [We] need to strengthen the feeling of solidarity between political parties. And for that, small local projects were more important than programmatic rallying. Local projects can proceed from within and function over the long term, whereas [great] programs may generate enthusiasm but will be disappointing in terms of practical results.[33]

The war was both a crisis and an opportunity: it "marked the entry of peoples into a new period of life."[34] In Bozi's view, whatever the outcome, Germany would be a radically different place after the peace, and preparations for this world were vitally necessary. Almost from the beginning of the conflict, his correspondence referred, however obliquely, to the challenges of demobilization, armistice, and economic and social restructuring.[35]

The GSR's alternative arbitration courts office were a product of their efforts to find and nurture the instinct for justice "rooted in the people." The courts allowed individuals to bring their conflicts before arbitration panels from the community. The parties to a dispute chose their own arbitrators from a list of "trustworthy" men and women. The city officials who compiled this list recruited from middle-class and working-class organizations, including the labor unions, and were supposed to seek individuals representing a wide range of social backgrounds. The arbitrators worked in pairs, serving alongside a professional judge trained specifically for this purpose. The arbitration panel, in turn, selected a researcher to investigate the social circumstances behind the case and produce a report. Lawyers could advise the parties to the dispute, but were not allowed to represent them at the proceedings.[36]

According to Bozi, the arbitration courts were an important step in bringing law "closer to the people." The nature of the cases to be arbitrated was, in principle, unlimited. The success of this more organic, more populist (volkstümlich) form of dispute resolution, he believed, would eventually force German criminal and civil judges to become more social and more attuned to the needs of the community. Judges "will only orient themselves to the modern worldview," he wrote the Minister of Justice in Saxony, "when they are confronted by the threat that justice will be taken out of the courts' hands."[37] The arbitration courts were thus an important element in his larger vision of criminal justice reform.

Another major concern for Bozi and the GSR was to enhance the role of women in the justice system. Working with the feminist reformer Anna Schütz, Bozi created a GSR committee for "the Promotion of Women's Participation in Justice." Schütz was the head of the League for Women's Legal Protection, an organization in Frankfurt that offered legal representation to women and agitated for gender equality.[38] Schütz initially expected the committee to advocate for professional opportunities for women in the law, including the judiciary. Bozi urged them to focus upon "women's duties" rather than their rights, and to consider the diverse ways in which women could influence legal proceedings without necessarily becoming legal professionals.[39] The committee ultimately focused upon the application of "women's particular sensibilities" to justice. Under this heading, they appealed not only to liberal feminists but conservative moral reformers and others from the Christian charities. Bozi seemed to recognize that history was on the side of the feminists. He believed that once society recognized the need for women's participation in justice, women's entry to the judiciary would be only a matter of time. Meanwhile, he argued, the commitment to "motherliness" was the common ground upon which a diverse group of reformers could come together.[40]

Bozi's strategy had startling success. His GSR committee was able to recruit prominent feminists like Camilla Jellinek and Margarethe Bennewitz, who advocated women's full legal and political equality.[41] At the same time, Bozi brought on leaders of Christian charitable organizations like Pastors Walter Thieme and Friedrich Onnasch, who were steadfast opponents of women's equality.[42] He also brought in Ruth van den Leyen, a pioneer in the juvenile justice movement and a forceful proponent of penal reform, who was one of many women in the group who considered herself to be anti-feminist.[43] The diversity of this committee was all the more impressive, given that many women's organizations on the national level were splitting apart during the last two years of the war.[44]

Their first aim was to gain access for women to serve as expert witnesses and lay-judges in cases involving female defendants, witnesses, or victims. There were "relevant particulars" about a woman's "spiritual condition," the committee argued, which only other women could evaluate.[45] Bielefeld became the first German city to formally recruit women as advisers to the court on the validity of women's testimony, the assessment of women's character, and the repercussions of judicial measures for men and women upon the lives of their families.

The committee's broader aims were in no small part symbolic. Women, they believed, had special expertise in regard to the social realm. For Bozi, as for the American reformers discussed by Michael Willrich, the very coupling of the terms "social" and "law" implied, in some measure, a turn to the domestic sphere or to women's worlds.[46] If most jurists saw no role for women at the court, Bozi argued, this was because of the essential flaw in their methodological training that prevented them from recognizing "the connection between the social and the juridical." Creating a space in criminal justice for women's "special expertise" was thus an important step in the broader campaign to bring social perspectives into courts.[47]

Thanks to the GSR, Bielefeld became increasingly important as a source of reformist ideas and a laboratory for institutional change. Two of Bozi's most important collaborators were Pastor "Fritz" von Bodelschwingh and Carl Severing. Each of these figures were symbols of local patriotism and the transcendence of party politics or "Überparteilichkeit."[48] As the director of Bethel, Bodelschwingh guided an institution marked by a self-conscious mixture of "modern" and "traditional" elements. By 1914, the complex included asylums and clinics for epileptics, the physically and mentally disabled, alcoholics, and, of course, vagrants and beggars. The work was becoming increasingly specialized, and every branch of the institution sponsored scholarly research by professionals of one sort or another.[49] At the same time, Bethel continued to rely upon a circle of male and female volunteers from Bielefeld, as well as theology candidates from all over Germany. While Bodelschwingh boasted of the institution's attention to scientific advances, he continuously stressed its rootedness in Protestant-activist tradition dating back to Wichern. He also helped to construct a popular mythology around the builder of the institution, his father, who died in 1910. In speeches, official publications, and a hagiographic biography published in the year of his father's death, "Bodelschwingh, the Elder" was turned into a kind of prophet for the industrial age and a modern Protestant saint.[50]

Carl Severing, a prominent union leader and editor of the Socialist *Volkswacht*, was becoming a legend in his own right.[51] He was mythologized among Bielefeld's bourgeoisie as the man who taught Bielefeld's working class to police itself, enabling the pragmatic and rational form of labor relations that supposedly typified the city after 1900. Severing became prominent in the 1890s after leading a campaign among the union rank and file to suppress strike activity and encourage the negotiation of collective agreements.[52] In 1896 he was publicly thanked by Bielefeld's chief of police for "helping to maintain order" during a strike of coach workers.[53] He was also credited with persuading the workers to divert their strike funds into unemployment and sickness funds. Overall, Severing was perceived as a symbol of the healing power of local patriotism and civic responsibility operating above and beyond class loyalty. He was the "good Socialist," the man who could lead the workers back into the "*Heimat*" (the local community or "home"), and, by extension, into the nation, or "*Volk*."

In Severing's memoirs, he proudly recalled how his respected position within the Bielefeld community helped him to play a role as a mediator across class and political boundaries on a national level. While serving as a Social Democratic Party (SPD) deputy in 1908, he wrote decades later, Father Bodelschwingh approached him in the halls of the Reichstag, addressing him as "Brother Severing" and using the informal "*du*." The pastor wanted Severing to arrange a meeting—over a "bowl of pea soup"—with the Socialist leader August Bebel and the liberal reformer Friedrich Naumann, in order to discuss Bodelschwingh's proposed measures against vagrancy and begging. According to Severing, the unlikely meeting was a complete success, with Bebel and Naumann promising Bodelschwingh their "moral support" in transforming the vagrancy laws, and the latter declaring himself heartened by the visit and promising to return to them often.[54] Severing's story was a perfect illustration of his faith that criss-crossing identities and an underlying commitment to the social question would ultimately allow Germans to transcend party boundaries. Naumann and Bodelschwingh were pastors, Naumann and Bebel were social thinkers, and of course Bodelschwingh and Severing were fellow Bielefelders. United around their bowls of pea soup—simple, hearty German fare—the parties could begin to address a matter of practical, national concern.

Bozi's forays into the realm of Bielefeld social policy reflected a taste for similar ideological gruel. He was instrumental in making Severing a lay-judge on the Bielefeld court and continued to correspond with him and to write of him admiringly, even after he had thrown his support to the Nazis in 1933.[55] Together with Severing Bozi founded the "Association for the Discussion of Social Policy Issues" in Bielefeld soon after the outbreak of war. The aim of this society was to facilitate the exchange of ideas among all strata of the population in Bielefeld and to find new avenues for cooperation.[56] Bozi reserved rooms in the town hall and invited a diverse group of local and national personalities to present papers on issues of common concern. At the first meeting, a liberal Bielefeld architect reported on the housing question, while the conservative chair of Bethel's membership, Count Wolf von Baudissin, discussed the proposal for a "work-service requirement" and its implications for the region.[57] According to Bozi's recollections, the association meetings marked a high point in the "nonpartisan," idealistic atmosphere of the *Burgfrieden*. The membership lists show a large contingent from Bethel, including pastors, teachers, nurses, and at least one missionary.[58] Bodelschwingh and Baudissin were among "the most enthusiastic" participants, and the asylum generally offered "lively support" to the enterprise. Bozi credited Severing with ensuring that "great national concerns" were never overshadowed by party-political contradictions."[59] A number of other union and SPD lawyers and editors were present for the discussions, and the membership list included four participants identified simply as workers. The group also included a contingent of manufacturers, factory directors, and their wives, and a large number of pastors and teachers. About one of eight participants were women, including the female police assistant, Clara Hermelbrecht, and other women affiliated with the German Evangelical Women's Association (DEF).[60]

While the Bielefeld Association had obvious parallels to the prewar social commissions and wartime working groups discussed by Ratz and Steinmetz, Bozi's and Severing's organization was committed to addressing local problems without relying upon a regime of government experts.[61] The Bielefeld reformers sought to mobilize local energies not simply to influence policy but to transform the relationship between the people and state institutions.

The participation of workers and diverse groups of women alongside the traditional Christian associations, in their view, provided the foundation for promising initiatives in welfare, health, and education. They expected the war to forge a new kind of voluntarism that transcended traditional barriers of religion, class, and politics.

Toward the Bielefeld System

As the number of participants in the Bielefeld association grew, Bozi divided them into smaller, more focused working groups.[62] The "Committee for a Social Approach to Criminal Justice," founded in early 1915, became an especially fertile ground for new ideas. Bozi and Bodelschwingh led the group. The female police assistant, Clara Hermelbrecht, was a regular participant, as were two members of the Bielefeld Prison Association. The committee's aim, however, was to move beyond the membership and beyond the assumptions of the traditional prison association. They sought to fundamentally reconsider how private organizations and individuals could play a part in criminal policy.[63] Bodelschwingh made the vagabond question into the committee's first order of business. The chairman of the Association of German Worker Colonies had asked the Bethel leader to investigate what could be done about colonists who departed prematurely, only to fall back into begging and vagrancy, then into the hands of the police and the workhouse, and eventually back into the colonies.[64]

According to the charities, a majority of these chronic offenders were "adult children": weak-willed, mentally deficient persons who were unprepared for the rigors of the workplace and the burden of freedom. Pastor Onnasch defined adult children as "persons who could not make their way in life without direction." They were especially vulnerable to alcohol and other temptations of life on the road.[65] In their effect on the colonies, Bodelschwingh compared the adult children to water leaking into the hold of a ship. All of the colonies' efforts at rehabilitating vagrants and beggars, he declared, were stymied by this constant flow of broken souls, who stayed only until the "drive to wander" drove them back to the highways and cities. Social labors that might "bear fruit," Bodelschwingh said, mixing the horticultural and nautical metaphors so loved by his father, could begin only after the hole in the ship had been "plugged."[66]

Plugging the hole meant keeping these weak and fragile souls under supervision until they were truly "cured" and ready to live independently. Bodelschwingh, more than ever, blamed the criminal justice system for failing to handle these offenders as anything more than juridical abstractions: punishing their crimes without taking account of their real flesh and blood needs. The constant cycle of colony, prison, highway, and return to prison could partly be blamed on the blindness of the legal system.[67]

In Judge Bozi, the critics of criminal justice had a judicial insider who shared their frustrations. Bozi saw the same cycle from his vantage point behind the bench, often confronting individual offenders sentenced for begging or prostitution multiple times within the space of a year. His fellow judges, he wrote Bodelschwingh, were not immune from the "spirit of the times," and, in fact, increasingly refused to authorize police supervision or the workhouse for vagabonds and prostitutes they perceived as social victims. The problem was that judges could not think or act outside the paradigm of punishment and responsibility. They imposed harsh administrative measures upon the most egregious offenders, while allowing the others to be set loose with a mere fine or a short stay in prison.[68]

Bozi wanted more supervision for vagrants, panhandlers, and prostitutes but believed that effective oversight and treatment must take place within a welfare framework. He chided the charitable organizations for thinking that the General Commandos might "clean up" German society. "Any unmediated intervention by the General Commandos," he wrote to Bodelschwingh, created "a momentary success" at the cost of long-term goals and visions. "We work more in the direction of your own endeavors, when we create a self-functioning system, that would not be superseded by the military's special authority [Kommandogewalt]."[69] Bozi's vision drew upon the growing popular conviction that "the police must be kept far away from social work." The eventual goal was to avoid any overt appearance of "administrative coercion [behördlicher Zwang]." The very institution of policing was too freighted with the tasks of security and control to be serviceable.[70] In Bozi's view, the evaluation and categorization of offenders and the design and implementation of corrective measures should be handled by people who were close to the populations they supervised: teachers, welfare agents, and clergy, of course, but also respectable citizens from the working class. In the same spirit as the arbitration initiatives, Bozi sought to open up the criminal courts to a wider range of social knowledge and influences.[71]

In seeking to address the vagabond question, Bielefeld's committee on social law looked at how private welfare associations could create a system of supervision backed up by the coercive authority of Justiz, while engaging the "finely meshed" social knowledge and resources of private organizations. To some extent, the committee found a model for such a system in the efforts by the local morality association and Fräulein Hermelbrecht, the police assistant, to "rescue" women arrested for venal sex.[72] The police assistant, in partnership with the association, had carved out a space for private disciplinary intervention as an alternative to direct police control—although she pursued her efforts only at the discretion of the local criminal police. The Social Law Committee wanted to invest greater and more routinized authority into the hands of the local associations, which meant they would need the approval of the District Office (*Regierungspräsident*) in Minden or the Army Command in Münster. Interestingly, however, no Prussian police or military authorities seem to have been invited to the Bielefeld discussions.[73] Instead the committee developed its own program and then presented it to the Prussian government, with Bodelschwingh and Bozi and their colleagues in Berlin lobbying for authorization.[74]

The Bielefeld proposal called for Bozi to inform the prison society of all the cases of vagrancy, begging, and homelessness coming before the criminal courts. Herr Bitter, the teacher on the criminal justice committee and a member of the Bielefeld Prison Association, would be called in to investigate the circumstances behind the individual's behavior and given immediate access to the case files. If Bitter concluded that the offender was a "adult child" and suited for the worker colonies, then he was to phone Wilhelmsdorf and arrange for the colony to take custody. The judge would impose the normal sentence—a short prison term, followed by transfer to police authority—but the offender would be given the option of a suspended sentence in return for welfare supervision. If the offender accepted this arrangement, then he was bound to conform to the directives of the prison association and the worker colony. The moment he failed in his promise, he would be arrested again and the original sentence would be imposed.[75]

The linchpin of this proposal was the worker colony. In a letter to the judicial authorities in Minden, the head of the prison society argued that Bielefeld's charities were specially equipped to deal with these offenders because of their proximity to Bethel. The worker colonies offered a "navigable path" for rescuing "even profoundly wayward persons." The colonies were already taking some of the burdens away from the prisons and poor relief. What charities lacked, however, was "the necessary means [*Handhabe*] to keep people within their institutions."[76] In essence, the Bielefelders proposed that the authorities put crucial decisions about a whole class of offenders into the hands of private associations. Welfare would displace the police, and the colony would displace the workhouse as the primary agent of discipline for the vagabond.[77] The police not only ceded their power over these vagrants and beggars, but they were required to take custody of those who failed to conform to the terms of their welfare supervision. The police were becoming a power of last resort, backing up the position of the private associations.

Not surprisingly, the police authorities in Minden had reservations about the reform. It was approved only after further interventions by Pastor Bodelschwingh, and with a number of conditions. Most important, the District President insisted on approving the suspension of police supervision on a case-by-case basis. There would be no blanket grant of authority to the welfare associations, though offenders could be immediately delivered to the worker colonies while awaiting word of their fate. Second, the police authorities made residency at Wilhelmsdorf into a specific condition of exempting them from the workhouse. Bethel, in other words, was the foundation of the system, ensuring the quality and intensity of supervision. The close cooperation between the housemaster at Wilhelmsdorf and the members of the Bielefeld Prison Association was to be a crucial link in the disciplinary nexus.[78] Finally, the police authorities balked at the principle of using the threat of police custody simply as a guarantee for the authority of the welfare associations. In the future, the Minden President insisted, the police would decide whether to impose police custody according to the same criteria that had always been used, that is, whether or not a particular individual represented a danger to public security and morals.[79]

State officials in Minden and Berlin were drawn to this reform, in spite of its drawbacks, because they saw it as a way to unburden the police, prisons, and workhouses, while guaranteeing some measure of social protection. The resources of the state were stretched thin by the war, and the "vigorous measures" introduced by the General Commandos simply begged the question of what would ultimately be done with this population over the course of the conflict. Moreover, there seemed to be general agreement that a "swarm" of new wanderers could be expected with the end of hostilities and the demobilization. The Commando in Münster declared that it could do nothing on its own to refine and improve the handling of accused vagabonds. This was a matter for the local prison and welfare associations.[80] Karl Finkelnburg, the head of the Prussian Department of Prisons, told Bodelschwingh that he "welcomed any measure leading to limitations upon corrective custody."[81] The Bielefeld reformers, while no less keen to see a reduction in the workhouse population, were also hoping that the reform would lead judges to increasingly authorize workhouse confinement for offenders, so that the threat of police intervention could uphold the authority of the welfare associations. Judges, in other words, should begin assigning more supervision over a wider population of persons, though without actually broadening the power of the police.[82]

The Prussian Minister of Justice supported the Bielefeld System as a step toward forcing greater numbers of vagrants and beggars into permanent guardianship. When asking Prussian state's attorneys to support the reform, the minister declared that the offender's stay in a worker colony was an opportunity to "observe his mental condition and gather material for an eventual proceeding to declare mental incompetency on the basis of weakness of will." The German Civil Code typically made it difficult for the state to initiate guardianship proceedings, since family members had the primary responsibility and right of care. If a vagrant or beggar had already been ordered to a worker colony, however, and then fled or disobeyed the house rules, the state could legitimately apply to become the authorized legal custodian.[83]

The new system, with all its limitations, was barely established in Bielefeld when Bozi and other members of the committee began lobbying for its expansion to other areas of Westphalia. Almost from the beginning, Bozi also envisioned generalizing the system to other categories of criminals.[84] He urged Bodelschwingh and Father Schmidt of the Hostel Association to contact Protestant and Catholic worker colonies in other regions that could enter comparable arrangements with the courts and the police in their districts.[85] The challenge for the reformers was twofold. First, they needed to overcome the resistance of worker colonies that questioned whether they could or should supervise convicted offenders on probation. Second, reformers needed to win over state and judicial officials, as well as liberal reformers, who feared that too large a role for private charities would undermine the authority of the police as a guarantor of public security. These factors would shape the debate over the Bielefeld innovations for years to come.

The Bielefeld System and the Regulation of Prostitutes

The obvious next step in the minds of Bielefeld's Social Law Committee was to expand the Bielefeld System to the other principal class of wartime asocial offenders, the prostitutes and "at-risk" women. In order to accomplish this, the committee had to persuade state officials to include such women within the special penal-welfare category now defined for "adult children." The immediate obstacle to such a move was that the worker colonies at Bethel did not accept women. Bodelschwingh himself claimed to have no direct experience with prostitution policy.[86] Given the institutional framework that defined "adult children," the category was, in essence, gendered male. In defining a female subject for protective supervision and in establishing a locus and a mechanism for protective supervision, the Bielefeld committee had to look beyond Bethel and even beyond the framework of "closed welfare."

The committee turned to one of its members, Clara Hermelbrecht, the city's female police assistant and a leader of the Evangelical Women's Association.[87] Since becoming Bielefeld's first female police assistant in 1907 (and one of the first in Germany), Hermelbrecht administered the association's asylum for women, advised the police on matters of sexual immorality, and counseled women and girls accused of sexual offenses. Hermelbrecht also found employment opportunities for women, ideally in domestic service, but frequently in local industry. Hermelbrecht's expertise and experience with "fallen women" provided the framework for the Bielefeld committee's plan for protective supervision in the case of female asocials. The police assistant, it was argued, could advise the criminal court directly on an accused woman's social condition and whether protective supervision was warranted. She could also oversee the development of a program of supervision, tailored to the social and individual particularities of the case.

The Bielefeld Social Law Committee believed that fallen women, like vagabonds, needed to be separated into at least two basic categories: those who suffered from a "habitual drive" toward venal sex and those whose behavior could be altered through moral persuasion and social interventions. The hardened prostitutes, the Prison Association stated, would have to be incarcerated in workhouses for "as long as possible." They firmly believed, however, that most women convicted of sex offenses during the war were "still not ripe for the workhouse."[88] Bozi went even farther in his rejection of standard practice. Even the most degenerate women, he argued, should be put to work on the land or in some other jobs "which are not in proximity to a city and in which the employer can guarantee constant but well-meaning supervision."[89] Private welfare, in any case, both the judge and the prison association agreed, was even more crucial in the case of female offenders than male, because the needs of first-time prostitutes and at-risk women were more diverse. Some of them simply needed a modicum of oversight from a responsible, respectable woman. Others would require shelter in a home, from which they would need "special permission to leave, except when they were on their way to work." Still others would require a longer-term residence in a worker colony.[90] Private associations for fallen women had been struggling for years to provide a correspondingly wide range of options in supervision.[91] The Bielefelders now sought to link such an emergent welfare complex directly to the criminal courts through the mediating role of the police assistant. Most of the at-risk women in Bielefeld were to be supervised through the local Evangelical Women's Association home for girls or through the oversight of volunteer ladies. For those who required long-term care and preparation for the labor market, worker colonies specifically for women would be built, while in the meantime the prostitutes might be sent to facilities in neighboring regions.[92]

One of the most important changes in this reform was in the power it granted to the police assistant. Hermelbrecht had previously been allowed to supervise women criminals only at the discretion of the local morals squad, who initiated her interventions when they saw fit. The police assistant furthermore had no leverage over the women she helped, whether at the police station or at the Evangelical Women's house, except in her power to denounce them to the administrative authorities. The proposed reform changed Hermelbrecht's primary orientation from the police to the criminal courts. Like Herr Bitter, she would be summoned by the judges to the court and given direct access to the case files in all cases involving female asocials. After meeting with the defendant and investigating the circumstances behind the offense, Hermelbrecht would advise the judge on the woman's suitability for the various available forms of supervision.[93] It was Bozi's intention that Hermelbrecht's title would also be changed to "city welfare agent," in order that she would no longer be perceived as an agent of the police.[94]

From a juridical standpoint, women criminals who were deemed suitable for protective supervision were officially transferred by the courts to police custody. This official transfer, however, was done with the understanding that police control was suspended as long as the women followed the terms of their welfare supervision. Hermelbrecht was responsible for choosing a female volunteer from the community to oversee the criminal's probation. Previously the police assistant had assembled a circle of "local ladies" to serve as informal advisers for the girls and women sent to her by the morals squad. Many of these women were members of Bielefeld's Morality Association or were referred to her by a local pastor. The spirit of the new reforms required Hermelbrecht to cultivate a wider pool of volunteer assistants, while the new regulations for the position called upon her to make contact with employers and employer associations, in order to draw upon their information, advice, and assistance whenever possible.[95] It was assumed that most of the female offenders would "happily submit themselves" to such care and oversight.

Others, however, would be likely to pull away from the welfare overseers over time, eventually to fall back into immoral behaviors. For this latter population, it was argued, the threat of police custody was clearly a precondition for effective supervision.[96]

While Hermelbrecht was elated at winning direct coercive power over her charges, she was also more committed than ever to ensuring that police considerations did not determine the measures necessary to the "renewal and recovery of national energies." Like many Protestant women activists, she believed that the police was far too preoccupied with a narrowly defined mission of protecting public hygiene. The war, she believed, created a growing awareness of prostitution as a "social question" rather than a "sanitary question."[97] Such a distinction—between the "social" and the "sanitary"—was evident in the rhetoric of secular women activists as well.[98] In an article for Bozi's 1916 collection, the leading abolitionist Anna Pappritz declared that "the state has seen [the prostitution] problem until now almost exclusively from the standpoint of sanitation, in that it has tried to eliminate health risks through regimentation." The goal of a new policy, she argued, must be to address the "heart of the social illness."[99] Doing so meant investing greater power and authority into welfare institutions, while removing the police from the process of "control" and "surveillance."[100] Like Hermelbrecht, Pappritz insisted that the issue of physically contaminated bodies could not be decoupled from the problem of the moral infection of the social.[101] Such an argument provided the groundwork for a growing alliance between conservative women and feminists, one that inspired Bozi to invest greater energies into promoting the role of women per se within criminal justice.[102]

For Hermelbrecht, as for Bozi, the perception of prostitution as a "social question" rather than a "sanitary question" required a solution based upon the mobilization of popular energies. The war, she declared, had caused the "loosening of public mores," and public health was now "endangered by the licentiousness of women and men." Protective supervision meant getting the community to step in where parents and family members had failed. Hermelbrecht was to be present at all court hearings involving women or girls as defendants, and like Herr Bitter, the teacher, she would be given immediate access to the case files. If it seemed there might be "extenuating circumstances" around the woman's criminal behavior, then Hermelbrecht assigned someone from the community to make contact with the offender and investigate her past. If it was decided to transfer the woman to the police, while granting a conditional waiver of police custody, then Hermelbrecht's helper became the person principally assigned with setting the terms and overseeing compliance in the woman's supervision.

Who would supervise the former prostitutes and the endangered girls? It was obvious, Hermelbrecht told one audience, that it could not be the "typical 'Lady' who sits in our theaters, salons, café-houses and similar social establishments and is at home with her unsocial doing-nothing." Instead, she called for "serious-minded women of all confessions and occupational groups willing to come together to organize a work, that the state . . . coarse-grained and never so fine-meshed . . . would never be able to do satisfactorily." This work was based on "self-help" for women and a sense of feminine solidarity that transcended class and politics.[103] Her later guidelines for volunteers described the new era of protective supervision with direct reference to the older tradition of poor-relief, citing a Protestant saying that "the soul of poor relief is the care of impoverished souls" (*Die Seele der Armenpflege ist die Pflege der armen Seele*). The helpers served as models and guides for the transformation of an entire way of life. This process was to start with practical matters, like money management and domestic skills, and move on to tending the vitally important area of "the external person: respectable, simple clothes, attention to the stockings, . . . learning to avoid false decoration."[104] The supervisors were also supposed to introduce their charges to good reading material and to speak with them about "the religious foundations of life."[105]

The role of the Church in Hermelbrecht's vision of social order was illustrated by her advice on mapping out urban areas for the organization and assignment of protective supervision. The typical course, she noted, was to follow the borders of police jurisdictions or the traditional municipal subdivisions. Hermelbrecht, however, argued for using the parish districts to subdivide the city into zones of practice. In this way, the spiritual and the practical purposes of welfare could be combined. "By depending upon the clergy," moreover, "it will be easier to mobilize the appropriate female force [*Hilfskraft*]."[106] Consciously or otherwise, Hermelbrecht's contribution to this decidedly modern innovation in criminal policy evoked Wichern's call for "geognostic maps" to divide and distribute the social energies of Christian lay-people.[107]

The Bielefeld System beyond Bielefeld

The Bielefeld model gained national recognition almost immediately. In the autumn of 1916, the Prussian Interior Ministry decreed the adoption of the Bielefeld System in all provinces. The decree invoked many of the themes from Bozi's writings, including the same paradoxical mix of voluntarism and coercion. "Adult children," the ministry argued, "were incapable of supporting themselves through consistent, orderly labor, because of their weakness of will." The only way to protect them from "total decline" was through an extended stay in a worker colony. However, the vagabonds' "irrepressible drive to wander [*Wanderdrang*]" usually lured them away from the colonies prematurely. The government authorized protective supervision in lieu of workhouse custody, but only upon the condition that the vagabonds "voluntarily" committed themselves to a worker colony.[108] The Interior Ministry also urged the Prussian Justice Ministry to make each judge specify in his decision whether the offender was a "weak-willed and unsteady" person. In the view of the Interior Minister, "a long criminal record would speak *in favor* of such a judgment." In other words, a greater incidence of recidivism should *improve* the individual's prospects of a suspended sentence—a striking departure from the principle that repeat offenders should be more severely punished.[109] Finally, the ministerial decree specifically called upon Prussian localities to follow the Bielefelders' model of a disciplinary system based upon collaboration between the criminal court, the prison association, and a local asylum. Since most Prussian districts did not have their own prison societies or worker colonies, a wider and denser net of such private institutions would have to be established.

Responses to the decree were divided. A leading member of the Deutsche Verein für Armenpflege protested against the implication that private charities were better suited than workhouses to assess and to treat the maladies of such offenders. Many of the so-called "adult children," he asserted, were actually dangerous individuals. Private associations would never be able to properly defend the public interest.[110] At the meeting of the Prison Society in Sachsen-Anhalt, Nordhausen's state's attorney argued that the minister's decree simply "created a new category of person, and thereby put still another burden on criminal justice."[111] He insisted that the courts in Sachsen-Anhalt had no need for "expert witnesses" from welfare. Pastor Hage, the director of the prison society, countered that the ministry's order was not "creating" a new category of person. Such a category, he argued, "is there, and one must reckon with it and treat it."[112] Pastor Just from the Rhenish-Westphalian Prison Society defended the principle of outside expertise at the courts. "We in the prison," he declared, "see people differently than the judges do; we know them better, and for that reason we can give psychologically worthwhile tips [*Fingerzeige*]."[113] A cautious compromise was suggested by August Finger, a professor of law in Halle and an occasional critic of reformers.[114] The Bielefeld System, he suggested, was legitimate and worthwhile to the extent that it enriched administrative and police practices of regulation. On the other hand, drawing upon the classical distinction between police and justice (*Polizei* and *Justiz*), Finger argued that welfare methods and principles must not interfere with the courts' responsibilities to determine guilt and innocence according to "objective" juridical standards. The administrative authorities, he declared, were obligated to understand the moral and social complexities behind a crime. Justice, however, "must paint in black." The society should beware of any reforms that might contribute to the "crumbling of the house of avenging justice."[115]

In practice, whether local courts adopted the Bielefeld System depended upon the initiative of the local prison associations and the asylums. Local governments, judges, and state's attorneys usually followed in their wake. In Württemberg the local clergy established a welfare advising office for the court through funding from the Robert Bosch Foundation. They used local "educational homes" for protective supervision and relied upon the Stuttgart police assistant as a welfare mediator.[116] In Hessen-Nassau, where local prosecutors controlled the prison society, the ministry's initiatives were resisted.[117] In Bozi's own district, the president of the higher court in Hamm initially refused to authorize the use of the Bielefeld System anywhere beyond the city and surrounding area of Bielefeld. The court president told the head of the Bielefeld prison association that he had written to the Ministry of Justice, but since he received no specific directions on the reforms, he saw no justification for action. The pastor was amazed that one justice could stymie the government's directive. "Is it the same in the judiciary as in the Church?" he asked Bozi. " 'Each did what seemed to him good, and there was no King in Israel?' "[118]

To many reformers, the ambivalence among jurists seemed to permeate the Prussian judicial bureaucracy, suggesting that tensions between the judicial and the administrative offices extended to the highest reaches of government. While the Bielefelders found a ready audience at the Department of Prisons in the Ministry of Interior, the Ministry of Justice was less responsive to Bozi's initiatives.[119] Ernst Rosenfeld, a professor in Münster with close ties to the Berlin Prison Association and the Westphalian Frauenhülfe, warned Bozi not to expect any assistance from the Justice Ministry.[120] It would be far more sensible, Rosenfeld urged Bozi, for him to concentrate on propaganda among individual judges and welfare associations. "In Münster," he added, the best ideas in criminal justice reform were frequently blocked or hindered by the justice officials.[121]

The ambivalence of judges helps explain the extremely modest results for the Bielefeld System during the war, particularly as it dealt with vagrants and panhandlers. Across Prussia, the Bielefeld System sent only 112 offenders to worker colonies. The colony in Hilmarshof complained that judges used the colonies as a dumping ground for physically and mentally disabled persons who were incapable of productive labor. The colonies in Weeze and Hohenhof reported that the offenders sent there were a bad lot who should have been sent to the workhouse instead. The Weeze director complained that these colonists were "mentally retarded, incapable of working without supervision, smoked in the hay barns, and harassed other colonists at work and at meals." Most of the colonies, nevertheless, gave positive reports about the experience, however limited the pool. Their main fear—that offenders on probation would have a negative influence upon the other colonists—proved groundless.[122]

In the summer of 1918, the Interior Ministry produced its most enthusiastic endorsement yet of the Bielefeld reforms. The July 15 decree was actually written in consultation with Bozi.[123] For the first time, the ministry adopted the reformers' perspective on the opposition between protective welfare supervision and police supervision and suggested that the former must, as far as possible, displace the latter. Protective supervision, the ministry explained, was about strengthening the social position of the ex-offender, whereas policing was a matter of sanitary or juridical control. The ministry warned that the "moral decline of a large number of girls and women" would be one inevitable element "among the damages resulting from the long-lasting war." With peace, they predicted, there would be "a precipitous rise" in the numbers of professional prostitutes and of women who were "on that path."[124] Such prophecies of moral decay were later picked up and propagated in the most overheated prose by journalists of the postwar inflation era, who produced a veritable panic about threats of bodily and cultural contamination. In the summer of 1918, the government's public articulation of these fears represented a declaration of support for the *social* agenda of popular justice-welfare organizations and associations.[125]

The Bielefeld System as a Broader Vision of Social Order

Most historical accounts of Germany society during the First World War describe a process of social dissolution as the war dragged on. It is not unusual to treat the last year and a half of the war as a prehistory to the revolution of November 1918. One thereby confronts a narrative of progressive fracturing, in which the *Burgfrieden* unravels and

Germany is increasingly divided into two (or more) irreconcilable camps.[126] The last eighteen months of the war, however, can also be seen as a prelude to new collaboration across historic class and political divides. Nowhere is this more apparent than in the case of criminal justice reform efforts, and Alfred Bozi was in many ways at the center of this reform work. Even as fractures in the *Burgfrieden* became apparent, the Bielefeld judge continued to mobilize remarkably broad coalitions behind his vision of social order for what, now more so than ever, he believed, would be a "New Germany."

Conclusion

Bozi's dream of an institution that drew upon welfare knowledge and applied it to a full range of criminal cases required a modicum of social stability and political support before it could be realized. But the idea spread and prospered during one of the most tumultuous periods in German history, providing an intellectual and political bridge to a new generation of reformers and a new age of experimentation in the Weimar Republic. The Bielefeld System struck a chord among those trying to piece together models of social order during times of social dissonance.[127] While quintessentially forward-looking in their view of criminal policy, the Bielefeld reformers gestured back to both the "spirit of 1914" and the ideals of community, solidarity, and mutual aid promoted by Wichern.

Borrowing Edward Dickinson's terminology, one might be tempted to describe the Bielefeld System of penal-welfare supervision as "restorationist." At its earliest stages of development, certainly, Bielefeld reformers invoked a vision of cultural leadership by social elites, or *Honoratioren*—even if the category of leaders had now been broadened to include an aristocracy of workers, women, and middle-class citizens. Yet to focus purely upon the Bielefeld vision as a project of reconstruction would be to miss two points in particular. First, the Bielefeld System opened a path for various discourses of "asocial behavior" to play a larger role in the courts. Bozi and Bodelschwingh stressed the importance of private volunteers in welfare for criminal offenders, but they also believed strongly in scientific training and knowledge. Proponents of the Bielefeld System eventually looked to sociologists, psychiatrists, and geneticists to assist in fine-tuning the advisers' social diagnoses of offenders. The second argument against interpreting the Bielefeld System as "restorationist" is that the Bielefeld reformers—Bozi and Severing in particular—believed they were part of a larger struggle to transform governance and authority in Germany along populist lines. The mobilization of "popular energies" to participate in criminal policy was supposed to represent a model for civic engagement that transcended class and party lines.[128]

This populist ideal of citizen activism in criminal policy provided legitimacy for the turn to welfare principles and welfare tools in criminal court practice. Lay-persons supposedly brought the external world and real existing conditions into the enclosed and artificial world of the courtroom. They forced the judges and prosecutors to turn their gaze outward and consider the individual within a broader framework. They gave a richer, more contextualized meaning to the concepts of guilt, innocence, and responsibility. In place of the traditional limits upon judicial discretion, judges could consider a potentially endless array of social factors as "extenuating circumstances." Along with the pardon, whereby sovereignty exercised its traditional right of mercy, the judge could arrange for a suspended sentence, whereby the criminal's symbolic debt to the sovereign was momentarily forgotten and welfare knowledge could determine the particularities of treatment.

These new modes of supervision were "rational" and "scientific" mainly in the sense that they were bureaucratically organized and, increasingly, centrally funded. They constituted a transfer of authority from the state to the community, moving the locus of discipline from the public sphere of the criminal courts and the carceral institutions to the private spheres of the home, the family, and the workplace. They illustrated the persistence of Protestant models of supervision and the difficulties of making a clear dichotomy between the roles of "progressive" and "traditional" discourses in the construction of regulatory mechanisms.

THE END OF JUSTICE?
Soziale Gerichtshilfe in the Weimar Republic

The end of World War I and the collapse of the Imperial system created unprecedented opportunities in legal reform. While there were sharp disagreements about how to remake government and society in Germany, there was broad consensus about the need to transform criminal justice. Jurists, charitable societies, and public welfare advocates agreed that punishment, to be legitimate, must become more than a reaction by the state to transgressions against the law. The common goal, wrote legal scholar Wolfgang Mittermaier, "was to treat the criminal according to his character [*Eigenart*], beginning with the first investigation of a crime and ending only when the criminal—so far as possible—is placed into ordered society."[1] In this vision, criminal justice was embedded within a broader network of state and private institutions that supported criminal policy. To realize this vision, the police, the courts, and the prisons had to "become social."

Soziale Gerichtshilfe, literally social court assistance, was pivotal to defining a social terrain for criminal justice. Growing out of the Bielefeld System for vagrants and prostitutes, Gerichtshilfe provided welfare advisers to create a "complete portrait" of accused offenders and their milieus. The advisers investigated the individual's work experience and prospects for employment, economic well-being, family life, community, religion, education, heredity, and physical and mental health. This information was then analyzed in the form of a "social diagnosis and prognosis," as well as recommendations on sentencing, pardoning, and protective supervision. In some cases, the Gerichtshilfe investigator was only a mediator between the court, the accused, and various welfare organizations. In other cases, the investigator was also the provider of welfare and the agent of supervision.

Soziale Gerichtshilfe, though initially controversial, spread across Prussia in the early 1920s and saw explosive growth after 1926. By 1929 there were over 300 such institutions in Germany. In Berlin, Gerichtshilfe advisers investigated over 6,000 cases in 1930, in Düsseldorf over 15,000. Gerichtshilfe became an important factor in smaller cities, too, and even in small towns. In Aachen, Gerichtshilfe handled 900 cases in 1930, while in tiny Limburg near Frankfurt (pop. 20,000) there were 300 cases in the same year. Across the ideological spectrum, reformers saw Soziale Gerichtshilfe as the first "creative accomplishment" in the struggle to bring social principles into criminal justice. Embattled government and judicial leaders seized upon Gerichtshilfe as a means to "draw the people closer to the justice system." By creating avenues for popular participation in criminal justice, officials hoped to resolve a seemingly endemic crisis of popular trust in the courts.

Surprisingly, Soziale Gerichtshilfe became established across Germany without the national government stepping in to determine its structure or even its role in criminal procedure. Officials encouraged experimentation, assuming that the legal codes would be rewritten within a few years and settle any outstanding questions. Legal scholar Gustav Radbruch urged lawmakers to let this "wild" plant continue to grow before "making use of the garden shears."[2] Prison associations seized the opportunity to make the institution their own, but faced competition from the growing state welfare offices. After initially resisting Soziale Gerichtshilfe altogether, judges and state's attorneys intervened in hopes of putting the institution under the control of the court. Eventually reformers were forced to choose sides in what became a fierce and wide-ranging argument over the future of the institution.

The stakes in this fight were large. The proponents of public welfare saw Gerichtshilfe as the first step in a series of reforms to transform criminal policy. They envisioned the courtroom of the future as a "working group" in which judges, welfare officials, doctors, and prison warders discussed and decided criminal cases as equals. "The judge," Mittermaier argued, "will climb down from his somewhat elevated seat," while the other participants will "climb up from the position of consultants." Ultimately, criminal justice per se would be integrated into social policy. Gustav Radbruch, a leading legal scholar of his day, argued that a "completely different" kind of judge must emerge, for whom the penal code was no longer a "guide" (Wegweiser), but rather a set of "limits" upon what were essentially social interventions. "The criminal court judge of the future," he wrote, "should see himself less as an executor of the law than as a social administrator."[3]

Welfare's utopia, however, was the judiciary's nightmare. Judges and prosecutors feared that socializing the courts would inevitably trample the essential principles of criminal justice. A key goal for them was therefore to keep Gerichtshilfe tightly under the control of the courts, limiting its role to the provision of raw social and personal data relevant to a given case. Public welfare agencies, in their view, were poised to use Gerichtshilfe as a Trojan horse to infiltrate and co-opt the machinery of justice.[4] Welfare for criminals would then become a right rather than a privilege. The logic of entitlement would undermine any effort to hold offenders responsible for their crimes.

With the onset of the Great Depression, differences over Gerichtshilfe threatened to tear apart the criminal law reform movement. As a participant at the International Penal Union (IKV) meetings in 1929 observed, "Between the judges and the representatives of public welfare there were utterly divergent viewpoints concerning the relationship between welfare and punishment."[5] Private charities tried for a time to stake out a compromise position between these camps, but they grew increasingly distrustful of public welfare interests and increasingly afraid of the consequences of state control of Gerichtshilfe. Appalled by a cultural drift toward empathy with the criminal, they allied themselves with the judiciary, hoping to assert control over the reform movement that they had helped fashion.

Anxieties of Disorder

The birth of Gerichtshilfe came in a context of deepening anxieties about social disorder. Criminologist Hans Hentig, a combat officer and military judge during the war, claimed that former prisoners had systematically deserted the frontlines and rushed back to wreck havoc on the domestic front.[6] Revolutionary crowds in November 1918 stormed a number of prisons and liberated ordinary offenders alongside political prisoners. Critics accused revolutionary governments of indiscriminately giving amnesty to thousands of habitual offenders. In the postwar chaos, fears of crime and political disorder easily became entangled.[7] Criminologists argued that the political upheaval in Germany, like other revolutions, "loosened the bonds of law and morality in all the circles of the people in which the feeling for law is not deeply, internally anchored." Deprived of their customary restraints and freed of inhibitions, it was suggested, a certain sector of the population inevitably turned to crime.[8] Moreover, the defeated country's inability to enforce "rigorous pass-controls" allowed international criminals, "the dregs of humanity," to stream into the country.[9]

Postwar observers were afraid not only that a collapse of authority bred crime, but that criminal elements exercised an unwholesome effect upon politics. According to Hentig's "applied criminal psychology," deviant psychopaths disrupted the political process by encouraging the most violent and irrational tendencies of the crowd.[10] When the Berlin press referred to a plague of "armed criminal bands" in the spring of 1919, it purposefully conflated the depredations of armed political organizations with gangsters engaged in robberies and other ordinary crimes.[11]

Alongside these political concerns, a series of moral panics in postwar Germany linked the discourse of criminal policy with a range of social and cultural anxieties. Historian Richard Bessel notes how Germans after World War I feared the dissolution of the family due to the huge numbers of widows and orphans, rising rates of divorce, and an overall surfeit of single women. Demobilization, furthermore, presaged the sudden release of millions of young men back into German society, many of them scarred or brutalized by the front experience, and a good number still armed.[12]

Prostitution, it was argued, operated upon a different scale than ever before. A common refrain was that the traditional borders of class and respectability had been breached. Increasingly, women from bourgeois households walked the streets, while healthy, attractive men from good families availed themselves of these services.[13] Night clubs, black markets and opium dens, it was alleged, lured decent people who in another era would have stayed far away. Policemen and journalists claimed (self-servingly) that it now took special expertise to distinguish between the gentleman and the swindler, the lady and the whore.[14] An obsession with venereal disease became a flashpoint for fears about the transgression of social boundaries and the spread of stealth infections more generally.[15] War, revolution, and defeat had supposedly destroyed the great walls protecting respectable society.

The Crisis of Trust in Justice
(Vertrauenskrise der Justiz)

While the disorders of the revolutionary period intensified the popular concern with deviance and crime, they did not produce a more favorable view of incarceration. In the spring of 1919, Alfred Bozi noted that popular opinion had only grown more hostile to the prison and the workhouse and more suspicious of the courts. "The judge who insists upon imposing prison sentences for the full range of offenses required by law," he wrote, "increasingly stands against popular opinion."[16] One of the first acts of the revolutionary Prussian state government was to abolish the Rawiczer system of prison discipline. Led by the Independent Socialists, the provisional Ministry of Justice ended corporal punishment, shackling, and the rule of silence. Prisoners were permitted to read newspapers regardless of political content and correspond more freely with the outside world. Prison personnel were called upon to engage in a "just and well-intentioned treatment of prisoners, aimed at their spiritual and moral uplift, so that they reenter life in a purified state."[17] On the national level, reform efforts were more cautious, but showed a similar trend. In 1919, a commission of the National Assembly considered a proposal to introduce conditional sentencing of offenders and allow judges to order protective supervision by prison associations as a substitute for imprisonment. Delegates to the National Assembly fretted about undermining the severity of punishment during a time when "legal norms were so confused, respect for the law was so shaken, and the authority of the legal order was so weakened." The commission argued, however, that conditional sentencing did not diminish the severity of punishment as long as protective supervision was properly implemented. Their goal, they said, was to replace the short prison sentence with a longer and "more effective" measure "of a different kind." As it turned out, the National Assembly was permanently adjourned before the law was enacted.[18]

The most far-reaching criminal justice legislation on the national level was the remarkable Law for the Purging of Criminal Records. This legislation sought to liberate all but the most serious criminal offenders from the burden of lifelong stigma and discrimination. After a period of time (which varied depending upon the offense), the justice authorities were prohibited from providing information about a criminal conviction to any outside agency or individual. After another lapse of time, all records of the conviction were essentially purged. While the act excluded major felons, it had a profound effect upon the status of many ex-offenders and carried enormous symbolic implications. Here the state declared that its interest in the resocialization of former offenders outweighed the right of employers, the public, and even the police to know about an individual's criminal past.[19]

The new government faced an awkward challenge in the widespread perception of the courts as bastions of a reactionary sensibility out of step with the spirit of the times. Critics referred to these popular misgivings about judges and prosecutors as the "crisis of trust in justice."[20] A primary reference point was the alleged bias of judges in a number of high-profile cases of political violence. Radical Socialists had long accused judges of practicing class justice, that is, of favoring bourgeois interests against the working class. In the postwar era, even many liberals and moderate Socialists argued that judges treated right-wing political violence with far greater lenience than political crimes from the left.[21]

Added to the charges of political bias were old and new accusations about the judiciary's insularity and aloofness and its fetish for legal formalism. At all ends of the postwar political spectrum, critics lamented the judiciary's ignorance of real life conditions and its slavish attention to "dry and bloodless legal paragraphs." The origins of this discourse could be traced back to the late Imperial era. Alfred Bozi had long decried specialization in judicial education. Franz von Liszt had demanded that criminal sociology and psychology become part of the basic judicial education. Gustav Aschaffenburg had called upon the judge to "leave the courtroom and the study and go out into life, among the people, so that he may learn to know criminals." During the war, when demands for a social perspective on crime became especially widespread, judges were seen as increasingly out of step. In 1917, Bozi asserted there were good reasons why so many Germans "perceived the law as an alien mechanism of coercion."[22]

Warnings about the crisis in justice reached a crescendo in the early Weimar period. In 1920, Gustav Radbruch warned the Reichstag that "there is deep mistrust, deep exasperation among the people, among the working class, against our justice system."[23] At the 1921 Socialist Party Conference in Görlitz, delegates declared that, "under the protection of judicial independence, a relic of the authoritarian state has been preserved: the courts are a foreign body in the popular social state [*soziale Volksstaat*] of today."[24] Later, in his inaugural address as Reich Minister of Justice, Radbruch referred to a "state of war" between the people and their courts. In 1922, Hugo am Zehnhoff, the Prussian Minister of Justice from the Catholic Center Party, made similar observations, particularly noting the working classes' animosity toward the judiciary.[25]

In time, the very term "crisis of trust" became a key word of German politics and culture. In 1926, the IKV planned to devote its annual meeting to the subject.[26] Literature, film, and theater propagated an image of judges and prosecutors as soulless technicians whose focus on legal norms drained them of all empathy, wisdom, and common sense. The stubborn loyalty to the law that had once made judges into heroes of progressives now made them into objects of ridicule and contempt. "Our judges are utterly and completely incorruptible," Brecht's Herr Peachum declares in the *Three-Penny Opera*. "No amount of money could corrupt them into doing justice."[27]

Restoring Trust: "Make Justice Social"

The solution to the crisis of trust, according to reformers, was to finally "make justice social." This meant both addressing the social origins of crime and creating stronger ties between the criminal justice system and civil society. In spite of their ideological differences with Christian charities, the new leaders looked to the prison societies, the transition stations, and the worker colonies for viable models of justice-welfare collaboration. Even the Socialist Party, which once vilified the worker colonies as "volunteer prisons," now saw such institutions as essential to criminal policy.[28] The governments of Prussia and the Reich supported a "mixed economy of welfare," with private charities of all kinds continuing to receive public financing.[29] Werner Gentz, a Socialist official in Kiel, declared that private prison associations were necessary to "supplement and animate" state welfare. "To bureaucratize charity-work [Liebesarbeit]," wrote Gentz in the journal of the prison societies, "is to remove the love: Welfare without love is control."[30]

Popular participation in justice was a key theme in early Weimar reform initiatives. The Prussian government established citizen advisory boards for the prisons and penitentiaries and promised there would be local citizen oversight of all carceral institutions eventually.[31] Reformers nationwide pressed for the introduction of a jury system on the Anglo-American model and greater use of lay-judges. In its historic Görlitzer Program of 1921, the SPD called for "the decisive engagement of elected people's judges" and the participation of women "in all branches of justice."[32] The so-called "laification" of justice was also supported for a time by the Prussian Judges Association, though it was fiercely resisted by national judicial organizations.[33] Max Alsberg, a celebrated author and defense attorney, argued that "we can no longer do without the lay element in criminal justice." He saw opportunities for a new era of popular participation in justice resulting from the fact that so many otherwise respectable Germans were prosecuted under wartime black market laws. "The sphere of those touched by the punishing power of the state has moved closer to the general consciousness," he wrote.[34] Journalist and activist Hans Hyan argued counterintuitively that increasing public involvement in criminal policy would provide a firmer scientific foundation. Only those who knew and understood the "life experiences" of the people, Hyan wrote, could gather social data from the private sphere and adapt it effectively to criminal justice.[35]

Civic activism was also a big part of the press's answer to the crisis in criminal justice. The liberal Berliner Morgenpost, a large-circulation daily, blamed the chronic state of insecurity in Berlin upon the public's failure to assist the police. "Daily there occur new, impudent robberies on the open street," the paper declared,

in densely populated apartments and even in hotels, while it remains impossible, in general, to catch the criminals and bring them to justice. Every week, at least one murder occurs in Berlin, which in many cases remains unsolved. The reason? No one watches out for others any more. . . . How many murders and felonies before the war were solved due to the watchful eye of the Berliners!

To rectify this situation, the paper announced its own contest, a sort of training exercise in public surveillance. One of the paper's reporters was sent forth to traverse the city on foot, while his photo was posted on advertising pillars across Berlin. The paper promised 2,000 marks to the first Berliner to recognize and "arrest" the man by shouting "eyes open!" (*Augen auf*).[36]

The populist direction in criminal policy reform was systematized in the 1922 draft for a German Penal Code written under the direction of Minister Radbruch. This draft went beyond previous proposals in its emphasis upon measures to reintegrate offenders into society. It greatly reduced the number of crimes requiring imprisonment, while also giving judges the long-sought power of conditional sentencing. Moreover, Radbruch's code abolished the death penalty and almost all the traditional sanctions associated with "civil death." The guiding principle was to restore the offender's sense of honor and dignity as quickly as possible and to lay the groundwork for his eventual return to family, community, and nation.[37]

The failure of the 1922 draft penal code—it died in a Reichstag committee—underscored the challenges of change from above during the Weimar era. With its unstable cabinets and dysfunctional parliaments, the Reich government was unlikely to provide sustained leadership in criminal reform. Gustav Radbruch, by far the most reform-minded Justice Minister in the Weimar Republic, fought long and hard to get women admitted to the judiciary—against the opposition of all the major judges' associations. Alfred Bozi initially invested hope in the numerous National Assembly and Prussian Landtag members from the SPD whom he knew from the Society for Social Law and especially from his wartime reform work. Max Quarck was supposed to be "his man" in Berlin. By the spring of 1920, however, Bozi despaired over the "complete failure" of parliamentary initiatives and had turned his attention back to the kind of local institution building that he called "small works."[38]

"Small works" indeed became the true engine of Weimar criminal policy reform. Local initiatives spawned institutional models that were eventually promoted through ministerial interventions, utterly bypassing parliamentary authority. This was both the strength and the weakness of Weimar reform. On the one hand, reformers accelerated the modernist reform currents of Wilhelmine and wartime Germany. In spite of its political, economic, and social crisis, Germany entered an era of unparalleled innovation in criminal policy. On the other hand, the lack of clear guidance from the state and the failure to articulate principles and standards for these new practices furthered the growth of separate ideological camps within the reform movement.

The Bielefeld System Postwar:
Practical Reform in Chaotic Times

Judge Alfred Bozi had strong misgivings about the revolution that deposed the Kaiser and destroyed the Imperial system. He nevertheless saw an opportunity in the upheaval of 1918–19 to realize dreams of a new Germany. "Anyone who had suffered as I did under the suffocating air of the juridical," he wrote the newly appointed minister, Wolfgang Heine, in December 1918, "finds the new spirit that wafts from the Justice Ministry to be a special relief."[39] Bozi knew Heine and other Socialists from their work with the Society for Social Law and felt that they shared many of his reform goals. Ironically, when it came to addressing systemic flaws in criminal justice, the new left-wing government turned out to be far too cautious in Bozi's estimation. The government asked its followers to wait until order in the country was reestablished. Bozi, by contrast, argued that institutional transformations were, in themselves, part of the very process of establishing social peace and political legitimacy.[40] Even in January 1919, in the days between the Sparticist Uprising and the elections to the National Assembly, Bozi rejected any postponement of reform measures. "We should use the crisis conditions to achieve change," he told Pastor Hage, the head of the Saxony-Anhalt Prison Society.[41]

Change for Bozi meant creating roles for private individuals and associations in all areas of criminal justice. Having established the Bielefeld System for vagabonds and prostitutes, the judge's next goal was to make welfare investigations and protective supervision possible in all criminal cases, regardless of the offense. This was necessary, he believed, in order to rationalize the granting of pardons and findings of extenuating circumstances. As discussed above, wartime circumstances caused a radical increase in administrative pardons for convicted felons. By the middle of the war, it was also clear that judges were stretching the definition of extenuating circumstances in order to send offenders to prison rather than the penitentiary and ensure their fitness to serve in the German military. Critics charged that such measures were arbitrary and unfair, as well as dangerous. They claimed that hardened criminals were let loose on society, while economically desperate men, women, and children were locked up for offenses that had not even been crimes before 1914.[42] Bozi thought that the Bielefeld System would make pardons legitimate and safe by allowing rational and scientific judgments to be made about each offender's guilt, moral worthiness, and ability to integrate into society.

As a judge, Bozi found the process of administrative pardons to be especially intolerable. It was a "horribly ceremonious and complicated proceeding," he told the liberal deputy and future Reich Justice Minister Eugen Schiffer in 1918.[43] Pardons were frequently "political," in as much as government administrators brought external considerations to bear on the process, and they were laden with the symbolic baggage of a sovereign power granting its beneficence to an obedient citizenry. Give this power to judges, he argued, since they were more independent, more focused on the rule of law, and better placed, under the proper circumstances, to distinguish between habitual criminals and those who could still be made into valuable and productive members of society.

In the last year and a half of the war, Reichstag deputies affiliated with Bozi's Society for Social Law played a leading role in reviving the idea of conditional sentencing.[44] Their most important success was the passage of the Lex Schiffer, an emergency measure giving judges the power to substitute fines for prison sentences in cases of "wartime offenses." Under this law, judges were supposed to consider whether incarceration was warranted, fair, and wise.[45] Technically, the law's application was restricted to offenses prosecuted under the "extraordinary" laws and regulations of wartime and not under the Imperial Penal Code. In practice, the Lex Schiffer could be applied to almost every kind of criminal and every kind of crime, from stealing food to forging documents to assaulting a state agent, and it continued to be in effect even after the war ended.

The unprecedented latitude and flexibility in sentencing afforded by the Lex Schiffer opened a door to new roles for welfare in ordinary criminal cases. Bozi put forward the Bielefeld model as a means for judges to gain insight about the criminal and the options for protective supervision. He foresaw that once the Lex Schiffer was widely used, pressure would build to have some form of supervision for the growing percentage of offenders who would be freed by the courts.[46] Of course prison associations already assumed protective supervision over vagabonds and prostitutes conditionally released from the workhouse under the terms of the Bielefeld System. For years now, a number of associations also supervised former penitentiary inmates whose conditional release from police supervision was contingent upon their "voluntary" acceptance of welfare oversight. The prison associations relished an opportunity to gain greater leverage over their clients. The director of the Saxony-Anhalt Prison Society, Pastor Hage, wrote that conditional sentencing by the courts would allow the transition stations in particular to exercise greater "psychological pressure" upon their residents.[47]

Heinrich Seyfarth, the director of the Deutsche Hilfsverein in Hamburg, told Bozi that the "only difficulty" he faced in his work was that most released prisoners "could not be forced" to make use of his institutions.[48]

Bozi wanted the prison associations to play a central part in the new arrangements, but he was also concerned that workers and women should serve as advisers to the courts. The prison associations were still predominantly male and had little or no working-class representation.[49] Bozi was proud of having arranged for the Socialist leader Carl Severing to serve as a lay-judge in Bielefeld. In 1918, he consulted with Severing and other Socialists to determine how best to recruit workers for these tasks. In the case of women's participation in justice, the challenge was to overcome centuries of prejudice and exclusion. "My judicial practice," Bozi wrote Wolfgang Mittermaier, "has brought me to the conviction that a stronger recruitment of women to work at the court is urgently necessary."[50] Privately, Bozi even expressed support for women's entry into the judiciary—a view that took him well out of the mainstream of Prussian judges.

The women's committee of the Society for Social Law (GSR) became an important vehicle for experiments in justice and welfare in Bielefeld. The committee recruited women volunteers and professional welfare workers to investigate the domestic circumstances of male offenders, evaluate the testimony of women witnesses, victims, and defendants, and assess the impact of punishment upon the lives of prisoners and their families. The committee sought to institutionalize this practice in 1919 by getting the city to establish communal welfare councils in each judicial district. The councils served as liaisons between the judges and various public and private health and welfare organizations. As judges tried to meet the requirements of the Lex Schiffer, they now turned to the councils for assistance. To help women volunteers understand the legal issues at stake, the GSR established the first legal training course for women at the adult education school (*Volkshochschule*) in Bielefeld. The instructors were Bozi and the female police assistant, Clara Hermelbrecht.[51]

The communal welfare councils worked well until political disagreements in Bielefeld and in the GSR undermined the local consensus. The GSR's committee on women fell apart when conservative members objected to the feminists' support for women's entry into the judiciary.[52] Bozi himself became entangled in a nasty dispute with local Socialists, who, after appointing him to the school board, demanded he support a Socialist candidate for headmaster. By the spring of 1920, strained relations between municipal officials and local charities made it impossible for the communal welfare councils to function as intended. Working with the Prison Society of Pomerania, Bozi developed a new model for welfare intervention at the courts that he hoped would circumvent such political tensions. In place of the publicly funded communal welfare councils, he created an independent agency called "Soziale Gerichtshilfe" that was funded directly by the GSR. Gerichtshilfe eventually employed two full-time officials who were supposed to be politically neutral, knowledgeable in legal affairs, and familiar with organizations and individuals in Bielefeld involved with the care and supervision of criminally at-risk persons. The first Gerichtshilfe employee was Fräulein Hermelbrecht, the former police assistant employed by the German Evangelical Women's Association.[53]

The Gerichtshilfe agency decided when the social investigation of a criminal defendant was warranted and then assigned the task to an adviser or "court helper" (Gerichtshelfer). A central assumption was that the welfare advisers should, as much as possible, come from the same community as their clients. Catholic defendants were referred to the local priest involved with the Bielefeld prison association, while Protestant defendants were handled by Protestant volunteers. Anyone who expressed a preference for public, nonsectarian assistance would be handled by the city welfare office, in consultation with Hermelbrecht.[54]

Typically, Bielefeld Gerichtshilfe entered the case after the prosecutor made a formal accusation. The advisers read the police report, interviewed the accused, and gathered information in the community. They then filled out a questionnaire on the accused and wrote a narrative report. As one advocate of Gerichtshilfe described it, the report could "start with neighbors and grandparents and end with the condition of his underwear." Its aim was to "allow the judge to see into the essence of the accused": not the immediate, ephemeral cause of the crime (*die Ursache*), but the deeper and more rooted elements of causality (*die Gründe*).[55] The report was delivered to the presiding judge prior to the "intermediate proceeding," where it was decided whether to accept the prosecutor's charge and proceed to trial. Thus a report that portrayed the accused in a sympathetic light could persuade the judge to dismiss the case entirely or recommend a lesser charge. Damning evidence, of course, might have just the opposite effect.

If the case went to trial, then the Gerichtshilfe report helped the Bielefeld judges decide which witnesses to call and what questions to pose. In some cases, the report also allowed a judge to check on the veracity of testimony. The report's most important function, though, was in regard to sentencing and pardoning. In addition to the presiding judge, the adviser submitted the report to the district court judge serving as state commissary for pardons

(*Gnadenbeauftragte*), a post created in 1919 to make the granting of pardons more fair and efficient. The report was also made available to the prosecutor, but not to the defendant or the defense attorney. The reformers did not want the reports to be subject to legal challenges or counter testimony. They believed that welfare could and should provide the courts and pardon officials with an objective picture of social reality.[56]

The Impulse from Above:
Justice in the New Republic

The Bielefeld experiment spread through local initiatives, initially without any help from the state. Prison associations in Saxony-Anhalt, Pomerania, and the Rhineland and Westphalia, where Bozi had contacts, created their own versions of Gerichtshilfe. The first major external boost came with a series of ministerial decrees by the Prussian government. A new Prussian Minister of Justice was appointed in 1920. Hugo am Zehnhoff was a lawyer from the Catholic Center Party, with close ties to Catholic social reformers in the Rhineland. He was considered conservative but also, as one subordinate described him, "especially pardon-happy." He focused the ministry's attention on integrating the pardon-process into judicial practice and giving it a strong social component.[57] To help shape the new policy, he turned to two energetic young followers of Franz von Liszt, Fritz Hartung and Albert Hellwig. Both were former judges from the famously progressive city of Frankfurt who had become assistants in the ministry. Hellwig was a longtime acquaintance of Judge Bozi, having been affiliated with his early reform project, the *Verein Recht und Wirtschaft*. Like Bozi, he was a strong proponent of broader training for judges.[58]

The decrees followed the basic outlines of the Lex Schiffer (which had applied only to wartime offenses) and the proposed National Assembly law on conditional sentencing. They gave judges the authority to suspend prison sentences when offenders promised to place themselves under the protective supervision of a welfare organization. The period of protective supervision was expected to last three years—regardless of the length of the original sentence. The decrees ordered judges to base their decisions on an assessment of the "circumstances of the act." Protective supervision was out of the question if the crime was "the result of depravity or a criminal inclination." The origins of the crime had to be in "recklessness, inexperience, seduction, or need." The judge must also ask: whether the offender was penitent and sought to make restitution, had served honorably in the military, and had a criminal record. No offender was to be given the option of protective supervision unless there were good reasons to expect that he or she would make "an actual demonstration of overall satisfactory behavior" during these three years. Only if the offender showed full compliance with the demands of the welfare agency could the judges then arrange for a full pardon.[59]

The linchpin of this new policy was Soziale Gerichtshilfe. Minister am Zehnhoff promised financial support to prison associations engaging in Gerichtshilfe and asked Bozi to write guidelines for judges and local officials, as well as charities. In announcing the initiative, Am Zehnhoff described Gerichtshilfe as an antidote to the crisis of trust in justice. He noted the "conviction among wide sectors of the working class that the judiciary cannot properly judge their circumstances and their struggles, because they are cut off from the people and therefore do not possess sufficient knowledge of their life conditions." While the minister defended the courts' efforts, he declared it "vitally necessary that we prove the state is doing everything in its power to provide for the insight of judges into all social conditions."[60] Gerichtshilfe was to be the bridge between the courts and civil society.

The theme of Gerichtshilfe as an antidote to the crisis of trust was picked up by other advocates for the institution—on the left and the right. Theodor Noetzel was a prominent state's attorney in Kassel who was involved with the conservative Prussian judges association and with Heinrich Seyfarth's national umbrella group for the prison societies. Noetzel told the leaders of the prison societies that the people's trust in criminal justice was "deeply shaken." They demanded institutions of justice, he declared, that were truly modern, appropriate to the times. Gerichtshilfe, he argued, was essential to restoring the reputation of criminal justice. Echoing Bozi, he envisioned the "work of Gerichtshilfe expanding into a great moral movement . . . for the education and improvement of criminals, the reduction of crime, the transcendence of class conflict, and thereby to the unity and reawakening of the people!" If there was something strange or incongruous about a conservative prosecutor waxing poetic about a legal utopia, no one bothered to comment on it.[61]

The Many Faces of Gerichtshilfe: 1922–1926

Minister am Zehnhoff hoped that Gerichtshilfe would reinvigorate the prison societies, which were struggling in the crisis conditions of the early Weimar Republic. The rising rate of inflation put enormous pressure on associations that relied upon income from endowments or gifts from wealthy donors. The growing levels of economic desperation among ex-offenders also added to their burden. In 1922, the prison association in Halle was saved from collapse only by a large donation from the United States and an influx of new dues-paying members from the local unions.[62] In the same year, the venerable Berlin Association complained it could not afford to replace the "bad, unkempt clothing" of homeless ex-offenders so that they could be admitted to the worker colonies. After warning the government repeatedly of its difficulties, the nearly one-hundred-year-old prison society was officially disbanded during the hyperinflation of 1922–23. A number of smaller associations also collapsed.[63]

Even as they faced these unprecedented financial challenges, the prison associations were struggling, like other private charities, to define their place in the new German social state. Increasingly, the societies complained, the families of prisoners and newly released offenders believed they were entitled to social assistance. The Berlin Society's last annual report grumbled that the families of offenders "think we have a duty to provide them with care-free lives."[64] Clergymen and volunteer advisers in cities and towns complained about the new "audacity" and "cheekiness" of their clients. Even as the prison associations were more important than ever from the perspective of re-formers and government officials, their moral authority among the populations they served had apparently been shaken.[65]

In spite of these challenges, most of the eighty Gerichtshilfe agencies founded before 1926 were administered directly by prison associations. The first and most successful of these agencies was in Halle, the home of the prestigious Prison Society for the Prussian Provinces of Saxony and Anhalt and a city known for its innovations in welfare for released prisoners. The director of the Halle association, Pastor Hermann Hage, was a close associate of Bozi. Just as the original Bielefeld System had made special use of Bethel, Hage expected Halle's impressive complex of welfare institutions to provide special options for protective supervision. These included separate transition stations for educated and working-class offenders, asylums for sexually en-dangered women, and two worker colonies in reasonable proximity to the city.[66] The Halle Prison Association pioneered what was called "continu-ous welfare," whereby the same adviser prepared the social diagnosis for Gerichtshilfe, assisted the offender and the offender's family through the period of incarceration, and directed the process of protective supervision upon the offender's release.[67] Gerichtshilfe in Halle thus became the gateway to a whole variety of welfare benefits. If the offender needed employment training, clothing, housing, or direct monetary support, the Gerichtshilfe adviser was expected to make these decisions and arrange for such assistance. Gerichtshilfe in Halle pursued "every means of binding the individual to his environment [*Umweltverknüpfungen verschiedenster Art*]."[68]

Gerichtshilfe could not succeed anywhere without the cooperation of the judiciary. In this respect, the Halle reformers were far more successful at first than the many reformers elsewhere who imitated their model between 1922 and 1926. Halle's judges allowed the Gerichtshilfe advisers to decide when to enter a case, shared court documents, and frequently relied on the advisers' reports in sentencing. In other cities and towns, by contrast, judges often questioned whether welfare had any role to play regarding adult offenders and resented the idea of the prison associations meddling in their affairs. Numerous judges insisted that they had their own contacts in the welfare and medical community whom they called upon as necessary. Judges, moreover, frequently complained that the advisers' reports were too emotional and showed too much sympathy for the accused. They also accused the advisers of playing detective, of investigating the act itself—and arguing about juridical issues—rather than pursuing a truly social investigation. The advisers, not surprisingly, complained of judges and prosecutors ignoring their reports.[69]

Relations between the judges and the welfare advisers were even worse in cities where Gerichtshilfe was administered by the public welfare offices. Often, as in Berlin, cities took over Gerichtshilfe when the local prison association was in crisis. Inevitably, the city officials brought a strong and unapologetically "welfarist" perspective into their work. In Berlin, the founders of Gerichtshilfe came mostly out of the juvenile justice movement. The first director of Berlin Gerichtshilfe, Else von Liszt (daughter of Franz), also directed city welfare for youth offenders. The first Gerichtshilfe advisers were female police assistants who otherwise worked with delinquent boys and sexually endangered girls.[70] Not surprisingly, Berlin Gerichtshilfe tended to define itself through a pedagogical and therapeutic ethos. One Berlin reformer declared they must make the judge into a "people's educator." Another reformer stated that the challenge of adult supervision was essentially the same as in youth supervision, except that juvenile institutions transformed the offender's underlying character (*Bildung*), while adult institutions focused upon adjusting the individual's behavior to real-life conditions.[71]

The aggressive posture of the city welfare offices frequently made judges and prosecutors uneasy, particularly when city governments were controlled by the Social Democrats. Even after two years of Gerichtshilfe in Berlin, judges only made use of the institution in 119 cases. In Düsseldorf, Gerichtshilfe took on a disappointing 143 cases in 1925. Even many judges who embraced the juvenile justice movement doubted whether its principles had any place in the world of adult criminal justice. They feared that city welfare's discourse of social entitlement would infect the judicial process, undermining the court's ability to hold individuals responsible for their crimes. Moreover, judges feared that city officials would "politicize" the pardon process, bringing government pressure to bear on judges when Gerichtshilfe felt that a pardon was justified.[72]

In the early Weimar Republic, it was an open question whether Soziale Gerichtshilfe would gain a solid footing in German criminal justice. Judges were clearly more open to the Halle model than the Berlin model, particularly if the prison association, as in Halle, was old and respected, had strong ties with the judiciary, and was richly supplied with numerous "safe" options for protective supervision. What judges most preferred was the Bielefeld model, where Gerichtshilfe was run by an independent agency that simply mediated between the court and the welfare organization, rather than performing welfare itself. In Kassel, state's attorney Theodor Noetzel assumed responsibility for Gerichtshilfe, choosing his own pool of welfare advisers and carefully setting the terms under which Gerichtshilfe would operate. Though significantly smaller than Düsseldorf, let alone Berlin, Kassel Gerichtshilfe had almost five times the number of cases in 1925. Few cities, however, followed the Bielefeld or Kassel models initially, and, true to his own principles of organic reform, Bozi refused to take a stand on how Gerichtshilfe should be structured. Instead, he advised the ministry that Gerichtshilfe should be "adapted to the conditions of local welfare organizations."[73]

Gerichtshilfe proponents tried to win over the judiciary by stressing its fealty to the established goals of welfare for offenders, especially to putting criminals to work. In Bielefeld, the founding principles of the Association for Gerichtshilfe described the recidivist offender as "an economic burden."[74] In a mailing to Prussian judges, Bozi summarized Gerichtshilfe's purpose as finding and preserving the offenders' "productive capacities."[75] The Prussian Minister of Welfare similarly declared that the aim of Gerichtshilfe was to get criminals, as quickly as possible, back into the workforce.[76] Reformers depicted Gerichtshilfe as part of a swelling tide of social reform that arrived at long last upon the courthouse steps. Judges were now forced to decide whether to barricade themselves inside, throw open the doors to whatever may come, or try to channel this movement into a direction they found acceptable.

Breakthrough: 1926 and After

In 1926 the Prussian Ministry of Justice finally forced the issue. A decree that year ordered judges and prosecutors to examine the relationship of each criminal act to the "personality of the offender." The courts must ask whether the crime was caused by an "abject sensibility [*ver-werflichen Gesinnung*] or inclination of the will" or whether it "rested upon causes which cannot be blamed upon the offender." The proclamation required that judges collect information on the defendant's early life, as well as the personal and economic relations at the time of the act; the impact of mental disease or disturbance; the motive, incentive, and purpose of the act; the level of remorse; the offender's present condition; and the likely impact of punishment upon the offender and any family relations.[77] This information, as much as possible, was to be factored into the sentence. Suddenly Gerichtshilfe was no longer an option but a requirement of the criminal justice process.

The ministerial decree was a breakthrough for Gerichtshilfe. The number of agencies subsequently rose every year, even during the depression, until the Nazi seizure of power. By 1930, there were over 300 Gerichtshilfe agencies across Germany. The new spirit of cooperation from judges and prosecutors could be seen in the rising caseloads. In 1930 Berlin Gerichtshilfe investigated more than 6,000 criminal cases. Hamburg, Cologne, and Frankfurt all saw increases of at least 15 percent per year in the volume of cases between 1927 and 1930. In many cities, the increase in Gerichtshilfe activity accompanied steady growth in the rate of conditional pardons and the ordering of protective supervision. In the relatively small city of Halle, Gerichtshilfe handled 500 protective supervision cases in 1928. In Düsseldorf, Gerichtshilfe processed 3,900 applications for conditional furloughs from prison.[78]

The success of Gerichtshilfe, as expected, brought new faces into the courts. In the district of Neuruppin in the province of Brandenburg, the woman social worker in charge of Gerichtshilfe recruited 178 advisers for 13 relatively small judicial districts, serving 355 towns and villages. Women and men of all social classes were targeted through a "comprehensive propaganda effort" using local papers and organizations.[79] When the chief state's attorney in Potsdam wrote draft regulations that prohibited women welfare advisers from working with male offenders, he was immediately reprimanded by the exasperated chief judge, Albert Hellwig. The prosecutor believed he must protect the "dignity" of the male offender, but Hellwig pointed out it was already the norm across Germany for women to be engaged as social workers for male and female offenders. In any case, he argued, women were generally more qualified than men for this kind of work.[80]

Why were judges suddenly so accommodating of an institution they had previously resisted? Obedience to the Ministry of Justice was only part of the explanation. Judges also took an increasingly active interest in determining the structure and practice of Gerichtshilfe agencies both locally and nationwide. The "spirit of the times," in Aschaffenburg's words, was affecting them profoundly. This spirit emphasized the importance of welfare over punishment. In 1927, the conservative Reich Minister of Justice, Oskar Hergt, called welfare for released prisoners "the most successful tool in the battle against criminality" and "the most important problem" in criminal policy.[81] Judges had good reason to fear that if they remained aloof from Gerichtshilfe, the institution would simply evolve without them—probably under the control of state welfare offices. Already, it was alleged, state and provincial governments were pressuring judges to use protective supervision more, to reduce prison sentences, and rely more upon fines. Bozi had once asserted that judges would only embrace reform when they faced the possibility of losing their traditional areas of authority. After 1926, when the very power to sentence seemed to be slipping away, Bozi's words seemed prophetic.[82]

Judges and prosecutors after 1926 were far more forgiving of the quality of Gerichtshilfe reports, particularly those that came via the prison associations. In Neuruppin and Potsdam they praised the advisers for uncovering important information and providing this to the courts in a clear and objective fashion. In Düsseldorf, a concerted campaign by the head of the appeals court and by the Rhenish-Westphalian Prison Society clearly made an impression on judges and prosecutors. The growing corps of experienced volunteer advisers convinced the courts that they could provide "thoroughly useful" and "objective" information. The growing reliance on printed forms for the advisers' reports also improved judges' and prosecutors' perceptions of the institution. The forms, which in some places were three or four pages long, included numerous multiple choice questions on the offender's family, work life, health, and lineage (*Abstammung*). They forced the advisers to choose particular categories—such as "criminal urges, depravity, recklessness, weakness of character, seduction"—and to pay attention to specific judicial concerns.[83]

The Question of Procedure

With the establishment of Soziale Gerichtshilfe in towns and cities across Prussia, new questions arose about precisely how the Gerichtshilfe reports would play a role in the criminal process. Seemingly technical issues of criminal procedure implicated a host of symbolic concerns about rights and authority within the courtroom and within criminal policy more broadly. The fight over criminal procedure exacerbated growing tensions between proponents of the three different models of Gerichtshilfe.

According to the Code of German Criminal Procedure, all evidence used in court decisions had to be publicly and orally presented at the main trial. This "principle of immediacy" was established in the great period of liberal reforms around German unification. Its purpose was to stop the use of secret dossiers, which had been standard practice under the old inquisitorial system. Prior to the 1860s, an investigating magistrate assembled the facts of a case by interrogating the defendant and witnesses in a "pre-trial investigation." The resulting dossier determined the structure and focus of the trial and heavily influenced the judges' verdict. Nevertheless, the defense had no right to see the dossier and thus little opportunity to challenge its content. The 1871 Code of Criminal Procedure reduced the importance of the pre-trial investigation and elevated the trial itself into the central moment in the criminal process. Henceforth defendants had a right to confront all the evidence against them, and the public had a right to see the engines of justice at work. In fact, the public aspect of criminal justice was so important to the reformers of 1871 that they made it a requirement for all cases to go to trial— even when the offender had already confessed. Plea-bargaining in Germany was (and is still today) an impossibility.

How were Gerichtshilfe reports to be made part of the trial? Under the Berlin model, the court advisers often read their reports aloud and thus into the court record. The adviser thus effectively served as a kind of expert witness, subject to questioning by the defense and the prosecution, as well as by the judges. This solution was adamantly opposed, however, by the charitable associations and by many judges and prosecutors. The charitable associations feared that integrating Gerichtshilfe into the adversarial process destroyed the "relationship of trust" between the court advisers and their clients. Judges and prosecutors objected to giving welfare agents an independent platform to influence the proceedings. Both groups believed that Gerichtshilfe's reports must be filtered by the legal authorities before they could be allowed as evidence.[84]

Under the Bielefeld and Halle models, the court advisers typically sent their reports to the judges and prosecutors and not to the defense. When defense lawyers insisted they were legally entitled to see all official court documents, judges simply responded that the reports were not in fact "official documents." Bozi advised presiding judges to use the reports as background reading for the interrogation of defendants at the pre-trial proceedings.[85] If the defendant's responses confirmed the content of the report, then his or her testimony at the main trial would presumably suffice as evidence. If the defendant contradicted the report, then the judge would have to call other witnesses to corroborate (or refute) the report's assertions. In a variation on the Bielefeld model, Gerichtshilfe in Kassel was placed entirely under the leadership of the head prosecutor, Theodor Noetzel. Noetzel recruited and trained a corps of advisers, made up mostly of volunteers. He personally oversaw the advisers' investigations and then made their reports part of the prosecutors' files (*Handakten*). Noetzel decided what aspects of the report were relevant to the cases and how this evidence would be introduced at trial. Like Bozi, Noetzel believed it violated the essential purpose of Gerichtshilfe for the advisers to be called as witnesses, and that this should be avoided.

The issue of trust—a key word in the debate over the legitimacy of justice— was the preeminent concern of the charitable associations. The prison societies argued that Gerichtshilfe achieved its potential only when the advisers maintained a strong personal relationship with the offenders and their families. "Trust" was the principal reason that welfare rather than police must play the role of investigating the social sphere. "Trust" was a main argument for the superiority of private welfare over public. If the advisers were dragged into the adversarial process, the charities claimed, their special relationship with their clients would be destroyed. Defendants would look to Gerichtshilfe to help them avoid their due punishment, and they would blame the advisers when a negative report contributed to a harsher sentence. In a survey conducted by the Evangelical Conference on Criminal Justice, sixty of seventy Gerichtshilfe agencies insisted that the defense should *not* have access to the advisers' reports. In Halle and Stettin, Gerichtshilfe advisers complained of being frequently called as witnesses by the defense and having to insist on their right of refusal. Stories poured in about advisers who were harassed, threatened, or sued by the families of offenders. A pastor in Rinteln described being confronted by the mother of one defendant. The woman cursed him as "black police" (a reference to the Pastor's frock) and rallied "radical political elements" in the town against him.[86]

The prison societies feared that good volunteers would quit if they risked facing such retaliation. As one jurist wrote, volunteers were inherently more vulnerable than professionals, since they did not have the protection of a government office or an official title. Volunteers invested time and energy into Gerichtshilfe because they saw it as "*Liebestätigkeit*," the labor of love. Even as they embraced the rhetoric of modern criminology, they adhered to the traditional sense of welfare as a moral enterprise to supplement justice with mercy.[87] Many of the charitable organizations even argued that court advisers should be granted a legal right to refuse being called as witnesses. It made no sense to them that the advisers could ever be forced into an openly partisan role.[88]

While judges, prosecutors, and charitable associations supported judicial control of Gerichtshilfe, others—including many scholars, trial attorneys, and public welfare officials—gravitated toward alternatives. Few of Liszt's students in the criminal law reform movement could have disagreed that the special relationship between welfare adviser and offender should be protected. On the other hand, many reformers feared that the rights of defendants would be compromised if Gerichtshilfe became an investigative arm of the court that was insulated from public scrutiny and challenges by the defense. For Gustav Radbruch, Gerichtshilfe exposed the underlying tension within the modern reform movement between liberal concerns with individual rights, fairness, and openness and social aspirations for a therapeutic system in which criminals were diagnosed and treated according to scientific criteria. Like most of Liszt's students, Radbruch had a liberal perspective on criminal procedure. As Minister of Justice, Radbruch generally supported adversarial principles, including the introduction of cross-examination. Nevertheless, Radbruch believed that the adversarial system was only suitable for creating a "clear picture" of the criminal act. "The picture of a personality," he declared, "cannot be constituted through the opposition of contesting parties. This work must lie in one hand." Radbruch called Gerichtshilfe a "neo-inquisitorial organ," because it reintroduced the idea of a neutral, objective authority—the welfare adviser—to create a "complete portrait" of the accused during the pre-trial investigation. The dilemma for modern reformers, Radbruch argued, was to carve out a space for Gerichtshilfe to work, without destroying the progress made in fifty years of liberal procedural reform.[89]

The trial lawyers were more emphatic. Across Germany, lawyers' associations overwhelmingly supported the right of the defense to access Gerichtshilfe reports. Writing on behalf of the Berlin Bar Association, Max Alsberg insisted that judges and prosecutors were violating the principles of fairness and openness at the heart of the Code of Criminal Procedure. If allowing defendants to scrutinize the reports made volunteer advisers uncomfortable, then so be it. According to Alsberg, the charitable associations frequently sought to place themselves between the clients and their lawyers: telling the defendants that lawyers were now "superfluous" and promising the defendants they would receive better treatment if they abandoned their adversarial approach. For the lawyers, the issue of procedural integrity intersected with the issue of professionalism. Perhaps, they argued, it was time for state-trained and state-administered welfare officials to exercise a steadying influence upon this new institution.[90]

Welfare Visions

After 1926, many Prussian state officials pressed openly for the "Berlin model" of Soziale Gerichtshilfe. Many chief justices for judicial districts, who were usually Socialist appointees, called upon their lower court judges to use the public welfare offices for both Gerichtshilfe and protective supervision. Officials argued that welfare for criminals had become too important to leave to the private associations. The security of the public and the rights and well-being of former offenders were at stake.[91] They pointed to the so-called "Frankfurt numbers," which showed that 65 percent of Gerichtshilfe clients in Frankfurt were previously wards of the public welfare office. If continuous welfare was a worthy goal—and that was something the prison societies and the public welfare advocates had once agreed on—then it seemed that the state was best positioned to mediate among the various sites of supervision in Weimar society.[92]

The advocates of public welfare were also eager to secure Gerichtshilfe's autonomy from the judges and prosecutors. They noted that the prison associations were frequently led by local judicial officials and wealthy members of the community. As a result, the members of these associations were easily bullied or manipulated by the bench. The scope and scale of Gerichtshilfe's activity was circumscribed by judicial and prosecutorial interest. Welfare concerns were subordinated to the juridical.

By 1926, welfare officials had grown frustrated with the persistence of an "artificial" separation between justice and welfare. In their view, criminal policy and social policy were a unified whole and should function with a more or less unified apparatus. "The criminal act is not a social phenomenon sui generis," wrote Werner Gentz,

> but rather only a special case of asocial behavior more generally. . . . One cannot pull the individual who has manifested this onto two different tracks: to attack the social distress by means of welfare . . . and the criminal act by means that are utterly indifferent to these matters. The conceptual distinction between these modes of procedure must not be allowed to grow into a discrepancy between the measures. *It concerns one and the same individual "person."* He is not separable into an object of criminal justice and one of welfare.[93]

For the "object" of criminal justice and welfare to be the same, judges would have to sacrifice once and for all their understanding of the offender as a free and rational individual. In the criminal policy of the future, Gustav Radbruch wrote, welfare and justice would be concerned with the individual "embedded in society, with all his intellectual and social constraints, with his total class-determined character."[94]

The implication was that welfare advisers would have a far more central role at the courts than judges had so far been willing to grant them. Reformers described the court of the future as a "working group" (*Arbeitsgemeinschaft*) in which judges and welfare officials enjoyed equal representation. According to Hans Muthesius, judges had to overcome their stereotype of welfare as weak and submissive caregivers, "blinded by tears of compassion." Welfare and justice, Muthesius insisted, used the same principles of fact-finding and were equally objective. Professional welfare advisers, no less than the judges, defended public security, upheld the authority of the state, and fairly and equitably resolved conflicts. Otto Krebs suggested that the name "*Gerichtshilfe*" (court assistance) be changed to "*Rechtshilfe*" (legal aid) in order to dispel the impression that the institution existed merely to assist judges and prosecutors: the new institution served a higher principle and a greater good.[95]

In the late 1920s, support for making Gerichtshilfe into a public welfare institution grew more vocal. A majority of local Prussian officials surveyed in 1927 were doubtful whether Gerichtshilfe could continue to rely on private volunteers. Now it was public officials who criticized the charities for their emotionalism, as well as their unprofessional demeanor. A recurring accusation was that welfare advisers from religious organizations used Gerichtshilfe to impose their morals upon offenders and even to proselytize. The advisers allegedly forced clients to confess their guilt and demonstrate repentance before they would be helped. Members of the Social Democratic Jurists Association argued that private Gerichtshilfe, for that reason, corrupted the adversarial process. In some cities, local officials undermined the ability of charities to practice Gerichtshilfe by forbidding the police from reporting the religious identity of detainees.[96]

A wave of professional meetings from 1928 to 1930 placed Soziale Gerichtshilfe at the center of their agendas. The question of where Gerichtshilfe should reside could have served as a litmus test for political affiliation. Organizations dominated by the left—the Congress of German Municipalities, Workers' Welfare, the Conference of Social Democratic Jurists, and the Association of German Juvenile Courts—passed resolutions calling for public welfare control. They were opposed by organizations with a politically conservative bent: the Prussian Judges Association, the National Association of Gerichtshilfe, Prison Welfare, and Welfare for Released Offenders, the Inner

Mission, and Caritas. In a short period of time, a movement whose origins were in the "anti-politics" of wartime and in the postwar populist consensus to "make justice social" had become the clearest illustration for the polarization of Weimar society.

A Crisis of Power?
The Discourse of Verweichlichung

Even as state welfare proponents became increasingly passionate about their vision for Soziale Gerichtshilfe, Prussian judges engaged in an unprecedented mobilization to demand that Gerichtshilfe be subordinated to the courts. For the judges, putting Gerichtshilfe under public welfare would lead to the ultimate softening or weakening—*die Verweichlichung*—of justice. The concept of *Verweichlichung* referred to both a decline in the severity of punishment and in the authority of the judiciary. Criminals received progressively lighter sentences, judges argued, even as incarceration became milder, and administrative release from prison became more widespread. The judges blamed this decline of punishment on the penetration of alien ideas into the once self-contained world of criminal justice. Principles of retribution and deterrence, they claimed, were undermined by therapeutic professionals who saw criminals as victims of social forces. The social state had made education, health, and employment into rights instead of privileges. Now the ideologues of entitlement were knocking on the door of the justice system. Judges saw themselves as the last embattled defenders of moral and legal principles against the "spirit of the times."

Two widely cited studies published in 1926 gave scholarly support to anxieties of *Verweichlichung*. Law professor Franz Exner presented a statistical analysis of sentencing practice since 1880, which found that most classes of felons were increasingly spared the penitentiary. The trend toward milder sentences, Exner demonstrated, began in the Wilhelmine era and accelerated after World War I, even as the frequency of many offenses increased. Part of the reason for this, he noted, was that judges were sympathetic to the widespread economic deprivation after the war and the effects of the ensuing hyper-inflation. Exner, however, rejected the idea that social distress was sufficient to explain or to justify the changes in judicial practice. He noted that judges also gave lighter sentences to multiple recidivists, and that the trend in milder sentences continued even after economic conditions improved.[97] In a more polemical attack on sentencing practice, criminologist Robert Heindl argued that justice institutions were infected by a "meaningless, exaggerated sentimentality." Heindl, who first rose to prominence in the Wilhelmine era as a critic of transportation, again attacked the "utopian assumptions" behind the belief in corrigibility. Heindl rejected the common interpretation of criminals as weak-willed, vulnerable individuals who could be transformed through supervision. A much greater percentage of offenders, he argued, were "professionals," that is, individuals who were committed to crime as a vocation and thoroughly socialized into a criminal lifestyle. The increase in pardons and the reduction in sentences, Heindl charged, simply consolidated the position of a powerful criminal underworld.[98]

Until the collapse of the Weimar Republic, critics complained of a steady drop in conviction rates, the increased use of fines in lieu of prison terms, and the increasing neglect of police supervision for released prisoners.[99] Conservative journalists and politicians decried the meddling of Prussian state administrators into judicial affairs. Judges feared that public Gerichtshilfe agencies would pressure them to be lenient or simply go over their heads to seek pardons from the state commissary for pardons.[100] Judges also complained about more diffuse cultural pressures, the "softness of the times," which subtly but consistently pushed them toward mildness. Even criminologist Gustav Aschaffenburg, a long-time advocate of flexible sentencing, argued in 1927 that the courts were "yielding too much to popular sensibilities."[101] He eventually rejected the very possibility that judges could assess an individual's personality, character, and environment during the course of a trial.[102] The consensus that punishment had become milder put judges on the defensive and made them the chief proponents of measures to reestablish the iron severity of justice.

The discourse of *Verweichlichung* also came out of the stalemate in efforts to create institutions of protective supervision. In contrast to the United States and the United Kingdom, Germany never created state agencies or institutions specifically to supervise ex-offenders. Part of the reason for this was fiscal. Prussian officials only started to plan asylums for released offenders at a point when the economy was in crisis. They never went beyond the discussion stage.[103] The larger problem, however, was ideological. Conservatives held on to the idea that prisoner welfare was essentially a matter of mercy and charity for "worthy" recipients, regardless of how much they would give "fallen" men and women a chance at moral redemption. The charities feared that state supervision of released prisoners would make welfare into an entitlement for all criminal offenders. Many leftists, on the other hand, feared that state supervision would inevitably become a repressive institution in the manner of the dreaded police supervision.[104]

Private associations faced their own challenges and contradictions in trying to provide supervision for ex-offenders. Local communities often feared that asylums for released offenders could turn their towns into gathering places for the worst elements. Many charitable activists, moreover, argued that asylums specifically for ex-offenders *undermined* the ability of released prisoners to integrate into society. Living in such homes, they claimed, prolonged the stigma of punishment and cut off former inmates from normal avenues of human interaction. By 1930, the prison societies had just twenty-three homes nationwide that were specifically for released offenders, while the Inner Mission had another twenty-eight. Catholic organizations had relatively greater capacity, with one hundred and eight homes serving a much smaller population. This marked an increase from prewar days, to be sure, but nowhere near what was required if protective supervision of released offenders were really to become the norm. The prisons alone released 150,000 inmates in 1929, almost 6,000 of them on parole. The courts meanwhile set free 30,000 convicted offenders as a result of conditional pardons.[105]

The worker colonies also disappointed reformers like Bozi, who expected them to supervise all classes of conditionally released offenders. Bozi caused an uproar in 1919, when he unilaterally announced that habitual felonious offenders could be assigned to protective supervision in the colonies as a condition of their pardon. The director of the Rhineland-Westphalian Prison Society, Theodor Just, warned Bodelschwingh that the character of the colonies would be "brought down" by a mass influx of these offenders. Most of the felons, Just argued, would enter the colonies only to avoid a more serious punishment or to find easy routes of escape. They would not readily conform to the moral and physical rigors of colony life. Pastor Just also doubted whether the police would pursue offenders under protective supervision who escaped from the poorly secured colonies. Offenders would have to be transferred across regional boundaries, he reasoned, yet the jurisdictions of the police and judicial authorities were local.[106] Bodelschwingh rejected these arguments—like his father, he upheld the principle of open access to the colonies—but he did worry that the colonies, over time, would be turned into institutions of forced confinement. The Bielefeld System did indeed create complications for the colonies when vagrants under protective supervision escaped. In a survey of colonies soon after the war, Bodelschwingh found that many directors were ambivalent about supervising offenders who were still serving a criminal justice sentence.[107]

During the Weimar Republic, it is likely that former offenders constituted a majority of the population in the worker colonies, but the colonies were determined not to be seen as mere adjuncts to criminal justice. Several colonies actually stopped keeping figures on the number of colonists with criminal records. Paul Braune, however, the leading figure in welfare for vagrants and beggars between the wars, estimated that 50 of the 480 colonists who resided in Hoffnungsthal in 1924 had come directly from prison, as did around one-third of the 50 women in the nearby Erkner colony. Typically no more than 10 colonists at a given time were there under the terms of a conditional pardon. Braune and most colony directors emphatically rejected the idea of segregating colonists who were under protective supervision or in any way subjecting ex-offenders to special restrictions. It was a basic principle of colony practice that released prisoners must be "assimilated as quickly as possible" into the larger community. In the spirit of Father Bodelschwingh, the directors were eager to avoid putting any stigma upon colonists because of their past mistakes.[108] When the Central Committee of the Inner Mission asked colony directors whether they would be willing to take in more ex-offenders, the responses were noncommittal. The focus of the worker colonies was impaired persons, "partial invalids," persons with limited employment potential. Former offenders were welcome as a subset of these groups but not as a category onto themselves.[109]

Ultimately, the private associations' dominant position in welfare for released prisoners and their perception of protective supervision as a charitable benefit were primary obstacles to the development of protective supervision as a means for ensuring the public safety against "dangerous individuals." Up until the Third Reich, the German state was a relatively anemic presence in this area of social control. Whether or not judges imposed protective supervision as a condition for pardoning criminal offenders depended upon the interests of local associations and their relationships to the courts. In the Düsseldorf region, protective supervision was used rarely, and then almost exclusively as a measure for underage offenders. In Bozi's regional center of Hamm, such supervision was quite common.[110] Overall in Germany, most offenders granted a conditional pardon could avoid supervision altogether.

While the limits of private associations sowed doubts about the efficacy of protective supervision in protecting society, the persistence of high unemployment in the 1920s undermined the moral and the practical arguments behind welfare for released offenders. Critics asked why offenders should receive benefits and job assistance while millions of ordinary, law-abiding Germans were forced to fend for themselves. As Georg Rusche and Otto Kirchheimer wrote in their classic study of punishment, "There is a contradiction between society's interest in the rehabilitation of the delinquent . . .

and its alleged interest in maintaining the deterrent function of impris-onment by not giving the prisoner special advantages."[111] If punishment improved the poor's conditions, then people had an incentive to commit crimes. This problem only increased with the onset of a new economic crisis in 1929. A working-class woman in 1930 wrote her imprisoned husband about layoffs at the local factory in Braunschweig. "You have it good," she said. "You are to be envied. When the time comes, you get your food." A former prisoner wrote the prison pastor in Celle that he and a fellow ex-offender had reached the well-considered conclusion that fifteen years in the penitentiary was preferable to fifteen years carrying potash under present conditions. The pastor concluded that punishment was "not a meaningful social institution" once the "level of civilization inside the prison was higher than the level outside in the worker's hovel."[112] The number of clients han-dled by the Prison Society in Berlin shot up from fewer than 8,000 in 1925 to more than 22,000 in 1929. The society declared that it no longer had the capacity to supervise these offenders or to test their "willingness to work."[113]

In Bozi's original plan for Gerichtshilfe, the growth of welfare supervision was supposed to offset a decline in rates of incarceration. With the failure to expand or even sustain the work of the prison societies, the state welfare offices, or the worker colonies, a generation of released criminals went un-supervised. Critics lamented the disintegration of traditional social controls. First, the Law for the Purging of Criminal Records put time limits on infor-mation in the criminal register. Then, state and local decrees limited the scope of police supervision to where it was no longer possible for the authori-ties to banish released prisoners from certain locales or even to visit them at their homes or in their places of employment. The 1927 draft penal code envisioned abolishing police supervision entirely.[114]

Critics of reform asserted that criminal offenders granted a conditional pardon or early release had few obligations beyond filling out forms and dropping by the police station now and then. Unless they sought direct financial assistance, it was alleged, the welfare agencies lost sight of them. Prosecutor Theodor Noetzel claimed that professional criminals had become mocking and contemptuous of the Weimar justice system. A "well-known" saying of the Berlin underworld, Noetzel declared, was "*erst klau' ick, dann bewähr' ick mir*" (first I heist somethin', then supervise me self).[115] Offenders perceived a sentence of protective supervision as equivalent to an acquittal. "I was acquitted for three years," was another supposed saying from Berlin. Since first offenses rarely led to prison terms, criminals believed that the first offense, in essence, did not count.[116] By the late 1920s, "the softening [*Ver-*

weichlichung] of justice" was as much a key word of right-wing politics as "the crisis of trust in justice" was for the left. When Prussia appointed a new Justice Minister in 1928, the liberal newspaper *Berliner Tageblatt* urged him to treat the question of *Verweichlichung* as the first topic of discussion during his introductory press conference.[117]

Judicial Offensive:
The Prussian Judges Association

In the meantime, judges and prosecutors sought to use the Prussian Judges Association (PRV) to stop welfare's alleged grab for power. A leading force in the effort to assert judicial control over Soziale Gerichtshilfe was Theodor Noetzel, the chief prosecutor and director of Gerichtshilfe in Kassel. Noetzel was popular among Prussian judges in ways that Bozi was not. In contrast to the Bielefelder, Noetzel was no critic of his fellow jurists or Prussian juridical traditions. He was solicitous regarding the misgivings of judges and prosecutors even as he urged them to embrace Gerichtshilfe. In a keynote address at a gathering of Christian reformers, Noetzel began by summarizing the arguments of Gerichtshilfe's critics. "In a time of the deepest moral decline [and] extraordinary indifference to justice and law," he cried,

> . . . do you want to support the criminal as against the law-abiding countryman [*unbestraften Volksgenosse*] who is also suffering? Do you want to take away the last vestige of the criminal's sense of responsibility through the punctilious investigation of the intellectual, spiritual, and economic foundations of a crime? Can you answer for the progressive weakening of criminal justice and, resulting from that, the reduction and the effacement of the internal restraints upon those countrymen with an asocial predisposition?

Noetzel responded that, "correctly practiced," Soziale Gerichtshilfe would never constitute aid and support for criminal offenders *against the court*, but rather assistance *to* the court *against criminals*.[118] Gerichtshilfe, he declared, must provide information and interpretations that were "unclouded" by one-sided concern for the criminal's "well-being." Helpers properly trained and administered would serve as eyes and ears of the prosecutors and judges within the social realm.[119]

Noetzel offered Prussian judges a vision of Gerichtshilfe in which romantic, utopian ideals of popular justice were contained by the firm hand of the prosecutor. The court helpers in Kassel included a factory director, two factory workers, an artisan, "ladies" from the Jewish, Catholic, and Protestant welfare associations, and one woman from the public welfare office. These voices of the people, however, along with the voice of the criminal, were introduced into the court record only after being analyzed, interpreted, and reformulated by the prosecutor's office. They impacted the proceedings only within the context of the prosecutor's case.[120]

Speaking to judges and charities, Noetzel argued that Gerichtshilfe was not a welfare institution at all, but an institution to mediate on behalf of the court with outside organizations. To avoid confusion about the purpose of Gerichtshilfe, he even argued that its official name should be changed, dropping the modifier "*soziale*" and calling the institution "adult Gerichtshilfe" or, better, simply "Gerichtshilfe." At best, he asserted, referring to Gerichtshilfe as a social institution was redundant or obvious. More often, he asserted, the name encouraged the "misconception" that Gerichtshilfe's principal loyalties were to the welfare realm.

In 1927, under Noetzel's leadership, the Prussian Judges Association took up the issue of Gerichtshilfe.[121] The PRV had barely existed since the Great War, having met only once in 1926 with a relatively diffuse agenda. The extreme statement of principles, however, garnered enormous attention and quickly thrust the organization into the center of reform debates. The judges demanded that all Gerichtshilfe agencies be subordinated to the courts, pursuing investigations only upon the orders of judges and prosecutors, and according to their guidelines. The agencies were to be administered either directly by the courts or by private associations with judicial oversight.

The PRV rejected all aspects of the Halle model of continuous welfare and the Berlin model of state administration, openness, and adversarial procedure. The judges demanded that Gerichtshilfe agencies stop proffering direct assistance to defendants and their families and stop practicing protective supervision. Under no circumstances, according to the PRV, were communal welfare offices or other public authorities to control Gerichtshilfe. Helpers' reports were not to be made available to the defense. In short, with the PRV's statement of principles, Prussian judges sought to domesticate the threat of welfare. Gerichtshilfe would be the arm of the courts, with the helpers clearly subordinated to the judges and prosecutors.

The Alliance of "Robe and Frock"

The PRV's statement of principles went too far for many leaders of the prison associations, which had embraced the Halle model of Soziale Gerichtshilfe and its ideal of "continuous welfare." These associations were already integrating the task of social investigation for the courts with the provision of welfare assistance to defendants, convicted offenders, and offenders' families.[122] After 1926, in fact, many prison associations changed their names so as to suggest that prison welfare, welfare for released prisoners, and "Gerichtshilfe" were all part of the same mission. Also in 1926, the prison societies formed a new umbrella organization with the title "National Association for Gerichtshilfe, Prison Welfare, and Welfare for Released Prisoners." How could these projects be so integrated and yet be kept separate?

Heinrich Seyfarth, the director of the National Association, initially seemed to support the continuous welfare model. Clearly, he had turned his back on the charitable tradition of keeping welfare and justice in separate spheres. At the founding of the association, Seyfarth noted how its predecessor organization in the Wilhelmine era had followed the principle that welfare is introduced "only after the punishment has ceased." By contrast, Seyfarth promised, the National Association would engage with "all problems encompassed by guilt and atonement . . . [and] stimulate changes . . . through which the entire penal system will be saturated with welfare ideals."[123] Their focus, he said, was to create "a connection between the criminal and the circles of people constituted as religious, professional or social communities." Gerichtshilfe, in his rhetoric, seemed to fit seamlessly with the other areas of association work. It was an anchor for welfare in the realm of the courts.

The leaders of the Inner Mission searched for a "synthesis" between the judges' insistently juridical viewpoint and the extreme social perspective of the proponents of public welfare.[124] They were concerned that charities not be made into tools of the judges and prosecutors and believed they had a Christian obligation to offer advice and comfort to the accused.[125] They also wanted Gerichtshilfe to be insulated from the adversarial process and even pressed for a law to give advisers immunity from being called as witnesses. At the same time, the charities shared the judges' belief that it would be catastrophic for Gerichtshilfe to be subordinated to the public welfare offices. Some kind of policy must be in place to guarantee the role of private welfare associations.

In spite of the ambivalence toward the judges' stance on Gerichtshilfe, Seyfarth decided that the National Association must ally itself firmly with the judiciary. His fellow clergy and the core of activists followed suit. The alliance between "robe and frock" was a product of shared concern with the ideology of entitlement that they associated with the Prussian state, municipal governments, and the proponents of public welfare. Ensuring judicial control of

Gerichtshilfe, they argued, was the only way to stop protective supervision from becoming a right for all offenders rather than a privilege for those who demonstrated some measure of moral worthiness.[126] Judges and clergy returned to the theme that assistance, care, and oversight could be proffered only when the offender was demonstrably ready for repentance and rehabilitation. They defended the need for punishment, the just measure of pain and its attendant suffering, as a means of upholding the authority of the law and educating the wrong-doer. Criminal justice, they insisted, was fundamentally different from social policy.[127]

The awkward situation of many charities in Germany was captured in Hermine Bäcker's notes from a 1932 meeting of reformers that included representatives of the various sides in the Gerichtshilfe debate. Bäcker directed the Inner Mission's newly founded Council on Welfare for At-Risk Persons and Criminal Offenders. At the meeting, Seyfarth represented the National Association, while a state's attorney named Mosler represented the PRV. Both, of course, supported the judges' proposal for Gerichtshilfe. The other participants were representatives from Jewish welfare and the Social Democratic workers' welfare organization, both of whom supported Gerichtshilfe as welfare.

Mosler opened the meeting in what Bäcker called a notably provocative tone, lecturing the group on why Gerichtshilfe must be purged of any welfare component. The representatives from Jewish Welfare and the workers' welfare association, according to Bäcker, immediately declared so much of the introductory comments to be "intolerable" that "we could heartily rejoice with the thought that the meeting would be over in half an hour." Instead Mosler "sat himself across from the delinquents," Bäcker wrote, "and addressed them in a truly motherly fashion, which, judging by their responses, did not have much influence upon their opinions." Bäcker, however, was again surprised to discover how much sympathy she felt with the representative from the workers' welfare association. The latter spoke from the conviction that welfare is about responsibility for the "whole person" and that this was the character of intervention toward which Gerichtshilfe was striving. Mosler, by contrast, represented a "pure formal juridical form of thinking which is completely alien to those of us coming out of welfare."

Bäcker, by her own account, found it hard to stay quiet. But she did. "What I would have said," she wrote to the Central Committee of the Inner Mission, "would have put us in the camp with the Jews and Workers' Welfare." Such a step at that point, 1932, was apparently unthinkable. She doubted she would have had enough time at the meeting to distinguish her position in ways that the jurists would have understood. She left the meeting, however, with a "bad conscience."[128]

Hermine Bäcker's fit of bad conscience must have been a common ailment among Christian welfare activists in the polarized atmosphere of depression-era Germany. Seyfarth's National Association increasingly sought to rally the charities against the proponents of state welfare. Writing in the association's monthly journal, Seyfarth condemned "sentimentality" and "excessive empathy" toward criminals as a disease of the left and, more and more, of popular culture. Bäcker's wry commentary on her meeting illustrated the dilemma for many reformers coming from the private welfare tradition: there was very little ground to stand on between the "delinquents" of the left and the law-and-order forces on the right.[129]

The Fractured Landscape of Reform

In the brewing fight over Gerichtshilfe, the National Association's most important recruit was Alfred Bozi. The leaders of the association anointed Bozi the "father of Gerichtshilfe" and provided him with a seat of honor at their functions. Before 1926, Bozi had refused to take sides in the debate between proponents of public welfare and the private charities. As recently as 1927, he supported experimentation with different Gerichtshilfe models. Over time, however, the success of Gerichtshilfe, the extraordinary momentum that he had fought so hard to create, made him uneasy. What if social policy truly swallowed criminal justice? Could the courts be reduced to handmaidens of the welfare system? Bozi's nervousness was captured in his preparations for a book in 1927–28 that was to be entitled "the great crisis." At a moment when he might have looked back cheerfully on a decade of accomplishments, the man who had shown such incredible optimism during the dark days of war and revolution now vented his pessimism, if not despair.

As a bulwark against the dangerous tide, Bozi in 1928, retired and ailing, endorsed the PRV's stance that Gerichtshilfe was "assistance to the court, but not a welfare measure."[130] He called upon reformers to insulate justice from the "political" concerns of the welfare agencies. He intimated that state administrative bodies were threatening to undermine and contaminate justice. A decade later, in his unpublished memoirs, the judge would cite his repugnance at the "politicization of justice" as a key experience driving him to embrace Adolf Hitler's promise of "national renewal."[131] Only in Hitler's Reich did Bozi rediscover the confident, upbeat tone of his earlier pronouncements.

Bozi's obsession with the "politicization of justice" demonstrates how the Gerichtshilfe debate had become a proxy for a larger conflict about the purpose of punishment and the locus of authority in criminal policy. In the final years of the Weimar Republic, Socialists and progressives lashed out at the judiciary for blocking the march of progress. The Congress of German Municipalities and the Association of German Juvenile Courts used their annual meetings in 1929 to denounce the PRV proposal. The Reich Conference of Socialist jurists accused the judges of "an attempted coup against the social state."[132] Werner Gentz wrote that subordination of Gerichtshilfe to the courts would be a "death sentence" for the institution. "Gerichtshilfe is welfare-work," Gentz insisted, "or it is nothing at all."[133] At the IKV meeting of 1929, also devoted to Gerichtshilfe, Theodor Noetzel represented the views of the PRV, but was steamrolled by a lineup of prestigious law professors and welfare proponents who criticized the judiciary's stance. A spokesman for the Reichsverband observed that "between the judges and the representatives of public welfare there were utterly divergent viewpoints concerning the relationship between welfare and punishment."[134]

Law scholar Wolfgang Mittermaier noted wearily that there was something "typically German" in having allowed an institution to develop informally without ever agreeing upon who would participate, what it would do, or even what it would be called. Such haphazard, grassroots development was possible and perhaps necessary in the context of postwar Germany, where the essential appeal of Gerichtshilfe was precisely in its "organic" roots and its populist character. By the late 1920s, Gerichtshilfe had become a basic element of German criminal justice. The question of who would shape and control this institution could no longer be postponed. "Perhaps hardly any area of the criminal sciences is so controversial as that of Soziale Gerichtshilfe," declared the *Berlin Börsen-Courier* in 1929.[135] A question of institutional structure and procedure had become the touchstone for two seemingly irreconcilable ideologies of social discipline.

CRISIS AND RENEWAL IN CRIMINAL REFORM

Over the course of the Weimar Republic, the postwar consensus in criminal policy was fractured, as reformers sought to institutionalize competing visions of *Soziale Gerichtshilfe*. On one side, mainstream judges and prosecutors saw Gerichtshilfe as a tool to expand judicial power into the social realm through the use of charitable volunteers. On the other side, public welfare organizations and Prussian government officials envisioned Gerichtshilfe as part of a comprehensive welfare complex under the control of the "social state." Events in the late Weimar Republic furthered the polarization of these camps. First, popular culture picked up the cause of criminal policy reform: celebrating welfare as a humane and effective solution to the crime question, while demonizing judges and prosecutors as reactionary holdovers from authoritarian times. Second, the onset of the Great Depression brought a collapse in the employment market and a crisis of solvency for charitable associations and local government agencies. In the wake of this disaster, the ideal of protective supervision became ever more implausible. The political left cast about for ways to rescue the legitimacy of criminal policy reform. The right used the crisis in reform as an opportunity to promote its own claims to leadership.

Even as the postwar reform coalition disintegrated, new alliances emerged around the use of racial hygienic technologies to evaluate criminal offenders and individualize criminal sanctions. Reformers embraced "criminal biology" because it claimed to provide a scientific and thus authoritative and objective means for identifying the hopeless cases among offenders and excluding them from protective supervision and other entitlements. Criminal biology promised to adjudicate in the debilitating and seemingly irresolvable struggle between justice and (public) welfare. Scientific experts would draw upon Gerichtshilfe reports and other data to evaluate the moral culpability of offenders and their fitness for a social, law-abiding existence. Offering ostensibly new tools and new interpretive frameworks, criminal biology would rescue criminal policy reform from its growing crisis of legitimacy and credibility.

Socialist Dreams

Behind the great fissures in Weimar's criminal reform movement was a cultural crisis: a clash of perspectives on the purpose of punishment, the authority of justice versus administration, and the rights and obligations of citizenship. During the Weimar Republic, Socialists and liberals abandoned their traditional affinity for the judiciary and reigned in their historic suspicions of administrative power. The left's faith in the courts was shaken by judges' alleged political bias in high profile cases and the aggressive opposition of judicial organizations to the growth of public welfare and the admission of women to the judiciary.[1] At the same time, the left showed a growing readiness to invest authority in administrative agencies, including its old bête noire, the police.

On a symbolic level, SPD leaders tried to reinvent the Prussian police as an arm of the social state. The leader of this effort was Carl Severing, Alfred Bozi's friend and fellow Bielefelder, who played an instrumental role in the wartime Bielefeld reforms. Severing served as Prussian Minister of the Interior from 1921 to 1926 and put enormous energies into changing popular impressions of the police. The "new Prussian police," its supporters argued, no longer merely enforced the laws and patrolled the borders of respectable society: the police was involved in every aspect of social life, promoting the general welfare, community, and security. While many of Severing's reforms were cosmetic, they helped overcome the stigma of the Imperial era police and promote the ideal of a modern, democratic police-welfare complex to supervise endangered persons.[2]

The Prussian state's discourse of the new police appropriated much of the rhetoric of the private charities. Severing insisted that since the overthrow of the Imperial system, the traditional understanding of public versus private institutions was no longer valid. The new police, he argued, was created by the people to serve popular social ends. As director of Prussia's new police academy, Severing appointed Ernst van den Bergh, an eloquent writer and speaker who shared Severing's romanticized view of policing. Van den Bergh argued that the Prussian police had evolved out of the unique conditions of postwar German life. It was an "organ of the social body" that served both as a "central nervous system" and a "healing agent."[3] The police, in his view, facilitated social development and protected social bonds. It was not, strictly speaking, a juridical institution at all, but a "people's police" (*Volkspolizei*).

This concept of the police as an organic institution was at the center of the Prussian government's most important propaganda event, the Great International Police Exhibition of 1926 in Berlin (GPA). Van den Bergh declared it a "cultural duty" for the state to correct popular misconceptions about the police and, by raising awareness, to create new avenues of cooperation. Severing personally directed the planning of the exhibition, postponing his retirement from the Interior Ministry in order to officiate at the opening ceremonies.[4] It was the first major international event in Berlin since the Great War and one of the largest exhibitions ever hosted in the city. Over 20,000 square meters of exhibits presented a comprehensive view of police work, including a detailed statistical and descriptive portrait of the many branches of the new police. In the course of four weeks, 500,000 people visited the GPA. Newspapers ranging from the left-wing *Vorwärts* to the reactionary *Deutsche Allgemeine Zeitung* praised it as both popular entertainment and national pedagogy. Books, films, and even toys would appear in the Berlin markets celebrating the central image of the policeman as "your friend and helper." For the radical journalist Egon Erwin Kisch, the scene in Berlin evoked Mirabeau's Paris in the days of Louis XVI: an entire city "excited by the monstrous offerings of a highly intricate, imperious, and costly police, which so many scoundrels praise and so many fools admire!"[5]

The Great Police Exhibition and its accompanying stream of publications argued that the police's regulatory domain could no longer be circumscribed as in the past. The police was a vital element of welfare, medical policy, economic growth, cultural affairs, and education, it was claimed. Charitable organizations, including the prison societies, were given their own stalls at the exhibition, but they were subordinated to state agencies in both their symbolic and substantive placement—much to the consternation of Inner Mission officials.[6] The GPA was about the synergy between the state and the *Volk*. It left little room for other mediating institutions. In the exhibition's wake, star detectives like Ernst Gennat and Ernst Engelbrecht became darlings of the big-city press and advised Germany's leading studio on the production of crime films. The exhibition also gave birth to a distinct piece of Weimar kitsch: the humble constable as a symbol of benevolent social order. The ubiquitous poster for the exhibition featured the policeman's raised hand, illustrating the "defensive, protective, and preventative action of the police." Weimar cinema adapted this image, ad nauseam, showing a constable parting the traffic—or halting the chaos of modernity—in order to pilot a small child or some other vulnerable individual to safety.[7]

A not-so-subtle subtext of this effort to remake the police's image was that Germans should now trust the state to take the leadership role in protective supervision. A socially oriented, "organic" police could assume the tasks historically defined by the charities—and more. The targets of this propaganda were on the left as well as the right. The new Prussian police had to overcome the traditional hostility and distrust of the working classes in general and Socialists in particular. They had to also counter the claims of conservative proponents of the charities that the police were inherently unsuited for social work, that there were moral, political, and practical reasons for leaving these tasks to private associations.[8]

The Ex-Convict in Weimar Culture and Society

While the leaders of the new Prussia cast the police into the role of benevolent supervisors, they also focused attention on the ex-offender as an object of special concern. The popular fascination with the ex-convict in Weimar culture was based upon a mixture of fear and empathy, as well as hope. The former offender was the quintessential outcast. He was both a victim of persecution and damaged human material in need of repair. A key promise of the social state was to integrate such persons into society while ensuring that they did not threaten public security.

The story of the captain from Köpenick—which had been largely forgotten since the war—became part of the democratic mythology that demonstrated the strengths of the new order against the failings of the old. Wilhelm Voigt's alleged suffering under the police machine of the Imperial era was a foil against which the proponents of the Republic defined their social integrationist ideal. Though Voigt died lonely, poor, and exiled in 1922, the captain from Köpenick made a triumphant and highly controversial return to the public limelight at the Great Police Exhibition of 1926. An exhibit featured a life-size portrait of Voigt borrowed from the Berlin wax museum. The accompanying text cast Voigt as the victim of a brutal and clumsy Imperial police system that was indifferent to human life.[9] In the same year and in a similar vein, UFA produced a film version of the Köpenick story. Carl Zuckermann's famous stage dramatization premiered in 1931, and another film and a novelized version of the story soon followed. In each retelling, the affair took on a broader symbolic and political resonance: linking the critique of authoritarianism to the current day's struggle against resurgent militarism (the "fetish" for uniforms) and the enemies of the Republic.[10] On the twenty-fifth anniversary of the affair, there were reenactments, interviews with surviving participants, and a carnivalesque spirit of celebration around the now mythic event. Wilhelm Voigt, the quintessential "old prison bird," was a potent symbol for the democrats and humanists struggling for a new era.[11]

Alongside the Köpenick industry, a wave of films, novels, and plays decried the fate of released prisoners in German society. The image of the ex-convict as a haunted and persecuted figure became a cinematic cliché in the Weimar years. In the 1927 film *Die Vorbestraften* (The Ex-Convicts), the protagonist explains why he has ended up back in prison by saying simply: "Because I am an ex-con."[12] Alfred Döblin's great novel *Berlin Alexanderplatz* (also a radio play and film) turned the former offender into a figure of epic tragedy, while Hans Fallada's *Wer Einmal aus dem Blechnapf frisst* put him at the center of realist social critique. Fallada's book included a devastating portrayal of an asylum and writing shop for ex-offenders in Hamburg with clear similarities to Pastor Seyfarth's famous halfway house.[13] To a remarkable extent, the discourse of criminal policy reform became art. A whole section of Jakob Wassermann's novel *The Case of Maurizius* is taken up with a glowing, romanticized description of social measures for delinquent youth in Chicago. The novels essential tension is between a prosecutor whose heart and soul is invested in the majesty of law and the principle of legality and the prosecutor's son, who believes in a social interpretation of crime and promotes social healing and forgiveness. Perhaps not surprisingly, a growing number of reform-minded jurists turned to literary pursuits. On the right, the leader of the Prison Association of Glückstadt on the Elbe wrote the screenplay for a film about the experience of a released prisoner and asked the Reichsverband to fund it. Heinrich Seyfarth liked the screenplay and provided practical suggestions for revision (he recommended that the protagonist, a released offender, first go to a halfway house), but he also wondered whether creating a film on this subject would simply play into the sensational currents of the time.[14]

The most noteworthy example of a criminal reformer turning to fiction was Karl Maria Finkelnburg, the head of the Berlin Prison Administration. Finkelnburg's play *Amnestie* opened in December 1929 at the Volksbühne, one of Berlin's leading theaters, to rave reviews and angry denunciations.[15] The drama, set in Imperial Germany, concerns a candidate for the clergy in Imperial Germany who is assigned to a penitentiary with a tough, law-and-order warden. Deeply moved by the plight of the inmates, the young hero tries to persuade officials to declare a general amnesty, excluding only those inmates who were demonstrably incorrigible. The candidate's essential decency and common sense crashes against the officials' rigid commitment to legal norms. "I am against amnesty in principle," the warden declares, "on the grounds of justice." In the end, the candidate quits the church and goes to fight for his ideals in politics and society at large. Like many literary works in the late Weimar years, *Amnestie* attacks the fetishization of law as a system of power and romanticizes a de-christianized ideal of mercy and grace. The ultimate tool of justice, in *Amnestie's* world, is welfare for the released prisoner.[16] The novelist Arnolt Bronnen attacked Finkelnburg for seeking the "destruction of law," while Thomas Mann, usually no friend of topical, confrontational theater, praised Finkelnburg as both artist and social critic for grappling with a vital issue of the time.[17]

Hedwig Wangel's "Gate of Hope"

Even as criminal reformers reached out to a new public sphere, public figures with no particular claim to knowledge or authority in criminal policy became active in reform. The most prominent, and perhaps the most eccentric, of these celebrity reformers was the actress Hedwig Wangel, who created an asylum for released women prisoners in 1926. Wangel had been a highly regarded member of Max Reinhardt's legendary Deutsches Theater, until her sudden retirement in 1903 at the age of twenty-eight to devote herself to caring for the homeless. Wangel worked at the Salvation Army and, in time, also became involved in welfare for women prisoners, visiting inmates in Berlin under the auspices of the Berliner Prisoner Association. In 1925, she returned to the theater and started a successful film career with the great German production company UFA. Her purpose, she declared, was to fund her new dream: a refuge for women prisoners in the environs of Berlin.

In spite of her time with Christian charities, Hedwig Wangel represented a different cultural universe. Rather than work through the prison associations, Wangel created a foundation in her own name and raised funds through lectures, performances, and appeals to Berlin's intellectual, artistic, and political elites. The poet Else Lasker-Schuler and the sexologist Magnus Hirschfeld became members of her board. The artist Kaethe Kollwitz designed the cover of her funding appeal. Albert Einstein wrote the preface for a book she planned to write, in which he praised the actress's "social-hygienic work on the highest plane." Her list of contributors included well-known actors, writers, and businessmen. According to Karl Finkelnburg, "overnight, Frau Wangel's plans were the talk of the ladies' rooms in every theater, the balconies of the movie houses, and the clipping room of every newspaper editorial office."[18] At the opening of the asylum, a well-known soprano entertained the guests and a popular poet read an ode.[19]

Wangel's somewhat studied eccentricities were part of her charismatic appeal. She was intensely religious, but made disparaging remarks about the church. A reporter declared that she would probably "lose herself in pietistic ecstasy" if not for her commitment to activism in the here and now. He had been invited to interview her at ten in the evening in her cluttered Berlin apartment. He stayed until three in the morning, as she laid out her spiritual principles, chatted with a writer friend, and allowed an artist to paint her portrait. The reporter was clearly smitten, describing her as a "priestess of pure humanity . . . an important, a remarkable woman."[20]

Wangel's most important advocate was Karl Finkelnburg. Long before his emergence as a controversial playwright, Finkelnburg was known as a disciple of Karl Krohne, the widely revered successor to Wichern as director of Prussian prisons. Finkelnburg's first leap into public discourse was his 1912 study of ex-prisoners, which famously demonstrated that one out of every six legally responsible adult German men was an ex-offender. Finkelnburg argued for less reliance on incarceration. During the Great War, Finkelnburg was instrumental in the establishment of the Bielefeld System.[21] In the early Weimar years, he became known as an advocate for prisoner rights, but also played an important role in promoting the prison associations to government officials.[22]

Finkelnburg helped Wangel gain access to members of the Prussian cabinet, including Minister President Otto Braun and Interior Minister Karl Severing. Within a year, Wangel secured government grants, as well as personal contributions and high-profile visits from government ministers and their wives. Finkelnburg also introduced Wangel to the administrators of women's prisons in Berlin.[23]

Wangel started the Gate of Hope in October 1926 with forty released women prisoners in Hübertshöhe bei Storkow, southeast of Berlin. The new home was just twenty miles from Gottesschütz in Erkner, the first worker colony for women. The contrast, however, was revealing. While Gottesschütz was simple and unadorned, Gate of Hope was like a *gemütlich* middle-class vacation lodge. The asylum sat on a beautiful wooded lake, visible through the grand windows in the main house's reception room. The two sleeping halls were each divided into nine separate spaces by brightly painted wood partitions and enclosed with colorful curtains. There was a library, a music room, and a screening area, with a radio and a film projector donated by UFA. There were also three rowboats that could be launched from a nearby pier.[24]

Like the worker colony, Gate of Hope offered a respite from the temptations of the modern city. In a period of four months to a year, the residents were supposed to rebuild their mental and physical resources and prepare for reintegration into society. Labor and education were the focus, and the week-day schedule was tightly regimented. Weekly reports measured the residents' progress. In contrast to Gottesschütz, however, Gate of Hope treated nature as a locus of discovery, pleasure, and contemplation rather than a testing ground for the will. In the quiet hours, residents strolled in the woods, "lay happily" around the grounds, or went rowing on the lake. An annual report referred to contact with the "beloved cattle" and the "wonderful garden" as "oppor-tunities to feel happy." A brochure for Gate of Hope showed residents dancing in step on a pier at daybreak and a young woman extending her arms raptur-ously over the lake while an old woman leans back on a chair smiling indul-gently. Publicity for Gottesschütz, in contrast, showed women digging peat or plowing a garden by hand. Gate of Hope's labor program was intended not as "moral therapy" but as an opportunity to develop the practical, marketable skills taught in Berlin's vocational training centers, which were off-limits to former convicts. On a revolving schedule, Gate of Hope offered classes in hairdressing, stenography, typing, bookkeeping, sewing, and tailoring.[25]

One of the most controversial aspects of Gate of Hope was its steady contact with the outside world. UFA frequently sent the asylum a film for Saturday screenings. At least some of the films were pedagogical in nature ("We saw a very worthwhile film about venereal disease," Wangel noted in an annual report), but most were presumably for entertainment. The asylum invited neighbors from the nearby town to join them for screenings. Wangel herself frequently came by with colleagues and friends after theater perfor-mances in the city. Late into the night, actors, playwrights, and other theater people mingled with released women prisoners while "the mother of the shipwrecked" held court.[26]

The response of Christian charities to Wangel's experiment went from cautious to skeptical to sharply condemnatory. Leaders of welfare for released prisoners saw Wangel as a dilettante who ignored the lessons of decades of practice. One of the most important of these lessons, they argued, was that asylums that were exclusively for ex-offenders were much less effective than "mixed" asylums. The Inner Mission in particular held up the worker colo-nies as a model. By taking in criminals alongside noncriminals, the colonies protected former prisoners from public stigma and provided them with positive role models and inspiration for improvement. The colonists, it was argued, were less likely to glorify their crimes and their punishment if they were among non-offenders.[27]

Hedwig Wangel's rejection of welfare orthodoxy in the question of mixed versus pure homes for ex-offenders was especially galling to Christian organizations because Gate of Hope did not screen its clients according to moral criteria or enforce the norms that were standard to the Christian homes. The charities accused Wangel of providing the women with daily cigarettes and candy just so they "have it good." While they never doubted her piety, they disdained her "ecstatic emotionalism," arrogance, and constant self-marketing.[28] The very charismatic qualities that won the support of journalists and prominent Berliners were anathema to the Christian charities. A Pastor who attended Wangel's presentation to Berlin school teachers found her self-produced film about Gate of Hope to be "in every aspect bad." It missed all of the important points, he wrote, and was "clearly made simply to heroize Frau Wangel, who . . . stands in the center of every picture."[29] A prison pastor from Rheinbach described Wangel's appeal for the "staging" of her project as "pretentious, arrogant, and ignorant." To the Pastors, Wangel was a living caricature of the great institution builders like Bodelschwingh and Wichern.[30]

The charities were willing to tolerate Wangel's experiment so long as she drew her support mainly from circles who were not ordinarily interested in welfare for released prisoners. They were alarmed, however, by the scope of her popularity, particularly when she began soliciting contributions door to door and making presentations across Germany to the same publics that were targeted by the prison associations, worker colonies, and the women's homes. Observers saw Wangel as part of a larger effort by a new breed of reformer to appropriate the criminal reform movement. Members of the Inner Mission deeply resented her dismissive references to "religious formalism."[31] At the meetings of the Rhenish-Westphalian Prison Society in 1930, Heinrich Seyfarth accused Wangel's supporters of "falsifying history" to make it seem that modern criminal policy was an invention of the Weimar Republic. Indeed, one newspaper, according to Seyfarth, had a headline "in large letters" referring to Wangel as the "founder of German welfare for released offenders." They have expunged names like John Howard, Franz von Liszt, Karl Krohne, and Adolf Fuchs from the historical record, he cried.[32]

The meteoric rise of Hedwig Wangel's Gate of Hope was followed by a similarly rapid fall. Disturbed by complaints, the conservative Catholic Prussian Welfare Minister demanded that Wangel add to her board two experienced private welfare administrators, Anna von Gierke and Elisabeth von Harnack. Gierke was the charismatic director of an asylum for endangered youth in Charlottenberg and, until 1920, a prominent figure in the Conservative Party. Harnack was the daughter of Adolf von Harnack, perhaps the most prominent German theologian of the early twentieth century and the leading

Sonnenaufgang

im Tor der Hoffnung

Regenerating Criminals: "Sunrise in Gate of Hope." (Bundesarchiv, Berlin)

theoretician of Protestant social activism.[33] Gierke and Harnack immediately demanded changes in the operations at Gate of Hope and called upon Wangel to remove herself from the asylum's day-to-day operations. Wangel dragged her feet, and Gierke and Harnack soon quit the board in frustration. In 1930, the state placed the Hedwig Wangel Association under receivership, citing "irregularities" at the home and the absence of authorization for Wangel's extensive fund-raising efforts. Wangel and her allies, in turn, accused religious-based charity organizations of a conspiracy to destroy her reputation and forcibly close the asylum.[34]

Sex and the Discourse of Prison Reform

For the charities, Hedwig Wangel's experiment in protective supervision illustrated how secular Weimar elites misappropriated the ideals and the institutional models of private welfare. The charities were similarly dismayed when a feature film and press campaign made the "sexual needs of prisoners" into a major topic in criminal reform. The film *Sex in Chains: The Sexual Needs of Prisoners* again took the prison associations' tropes and fashioned them into a message that conflicted utterly with the charities' moral and social predilections.

Sex in Chains was directed by Wilhelm Dieterle, like Hedwig Wangel an actor from Max Reinhardt's Deutsches Theater. The film starred Dieterle himself as Sommer, a decent middle-class man, who gets into an altercation defending his wife against the advances of a stranger. Sommer unintentionally pushes the man to his death down a flight of stairs. He is convicted of manslaughter and sent to prison for three years.

While in prison, sexual yearnings drive the hero to the point of mental and physical collapse. Sommer confronts the temptations to masturbate and to find physical comfort with a fellow inmate. Ultimately, the film makes clear, he succumbs to both. Meanwhile Sommer's wife struggles to remain loyal to her husband, but eventually submits to an opportunistic male seducer. While most of the film's action takes place in prison, the central didactic message plays out upon Sommer's release. Husband and wife are alienated from each other and cannot find a path of reconciliation. At the end of the film, the reunited couple commits suicide in despair over their sense of degradation and loss of meaning.[35] In a postscript, the filmmaker calls for the reform of prison regulations to address the sexual rights of prisoners.

Sex in Chains was inspired by the writings of Karl Plättner and Erich Mühsam, Communists who were incarcerated during the Weimar Republic.

In fact, the film's seemingly radical message was a twist on older themes in the literature of criminal reform. Since Wichern, Christian reformers had been concerned about sexual transgressions among male prisoners held in group confinement. Karl Krohne's 1889 textbook on prison practice emphasized the risk of homosexuality as a principal justification for solitary confinement. The question of masturbation was more controversial and less broadly discussed, but was frequently alluded to in critiques of modern justice. Most important, perhaps, *Sex in Chains* drew upon the charities' sanctified view of "healthy family relations" as the key element in the salvation and rehabilitation of the criminal.[36]

Like Hedwig Wangel's experiment in welfare, Wilhelm Dieterle's foray into prison reform found a particularly receptive audience in 1928. Sigmund Freud's sexual repression thesis had gained a wide following among the educated urban middle class. Popular criminology had sold the idea of crime as a medical problem. Most important was the rise of the Weimar social state and the discourse of welfare entitlement. If society had an obligation to rehabilitate offenders, it was argued, then prisoners had a right to those freedoms and opportunities that made rehabilitation possible. It was commonplace in the late Weimar Republic to argue that prisoners and former prisoners had a right, perhaps even a preferential right, to employment. Arguing for the right to sex was a surprising but in some ways a logical extension of rehabilitative ideals.[37]

Dieterle's film was promoted by some of the same left-wing intellectuals who helped to legitimate Hedwig Wangel. The League for Human Rights, an organization that included Albert Einstein and Magnus Hirschfeld, gave *Sex in Chains* its "patronage."[38] In the film's wake came a host of publications. Karl Plättner's 1930 memoir of penitentiary life presented vivid testimony about bestiality, "bread and beef as sexual-instruments," and "functional fetishism," and offered an impassioned case for the long-term consequences of such deviant behavior. A best-selling memoir by an anonymous member of the Berlin underworld asserted that 50 percent of prison inmates engaged in homosexual acts and that a significant percentage lost all desire for women as a result of incarceration. Adopting the sober tone of the social reformer, the gangster-turned-author declared the prisons to be a failure, then added: "A more humane penal system must give us access to prostitutes from our circles."[39]

Such accounts of sexual corruption seemed to expose deeper truths about the irrationality and inhumanity of incarceration. Weimar newspapers and magazines reported on discussions of prisoner sexuality with the usual mix of earnest social concern and overheated sensationalism. Women readers sent erotic letters to Erich Mühsam, one of the prison memoirists who had written about sexual deprivation.[40] In the Reichstag, reformers called for giving prisoners access to "normal sexual relations." One proposed law would have given all inmates the right to intimate visits from persons of the opposite sex, while allowing privileged inmates—those who did not pose a risk to society—regular furloughs for this purpose. Another proposal, less popular but remarkable simply for coming under discussion, was to create coed prisons.

Most of these proposals came from the political left, with Communists in particular supporting policies that had supposedly been introduced to great effect in the Soviet Union. Few of the advocates of sexual rights for prisoners were criminal justice professionals, and few of them had participated in past criminal justice debates. Nevertheless, the movement gained enough attention, from the press in particular, that justice professionals felt obligated to respond. Karl Finkelnburg asked wardens and other prison officials to consider the impact of sexual deprivation upon prisoners. In one of his last acts as a Prussian official, Finkelnburg loosened the requirements on the display of pornography in prison cells, reasoning that easy access to images of naked women would help male inmates to maintain a healthy sex drive and avoid homosexual encounters. Another Prussian official, Werner Gentz, published an article in Germany's most prestigious criminal law journal exploring the problem of the sexual needs of prisoners. Gentz confirmed many of the basic contentions of the sex reformers. Probably 80 percent of the prison population practiced masturbation, he asserted, while 10 to 20 percent engaged in "mutual masturbation or homosexual acts." Gentz furthermore agreed that such evidence had disastrous implications. Medical research, he claimed, demonstrated the long-term "characterological" effects of deviant sexual activity, especially for young inmates. Gentz stopped short of concluding that prisoners had a right to sex, but having painted a picture of crisis and desperation, the alternatives he proposed—more sports and a more fulfilling work program—were hardly comforting. Gentz's essay conceded the radicals' most important claim: that if the prison system failed to address the "sexual needs of prisoners" it would continue to produce individuals who were incapable of reintegration into society.[41]

Sex in Chains and the ensuing discussion infuriated conservatives both within and beyond the criminal reform movement. In Bavaria, clergy, justice officials, and private citizens flooded the Interior Ministry with complaints, which were duly forwarded to the Federal Office of Film Censorship in Berlin. The Bavarian government asked the authorities to reverse their decision allowing the film's distribution. Audience reaction, they argued, made clear that the film undermined public trust in justice, denigrated religious values, and

The prison as morally corruptive. From the film Sex in Chains.

had a deleterious effect upon public morality.[42] Charitable leaders expressed their horror over reform proposals that would "transform prisons into brothels."[43] Looking back from the vantage point of 1933, Heinrich Seyfarth claimed that the campaign for prisoners' sexual rights convinced him of the hopelessness of trying to work with the left on matters of reform. The sexual rights movement, Seyfarth wrote, demonstrated the Marxist influence upon criminal policy, and thus "typified the wrong path that [reformers] had taken."[44]

The campaign for prisoners' sexual rights and Hedwig Wangel's Gate of Hope each had a utopian quality. The chances that German society would support a vacation-like home for ex-convicts or sexual opportunities for prisoners were slim indeed. Both projects, however, were rooted in the idea that punishment, however severe, must preserve the "natural bonds" between the offender and society. Wangel and Dieterle each appropriated the discourse of protective supervision and fleshed out its consequences for an age of social entitlement. If the state had an obligation to do everything possible to rehabilitate the criminal, they reasoned, then criminals had a right to those benefits necessary to their success—including the development of marketable skills, fellowship with ordinary people, and, of course, physical

Beyond prison: the destruction of the family. From the film Sex in Chains.

and mental health. For the charities, this logic of entitlement marked the abandonment of welfare's traditional obligation to judge the offenders' level of repentance and respect for authority before tendering assistance.

It is hard to find a significant overtly "Marxist influence" in German criminal reform, but there is no question that the discourse of secular welfare advocates carried increasingly radical implications for criminal policy. In their struggle for new tools and broader powers, welfare proponents placed crime on a continuum with a range of "asocial behaviors." This step of course pathologized and potentially criminalized various forms of behavior that were previously tolerated. At the same time, if crime was just one of many possible expressions of social marginalization and discontent, then the criminal offense lost its significance as a unique marker of immorality and deviance. Karl Finkelnburg wrote:

> Criminality is a universal phenomenon. One should not consider the delinquent person to be abnormal. Rather, it could be much more seriously asked whether an abnormal person is not the one who decade after decade, in the press and pressure of life . . . never committed a criminal offense.[45]

Finkelnburg's colleague Werner Gentz challenged the principle that punishment and welfare must be pursued on separate tracks. The object of punishment and welfare, Gentz argued, was the same: the resocialization of those who were ready to live productive and orderly lives, the long-term treatment under humane conditions of confinement for those who were not.[46]

These were not the sentiments of political radicals or marginal figures. Finkelnburg held powerful positions in the Imperial era and the Republic. Gentz was an up-and-coming star in Prussian administration who frequently contributed to prison society publications. Members of the International Penal Union (IKV), still Germany's most prestigious reform society, expressed similar views. They spoke of "overcoming punishment," abolishing the penitentiaries, and removing all elements of dishonor in punishment. Alwin Sänger, a moderate Reichstag deputy from the SPD, captured the zeitgeist during the Republic's relatively happy middle years. "One should finally cease to treat the battle against criminals from the perspective of morality," Sänger declared. "The time will hopefully come soon where we will have not penal institutions but clinics for criminals."[47]

Backlash and the Search for a New Consensus

The effacement of the borders between punishment and social policy provoked a backlash from right-wing jurists and publicists. Adolf Baumbach, the president of the Berlin Senate and a former high court judge, declared that criminal justice was "bankrupt" and that "the softening of the backbone was the sickness of our times." Years of reform, he argued, had reduced the German state to the role of a "scolding old man." Baumbach accused Weimar legislators and administrators of pressuring judges to be mild and undermining them when they were firm. The pardon authorities, Baumbach claimed, now granted probation "almost systematically, without considering the offender's character and dangerousness." For him, there was indeed a "crisis of trust," but it was the product not of the judiciary but of a government subservient to the "horrible, false humanity of our time."[48]

Baumbach's fusillade and attacks from other high-status jurists opened a space for anti-reformist manifestos by popular writers and propagandists.[49] Heinrich Berl wrote that "the press, the theater, art, and literature . . . all vie with each other for the glorification of the criminal." He accused reformers of seeking the "psychological determinants of the criminal" in order to strip him of free will and find a justification for letting him go."[50] Karl Fees claimed that the dominant "sociological" approach to criminal policy failed utterly.

Society could not possibly reintegrate this great mass of offenders, he argued. Instead, criminals were forming their own ever-more sophisticated and dangerous alternative organizations.

There was a grain of truth in even the most intemperate diatribes. Indeed, prostitutes for the first time had their own representative organizations. Vagrants and beggars from across Germany gathered in 1930 for what was billed as the first annual "Vagabond Congress." In the big cities, former prisoners created their own mutual aid associations. Hans Pitak, an unemployed six-time offender, founded an association for released prisoners in Berlin with support from many of the same prominent intellectuals who helped Wangel, including Albert Einstein, Magnus Hirschfeld, and Käthe Kollwitz.[51] The most notorious of the ex-offender mutual aid organizations were called "Ring Associations." According to their members, these associations were athletic clubs and mutual aid societies that carried out many of the same functions as the prison associations. For Fees and other detractors, however, the Ring Associations were "Chicago-style" syndicates that sponsored illegal gambling, burglary, and theft. Such criminal societies, it was argued, were filling a vacuum created by the collapse of traditional justice and police controls.[52]

In their march toward political power, the National Socialist propagandists also vilified the progressive criminal reform movement for holding society rather than criminals responsible for crime. Local Nazi papers relished describing crimes by repeat offenders who were furloughed from prison or had been sentenced to protective supervision in lieu of incarceration. They promised that Hitler would restore German judges to their rightful place as moral arbiters and defenders of public safety. While there were few specifics behind the Nazi program, they were often hostile toward pardons, welfare in lieu of punishment, and the rehabilitative ideal in general.[53]

Much of the criticism of reform by the Weimar right was similar to prewar accusations of "excessive mildness" in criminal justice, but the differences were important. First, the critics no longer attacked the prison societies, the clergy, or the judiciary. Instead, they focused their ire upon progressives and socialists. The right's fear of an emasculated justice was linked in particular to anti-feminist perspectives. It was certainly no coincidence that Heinrich Berl was the author of an infamous anti-feminist manifesto, or that right-wing judges vigorously opposed the admission of women into the judiciary down to the end of the Weimar Republic.[54] Second, the hyperbolic and undiscriminating attacks by journalists and propagandists in the Weimar Republic found a surprising echo in the writings of pastors, scholars, and members of the prison societies themselves. A significant branch of the reform movement, in other words, was aligning itself publicly with an anti-reformist posture.

The rhetoric of backlash was especially strong after 1929, when mass unemployment and the fiscal crisis of the prison associations and local governments further undermined the plausibility of protective supervision. Ellen Scheuner, a prominent advocate of Gerichtshilfe in the Inner Mission and a regular contributor to Seyfarth's journal, wrote glowing reviews of Fees and Berl.[55] A new generation of legal scholars assailed the "bankruptcy" and "corruption" of the reform movement and called for an "authoritarian criminal justice" that could overcome the naive faith in rehabilitation that allegedly typified the dominant schools of criminology in Germany.[56] Fresh upon the Nazi seizure of power in 1933, Seyfarth wrote sycophantic letters to officials at all levels of the new government, offering his services and asserting that his focus, like the Nazis, had always been on identifying incorrigible criminals and removing them permanently from society. Even Alfred Bozi, whose reform program was built on the concept of collaboration across ideological boundaries, wrote paeans to the Nazis in their first few years of rule, arguing that Hitler was the only leader who could bring back the spirit of 1914 and reunite German society behind a program of comprehensive reform.[57]

Meanwhile, the prison societies went from boasting about generous assistance to needy ex-offenders to boasting about their tough-minded rejection of less than worthy applicants. In 1930, the new chairman of the Berlin Prison Association, Friedrich Ulrich, announced the organization's commitment to reducing the overall number of ex-offenders receiving assistance—in spite of the documented increase in need. The prison society of Frankfurt on the Main, likewise, reported proudly on its success in preventing former offenders from settling in that city.[58] In its 1932 report, the Berlin Association declared that the "burning" question in criminal policy was the selection of ex-offenders. The crisis in the employment market made it impossible to test the offenders' capacity and willingness to work, the report declared. In this environment, the prison societies needed new techniques and criteria to determine who was and who was not deserving of welfare.

Seyfarth's National Association for Gerichtshilfe, Prison-Welfare, and Welfare for Released Prisoners placed the problem of selection increasingly at the center of attention. Writing in the association's journal, Theodor Noetzel argued that Soziale Gerichtshilfe must liberate itself from the "stigma" of arranging for pardons and conditional release. The task of Gerichtshilfe, he argued, was to provide judges with an objective picture of the offender's "personality, inherited characteristics, and environmental influences." Gerichtshilfe was supposed to make the courts more cautious and discriminating about whether to acknowledge extenuating circumstances and lessen the punishment.[59]

Noetzel's reference to "inherited characteristics" was no accident. Gerichtshilfe had always been concerned with how family backgrounds helped to explain an offender's "disposition." The question of whether these factors were biological or environmental, however, was generally left open. If the offender's father and grandfather were heavy drinkers, then the adviser would say that he was "burdened," and that this might be considered extenuating circumstances. It was a secondary matter whether the burden was passed on through nature or nurture. In the late twenties and early thirties, however, at least some reformers pushed Gerichtshilfe to search for biological factors in crime. New questionnaires for advisers issued in these years had a more explicit concern with biology. Gerichtshilfe was also supposed to play a role in a key innovation of the late Weimar Republic: the spread of criminal biology.[60]

Criminal Biology

Most historical accounts of social policy in the Weimar Republic note the rising tide of eugenic approaches to deviance in the Depression era.[61] Historians often describe the resurgent interest in heredity as a repudiation of humanist principles and social integrationist ideals. Young Sun Hong, for example, argues that eugenic reformers rejected the "spiritual foundations of the republican welfare system." Looking toward the "supragenerational entities of *Volk* and race," she writes, these right-wing reformers saw "social pedagogy and social hygiene as wasteful." Richard Wetzell argues that traditional prison reformers were isolated in the late Weimar Republic, fighting a rear-guard battle against the charge of hereditarian thinkers. Overall, historians suggest that a great era of social optimism came to a close in the Depression, with the incredible accumulation of Weimar experiments—in saving souls, regenerating "human material," and rebuilding community—unceremoniously swept into the dustbin of history.[62]

The leading proponents of criminal biology in the Weimar Republic, however, aimed not to repudiate "traditional prison reform" but to realize its most cherished goals. They envisioned a symbiotic relationship with both Soziale Gerichtshilfe and welfare for released prisoners. The charities were to provide researchers with essential data about offenders and their communities.[63] The researchers, in turn, would offer charities their assessments of the social, psychological, and biological factors that influenced the individual's behavior. State officials hoped that criminal biological research could help prevent the allocation of social benefits to incorrigible and potentially dangerous offenders. It would provide an unassailably rational, scientific, and politically neutral supplement to the work of Gerichtshilfe. For advocates of a social criminal policy, criminal biology would provide new legitimacy and a unified foundation to an increasingly floundering and divided reform movement.[64]

What was criminal biology? From the standpoint of many criminologists, it was nothing new, merely another label for the kind of clinical and ethnographic research into the etiologies of crime that had been taking place for decades. For social reformers, criminal biology meant applied criminological research. Even if criminal biological diagnoses were not immediately used in sentencing, treatment, or pardoning decisions, the long-term goal of the research was to provide a database for precisely such decisions. It was "biology" inasmuch as it made a claim to scientific rigor, but its concerns encompassed social, cultural, and economic factors that contemporaries would not usually include within the life sciences.

Criminal biology began in the conservative, primarily Catholic state of Bavaria. Later a researcher with support from the Rockefeller Foundation established another criminal biological project in the more progressive and predominantly Protestant state of Saxony. Reformers in Prussia, including Heinrich Seyfarth and Alfred Bozi, paid close attention to these experiments. In the late 1920s, pressure grew on the Prussian government to follow the example of its southern neighbors. It is therefore worth looking closely at each of these cases.

The goal of criminal biology in Bavaria was to support the so-called "progressive" or "levels" system of punishment that was introduced into Bavarian prisons after 1921. In this system, prisoners were housed according to their prognosis for rehabilitation. The highest level was reserved for offenders who were almost ready to be released. They received special benefits, incentives for good behavior, and preparation for living again as free citizens. The bottom level was where prisoners started and where they stayed if they proved to be incorrigible. Conditions there were raw and unpleasant, even compared to other German penitentiaries. The middle level had only basic comforts and was supposed to be a stopping-off point as the inmate progressed upward.[65]

Historians note that the prison reforms in Bavaria were as much about hardening the punishment for incorrigibles as about benefiting those with good prospects for the future. Nikolaus Wachsmann demonstrates that the highest levels were not significantly better than what had once been normal for all inmates. Moreover, the average inmate's chances of reaching the highest level in the Bavarian prison were slim. Wachsmann concludes that the system mainly "helped institutionalize the distinction between 'reformable' and 'incorrigible' offenders."[66] Nevertheless, the triumph of a rehabilitative ethic provided the backdrop for these reforms. The Bavarians poured enormous resources into a project that only made sense within that context. In Bavaria, as in Prussia, the rate of incarceration fell throughout the middle years of the Weimar Republic. The government of Bavaria was under pressure to develop its infrastructure for protective supervision. It resisted some reforms—like Gerichtshilfe—but nervously expected a host of liberal-oriented changes to be forced upon the "Free State" once a new penal code and unified code of punishment were instituted by the Reich. The levels system in Bavarian prisons created a safety valve to control the flow of offenders through the justice system and into the welfare system.

The Criminal-Biological (KB) Service was established by the state in order to further refine the labeling and sorting of offenders under the levels system. Bavarian officials were concerned that many offenders could move up through the levels system by simulating rehabilitation or simply conforming to the prison regime without actually modifying their anti-social perspectives.[67] The leader of the KB project in Bavaria, Theodor Viernstein, was a former prison doctor who was convinced that the analysis of a full range of data about every prisoner would allow experts to see past the prisoner's superficial exterior. Viernstein stressed that criminal biology was a new departure because of its comprehensive collection of data and its sensitivity to genetics and other biological "facts."

In practice, however, many aspects of the criminal biological investigation were indistinguishable from the social investigations carried out by Gerichtshilfe. Like the court welfare advisers, Viernstein's investigators were more often chaplains or teachers than trained investigators. They relied upon a questionnaire for each case that, again like Gerichtshilfe, mostly consisted of questions about education, family, religion, and upbringing. Even the genealogical and physical data collected by Viernstein was increasingly present in Gerichtshilfe forms as well. The investigators' guidelines for formulating their reports were familiar as well: their goal was to understand the individual's "personality" and "character" (*Gesinnung*) and to formulate a social prognosis based on this material.

What distinguished criminal biology from Gerichtshilfe was its posture of scientific neutrality. In spite of the efforts of judges and prosecutors to strip Gerichtshilfe of welfare responsibilities, the institution was still colored (or, for some, "tainted") by its association with traditional charity and the public welfare agencies. Its foundations were not in science but in social practice and the discourse of solidarity. Gerichtshilfe advisers were often just upstanding members of a community with no special training and not necessarily any experience with crime or criminal justice. Criminal biology, on the other hand, promised to give scientific professionals a voice in the criminal process.

Whether criminal biology really introduced greater scientific rigor into criminal justice, of course, is a different question. Historian Richard Wetzell notes that the guidelines for investigators offered nothing in the way of a methodology, and Viernstein himself seemed to make only the most haphazard and superficial use of his vast store of data. Ultimately Viernstein admitted that in each case he "determined corrigibility through an intuitive assessment of whether the criminal was 'good or bad.' "[68] Thus, as in Gerichtshilfe, the narrative of the criminal's life and the portrait of the criminal's place in society were at the center of each diagnosis. Historian Christian Mueller concludes that the Bavarian penal system relied upon criteria of judgment that were not so much modern at all as rooted in "traditional Christian-Conservative concepts." As Oliver Liang suggests, biological language reinvigorated moral and social judgments and bolstered the arguments for excluding certain types of offenders from entitlements.[69]

Criminal biology's mixing of moral, social, and scientific discourse ultimately furthered its appeal to reformers like Heinrich Seyfarth and Alfred Bozi. For the pastor and the judge, modernizing criminal policy meant facilitating the evaluation of offenders as complex moral and social beings—rather than the mere juridical abstractions of classical liberalism. Seyfarth and Bozi admired criminal biology because it addressed the most challenging and disruptive aspect of penal modernity: the tendency to shift offenders from justice to welfare. Few reformers questioned the need for more welfare for criminals, but the continued growth of such welfare only made the need for greater and cleaner mechanisms of discrimination more pressing.

Criminal Biology and the Progressives

While Viernstein's project had a largely unspoken debt to Soziale Gerichtshilfe, criminal biology in the state of Saxony explicitly defined itself as an effort to both build on Gerichtshilfe's successes and refine its future practice. In contrast to Bavaria, Saxony was considered possibly the most progressive state in Germany in areas of welfare and penal reform. Eugenics in Saxony, according to Michael Schwartz, was the product of a Social-Democratic, liberal, and Protestant constellation. Between 1926 and 1930, a coalition of liberal parties in Saxony ruled together with a breakaway conservative wing of the Social Democrats. In spite of its left-liberal profile, the coalition had strong support from Protestant welfare associations. Saxony created the most extensive system of Soziale Gerichtshilfe outside of Prussia and was the only state to subject both Gerichtshilfe and welfare for released prisoners to public control. For reasons peculiar to Saxony, this arrangement was completely accepted by the private charities, who worked closely with state agencies in a variety of contexts.[70] The regime offered generous support to criminal biology specifically in hopes of strengthening the role of welfare in criminal policy.

Criminal biology in Saxony originated with one man, Rainer Fetscher, a young researcher in Dresden. Fetscher started in 1923 with a grant from the Rockefeller Foundation to study the hereditary defects of convicted prostitutes and other sex offenders. He approached the Justice Ministry in 1925 with a proposal for a "comprehensive card-file on asocial families in Sachsen, which should become a permanent collection for all pertinent information." Initially, the collection would serve purely scientific purposes. Over time, however, Fetscher hoped to make it available for public offices to gather information about individuals and families.[71] Fetscher expected the cardfile to serve as a resource in particular for Gerichtshilfe and welfare for released prisoners in order for them to "adapt their measures more to the particularities of individual cases." Like the project in Bavaria, criminal biology in Saxony functioned primarily through questionnaires that were distributed in the home communities of prison inmates. Investigators approached families and friends, local welfare agencies, churches, schools, and former employers. Fetscher sought to accumulate data not only about "hereditarily defective material," but about all aspects of the offenders' personal history and the "social conditions" under which they lived.[72]

Fetscher's questionnaires were built upon the theories of characterological science, a synthesis of sociology, psychology, and hereditary biology.[73] The five-page forms included a single page devoted to the offender's "urges" (*Triebleben*), while another section focused on "character build" and "life attitude," including, as a subsection, the "relationship of the Id to the outside world." The page devoted to "sociological behavior" included subsections on "special sociological defect-types," "ethical predisposition," and religious and political behavior.[74] The initial newspaper reports highlighting Fetscher's work described criminal biology as a tool in the service of rehabilitative aims. At least one report described it enthusiastically as an Anglo-American import.[75]

New Horizons

The association of criminal biology with a left-liberal reform government in Saxony undoubtedly strengthened its credibility among Social Democratic leaders in Prussia. Nevertheless, the Prussians were cautious about supporting this kind of research. It was the prison societies that put particular pressure on the Justice Ministry to create some sort of clinical laboratory in the prisons and begin the central collection of data on criminals. Speaking on behalf of the associations, Heinrich Seyfarth made direct appeals to officials. His journal, *Die Monatsblätter des deutschen Reichsverbandes für Gerichtshilfe, Gefangenen- und Entlassenenfürsorge*, vigorously promoted the work of Viernstein and Fetscher and offered a platform for a diverse array of scholars and activists to advocate for a state-supported project.[76] Seyfarth described a lifetime of frustration trying to ensure that the energy of volunteers was "reserved for those ex-offenders . . . who were still suited to a social existence." Germany required criminal biology, he argued, in order to identify the large numbers of people who were fundamentally "uneducable." The exclusion of these elements, he wrote, "was vitally necessary for the success of welfare."

In Seyfarth's imagined future, Gerichtshilfe's court advisers would refer offenders to criminal biological laboratories set up in every local jail. The criminal biological evaluation would then be included in the case file, which judges could use to ensure that incurable persons were not unwittingly funneled into the welfare system. For Seyfarth, then, even more so than for Fetscher and Viernstein, criminal biology was essentially a tool for screening and exclusion. In this way, however, it guaranteed the viability of social measures. The crisis of Gerichtshilfe, after all, centered upon two related fears: that welfare could mar the social diagnosis of offenders and corrupt the criminal process and that dangerous elements would be let loose on society. Criminal biology, which was a form of social diagnosis but was not welfare, could address both of these fears here and now—even if the technology was still in some ways unscientific and a long way from offering a consistently accurate form of diagnosis.[77]

In 1927 Seyfarth, along with Fetscher and Viernstein, leaders of private and public welfare, criminologists, and jurists met to form the Criminal Biological Society. From its inception, the organization maintained a distance from the political conflicts swirling around criminal justice issues. In spite of their extreme differences in ideology, the government representatives from Saxony and Bavaria each lavished praise upon criminal biology as a vital tool in legitimating the transformation of judicial practice and guaranteeing the effectiveness of protective supervision.[78]

In Prussia, state officials finally agreed to support a criminal biological project in 1930. Earlier, Prussia had made its commitment to the levels system in the prisons, and even started building the first postwar penitentiary, which was designed on humanist, rehabilitationist principles, with a tri-partite division of the inmates. There was no doubt that the Justice Ministry's embrace of criminal biology was a response to fears about excessive pardoning and early release from prison in a time when employment was scarce and the prison associations were reeling from a new economic crisis. "Measured by the present-day . . . socio-economic standard," an official of the Justice Ministry stated, "there are offenders who are . . . unsuited for freedom as a result of endogenous limits." Allowing these offenders to reenter society, he stated, was a "license for recidivism." Criminal biology could save the "pedagogical approach" to punishment by stanching the flow of repeat offenders coming before the courts and giving prosecutors and judges a base of scientific data to complement the reports of Gerichtshilfe agencies. Racial-hygienic screening was to allow public and private welfare associations to focus upon the needs of the "truly deserving," corrigible offenders.[79]

Prison pastors, progressive judges, and public welfare officials supported criminal biology in hopes of overcoming the debilitating and seemingly chronic conflicts over protective supervision in the late Weimar Republic. The comprehensive screening of offenders according to scientific criteria would finally render criminal policy safe for the liberal pardon policies and welfare interventions essential to modern punishment. The Prussian state would be assured of a larger and better defined role in the assessment of criminals and the determination of treatment. At the same time, Christian charitable institutions believed that criminal biology represented the last and best hope for realizing their hundred-year-old project of building seamless nets of care and supervision.

CONCLUSION

In November 1933, Judge Alfred Bozi, now an enthusiastic supporter of the Nazis, wrote to his friend Carl Severing, the former Socialist and union leader. Bozi had been looking over his archive of personal papers and was struck by his friend's important contributions to the reform movement in wartime Bielefeld. Severing had helped organize and sustain the remarkable collaboration between jurists, Christian social reformers, feminists, and union leaders that produced the Bielefeld System for the regulation of asocials and, ultimately, *Soziale Gerichtshilfe*. Bozi wrote Severing that he looked forward to the day when historians would have some distance from recent events and "observe matters . . . from the standpoint of historical necessity." They will realize, wrote Bozi, that many of those now on the Nazis' enemies list "laid the foundation stones upon which the new builders build."[1] Severing, in other words, would one day be recognized as a forerunner of the Nazi revolution.

For Severing—harassed by storm troopers and threatened with imminent arrest—Bozi's lavish praise must have been slightly surreal.[2] He would surely have rejected any connection between his own reform efforts and the Nazis' recasting of criminal policy in the years after 1933. The new regime, after all, rejected all ideological coalitions and promised to purge any trace of Marxism and feminism from German social policy. Moreover, the Nazis attacked the very principles of legality and individual rights that were the context for the Bielefeld reforms and for Severing's later work as Prussian Interior Minister. In their first year in power, the Nazis incarcerated over 100,000 people without formal charges, including thousands of homeless men and women seized during the so-called "beggars' week" actions in September 1933.[3] The regime also rescinded many postwar prison reforms and tightened the requirements for pardons and parole. In the summer of 1933, they placed the position of state commissary for pardons (*Gnadenbeauftragte*) into the hands of the state's attorney and abolished the penal affairs bureaus (*Strafvollzugsämter*) that had played such an important role in the acceleration of the pardon rate.[4]

The new government was initially uncertain about Gerichtshilfe. In the first months of the regime, it was left to local authorities to decide how to restructure the institution. In Berlin, judges and private associations finally succeeded in putting Gerichtshilfe firmly under the control of the courts and more or less blocking the participation of communal welfare offices. By the end of 1933, however, the Prussian Justice Ministry decided that Gerichtshilfe in any form was inconsistent with the principles of an authoritarian state. A ministry decree forbade judges from collaboration with any outside welfare advisers.[5]

In spite of these measures, Judge Bozi and many other prominent Weimar-era reformers continued to believe that the Nazis represented the great hope for the realization of social principles in criminal policy. These were reformers who had grown exasperated with the entrenched power of the left. They blamed state welfare agencies for undermining judicial and prosecutorial authority; criticized the dogmatic support for individual rights that prevented the enactment of security measures against dangerous individuals and chronic recidivists; and condemned the "Marxist" antagonism toward Christian social reformers that prevented a consensus regarding goals and methods for protective supervision. For Bozi, Pastor Heinrich Seyfarth, and other criminal policy reformers, the Nazis' assault on certain legacies of the Weimar Republic was not a repudiation of reform but a necessary step in the path toward renewal. By smashing the left, the Nazis made it possible for German society to transcend partisanship and class divisions and to "bring the national community [*Volksgemeinschaft*] into the fight against criminality."[6]

It was in this sense that the Nazi revolution was supposed to herald a return to the "spirit of 1914." These reformers saw the Nazis as mobilizing people of all classes behind an ethic of sacrifice and national struggle. Just as the wartime mobilization had provided every decent and healthy German with a role and an opportunity for heroism, the Nazis promised to give every true comrade a secure place in the social fabric. Once again—or so it seemed to Bozi and Seyfarth—there was a plausible and compelling narrative for how outcasts would become citizens. In this environment, Seyfarth asserted in 1933, it could not be tolerated that offenders were "hermetically sealed off" from society. "Prison affairs must be the people's affairs," he wrote.[7] A populist age would include a populist approach to criminal policy.

If the spirit of 1914 was about solidarity, however, it was also about national purification. There were few protests during the Great War when the police and the army arrested thousands of vagrants, beggars, and prostitutes. The revitalization of national community under the Nazis included more sustained measures aimed at purging "alien" elements from the *Volk*. Pastor Paul Braune, the widely revered director of the Worker Colony Association, praised Hitler's government for its vigorous measures against "professional" beggars and vagrants. Speaking for his colleagues, he endorsed the state's internment of beggars in concentration camps and looked forward to measures that would force alcoholics and mentally ill vagrants to stay in treatment centers. Charities would support this regime, he argued, even if it sometimes relied excessively upon the police, because they were all too aware of excessively lax standards during the Weimar Republic. The Nazis had liberated Germany from the era of "false humanitarianism" and the dogma of an "inalienable right to individual freedom."[8] The prison societies showed similar enthusiasm for the government's introduction of security confinement for "dangerous habitual criminals" in November 1933. Their leaders thanked the state for removing the crushing burden of so many hopeless and potentially dangerous cases.[9]

While the first year of Nazi rule was dominated by harsh measures against chronic offenders, subsequent years witnessed a clear reassertion of the social principles and the social agenda that characterized the efforts of reformers in decades past. With the left eviscerated and the economy recovering, Hitler's government turned to the question of how precisely good human material should be culled from the overall population of offenders. The Pardon Ordinance of 1935 gave judges formal power to pardon offenders without the approval of the administrative authorities. Historian James Whitman argues that this step marked the true beginning of "regularized probation" in Germany. According to Whitman, the Pardon Ordinance "set the basic framework for the liberalizing reforms of the postwar period."[10]

The new emphasis on pardons helped reopen the question of Gerichtshilfe in the Third Reich. When they banned the institution in 1933, Nazi officials were concerned that welfare agencies, including Christian charities, showed too much sympathy with offenders and undermined efforts to vigorously prosecute criminal behavior. Within a few years, however, such concerns were outweighed by the growing need for laborers and soldiers and the renewal of optimism regarding German society's capacity to physically and morally discipline youth and young adults.

In 1937, the Ministry of Justice announced the return of Gerichtshilfe, rechristened *Ermittlungshilfe* (mediation assistance) and placed under the control of a private association linked to the National Socialist Welfare Association.[11] Ministry official Roland Freisler indirectly praised Bozi's early speeches and essays on Gerichtshilfe as offering a useful direction for National Socialist reformers. Gerichtshilfe properly conceived, he asserted, would help the courts determine offenders' "attitude toward the national community" and whether reintegration to the *Volk* was possible and desirable. The prison societies would play a central role, but under the oversight of the National Socialist welfare association. This would prevent what Freisler saw as the Weimar reformers' mistake of giving Gerichtshilfe a "crypto-judicial" function and allowing it to evolve into a "one-sided" tool of the defense. *Ermittlungshilfe*, as its name implied, would be solely about mediation between criminal justice and social organizations.[12]

Like National Socialist pardon policy, the resuscitation of Gerichtshilfe drew upon the social reform aspirations of thinkers and activists since the mid-nineteenth century. The new institution had strong political overtones both in its criteria for evaluating human material and in the nature of the protective supervision it could recommend. Nevertheless, the essential structure and goals of *Ermittlungshilfe* were consonant with the early Weimar consensus. It still embodied the dream of making justice social by creating new contexts for popular participation, popular judgment, and popular supervision. And the Nazi state undoubtedly generated broad popular support for its criminal policy. As Reich Security Chief Reinhard Heydrich boasted, security in the Third Reich depended less upon the state than upon the "watchful eye of the entire public."[13]

Social approaches to criminal policy survived the collapse of the Third Reich and, indeed, flourished as never before under the Federal Republic of Germany. At a conference on conditional sentencing in 1952, a prestigious group of law professors argued that sentencing and pardoning were a unified aspect of criminal policy. The participants proposed a law to make probation part of the penal code and standardize its practice. Two goals, once deemed contradictory, were now coupled and treated as basic assumptions: that criminal policy should be an aspect of social policy, and that the apparatus of social diagnosis and supervision should be under the control of judges and prosecutors.[14]

One leading conference participant, Hamburg law professor Rudolf Sieverts, had also been a leading proponent and theorist of Gerichtshilfe. At the first postwar conference on Gerichtshilfe in November 1952, Sieverts surveyed the institution's history and reiterated the prewar critique of Weimar Gerichtshilfe as too oriented toward helping offenders. He disparaged the traditional effort at using lay-people from all walks of life to advise the courts on social issues. For Sieverts, the Nazis' instrumentalization of Gerichtshilfe as a tool of political conformity only underscored the importance of putting the institution firmly into the hands of professional civil servants under the oversight of judges and prosecutors.[15] Sieverts was either ignorant or, more likely, in denial about the judiciary's own instrumentalization of justice during the Third Reich.[16] In any case, his defense of judicial control and welfare professionalization captured the spirit of postwar German culture. The crisis of trust in justice was forgotten, while the conflict between public and private welfare models was largely resolved in the conservative-progressive compromise at the heart of the new Federal system.[17] Welfare experts trusted judges to understand and appreciate social criteria in the assessment of offenders. Judges (and charities) trusted state welfare professionals to uphold moral and legal standards and defend public security.

Gerichtshilfe was reestablished in all the successor states to Prussia within the Federal Republic of Germany. Shorn of its utopian aspirations and used at the pleasure of the prosecution, it nevertheless contributed mightily to the dominance of a social discourse in German criminal policy since the 1950s. In contrast to the United States, social approaches to crime in Germany maintained their legitimacy throughout the 1980s and 1990s and into the twenty-first century. This is reflected in the stunning divergence in rates of incarceration and the nature of the carceral experience in the United States and Germany. While the United States in 2003 had more than 700 prisoners for every 100,000 Americans, the rate in Germany was less than 100 prisoners per 100,000. Moreover, a significant percentage of American prisoners were nonviolent offenders: almost one quarter of all inmates in 2003 were incarcerated for drug-related crimes.[18] In Germany, prison has been increasingly reserved for violent offenders, while nonviolent offenders receive an extensive range of specialized therapeutic and economic services.[19]

Why has criminal policy in Germany and the United States diverged so profoundly? Legal historian James Whitman argues that the relative mildness of punishment in Germany can be traced to the "impulse toward mercy," which survives thanks to the isolation of European criminal policy from democratic influences. "Harshness and democratization go hand in hand," he writes, because "voters never have individual offenders before their eyes." In the United States, the most severe and degrading forms of punishment, those traditionally reserved for "low status" criminals, have, in the spirit of democratization, been extended to all criminals. In Germany and France, Whitman argues, the trend toward mildness originated with the treatment of aristocrats and gentlemen offenders (a natural focus of empathy for criminal justice reformers). The milder treatments reserved for these high-status criminals were gradually extended to all classes of criminals who were deemed "morally worthy" and "honorable."[20]

Whitman's argument has many strengths, but it fails to give sufficient weight to the role of welfare in the transformation of criminal policy or account for the tremendous popular support in Germany for "merciful" qualities in justice. Mercy was not—as Whitman suggests—simply an expression of spiritual enthusiasm and empathy for criminals. It was part of an alternative vision of social discipline. This book has essentially traced the opposite trajectory from Whitman's. Mildness in its modern incarnation, I argue, originated in special welfare measures for vagabonds, prostitutes, and juvenile delinquents—the lowest of the low in terms of status. Institutions like the Bielefeld System, judicial pardoning, and, especially, Soziale Gerichtshilfe gradually extended the practice of mildness, that is, the practice of welfare or "protective supervision," to broader and broader classes of offenders, including adult felons.

The ideal of protective supervision in Germany emerged not from a cloistered committee of bureaucrats, but from a popular movement for social reform. It survived due to the shared animosities toward state carceral institutions in the Wilhelmine era among conservatives, progressives, and Socialists. It flourished when wedded to a discourse of national strength and improvement, particularly around World War I. Reformers like Alfred Bozi and Heinrich Seyfarth reinvented criminal policy as a means to rescue damaged human material and better allocate energies and resources. Finding and excluding "bad material" from the benefits of supervision was essential to their project, but the project itself was built upon a remarkable foundation of optimism.

Writing in the wake of the American prison boom, such optimism is exotic indeed. Social criminal policy in the United States has largely retreated in the face of chronic despair about the "pathologies" of the inner city. Where there are no stable jobs and (according to mainstream perceptions) no stable families or recognizable social networks, there can be no plausible narrative of discipline and resocialization. The absence of a welfare safety net in the United States makes the concept of rehabilitating released offenders seem fantastical.

In Germany, faith in society's capacity to discipline and resocialize former offenders has waxed and waned over time, but has remained strong relative to other countries. Contrary to conventional wisdom, such optimism was furthered in the twentieth century by the intervals of war and National Socialism with their powerful ideologies of solidarity and popular mobilization. Progressives in the United States today may look longingly at how social perspectives still dominate criminal policy in Germany, but one must also keep in mind the twisted paths along which these social ideals have traveled.

NOTES

Abbreviations

ADW	Archiv des Diakonischen Werkes der Evangelischen Kirche
BA	Bundesarchiv
BL	Brandenbürgisches Landeshauptstaatsarchiv
CA	Central Ausschuss
DJZ	*Deutsche Juristen-Zeitung*
GF/St	Gefährdetenfürsorge und Straffälligenhilfe
GStA	Geheimes Staatsarchiv Preussischer Kulturbesitz
HBAB	Hauptarchiv von Bodelschwinghsche Anstalt Bethel
IKV	Internationale Kriminalistische Vereinigung
JGGSA	*Jahrbuch der Gefängnis-Gesellschaft für die Provinz Sachsen und Anhalt*
LAB	Landesarchiv Berlin
MDRG	*Monatsblätter des Deutschen Reichverbandes für Gerichtshilfe, Gefangenen- und Entlassenenfürsorge*
MKS	*Monatschrift für Kriminalpsychologie und Strafrechtsreform*
NB	Nachlass Bozi
SB	Stadtsarchiv Bielefeld
SWA	German Southwest Africa
ZStW	*Zeitschrift für die gesamte Strafrechtswissenschaft*

Introduction

1. GStA 84a no. 8195, Albert Hellwig, "Verbrechensbekämpfung und Ausbildungs-reform," 23 September 1919 (the title of the newspaper is illegible); Hans von Hentig, *Aufsätze zur Revolution* (Berlin: Springer, 1919), 2.

2. *Statistisches Jahrbuch für den Preussischen Staat* (Berlin: Landesamt, 1920–1924). In the same period, the number of convictions across Germany increased by 40 percent. Undoubtedly, "massive overcrowding" in some Prussian prisons contributed to the increase in pardoning, but higher pardon rates continued even after the prison population declined. Nikolaus Wachsmann, "Between Reform and Repression: Prisons in Weimar Germany," *Historical Journal* 45, no. 2 (2002): 414.

3. Soziale Gerichtshilfe is sometimes translated as "probation," but this can be misleading. In the American context, "probation" refers to the practice of supervising

offenders in lieu of incarceration and to the government office that investigates and supervises offenders. Gerichtshilfe was mainly an investigatory office. It was controversial whether Gerichtshilfe should be state-run (it usually was not) and whether it should practice welfare or simply mediate between welfare agencies and the courts. At least one contemporary American observer appreciated this distinction and translated Gerichtshilfe as "social case work auxiliaries to the court." Nathaniel Cantor, "Prison Reform in Germany—1933," *Journal of Criminal Law and Criminology* 24 (1933–34): 89.

4. Erwin Bumke, "Wandlung der Strafen," *MKS* 17 (1926): 359–65; Wolfgang Mittermaier, "Grundgedanken der Gerichtshilfe," *Die Justiz* 6, no. 1 (1930): 7; Paul Troschke, "Die Reformbedürftigkeit der Behandlung Asozialer Personen vom Standpunkt der Sozialpädagogik," *Die Versorgung Asozialer Personen. Gekürzter Bericht über die Tagung der Vorbereitenden Kommission zur Prüfung der Frage der Versorgung Asozialer Personen am 7. und 8. Juli 1922 in Bielefeld* (Frankfurt: Deutscher Verein für öffentliche und private Fürsorge, 1922), 8–16.

5. Detlev Peukert helped reframe the periodization of reform, describing the years 1880–1929 as the "age of classical modernity." Peukert, *Grenzen der Sozialdisziplinierung. Aufstieg und Krise der Deutschen Jugendfürsorge 1878–1932* (Cologne: Bund-Verlag, 1986); Richard Wetzell, *Inventing the Criminal: A History of German Criminology 1880–1945* (Chapel Hill: University of North Carolina Press, 2000); Peter Becker, *Verderbnis und Entartung. Eine Geschichte der Kriminologie des 19. Jahrhunderts als Diskurs und Praxis* (Göttingen: Vandenhoeck und Ruprecht, 2002); Christian Müller, *Verbrechensbekämpfung im Anstaltsstaat. Psychiatrie, Kriminologie und Strafrechtsform in Deutschland. 1871–1933* (Göttingen: Vandenhoeck und Ruprecht, 2004).

6. Jacques Donzelot, *The Policing of Families* (Baltimore: Johns Hopkins University Press, 1997), xxvi–xxvii.

7. An important exception is James Q. Whitman, *Harsh Justice: Criminal Punishment and the Widening Divide between America and Europe* (Oxford: Oxford University Press, 2003).

8. Roy Walmsley, "World Prison Population List," <*www.kcl.ac.uk/depsta/rel/icps/world-prison-population-list-2006.pdf*>; Whitman, *Harsh Justice*, 69–95.

9. Margaret Sommer, *Die Fürsorge im Strafrecht* (Berlin: C. Heymann, 1925), 33. The fact that a shocking 28 percent of German prisoners in 2006 were foreigners in some sense underscores the legacies of Weimar reform. Foreign offenders are far more likely to be perceived as unassimilable or at least unresponsive to the social measures available for German offenders. Amnesty International, *Federal Republic of Germany: The Alleged Ill-Treatment of Foreigners—An Update to the May 1995 Report* (London, 1996), and "Prison Brief for Germany," International Centre for Prison Studies, <*www.prisonstudies.org*>.

10. Dietrich Oberwittler argues that juvenile justice reformers' creation of a system with greater flexibility and informality ultimately worsened legal conditions for German youth by depriving them of traditional juridical protections. Oberwittler, *Von der Strafe zur Erziehung* (Frankfurt am Main: Campus, 2000), 336–37.

11. On the competition between private and public welfare advocates in general and its importance to politics in the Weimar Republic, see Young-Sun Hong, *Welfare, Modernity and the Weimar State, 1919–1933* (Princeton: Princeton University Press, 1998), and Edward Ross Dickinson, *The Politics of German Child Welfare From the Empire to the Federal Republic* (Cambridge, Mass.: Harvard University Press, 1996).

12. See especially Sommer, *Fürsorge*, 97–99.

13. Franz von Liszt, "Bedingte Verurteilung und Bedingte Begnadigung," *Vergleichende Darstellung des Deutschen und Ausländischen Strafrechts*, eds. Karl Birkmeyer et al. (Berlin: Verlag von Otto Liebmann, 1908), 74–75. On the American experience, see Michael Willrich, *City of Courts: Socializing Justice in Progressive Era Chicago* (Cambridge: Cambridge University Press, 2003), 89–95; David J. Rothman, *Conscience and Convenience: The Asylum and Its Alternatives in Progressive America* (Boston: Little, Brown, 1980), 82–113.

14. Edward Ross Dickinson, "Biopolitics, Fascism, Democracy: Some Reflections on Our Discourse about Modernity," *Central European History* 37, no. 1 (2004).

15. Paul Weindling, *Health, Race and German Politics between National Unification and Nazism 1870–1945* (Cambridge: Cambridge University Press, 1989), 1; Weindling, "The Medical Profession, Social Hygiene and the Birth Rate in Germany 1914–1918," in *Upheaval of War: Family, Work and Welfare in Europe, 1914–1918*, eds. Richard Wall and Jay Winter (Cambridge: Cambridge University Press, 1988).

16. Christoph Sachße and Florian Tennstedt, *Geschichte der Armenfürsorge in Deutschland. Band 2. Fürsorge und Wohlfahrtspflege 1871 bis 1929* (Stuttgart: Kohlhammer, 1988).

17. Detlev Peukert, "Die Genesis der Endlösung aus dem Geist der Wissenschaft," in *Max Webers Diagnose Der Moderne* (Göttingen: Vandenhoeck und Ruprecht, 1989), 102–21.

18. Richard J. Evans, *Tales from the German Underworld: Crime and Punishment in the Nineteenth Century* (New Haven: Yale University Press, 1998), 78–79; Richard Evans, *Rituals of Retribution: Capital Punishment in Germany 1600–1987* (New York: Oxford University Press, 1996), 528–29; Becker, *Verderbnis*, 25–27, 365–71; Müller, *Verbrechensbekämpfung*, 14, 23; Richard Wetzell, "The Medicalization of Criminal Law Reform in Imperial Germany," in *Institutions of Confinement: Hospitals, Asylums, and Prisons in Western Europe and North America, 1500–1950*, ed. Norbert Finzsch and Robert Jütte (Cambridge: Cambridge University Press, 1996).

19. Eric J. Engstrom, "Review of Christian Müller, Verbrechensbekampfung im Anstaltsstaat: Psychiatrie, Kriminologie und Strafrechtsreform im Deutschland, 1871–1933," H-German, H-Net Reviews (July 2006).

20. Wetzell, *Inventing the Criminal*, 140.

21. Andrew Lees, *Cities, Sin, and Social Reform in Imperial Germany* (Ann Arbor: University of Michigan Press, 2002).

22. Whitman, *Harsh Justice*, 120–50. Oberwittler notes the growth in pardons for youth offenders, but argues that there was nevertheless a "refinement of social con-

trol" as the courts increasingly granted guardianship over wayward youth and subjected them to forced education. Oberwittler, *Strafe*, 296–314.

23. Kevin Repp, *Reformers, Critics, and the Paths of German Modernity: Anti-Politics and the Search for Alternatives* (Cambridge, Mass.: Harvard University Press, 2000); Hong, *Welfare*.

24. Wetzell, *Inventing the Criminal*, 299–300; Becker, *Verderbnis*, 369–71; Peukert, "Genesis." In his empirical work, however, Peukert's analysis of creeping fascism and biological determinism in social policy circles is grounded in an argument about economic and cultural crises in the Weimar era and their impact upon social reform. Peukert, *Grenzen*, 292–317. Oberwittler also stresses the importance of specific conditions in the Weimar era and growing disillusionment with the failures of juvenile reform institutions. His argument that these institutions were characterized by a "deficit of modernity"—whether or not that is accurate in the case of juvenile institutions—seems inapplicable to the institutions for adult offenders discussed in this book. Oberwittler, *Strafe*, 215–41.

Chapter 1

1. Johann Fichte, "Thirteenth Address," *Addresses to the German Nation* (New York: Harper and Row, 1968), 190.

2. Hannah Arendt, *The Origins of Totalitarianism* (New York: Harcourt, Brace and Company, 1973), 166.

3. Leonard Krieger, *The German Idea of Freedom: History of a Political Tradition from the Reformation to 1871* (Chicago: University of Chicago Press, 1957), 176–92; James Sheehan, *German History 1770–1866* (Oxford: Clarendon Press, 1989), 375–79. For an alternative reading, see Etiene Balibar, "Fichte and the Internal Border: On Addresses to the German Nation," in *Masses, Classes, Ideas* (New York: Routledge, 1994).

4. Krieger, *German Idea*, 192.

5. Sheehan, *German History*, 378.

6. For a more nuanced argument regarding the relationship between the romantic ideal of "*Kulturnation*" and "the liberal image of the *Staatsnation*," see Thomas Nipperdey, *Deutsche Geschichte 1866–1918*, vol. 1, *Arbeitswelt und Bürgergeist* (München: C. H. Beck, 1991), 303–7. Also Louis Dumont, *The German Ideology: From France to Germany and Back* (Chicago: University of Chicago Press, 1994), which explores the relationship between "German romantic liberalism" and the supposedly "purer" French varieties.

7. K. T. Schwenken, *Aktenmäßige Nachrichten von dem Gauner und Vagabunden-Gesindel* (1822; reprint, Leipzig: Zentralantiquariat der DDR, 1981), 8–9, 1. On Gaunertum as a counterworld to the bourgeoisie, Peter Becker, *Verderbnis und Entartung: Eine Geschichte der Kriminologie des 19. Jahrhunderts als Diskurs und Praxis* (Göttingen: Vandenhoeck und Ruprecht, 2002), 177–254. On the nexus of Jewishness and

criminality, see Sander Gilman, *The Case of Freud: Medicine and Identity at the Fin de Siecle* (Baltimore: Johns Hopkins University Press, 1993), 169–70, and "The Jewish Murderer: Jack the Ripper, Race, and Gender," in *The Jew's Body* (New York: Routledge, 1991).

8. On the role of "Bildung" in developing capacities for citizenship, see Peter Uwe Hohendahl, *Building a National Culture: The Case of Germany 1830–1870* (Ithaca: Cornell University Press, 1989). The very word "citizen" (*Bürger*) in German already contained inherent connotations of rootedness in some kind of local middle-class community. Jürgen Kocka, "Bürgertum und Bügerlichkeit als Probleme der deutschen Geschichte vom späten 18. zum frühen 20. Jahrhundert," in *Bürger und Bürgerlichkeit im 19. Jahrhundert* (Göttingen: Vandenhoeck und Ruprecht, 1987).

9. Peter Becker, "Vom Haltlosen zur Bestie. Das polizeiliche Bild des Verbrechers im 19. Jahrhundert," *Sicherheit und Wohlfahrt. Polizei, Gesellschaft und Herrschaft im 19. und 20. Jahrhundert*, ed. Alf Lüdtke (Frankfurt am Main: Suhrkamp, 1992). According to Gilman, the identification of "the language of the Jews" with criminals goes back to the Renaissance. The tradition was given new life by Martin Luther in his *Book of Thieves* and then revised in the context of the German Enlightenment. Gilman, *Jewish Self-Hatred: Anti-Semitism and the Hidden Language of the Jews* (Baltimore: Johns Hopkins University Press, 1986).

10. Eberhard Schmidt, *Einführung in die Geschichte der deutschen Strafrechtspflege* (Göttingen: Vandenhoeck und Ruprecht, 1947); Hinrich Rüping, *Grundriß der Strafrechtsgeschichte* (München: C. H. Beck, 1981); Gustav Radbruch, *Paul Anselm Feuerbach. Ein Juristenleben* (Göttingen: Vandenhoek und Ruprecht, 1969).

11. Schmidt, *Einführung*, 20. Also see Isabel V. Hull, *Sexuality, State, and Civil Society in Germany, 1700–1815* (Ithaca: Cornell University Press, 1996), 342–70.

12. Paul Johann Anselm Feuerbach, *Lehrbuch des gemeinen in Deutschland gültigen Rechts* (Giessen: G. F. Heyes, 1801), 3.

13. Schmidt, *Einführung*, 214.

14. Feuerbach, *Lehrbuch*, 164.

15. Ibid., 16–45. On the corporealization of sovereignty in earlier eras see Ernst Kantorowicz, *The King's Two Bodies: A Study in Medieval Political Theology* (Princeton: Princeton University Press, 1997).

16. Otto Mittelstädt, "Schuld und Strafe: Zur Kritik der heutigen Reformbestrebungen," *Gerichtsaal* (1892): 238–239; Karl Binding, *Handbuch des Strafrechts* (Leipzig: Duncker und Humboldt, 1885), 13; Binding, *Grundriss des Deutschen Strafrechts* (Leipzig: Meiner, 1913), xvi–xvii.

17. Pasquale Pasquino, "Criminology: The birth of a Special Knowledge," in *The Foucault Effect: Studies in Governmentality*, ed. Graham Burchell et al. (Chicago: University of Chicago Press, 1991), 237.

18. Ibid., 240.

19. Paul Johann Anselm Feuerbach, *Aktenmäßige Darstellung merwürdiger Verbrechen*, 3rd ed. (Frankfurt: G. F. Heper, 1849).

20. Which is not to say that the work was obscure. The narratives were admired by nineteenth-century crime writers and by a later generation of criminologists. Joachim Rückert, "Zur Rolle der Fallgeschichte in Juristenausbildung und juristischer Praxis zwischen 1790 und 1880," in *Erzählte Kriminalität. Zur Typologie und Funktion von narrativen Darstellungen in Strafrechtspflege, Publizistik und Literatur zwischen 1770 und 1920*, ed. Jorg Schönert (Tübingen: Niemeyer, 1991). The *Narratives* was republished in 1913 with an introduction by a prominent criminologist. See the review by Hans von Hentig in *Monatschrift für Kriminalpsychologie und Strafrechtsreform* 10 (1913).

21. Feuerbach, *Darstellungen*, 6.

22. Ibid., 4–5.

23. Radbruch, *Feuerbach*, 3–12.

24. Feuerbach, *Darstellungen*, 6.

25. Peter Becker argues that Feuerbach's criminal portraits ultimately reinforced the distinction in his jurisprudence between criminally responsible and criminally insane offenders; see Becker, "Randgruppen im Blickfeld der Polizei," in *Archiv für Sozialgeschichte* 32 (1992): 290. In contrast to later criminologists, he argues elsewhere, Feuerbach clung to a moral discourse. Becker, *Verderbnis*, 266–67.

26. Feuerbach, *Darstellungen*, iv.

27. Feuerbach himself was ambivalent and often ambiguous about the role of pardons, arguing in his early work that "the duty of the state" and the majesty of the law should take precedence over moral considerations in a particular instance. See Feuerbach, *Revision der Grundsätze und Grundbegriffe des positiven peinlichen Rechts* (Erfurt: Hennings, 1799–1800), especially vol. 1, 25–28; see also the introduction to the 1849 edition of *Darstellungen* by Feuerbach's protégé, C. J. A. Mittermaier.

28. James Q. Whitman, *Harsh Justice: Criminal Punishment and the Widening Gap between America and Europe* (New York: Oxford University Press, 2003), 145–46; Franz von Liszt, "Bedingte Verurteilung und Bedingte Begnadigung," *Vergleichende Darstellung des Deutschen und Ausländischen Strafrechts* (Berlin: Verlag von Otto Liebmann, 1908), ed. Karl Birkmeyer et al., 58–63.

29. Feuerbach, *Darstellungen*, 43–56, 69–75.

30. This literature is cataloged, summarized, and discussed in Friedrich Christian Benedikt Avé-Lallemant, *Das Deutsche Gaunerthum in seiner social-politischen, literarischen und linguistischen Ausbildung zu seinem heutigen Bestande*, Bd. 1 (Leipzig: Brockhaus, 1858). See also Becker, *Verderbnis*, 177–212, and Joachim Lindner, "Deutsche Pitavalgeschichten in der Mitte des 19. Jahrhunderts. Konkurrierende Formen der Wissensvermittlung und der Verbrechensdeutung," in *Erzählte Kriminalität*. The editors of the "New Pitaval," a long-running, popular series on "true-life" crimes, were initially inspired by Feuerbach's *Darstellungen*.

31. Avé-Lallemant, *Deutsche Gaunerthum*, vol. 4, 314–18.

32. Richard Wetzell, *Inventing the Criminal* (Chapel Hill: University of North Carolina Press, 2000), 31–33.

33. Adolf Merkel, *Kriminalistische Abhandlungen. I. Anhang: Über vergeltende Gerechtigkeit* (Leipzig: Breitkopf und Härtel, 1867), 4–10. Franz von Liszt, "Kriminalpolitische Aufgaben," republished in *Strafrechtliche Aufsätze und Vorträge* (Berlin: Guttentag, 1905).

34. One sign of this was the carelessness with which classical liberal jurists used the term "criminal." From Feuerbach to Holtzendorff to Binding, jurists known for their precise attention to legal categories referred to any once-convicted person as a "Verbrecher." Richard Evans points out that, for liberals, the actual circumstances of punishment lacked the "larger political importance" of arrests and trials. Richard J. Evans, *Tales from the German Underworld: Crime and Punishment in the Nineteenth Century* (New Haven: Yale University Press, 1998), 121.

35. Franz von Holtzendorff and Heinrich Jagemann, eds., *Handbuch des Gefängniswesens* (Hamburg: Richter, 1888).

36. Karl Krohne, *Lehrbuch der Gefängniskunde unter Berücksichtigung der Kriminalstatistik und Kriminalpolitik* (Stuttgart: Enke, 1889); Erwin Bumke, "Die Freiheitsstrafe als Problem der Gesetzgebung," and L. Freudenthal, "Die Rechtliche Stellung des Gefangenen," *Handbuch Deutsches Gefängniswesen*, ed. Erwin Bumke (Berlin: F. Vahlen, 1928).

37. In theory at least, the *Gefängnis* was less harsh and less degrading. Prisons did not necessarily have forced labor and usually held offenders sentenced for less than two years. The *Zuchthaus* (from *züchten*—to breed or cultivate) had its origins in a Dutch Calvinist tradition of moral reformation. Robert von Hippel, "Beiträge zur Geschichte der Freiheitsstrafe," *ZStW* 18 (1898): 419–25. See also Peter Spierenburg, *The Spectacle of Suffering: Executions and the Evolution of Repression* (New York: Cambridge University Press, 1984).

38. Schmidt, *Einführung*.

39. Thomas Berger, *Die Konstante Repression. Zur Geschichte des Strafvollzugs in Preussen nach 1850* (Frankfurt: Verlag Roter Stern, 1974), 292–95.

40. Bumke, "Die Freiheitsstrafe," and Hasse, "Gefangenenanstalten in Deutschland und die Organisation ihrer Verwaltung," in *Deutsches Gefängniswesens*.

41. Georg Gradnauer, *Das Elend des Strafvollzuges* (Dresden: Vorwaerts, 1905), 34–58.

42. Thomas Mann, *Der Zauberberg* (Frankfurt am Main: Fischer, 1974), 457. In the Gefangnis, prisoners were still addressed with the formal "Sie," ostensibly a representation of the fact that they were not yet truly "outcast." On the role of honor and degradation in German punishment, see Whitman, *Harsh Justice*.

43. Johann Hinrich Wichern, "Über die Einzelhaft und die Tätigkeit der Brüderschaft des Rauhen Hauses in dem Strafgefängnis zu Moabit. Rede gehalten in der 57. Sitzung des Preußischen Abgeordnetenhauses," *Sämtliche Werke* (Hamburg: Luther Verlag, 1973), vol. 6, 340.

44. Heinrich Jagemann, "Organismus der Gefängnis-Verwaltung," in *Handbuch*, ed. Jagemann and Holtzendorff, 15–17.

45. In the views of some scholars and state officials, the police was an arm of the military, the immediate and principal agent for ensuring the state's monopoly of force. During the 1890s the police itself became increasingly trained and equipped for military-like engagements, especially in the western industrial areas of the Ruhr. See Hsui-huey Liang, *The Berlin Police Force in the Weimar Republic* (Berkeley: University of California Press, 1970); Ralph Jessen, *Polizei im Industrierevier: Modernisierung und Herrschaftspraxis im westfälischen Ruhrgebiet 1848–1914* (Göttingen: Vandenhoeck und Ruprecht, 1991); Albrecht Funk, *Polizei und Rechtsstaat: Die Entwicklung des staatlichen Gewaltmonopols in Preussen 1848–1918* (Frankfurt am Main: Campus, 1986), 233–35.

46. Hans Eichler, "Strafvollzug als Rechtsangelegenheit," in *Handwörterbuch der Kriminologie*, ed. Alexander Elster and Heinrich Lingemann (Berlin and Leipzig: de Gruyter, 1933), 703–4.

47. Karl Fuhr, *Strafrechtspflege und Sozialpolitik* (Berlin: Liebmann, 1892); Krohne, *Lehrbuch.*

48. Robert von Hippel, *Die strafrechtliche Bekämpfung von Bettel, Landstreicherei und Arbeitsscheu. Eine Darstellung des heutigen deutschen Rechtszustandes nebst Reformvorschlägen* (Berlin: Otto Liebmann, 1895), 52–68.

49. GStA 84a no. 7888, "Überweisung entlassener Strafgefangener an die Polizeibehörden. 1862–1900."

50. Doris Kaufmann, "Irre und Wahnsinnige: Zum Problem der sozialen Ausgrenzung von Geisteskranken in der ländlichen Gesellschaft des frühen 19. Jahrhunderts," in *Verbrechen, Strafen und soziale Kontrolle*, ed. Richard van Dülmen (Frankfurt am Main: Fischer-Taschenbuch-Verlag, 1990). Also Dirk Blasius, *Der Verwaltete Wahnsinn* (Frankfurt am Main: Fischer-Taschenbuch-Verlag, 1980) and *Kriminalität und Alltag* (Göttingen: Vandenhoeck und Ruprecht, 1978); and Alf Lüdtke, *Gemeinwohl, Polizei und Festungspraxis* (Göttingen: Vandenhoeck und Ruprecht, 1982).

51. Georg Steigerthal, "Die Bekämpfung asozialer Elemente durch die Nachhaftsstrafe," *41. JGGSA* (1925); Hippel, *Bekämpfung*, 198–205.

52. Fuhr, *Strafrechtspflege*, 328; the full text of the law is in the appendix. It was common for police supervision to prohibit visits to certain pubs, clubs, or associations.

53. Becker, *Verderbnis*, 214–19.

54. Until the end of the eighteenth century, a defendant could not be convicted without a confession, usually attained through torture, or two sworn witnesses to the crime. John L. Langbein, *Torture and the Law of Proof* (Chicago: University of Chicago Press, 1972). Feuerbach quoted in Fuhr, *Strafrechtspflege*, 20.

55. Proposals to condemn police supervision were beaten back at the annual meeting of the Association of Prison Officials. *Verhandlungen der Versammlung des Vereins der Deutschen Strafanstaltsbeamten* (Heidelberg: Weis, 1880); classical liberal scholars Holtzendorff and Binding also defended the practice. Fuhr, *Strafrechtspflege*, 279–82.

56. Funk, *Polizei und Rechtsstaat*, 32–33; Georg Steigerthal, "Besserungs- und Bewahrungsanstalten," in *Handwörterbuch*, Elster and Lingemann, 143–53.

57. W. O. Shanahan, *German Protestants Face the Social Question, vol. 1, The Conservative Phase, 1815–1871* (Notre Dame: University of Notre Dame Press, 1954).

58. Martin Gerhardt, *Johann Hinrich Wichern. Ein Lebensbild*, vols. 1–3 (Hamburg: Rauhes Haus, 1927–1931), contains useful detail but is unabashedly hagiographic. See also Peter Meinhold, *Wichern und Ketteler. Evangelische und katholische Prinzipien kirchlichen Sozialhandelns* (Wiesbaden: Steiner, 1978).

59. Sheehan, *German History*, 561; George L. Mosse, *Nationalism and Sexuality* (Madison: University of Wisconsin Press, 1985), 70–75. On the intellectual context of Protestant social activism, see Hermann Beck, "Conservatives and the Social Question in 19th Century Prussia," and Wolfgang Schwentker, "Viktor Aimé Huber and the Emergence of Social Conservatism," in *Between Reform, Reaction and Resistance: Studies in the History of German Conservatism from 1789 to 1945*, ed. L. E. Jones and James Retallack (Providence: Berg, 1993).

60. Gerhardt, *Wichern*, vol. 1; Gunther Brakelmann, *Kirche und Sozialismus im 19. Jahrhundert* (Witten: Luther, 1966).

61. Shanahan, *Protestants*, 237–38.

62. Gerhardt, *Wichern*, vol. 2, 137–272; Detlev Peukert, *Grenzen der Sozialdisziplinierung* (Cologne: Bund Verlag, 1986), 47–48.

63. Shanahan, *Protestants*, 225.

64. Johann Hinrich Wichern, "Rede auf dem Wittenberger Kirchentag" (1848), in *Sämtliche Werke*, vol. 1, 156–65.

65. Ibid., 158. The story is apparently taken from the memoir of Carsten Hinrich Hinz, *Das Leben des Verbrechers und die Bekehrung* (Hamburg, 1842). In an earlier essay, Wichern asserts that prison "made" Hinz into a criminal. Wichern also claims to have evidence of numerous other cases in which prisoners, out of desperation and longing for spiritual assistance, created their own gods and protective spirits. Johann Hinrich Wichern, "Notstände der protestantischen Kirche" (1844), *Werke*, vol. 4, pt. 1, 255.

66. Johann Hinrich Wichern, "Denkschrift über die Einzelhaft" (1861), in Wichern, *Werke*, vol. 6, 280.

67. Ann Stoler and Frederick Cooper, "Between Metropole and Colony: Rethinking a Research Agenda," and Susan Thorne, "The Conversion of England and the Conversion of the World Inseparable: Missionary Imperialism and the Language of Class 1750–1850," in *Tensions of Empire: Colonial Cultures in a Bourgeois World*, ed. Frederick Cooper and Ann Stoler (Berkeley: University of California Press, 1997).

68. Johann Hinrich Wichern, "Der Verein für innere Mission in Hamburg," *Werke*, vol. 2, 46. Emphasis in the original.

69. See Johann Hinrich Wichern, *Die innere Mission der deutschen evangelischen Kirche. Eine Denschrift an die deutsche Nation* (1849; reprint, Hamburg: Agentur des Rauhen Hauses, 1948), and, in particular, the second chapter, entitled "Die geographischen Grenzlinien auf dem Gebiete der inneren Mission."

70. Wichern, "Notstände," *Werke*, vol. 4, 235–37.

71. Johann Hinrich Wichern, "Denkschrift über die Einzelhaft," *Werke*, vol. 1, 287–89.

72. Michel Foucault, *Discipline and Punish* (New York: Vintage Books, 1979), 124–26.

73. Wichern, "Denkschrift," 279.

74. Wichern was instrumental in the building of the "New Prison" at Moabit between 1844 and 1849 but was quickly disappointed in its conventional administration. In 1854, King Friedrich Wilhelm of Prussia called upon him to transform Moabit in line with his original vision. Johann Hinrich Wichern, "Separatvotum zu dem Kommisionsbericht über die neue Strafanstalt zu Moabit, die Durchführung des pennsylvanischen Systems daselbst und die in Moabit vorgekommenen Wahnsinnsfälle und Selbstmorde" (1854), *Werke*, vol. 6.

75. Johann Hinrich Wichern, "Gutachten über die Neuorganisation des Personals der Strafanstalt zu Moabit," (1856), *Werke*, vol. 6, 80–81.

76. Johann Hinrich Wichern, "Zur Frage der Einzelhaft. Rede gehalten in der 62. Plenarsitzung des Preuß. Abgeordnetenhauses" (1861), Wichern, *Werke*, vol. 6, 317.

77. Wichern, "Über eine Vorbereitungsschule für Strafanstaltsaufseher" (1875), *Werke*, vol. 6, 378–79.

78. Wichern, "Die Behandlung der Verbrecher in den Gefangnissen und der entlassenen Straflinge," *Werke*, vol. 6, 31.

79. Wichern, "Gutachten über die Polizeiaufsicht" (1868), *Werke*, vol. 6, 372.

80. GSta 84a no. 7888, "Überweisungen entlassener Strafgefangener an die Polizeibehörden."

81. Wichern, "Gutachten," 373.

82. Ibid., 374; Theodor Just, *Festschrift zum 100-jährigen Geschichte der Rheinisch-westfälischen Gefängnis-Gesellschaft* (Düsseldorf: Selbstverl. d. Gesellschaft, 1926).

83. Wichern, "Die Gefangene in den Gefangnisse und nach ihrer Entlassung," *Werke*, vol. 6, 29; and "Die Behandlung," 43–49.

84. Wichern, "Rede auf dem Wittenberger Kirchentage," *Gessamelte Schriften*, 242.

85. Funk, *Polizei und Rechtsstaat*, 106–8.

86. Avé-Lallemant, *Deutsche Gaunerthum*, vol. 2, 3.

87. Ibid., vol. 3, esp. 193ff.

88. Ibid., vol. 1., 13–18; vol. 4, 313–17.

89. Ibid., vol. 1, vol. 2, 376. On the relationship between anthropology and liberalism between 1848 and 1885, see Woodruff D. Smith, *Politics and the Sciences of Culture in Germany 1840–1920* (New York: Oxford University Press, 1991), esp. 13–51 and 91–100.

90. Avé-Lallemant, *Deutsche Gaunerthum*, vol. 2, 369–75; Avé-Lallemant, *Die Krisis der deutschen Polizei* (Leipzig: Brockhaus, 1861). His influence on a new generation of police reformers can be gauged in Kurt Wolzendorff, *Der Polizeigedanke des modernen Staates. Ein Versuch zur allgemeinen Verwaltungslehre unter Berücksichtigung Preußens* (Breslau: Markus, 1918), 160–80.

91. Theodor Just and Gustav von Rohden, *Hundert Jahre Geschichte*, 191–93.

92. Ernst Rosenfeld, *Zweihundert Jahre Fürsorge der Preußischen Staatsregierung für die Entlassene Gefangenen* (Berlin: J. Guttentag, 1905), 40–46.

93. Franz von Holtzendorff, *Gesetz oder Verwaltungsmaxime? Rechtliche Bedenken gegen die Preußische Denkschrift betreffend die Einzelnhaft* (Berlin, 1861); Wichern, "Die Auseinandersetzung mit Professor Franz von Holtzendorff" (1861), *Werke*, vol. 6, 329–33; Gerhardt, *Wichern*, vol. 3.

94. On Mittermaier and the death penalty, see Richard J. Evans, *Rituals of Retribution: Capital Punishment in Germany 1600–1987* (New York: Oxford University Press, 1996), 254–57. Holtzendorff was also a prominent advocate of liberalism in Protestant ideology and practice as a member of the Protestant Unionsverein in Berlin. Claudia Lepp, *Protestantisch-Liberaler Aufbruch in die Moderne. Der deutsche Protestantenverein in der Zeit der Reichsgründung und des Kulturkampfes* (Gütersloh: Albert Teichmann, 1996).

95. Holtzendorff, "Einige Bemerkungen." Juvenile justice thus was not inherently a departure from principles of legality, rationalism, and responsibility. The special exceptions for youth offenders, in many cases, reinforced the dichotomy between (rational and autonomous) legal subjects and (irrational and dependent) pedagogical objects.

96. Holtzendorff, *Deportation*, 276.

97. Ibid., 618–19.

98. Ibid., 277ff., 669.

99. Holtzendorff, *Gesetz oder Verwaltungsmaxime*; Wichern, "Die Auseinandersetzung." Also, Gerhardt, *Wichern*, 137–272.

100. Funk, *Polizei*, 145–48.

101. Ibid., 153.

102. Otto Mittelstädt, "Die Reform des deutschen Gefängniswesens," *Preussische Jahrbücher* 40 (1877).

103. Otto Mittelstädt, *Gegen die Freiheitsstrafen. Ein Beitrag zur Kritik des heutigen Strafsystem* (Leipzig: S. Hirzel, 1879).

104. Mittelstädt, *Die Freiheitsstrafe*, iii. Mittelstädt's passionate support of classical liberal tenets of justice cost him an opportunity to serve as deputy to the first Imperial Minister of Justice. Bismarck declared Mittelstädt to be unsuited for the role because of his "idealistic exaggeration of the mission of justice, which I see as a sickness of today's judiciary." Hans Hattenhauer, "Justizkarriere durch die Provinzen: Das Beispiel Otto Mittelstädt (1834–1899)," *Preußen in der Provinz: Beiträge zum 1. deutsch-polnischen Historikerkolloquium im Rahmen des Kooperationsvertrages zwischen der Adam-Mickiewicz-Universität Poznan und der Christian-Albrechts-Universität zu Kiel*, ed. Peter Nitsche (Frankfurt: Peter Lang, 1991), 49.

105. Mittelstädt, *Die Freiheitsstrafe*, 29–35, 56–62.

106. Ibid., 25, 58.

107. Ibid., 62.

108. Ibid., 73.

109. Ibid., 72.

110. Karl Krohne, "Der gegenwärtige Stand der Gefängniswissenschaft," *ZStW* 1 (1881): 59–60; See the collection of newspaper articles at Bundesarchiv. 30.01. no.

5657–58, "Äusserungen der Presse über die Strafvollstreckung und das Gefängnis-wesen."

111. Franz von Liszt, "Der Zweckgedanke im Strafrecht" (1882), in *Strafrechtliche Aufsätze und Vorträge* (Berlin: Guttentag, 1905), vol. 1, 130.

112. Richard Sontag, "Beiträge zur Lehre von der Strafe," *ZStW* 1 (1881): 480–86. Monika Frommel points out that both the "Modern School" and their "classical school" opponents sought to portray themselves as "modern." Frommel, *Präventionsmodelle in der deutschen Strafzwecksdiskussion: Beziehungen zwischen Rechtsphilosophie, Dogmatik, Rechtspolitik und Erfahrungswissenschaften* (Berlin: Duncker und Humboldt, 1987).

113. Hattenhauer, "Justizkarriere," 37.

114. Heinrich Seyfarth, "Über die Deportation von Verbrechern," *Blätter für Gefängniskunde* 34 (1900): 4.

115. Otto Mittelstädt, *Vor der Fluth: Sechs Briefe zur Politik der deutschen Gegenwart* (Leipzig: Hirzel, 1897), 38–39. Heinrich Treitschke also argued that Germany, as a new country, was plagued by disunity and needed to be especially vigilant in dealing with its internal enemies.

116. Ibid., 32.

117. Ibid., 37.

118. Andrew Lees, *Cities, Sin, and Social Reform in Imperial Germany* (Ann Arbor: University of Michigan Press, 2002), 138, 149.

119. James Sheehan, *German Liberalism in the Nineteenth Century* (Chicago: University of Chicago Press, 1978), 154.

120. Liszt, "Bedingte Verurteilung," 6.

121. Mittelstädt, Otto, "Schuld und Strafe. Zur Kritik der heutigen Reformbestrebungen," *Der Gerichtssaal* 46–47 (1892): 237–38.

122. Reinhard Frank, *Freiheitsstrafe, Deportation und Unschädlichmachung. Ein Wort zur Verständigung* (Giessen: J. Ricker'sche, 1895), 1. See also Frank's comments at 10. *JGGSA* (1895): 105.

Chapter 2

1. Richard Wetzell, "The Medicalization of Criminal Law Reform in Imperial Germany," in *Institutions of Confinement: Hospitals, Asylums, and Prisons in Western Europe and North America, 1500–1950*, ed. Norbert Finzsch and Robert Jütte (Cambridge: Cambridge University Press, 1996); Peter Becker, *Verderbnis und Entartung. Eine Geschichte der Kriminologie des 19. Jahrhunderts als Diskurs und Praxis* (Göttingen: Vandenhoeck und Ruprecht, 2002).

2. Michel Foucault, *Discipline and Punish: The Birth of the Prison* (New York: Pantheon, 1977); See also the exchange between Foucault and historian Michelle Perrot regarding the creative role of architecture: "The Eye of Power: A Conversation with Jean-Pierre Barou and Michelle Perrot," in Michel Foucault, *Power/Knowledge: Selected Interviews & Other Writings 1972–1977* (New York: Pantheon, 1980), 148–49.

3. See chapter 1 above.

4. James Q. Whitman, *Harsh Justice: Criminal Punishment and the Widening Gap between America and Europe* (New York: Oxford University Press, 2003). For an argument on the role of pardons in constituting authority, see Douglas Hay's classic essay on early modern England. Douglas Hay, "Property, Authority and the Criminal Law," in *Albion's Fatal Tree: Crime and Society in Eighteenth Century England*, ed. Douglas Hay et al. (London: Pantheon, 1975).

5. An 1878 report for the Merseburg aristocracy declared that public interest had "grown cold." *1. JGGSA* (1885): 1; the Prussian government's role is described in Ernst Rosenfeld, *Zweihundert Jahre Fürsorge der Preußischen Staatsegierung für die entlassene Gefangenen* (Berlin: J. Guttentag, 1905), 44–46.

6. Jahres-Bericht des Zentralamts für den Gefangenenfürsorgeverein in der Provinz Hessen-Nassau (1916); *10. JGGSA* (1895): 1; Theodor Just and Gustav von Rohden, *Hundert Jahre Geschichte der Rheinisch-Westfälische Gefängnis-Gesellschaft 1826–1926* (Düsseldorf: Gesellsch, 1926).

7. Adolf Fuchs, *Die Gefangenen-Schutzthätigkeit und Verbrechens-Prophylaxe* (Berlin: Carl Heymanns Verlag, 1898), 33–35.

8. The professions stated on the membership lists are sometimes ambiguous. The membership lists that were examined are a mix of regional prison societies and local prison associations: Rhineland-Westphalia, Saxony-Anhalt, Hesse-Nassau; Elberfeld-Barmen, Magdeburg, and Halle.

9. It is the task of society to "lead the offender toward an ordered social life in which he is protected from the commission of new crimes"; Karl Krohne, *Lehrbuch der Gefängniskunde* (Stuttgart: Enke, 1889). See also Heinrich Seyfarth, *Hinter eisernen Gittern. Ein Blick in die Verbrecherwelt. Zuchthausstudien* (Leipzig: Verlag von Fridrich Richter, 1898).

10. Fuchs, *Gefangenen-Schutzthätigkeit*, 1–2; Ellen Scheuner, *Die Gefährdetenfürsorge* (Berlin: C. Heymann, 1930).

11. Fuchs, *Gefangenen-Schutzthätigkeit*, 52–82.

12. ADW CA 554, vol. 3. Heinrich Seyfarth, "Die Tätigkeit des deutschen Hilfsvereins für entlassene Gefangene. Vortrag auf der Generalversammlung des Verbandes der Deutschen Schutzvereine in Halle, 22 September 1904."

13. Ibid., 5, 16. See also Speck, "Der neueste Angriff auf die Fürsorge für entlassene Strafgefangene," *16. JGGSA* (1900): 64–78.

14. *18. JGGSA* (1902): 5–7; *Jahresbericht des Deutschen Hilfsvereins für entlassene Gefangene* (1901–04).

15. Ephrem Ricking, *Die deutschen Wanderarbeitsstätten* (Mönchen-Gladbach: Volksvereins, 1912), 41.

16. Frank B. Tipton, *Regional Variations in the Economic Development of Germany During the Nineteenth Century* (Middletown, Conn.: Wesleyan University Press, 1976), 88–94. Steve Hochstadt, *Mobility and Modernity: Migration in Germany 1820–1988* (Ann Arbor: University of Michigan Press, 1999).

17. Klaus J. Bade, "From Emigration to Immigration: The German Experience in

the Nineteenth and Twentieth Centuries," *Central European History* 28, no. 4 (1996); David Crew, *Town in the Ruhr* (New York: Columbia University Press, 1979), 59–74.

18. Dieter Langewiesche and Friedrich Lenger, "Internal Migration: Persistence and Mobility," in *Population, Labour and Migration in 19th and 20th Century Germany*, ed. Klaus J. Bade (New York: Berg Press, 1987), 94; Tipton, *Variations*, 91.

19. Tipton, *Variations*, 91.

20. James H. Jackson Jr., "*Alltagsgeschichte*, Social Science History, and the Study of Migration in Nineteenth-Century Germany," *Central European History* 23, nos. 2–3 (1990): 251–56.

21. See especially the poetry, songs, and artwork gathered in *Wohnsitz, Nirgendwo: vom Leben und vom Überleben auf der Strasse*, ed. Kunstlerhaus Bethanien (Berlin: Frölich und Kaufmann, 1982). Wilhelm Riehl wrote that "German folk humor praised only 'the holiness of beggars, of do-nothings, of propertylessness.'" Quoted in Anson Rabinbach, *The Human Motor: Energy, Fatigue and the Origins of Modernity* (Berkeley: University of California Press, 1990), 30.

22. Josiah Flynt, *Tramping with Tramps: Studies and Sketches of Vagabond Life* (New York: The Century Co., 1900), 169–99; Hans Ostwald, *Landstreicher* (Berlin: Bard Marquartdt und Co., 1904).

23. Wolfgang Köllmann, *Bevölkerung in der industriellen Revolution* (Göttingen: Vandenhoek und Ruprecht, 1974), 115–16; Mack Walker, *German Home Towns: Community, State and General Estate 1648–1871* (Ithaca: Cornell University Press, 1971); Steve Hochstadt, "Migration in Preindustrial Germany," in *Central European History* 16 (1983).

24. Flynt, *Tramping*, 186–87.

25. Jürgen Kocka, *Arbeiter und Burger im 19. Jahrhundert: Varianten ihres Verhaltnisses im europaischen Vergleich* (München: Oldenbourg, 1986); David Blackbourn, *The Long Nineteenth Century: A History of Germany 1780–1918* (New York: Oxford University Press, 1998), 114–16. In many trades, the length of the journey doubled between the eighteenth century and the 1840s. Jonathan Sperber, *The European Revolutions, 1848–1851* (Cambridge: Cambridge University Press, 1994), 44.

26. Johann Hinrich Wichern, "Festrede zur Einweihung der Herberge zur Heimath in Hamburg," *Fliegende Blätter aus dem Rauhen Hause* 29 (1872): 289–301.

27. Wolfgang Ayass, *Das Arbeitshaus Breitenau* (Kassel: Gesamthochschule Kassel, 1992), 93–94.

28. Ayaß, *Arbeitshaus*, 92.

29. Ludwig Fuld, "Zur Vagabundenfrage," *Gerichtssaal* 36 (1884): 553.

30. Robert von Hippel, *Die strafrechtliche Bekämpfung von Bettel, Landstreicherei und Arbeitsscheu. Eine Darstellung des heutigen deutschen Rechtszustandes nebst Reformvorschlägen* (Berlin: Otto Liebmann, 1895).

31. Ibid., 3–4.

32. Ibid., 48–50. The police's routine harassment of traveling apprentices is described in August Bebel, *Aus meinem Leben* (Frankfurt: Europäische Verlaganstalt,

1964), 42–44, and Theodor Wangemann, "Aus meinem Wandertagebuch," in *Die Arbeiter-Kolonie. Organ des Gesamt-Verbands der Deutschen Natural-Verpflegungs-Stationen und Herbergsverein* 10–11 (1893).

33. Bettina Hitzer, *Im Netz der Liebe. Die protestantische Kirche und ihre Zuwanderer in der Metropole Berlin (1849–1914)* (Köln: Böhlau Verlag, 2006), 336–39; Joachim Schlör, *Nights in the Big City: Paris, Berlin, London 1840–1930* (London: Reaktion Books, 1998), 147–53.

34. "Aus der Arbeit des Centralausschußes," *Fliegende Blätter aus dem Rauhen Hause* 45 (1888): 200; Flynt, *Tramping*, 175–92.

35. Hermann Stursberg, *Die Vagabundenfrage* (Düsseldorf: Rheinisch-Westfällisches Gefängnisverein, 1882). The 1881 meeting of the Rhenish prison society, where this lecture was given, centered on the vagabond issue.

36. HBAB, no. 8/3–32a, Bodelschwingh, "Referat." On alcoholism as a preoccupation of social reformers, see James S. Roberts, *Drink, Temperance and the Working Class in Nineteenth-Century Germany* (Boston: Allen and Unwin, 1984), chaps. 2–4; and Heinrich Tappe, *Auf dem Weg zur modernen Alkoholkultur: Alkoholproduktion, Trinkverhalten und Temperenzbewegung in Deutschland vom frühen 19. Jahrhundert bis zum Ersten Weltkrieg* (Stuttgart: Steiner, 1994).

37. *Die Arbeiter-Kolonie.* 1, no. 1 (April 1884): 3.

38. Rüdeger Baron, "Die Entwicklung der Armenpflege in Deutschland vom beginn des 19. Jahrhunderts bis zum Ersten Weltkrieg," in *Geschichte der Sozialarbeit. Hauptlinien ihrev Entwicklung im 19. und 20. Jahrhundert*, ed. Rolf Landwehr and Rüdeger Baron (Weinheim: Beltz, 1983), 29–32.

39. In direct contrast to classical liberals like Mittelstädt, Riehl insisted that forced labor *"can* educate [one] for free labor." Wilhelm Heinrich Riehl, *Die Deutsche Arbeit* (Stuttgart: G. J. Cotta, 1862), 260. Riehl, who researched the social question for the king of Bavaria, revised and republished his book on work during the 1880s. See Joan Campbell, *Joy in Work, German Work* (Princeton: Princeton University Press, 1989), 28–46.

40. Friedrich Nietzsche, *The Dawn*, in *The Portable Nietzsche* (New York: Viking, 1959), 82. Paul Lafargue, *Das Recht auf Faulheit* (1880), in *Arbeit und Müßigang 1789 bis 1914. Dokumente und Analysen*, ed. Wolfgang Asholt and Walter Fähnders (Frankfurt: Fischer, 1991), 96–97. Nietzsche and Lafargue were rare critics of the discourse of labor.

41. Carl Albert Kemmler, *23 Thesen gegen Vagabondage*; Ricking, *Wanderarbeitsstätten*, 38–39; Bodelschwingh, "Die Ackerbaukolonie," in *Ausgewählte Schriften. Veröffentlichungen aus den Jahren 1872 bis 1910* (Bethel: Verlagshandlung der Anstalt Bethel, 1964).

42. Bodelschwingh, "Rede zur Einweihung der Arbeiter-kolonie Wilhelmsdorf," 15 August, 1882, *Ausgewählte Schriften*, vol. 2, 431.

43. Francis Greenwood Peabody, "The German Labor-Colonies for Tramps," *The Forum* (February 1892): 752. Ricking, *Wanderarbeitsstätten*, 34–35.

44. *Die Arbeiter-kolonie.* 1, no. 1 (April 1884): 86–89. Peabody, "Labor-Colonies," 752–53.

45. W. O. Shanahan, *German Protestants Face the Social Question, vol. 1, The Conservative Phase, 1815–1871* (Notre Dame: University of Notre Dame Press, 1954), 380.

46. Ibid., 165.

47. Martin Gerhardt, *Johann Hinrich Wichern, ein Lebensbild* (Hamburg: Agentur des Rauhen Hauses, 1927–31), 429.

48. Friedrich von Bodelschwingh, *Saat und Segen in der Arbeit von Bethel: ein Ruckblick auf die Zeit seit dem Tode des Anstaltsvaters* (Bethel: Verlagshandlung der Anstalt Bethel, 1932).

49. I have translated *Arbeiterkolonie* as "worker colony" rather than the commonly used "labor colony" because it is more literal. Bodelschwingh indicated that the name was carefully chosen to put the focus on the workers rather than the work.

50. Friedrich von Bodelschwingh, "Die Arbeiterkolonien und Verpflegungsstationen," in *Die Arbeiter-kolonie. Organ des Gesamt-Verbands der Deutschen Natural-Verpflegungs-Stationen und Deutscher Herbergsverein* no. 3 (1884): 85; and "Bericht über die erste Hauptversammlung des Deutschen Herbergsvereins," ibid., 170.

51. "Einheitliche Hausordnung für alle Arbeiterkolonien," *Die Arbeiterkolonie* (1886): 36–37. Also Kurt Erdlenbruch, "Die Wirtschaftliche und soziale Bedeutung der Deutschen Arbeiterkolonien" (Ph.D. diss., University of Giessen, 1929), 52–55.

52. Peabody, "German Labor Colonies," 754.

53. "Wo liegt die Arbeiter-Kolonie," in *Die Arbeiter-Kolonie* 1, no. 3 (1884): 75–78.

54. Friedrich von Bodelschwingh, "Soziale u wirtschaftliche Leistungen der Arbeiterkolonien," in *Der Wanderer* 30 (1913).

55. Friedrich von Bodelschwingh, "23 Thesen über Ziel und Zweck der Arbeiter-Kolonien und Verpflegungsstationen," in *Die Arbeiter-Kolonie* 1, no. 9 (1884). In contrast, Rabinbach argues that during the same era, "the ideal of a worker guided by either spiritual authority or direct control and surveillance gave way to the image of a body directed by its own internal mechanisms, a human 'motor.'" Rabinbach's evidence, however, comes almost exclusively from scientific writers and the still rather narrow realm of factory production. Rabinbach, *Human Motor*, 35. Campbell, similarly focused upon the "science of work," argues that reformers had turned away from the "tradtional Christian belief in the value of work done for its own sake." Campbell, *Joy in Work*, 66–67.

56. Legal scholar Wilhelm Kahl quoted in Ricking, *Wanderarbeitsstätten*, p.45.

57. Hugo Friedländer, "Die Vorkommnisse in der Fürsorgeanstalt Mieltschin," in *Interessante Kriminal-Prozesse von kulturhistorischer Bedeutung. Darstellung merkwürdiger Strafrechtsfälle aus Gegenwart und Jüngstvergangenheit* (Berlin: Hermann Barsdorf Verlag, 1911–21), vol. 5, 167–68.

58. "Bericht," 175–76; "Aus der Arbeit des Centralausschusses," *Fliegende Blätter aus dem Rauhen Hause* 45 (1888): 202; "Instruktionen für den Bürovorsteher in Wilhelmsdorf vom 13.3.1895," reprinted in *Ein Jahrhundert Arbeiterkolonien: "Arbeit statt*

Almosen"—Hilfe für Obdachlose Wanderarme 1884–1984, 36–40 (Freiburg: Zentral-verband Deutscher Arbeiterkolonien, 1984), 35.

59. Robert von Hippel, "Der Hauptmann von Köpenick und die Aufenthalts-beschränkungen bestrafter Personen," *DJZ* 11, no. 23 (1 December 1906): 1303–4.

60. Bodelschwingh, "Rede," 430.

61. Schwarz, "Ist die Aufnahme der nach par 361 und par 362 StGB der Landespoli-zeibehörde überwiesenen Personen in Arbeiterkolonien unter Aufschub der Über-weisung in ein Arbeitshaus zulässig und zu empfehlen?" *Jahresbericht. Rheinisch-Westfälischen Gefängnis-Gesellschaft über das Vereinsjahr 1894.* (Düsseldorf, 1895), 48–50; Levin Freiherr von Wintzingeroda-Knorr, *Die Deutschen Arbeitshäuser, ein Bei-trag zur Lösung der Vagabonden-Frage* (Halle: Hendel, 1885).

62. Bodelschwingh, "Rede über die Fürsorge für arbeitsuchende Wanderer im Preussischen Abgeordnetenhause am 17. Juni 1904," in *Ausgewählte Schriften*, 565; Schwarz, "Aufnahme." Critics also seized upon the writings of Pastor Otto Fleisch-mann, who served over thirty years in a workhouse before publishing his damning exposes. Otto Fleischmann, *Deutsches Vagabunden und Verbrechertum in Neunzehn-ten Jahrhundert* (Barmen: Hugo Klein, 1887).

63. Hans Ostwald, "Das Leben der Wanderarmen," *Archiv für Kriminalanthropo-logie* 13 (1905): 309–10; Karl Kautsky, "Literarische Rundschau," in *Neue Zeit* 5 (1887).

64. Heinrich Holtmannspötter, "Wanderarmenhilfe und Arbeiterkolonien zwi-schen 1912 und 1933," and Jürgen Scheffler, "Die Gründungsjahre 1883–1913," in *Ein Jahrhundert Arbeiterkolonien*.

65. Bodelschwingh, "Rede zur Einweihung der Arbeiterkolonie Wilhelmsdorf," in *Ausgewählte Schriften*.

66. This discounted the common practice of withholding wages from refractory colonists.

67. Schwarz, "Aufnahme," 50.

68. Wangemann, "Wandertagebuch"; Friedrich von Bodelschwingh (the younger), *Friedrich von Bodelschwingh. Ein Blick in ein Leben* (Bielefeld: Pfennigverein, 1924).

69. HBAB, no. 8/3–32a, Bodelschwingh. "Leitsätze."

70. Bodelschwing, "Liebe Bruder auf die Landstraße," in *Gesammelte Schriften*; Ricking, *Wanderarbeitsstätten*.

71. *Protokoll über die achtzehnte ordentliche Sitzung des Central Vorstandes Deut-scher Arbeiter-Kolonien am 14. November 1907*, 49–50.

72. *Neueste Mittheilungen* 2, no. 62 (6 June 1883); Hebung der Arbeiterkolonien und Verpflegungsstationen, *Neueste Mittheilungen* 8, no. 17 (1 March 1889).

73. Regina Schulte, *Sperrbezirke: Tugendhaftigkeit und Prostitution in der bürger-lichen Welt* (Frankfurt: Syndikat, 1979), 206.

74. Amtlichen Drucksachen des Reichstages, no. 173, 931. See Gustav Aschaffen-burg, *Das Verbrechen und seine Bekämpfung* (Heidelberg: Winter, 1906), 80; Hans Ostwald, *Prostitutionsmärkte* (Leipzig: Fiedler, 1907).

75. K. Walser, "Prostitutionsverdacht und Geschlechterforschung: Das Beispiel der

Dienstmädchen um 1900," *Geschichte und Gesellschaft* 11 (1985); Kathleen Canning, "Social Policy, Body Politics: Recasting the Social Question in Germany, 1875–1900," in *Gender and Class in Modern Europe*, ed. Laura Frader and Sonya Rose (Ithaca: Cornell University Press, 1996); ADW CA GF/St no. 325. "Evangelischer-Wohlfahrtsdienst für die Mark Brandenburg. Leitsätze für nachgehende Fürsorge für ortsfremde Mädchen," n.d.

76. Alain Corbin, *Women for Hire: Prostitution and Sexuality in France after 1850* (Cambridge, Mass.: Harvard University Press, 1990); Sander Gilman, *Picturing Health and Illness* (Baltimore: Johns Hopkins University Press, 1995), and Sander Gilman, "The Hottentot and the Prostitute: Toward an Iconography of Female Sexuality," in *Difference and Pathology: Stereotypes of Sexuality, Race, and Madness* (Ithaca: Cornell University Press, 1985).

77. Alain Corbin, "Commercial Sexuality in Nineteenth Century France: A System of Images and Regulations," *Representations* 14 (1986): 212.

78. Paul Weindling, *Health, Race and German Politics between National Unification and Nazism 1870–1945* (Cambridge: Cambridge University Press, 1989), 182.

79. Schulte, *Sperrbezirke*, 174–85.

80. Abraham Flexner, *Prostitution in Europe* (New York: The Century Company, 1914), 276–77, 416; Schulte, *Sperrbezirke*, 175–76; Becker, *Verderbnis*, 163.

81. Nancy R. Reagin, "'A True Woman Can Take of Herself': The Debate over Prostitution in Hanover, 1906," *Central European History* 24, no. 4 (1981); Ursula Baumann, *Protestantismus und Frauenemanzipation in Deutschland 1850 bis 1920* (Frankfurt am Main: Campus Verlag, 1992) On the practice of regulation, see Schulte, *Sperrbezirke*, 157–204, and Lynn Abrams, "From Control to Commercialization," *German History* 8, no. 3 (1990).

82. Elisabeth Meyer-Renschhausen, *Weibliche Kultur und Sozialarbeit: Eine Geschichte der Frauenbewegung am Beispiel Bremens 1810–1924* (Cologne: Boehlau, 1989), 313–15, and Elisabeth Meyer-Renschhausen, "Die Weibliche Ehre. Ein Kapitel aus dem Kampf von Frauen gegen Polizei und Ärzte," in *Frauenkörper, Medizin, Sexualität*, ed. Johanna Geyer-Kordesch and Annette Kuhn (Düsseldorf: Shwann, 1986), 87; Reagin, *German Women's Movement*, 164–66.

83. Ursula Nienhaus, "Einsatz für die 'Sittlichkeit': Die Anfänge der weiblichen Polizei im Wilhelminischen Kaiserreich und in der Weimarer Republik," in *'Sicherheit' und 'Wohlfahrt:' Polizei, Gesellschaft und Herrschaft im 19. und 20. Jahrhundert*, ed. Alf Lüdtke (Frankfurt am Main: Suhrkamp, 1992), 245; Meyer-Renschhausen, *Weibliche Kultur*, 219–24; Nancy Reagin, *A German Women's Movement: Class and Gender in Hanover, 1880–1933* (Chapel Hill: University of North Carolina Press, 1995), 149–52.

84. Meyer-Renschhausen, *Weibliche Kultur*, 271–74; Andrew Lees, *Cities, Sin, and Social Reform in Imperial Germany* (Ann Arbor: University of Michigan Press, 2002), 106–8.

85. Meyer-Renschhausen, *Weibliche Kultur*, 126–39; Reagin, *German Women's Movement*, 81–89; Lees, *Cities*, 18.

86. Baumann, *Protestantismus*, 117–18, 130–31; Reagin, *German Women's Move-*

ment, 44–49. The Morality Associations, by contrast, were predominantly lower middle class. Richard Evans, "Prostitution, State and Society in Imperial Germany," *Past and Present* 70 (1976).

87. Edward Ross Dickinson, "The Men's Christian Morality Movement in Germany, 1880–1914: Some Reflections on Politics, Sex, and Sexual Politics," *Journal of Modern History* 75, no. 1 (March 2003). In fact, a great number of pastors called for the prosecution of male solicitors. See especially Hötzel, "Die Prostitution," 8. *JGGSA* (1892): 41–42.

88. "Verhandlungsbericht," 8. *JGGSA* (1892): 457ff.

89. Hong, "World War I," 353; Andrew Lees notes in particular the strong social emphasis in the writings of Pastor Ludwig Weber, a leader of the male morality movement. Lees, *Cities*, 84, 100.

90. Reagin argues that DEF reformers in Hannover did not see women as victims since they did not demonize bourgeois men. (Richard Evans cites Reagin while making the same assertion.) But the whole point of a social comprehension of crime was that it assigned guilt and responsibility to intermediary structures. It would have been surprising (and rather banal) if the reformers had simply blamed "bourgeois lust" for the moral decline of local women. Reagin, *Women's Movement*; Evans, "Prostitution," 125.

91. Scheuner, *Die Gefährdetenfürsorge*, 156–62; Meyer-Renschhausen, *Weibliche Kultur*, 274–300; ADW, CA GF/St no. 325. Leitsätze für nachgehende Fürsorge für ortsfremde Mädchen. n.d.

92. Kathleen Canning, *Languages of Labor and Gender: Female Factory Work in Germany, 1850–1914* (Ithaca: Cornell University Press, 1996), 301–8; Scheuner, *Gefährdetenfürsorge*, 167–68.

93. Andreas Wollasch, "Von der Bewahrungsidee der Fürsorge zu den Jugendkonzentrationslagern des NS-Staates—Der Katholische Fürsorgeverein und die Debatte um ein Bewahrungsgesetz zwischen 1918 und 1945," *Wolfahrtsverbände im Wohlfahrtsstaat* (Kassel: Universität-Gesamthochschule Kassel), ed. Christoph Sachße, 51–54; Wollasch, *Der Katholische Fürsorgeverein für Mädchen, Frauen und Kinder (1899–1945). Ein Beitrag zur Geschichte der Jugend- und Gefährdetenfürsorge in Deutschland* (Freiburg: Lambertus, 1991).

94. Wollasch, *Katholische Fürsorgeverein*, 58.

95. Reagin, *German Women's Movement*, 85; Richard J. Evans, *Tales from the German Underworld: Crime and Punishment in the Nineteenth Century* (New Haven: Yale University Press, 1998), 194.

96. Wollasch, *Katholische Fürsorgeverein*, 59; Pastor Fischer, "Die Seelsorgerliche Behandlung der Prostituierten nach der Haft," and Hötzel, "Die Prostitution," 8. *JGGSA* (1892).

97. Ayass, *Arbeitshaus*, 210–15; Schulte, *Sperrbezirke*, 196–97. Workhouses in some parts of Germany even allowed corporal punishment. Evans, *Tales*, 122.

98. Jahresberichte über das Diakonissenhaus "Evangelisches Magdalenenstift" zu Berlin-Teltow (1903–1913); Scheuner, *Die Gefährdetenfürsorge*, 160, 168.

99. Baumann, *Protestantismus*, 159; Meyer-Renschhausen, *Weibliche Kultur*, 279–302. See also her description of women's coalitions inside the temperance movement, 227–52.

100. Three of Georg Berthold's studies were published in book form: *Die Entwicklung der deutschen Arbeiter-Kolonien* (Leipzig, 1887); *Statistik der deutschen Arbeiter-Kolonien für 1887/89* (Berlin: M. Priber, 1891); and *Die deutschen Arbeiter-Kolonien. Sechste Folge für die Jahre 1889/91. Mit Rückblicken auf die Entwicklung und Bedeutung derselben seit ihrer Eröffnung* (Berlin: M. Priber, 1893).

101. Berthold suggested paying less to repeat visitors in hopes of discouraging them. Berthold, *Deutschen Arbeiter-Kolonien*, 70–71.

102. Konrad Von Massow, *Der Wanderer* (1908), 315.

103. Karl Kautsky, "Literarische Rundschau," in *Neue Zeit* 5 (1887).

104. "Über die Behandlung erwerbsbeschränkter und-unfähiger Wanderarmen," *Tagung des Vereins für Armenpflege und Wohltätigkeit* (1908); Hans Ostwald, "Das Leben der Wanderarmen," *Archiv für Kriminalanthropologie* 13 (1905): 309–10.

105. Konrad von Massow, *Der Wanderer* (1908): 315.

106. Friedrich von Bodelschwingh, "Grosse Kinder," *Bethel* 3, no. 1 (1911).

107. Ibid., 19–21; on the influence of Bodelschwingh's essay see chapter 6 below and GStA 1104 18 Adh 3 Justizminister to Oberstaatsanwälte, 23 December 1916.

108. Georg Steigerthal, Georg, "Die Bekämpfung asozialer Elemente durch die Nachhaftsstrafe," *41. JGGSA* (1925); Otto Mönkemöller, "Die Bewahrung Asozialer," *MKS* 15, nos. 8–12 (1924).

109. Erdlenbruch, *Wirtschaftliche und soziale Bedeutung der Deutschen Arbeiterkolonien*, 55–58.

110. "Bereitstellung der Arbetierkolonien zur aufnahme erstmalig zur Nachhaft Verurteilter," *Die Arbeiter-Kolonie* 10 (1894): 129–34.

111. Robert von Hippel, *Zur Vagabundenfrage* (Berlin: Verlag von Otto Liebmann, 1902), 24–25; Schellmann und Preetorius, "Gutachten," in *Blätter für Gefängniskunde* 33 (1899): 254–60.

112. "Bereitstellung," *Die Arbeiter-Kolonie* 10 (1894): 130, 132. Bodelschwingh, *Die Wanderarmen und das Reichsgesetz par. 28*, Bethel, 1899.

113. *Die Arbeiterkolonie* 11 (1894): 298ff.

114. Hippel, *Vagabundenfrage*, 28–29.

115. Hippel, *Bekämpfung*, 262–64.

116. Conrad von Massow, *Das Preussische Fürsorgeerziehungsgesetz vom 2.Juli 1900 und die Mitwirkung der Bürgerlichen Gesellschaft bei Seiner Ausführung. auf Grund der Ausführungsbestimmungen vom 18.Dezember 1900* (Berlin, 1901), 1–8; Peukert, *Grenzen*, 146.

117. von Massow, *Preussische Fürsorgeerziehungsgesetz*, 1–5.

118. "Tabellarische Zusammenstellung der deutschen evangelischen Magdalenenasyle, Zufluchtshaeuser, Frauenheime und Versorgungshaeuser nach dem Stande

vom 1. Januar 1908," *Der Armen- und Krankenfreund* (January–April 1908): 14–41; Wollasch, *Katholische Fürsorgeverein*; see also Reagin, *German Women's Movement*, 33–35, 85–88.

119. Fuchs, *Gefangenen-Schütztätigkeit*, 214–16; "Bestimmungen über die Fürsorge für entlassene Gefangene," Ministerium des Innern, 13 June 1895, reprinted in Fuchs, *Gefangenen-Schütztätigkeit*, 23–24.

120. *5. Jahrbuch der Gefängnis-Gesellschaft für die Provinz Sachsen und Herzogtum Anhalt* (1889): 3; Rosenfeld, *Zweihundert Jahre*, 54–57.

121. GStA 84a, no. 7935, "Polizeiaufsicht. 1870–1931."

122. GStA 84a, no. 7935, *Hannoverschen Courier*, 16 September 1900. "Ablösung der Polizeiaufsicht durch Fürsorgevereine"; Minister des Innern von Bischoffshausen an den Herrn Regierungspräsidenten in Merseburg. 9 January 1903; GStA 84a, no. 50904; Wolf, "Schutzaufsicht über die unter Polizei-Aufsicht gestellten Personen," *Jahresbericht, Gefängnisgesellschaft Hesse-Nassau* (1907).

123. "Verhandlungsbericht," 8. *JGGSA* (1892): 457ff.; Wollasch, *Katholische Fürsorgeverein*, 28, 79.

124. At least one leading reformer argued insistently for changing the title of the position to "city welfare worker." SB NB no. 38.

125. Quote in Reagin, *German Women's Movement*, 84.

126. Irene Stoehr, "Organisierte Mütterlichkeit: Zur Politik der deutschen Frauenbewegung um 1900," in *Frauen suchen ihre Geschichte: Historische Studien zum 19. und 20. Jahrhundert*, ed. Karin Hausen (München: C. H. Beck, 1982).

127. Meyer-Renschhausen, *Weibliche Kultur*, 337; Nienhaus, "Einsatz," 243–48.

128. SB. Magistrat—Wohlfahrtsamt. MV 416, "Vortrag gehalten im Evangelische Diakonie-Verein zu Zehlendorf und in der Ortsgruppe Bielefeld des Deutschen Evangelischen Frauenbundes von Clara Hermelbracht. 1909."

129. SB. Wohlfahrtsamt. MV 416, "Vortrag."

130. SB. Wohlfahrtsamt. MV 416, "Dienstanweisung betr. die bei der Polizeiverwaltung in Bielefeld tätige Polizeiassistentin. Dec. 4 1907."

131. According to Meyer-Renschhausen, the female police assistant in Bremen was supposed to defend "female honor" by preventing innocent, respectable women, falsely accused of prostitution, from being subjected to humiliating investigations and examinations. Moreover, the police assistant helped distinguish between hardened professional prostitutes and the "at-risk" women who may have been lured or even forced into venal sex. Meyer-Renschhausen, "Weibliche Ehre," 94–96. On the indiscriminately wide swath of police suspicions against lower class, working women, see Walser, "Prostitutionsverdacht."

132. SB. Wohlfahrtsamt. MV 426, "Vortrag."

133. The rhetoric of the women police assistants further contradicts Nancy Reagin's claim that the DEF rejected any identification with the fate of accused prostitutes, fearing that they might antagonize bourgeois men. The women assistants perhaps avoided criticizing "their own," but they certainly demonized lower class par-

ents, unscrupulous seducers, and nameless police functionaries. See Reagin, "A True Woman," 352–53.

134. Monika Frommel, "Internationale Reformbewegung zwischen 1880 und 1920," in *Erzählte Kriminalität: Zur Typologie und Funktion von narrativen Darstellungen in Strafrechtspflege, Publizistik und Literatur zwischen 1770 und 1920*, ed. Jörg Schönert, 467–96 (Tübingen: Max Niemeyer Verlag, 1991), 467–70.

135. Franz von Liszt, "Der Zweckgedanke im Strafrecht." in *Strafrechtliche Aufsätze und Vorträge* (Berlin: Guttentag, 1905), 127–79.

136. Franz von Liszt, "Die Zukunft des Strafrechts," in *Strafrechtliche Aufsätze*, 3; Karl Binding, "Vorwort," *Grundriß des deutschen Strafrechts* (Leipzig: Engelmann, 1900). The term *Humanitätsdusselei* is used by both Mittelstädt and Liszt. On Liszt's rejection of the humanitarian label, see Richard Wetzell, *Inventing the Criminal: A History of German Criminology 1880–1945* (Chapel Hill: University of North Carolina Press, 2000), 87.

137. Franz von Liszt, "Zukunft," 13–16, and "Das Verbrechen als sozialpathologische Erscheinung," in *Strafrechtliche Aufsätze* (Berlin: Guttentag, 1905). On Liszt's mixture of left-liberal affinities with a "supra-individualist social-reformist tendency," see Eberhard Schmidt, *Einführung in die Geschichte der deutschen Strafrechtspflege* (Göttingen: Vandenhoek, 1947), 331–32.

138. Liszt, "Zukunft," 12.

139. Gustav Aschaffenburg, *Das Verbrechen und seine Bekämpfung* (Heidelberg: Winter, 1906), translated as *Crime and Its Repression* (Montclair, N.J.: Patterson Smith, 1968); Aschaffenburg is generally regarded as the most influential German criminologist of his generation. Richard J. Evans, *Rituals of Retribution: Capital Punishment in Germany 1600–1987* (New York: Oxford University Press, 1996), 435–36; Wetzell, *Inventing the Criminal*, 63–64.

140. Aschaffenburg, *Gefängnis Oder Irrenanstalt*, Vortrag gehalten in der Gehe-Stiftung zu Dresden am 11 January 1908, 12.

141. Ibid., 13.

142. Robert Sommer berated his fellow psychiatrists for borrowing the term "Minderwertige" from the realm of business transactions. Becker, *Verderbnis*, 261. "Weakness of will" was a common topic in moral philosophy. See J.C.B. Gosling, *Weakness of the Will* (London: Routledge, 1990).

143. Aschaffenburg, *Das Verbrechen*, 175–78, 170–71.

144. Ibid., 181; *Die Versorgung asozialer Personen. Gekürzter Bericht über die Tagung der Vorbereitenden Kommission zur Prüfung der Frage der Versorgung asozialer Personen am 7. und 8. Juli 1922 in Bielefeld* (Frankfurt: Deutsche Verein für öffentliche und private Fürsorge, 1923), 89.

145. Liszt, "Verbrechen," 243.

146. Ibid., 243.

147. Ibid., 245.

148. Karl Wilmanns, *Über Gefängnispsychosen* (Halle: Marhold, 1908).

149. Karl Bonhoeffer, "Ein Beitrag zur Kenntnis des großstädtischen Bettel und Vagabondentums. Eine psychiatrische Untersuchung," *ZgStW* 21 (1900); Mönkemöller, "Die Bewahrung"; Otto Mönkemöller, *Korrektionsanstalt und Landarmenhaus; Ein soziologischer Beitrag zur Kriminalität und Psychopathologie des Weibes* (Leipzig: 1908); Otto Mönkemöller, "Eine Vagabundenfamilie," *MKS* 4 (1908); Karl Wilmanns, "Das Landstreichertum, seine Abhilfe, und Bekampfung. Vortrag, gehalten in der Versammlung der sudwestdeutschen Irrenärzte in Freiburg am 30. Okt 1904," *MKS* 1 (1904); Karl Wilmanns, *Zur Psychopathologie des Landstreichers. Eine klinische Studie* (Leipzig, 1906); see also Adolf Riebeth, "Über den geistigen und körperlichen Zustand der Korrigenden," *MKS* 5 (1908–9).

150. Liszt, "Zukunft," 12.

151. Franz von Liszt, "Bedingte Verurteilung und Bedingte Begnadigung," in *Vergleichende Darstellung des Deutschen und Ausländischen Strafrechts*, ed. Karl Birkmeyer et al. (Berlin: Verlag von Otto Liebmann, 1908), 15; Franz von Liszt, "Die Aufgaben der Gefängnis Gesellschaft," *10. JGGSA* (1895).

152. Fuhr, *Strafrechtspflege*; Rosenfeld, *Zweihundert Jahre*.

153. Welfare reformer Hans Maier later argued that private charities were historically the innovators, while the state usually stepped in to institutionalize and juridicalize good ideas. *Gefährdetenfürsorge und Sittlichkeits-Gesetzgebung. Bericht über die Tagung am 10. und 11. Oktober 1918 in Frankfurt a.M.* (Frankfurt: Reitz und Köhler, Schriften des Frankfurter Wohlfahrtsamtes, 1919), 57.

154. Paul Troschke, "Die Reformbedürftigkeit Der Behandlung Asozialer Personen Vom Standpunkt Der Sozialpädagogik," *Die Versorgung Asozialer Personen. Gekürzter Bericht über die Tagung der Vorbereitenden Kommission zur Prüfung der Frage der Versorgung Asozialer Personen am 7. und 8. Juli 1922 in Bielefeld* (Frankfurt: Deutscher Verein für öffentliche und private Fürsorge, 1922), 9.

155. *Gefährdetenfürsorge*, 6–8.

156. Troschke, "Reformbedürftigkeit," 195.

Chapter 3

1. Deportation was debated at the meeting of the Prison Society for the Province of Sachsen-Anhalt in June of 1914. *30. JGGSA* (1914): 6; Otto Jöhlinger, "Kolonialpolitik," *Recht, Verwaltung, und Politik im neuen Deutschland*, ed. Alfred Bozi and Hugo Heinemann (Stuttgart: Ferdinand Enke, 1916); Hans Hyan, *Verbrechen und Strafe im neuen Deutschland* (Berlin: Verlag für Sozialwissenschaft, 1919), 26.

2. Michel Foucault, *Discipline and Punish: The Birth of the Prison* (New York: Pantheon, 1977), 195–99.

3. Richard J. Evans, *Tales from the German Underworld: Crime and Punishment in the Nineteenth Century* (New Haven: Yale University Press, 1998), 78–79.

4. Evans, likewise, notes the role of eugenic arguments in de-legitimizing deportation, but this recognition plays no part in his overall argument. Ibid., 80–81.

5. Ibid., 45, 56–75.

6. Proponents of draconian measures against crime frequently drew upon the work of W. E. Wilda, a legal scholar from the Romantic School, who argued that "Germanic" practice (prior to the introduction of Roman Law) was based upon principles of expulsion. Cast forth from the tribe, outlaws were rendered "*vogelfrei*," that is, deprived of the protections of the *Volk*. W. E. Wilda, *Geschichte des deutschen Strafrechts. 1. Das Strafrecht der Germanen* (Halle: Schwetschke 1842). See H. H. Jakobs, *Wissenschaft und Gesetzgebung im bürgerlichen Recht nach der Rechtsquellenlehre des neunzehnten Jahrhunderts* (Paderborn: Schöningh, 1983).

7. Otto Mittelstädt, *Gegen die Freiheitsstrafen. Ein Beitrag zur Kritik des heutigen Strafensystems* (Leipzig: S. Hirzel, 1879).

8. Ibid., 77–80. As a neo-Kantian, Mittelstädt shared many of the "classical" liberal conceptions of the French Opportunist Republicans described by Robert Nye. Drawing upon the work of Charles Renouvier, French reformers supported deportation based on the criminal's violation of the social contract and society's "right . . . to defend itself in the 'state of war' that is the normal condition of modern life." Robert Nye, *Crime, Madness, and Politics in Modern France: The Medical Concept of National Decline* (Princeton: Princeton University Press, 1984), 69.

9. Mittelstädt, *Gegen die Freiheitsstrafe*, iv. Reformer Karl Krohne explained Mittelstädt's popularity in terms of the "materialist tendencies . . . which rule our time." The judge, he claimed, sought to defend property at all costs. K. Krohne, "Die gegenwärtige Stand der Gefängniswissenschaft," *ZStW* 1 (1881): 60.

10. Klaus Bade, *Friedrich Fabri und der Imperialismus in der Bismarckzeit: Revolution, Depression, Expansion* (Freiburg: Atlantis-Verlag, 1975), 92–93. For a critique of the concept of "social imperialism," see Geoff Eley, "Social Imperialism in Germany: Reformist Synthesis or Reactionary Slight of Hand," in *From Unification to Nazism: Reinterpreting the German Past* (Boston: G. Allen and Unwin, 1986).

11. *52. Jahresberichte. Rheinisch-Westfälischen Gefängnis-Gesellschaft* 52 (1880); "Karl Krohne. Zum 75. Geburtstag und sein Einfluß," *Blätter für Gefängniskunde. Organ des Vereins der deutschen Strafanstaltsbeamten* 46 (1912); Wolfgang Mittermaier, "Kann die Deportation im deutschen Strafstystem Aufnahme finden?," *ZStW* 19 (1899).

12. Krohne, "Gegenwärtige Stand."

13. Sebastian Conrad's recent essay also compares these movements, presenting a more chilling picture of both the worker colonies and the deportation movement. Sebastian Conrad, " 'Eingeborenenpolitik' in Kolonie und Metropole. Erziehung zur Arbeit in Ostafrika und Ostwestfalen," in *Das Kaiserreich Transnational. Deutschland in der Welt 1871–1914*, ed. Sebastian Conrad and Jürgen Osterhammel (Göttingen: Vandenhoeck und Ruprecht, 2004), 107–28.

14. Felix Friedrich Bruck, *Fort mit den Zuchthäusern!* (Breslau: W. Koebner, 1894); *Neu-Deutschland und seine Pioniere. Ein Beitrag zur Lösung der sozialen Frage* (Breslau: W. Koebner, 1896); and *Die gesetzliche Einführung der Deportation im Deutschen Reich* (Breslau: M. & H. Marcus, 1897). On Bruck's role in the wider debate, see

Wolfgang Mittermaier, "Literaturbericht. Deportation," *ZStW* 20 (1900): 613–16; and Bruck, *Noch einmal die Deportation und Deutsch-Südwestafrika* (Breslau: M. & H. Marcus, 1906). Prior to his work on deportation, Bruck wrote on the question of negligence, helping to codify the trend in German legal practice away from holding individuals criminally responsible for negligent behavior. Felix Friedrich Bruck, *Zur Lehre von der Fahrlässigkeit im heutigen deutschen Strafrecht* (Breslau: Koebner, 1885).

15. Bruck, *Zur Lehre*. Mittelstädt, for one, used the decriminalization of accidents as a model for the project of decoupling law and ethics. As Francois Ewald notes, such a shift in policy furthered the rise of insurance and made "risk-management" into a touchstone of the state's legitimacy. Francois Ewald, *L'Etat Providence* (Paris: Grasset, 1986), 352–53.

16. Bruck, *Fort mit den Zuchthäuser!*, 1–6, 61–67.

17. Bruck, *Neu-Deutschland*; Bruck, *Gesetzliche Einführung*.

18. Judges were actually supposed to pronounce two sentences, one specifying deportation, the other indicating a sentence for incarceration in the event that the offender could not be deported. Bruck, *Gesetzliche Einführung*, 4.

19. The other offenses were assault, theft, fraud, embezzlement, blackmail, and conspiracy (*Hehlerei*). Bruck, *Gesetzliche Einführung*, 5, 7.

20. Bruck, "Zur Deportationsfrage," *Die Kreuzzeitung*, 27 March 1897.

21. Felix Friedrich Bruck, *Die Gegner der Deportation* (Breslau: M. & H. Marcus, 1901), 7.

22. Bruck, *Gesetzliche Einführung*, 12–14.

23. Ibid., 15–16.

24. Ibid., 21.

25. Bruck, *Die Gegner*, 4–9.

26. Bruck, *Gesetzliche Einführung*, 19–21.

27. On Bruck's role in particular, see *Deutsche Tageszeitung*, 22 July 1897; *Münchener Allgemeiner Zeitung*, 22 June 1898. BA R30.01 no. 6101. Petition to the Reichstag from Casimir Wagner (Zweibrücken), Chairman of the Westpfälzischen Zweigvereines der Deutschen Kolonialgesellschaft. 6 December 1901.

28. Reinhard von Frank, "Freiheitsstrafe, Deportation und Unschädlichmachung," *Jahrbuch für Kriminalpolitik und innere Mission*, 50 (1895), republished in book form as *Freiheitsstrafe, Deportation und Unschädlichmachung. Ein Wort zur Verständigung* (Giessen: J. Ricker, 1895); Bennecke, "Ist die Forderung 'Fort mit den Zuchthäusern!' berechtigt und durchführbar?," *Verhandlungen der 15. General-Versammlung.Gefängnisverein für Schleisien und Posen* (1894): 12–30.

29. Friedrich Freund, "Über Strafkolonisation und Einrichtung überseeischer Strafanstalten," *Preußische Jahrbücher* 81 (1895); 68. *Jahresberichte. Rheinisch-Westfälischen Gefängnis-Gesellschaft* (1895): 21–24.

30. BA R30.01 no. 6101. The award went to an essay by Adolph Korn, which attacked Bruck's proposal on the grounds that oversight in the colonies could never be sufficient to uphold work and social disciplinary standards. A. Korn, *Ist die Deportation*

unter den heutigen Verhältnissen als Strafmittel praktisch verwendbar? (1898); *Frankfurter Zeitung*, 5 September 1898.

31. Bruck eagerly courted Liszt's support and was appalled when his 1905 textbook made only a passing reference to deportation, describing it as a "prophylactic" measure, in the same context as what Bruck termed the "scurrilous idea of castration." Bruck, *Noch Einmal*, 2–3.

32. Joachim Graf Pfeil, "Betrachtungen über Anlegung einer Strafkolonie," *Kolonialen Jahrbücher* 9 (1897); Franz von Bülow, untitled, *Die Post*, nos. 185, 196 (1894). The issue was discussed at the annual meeting of the German Colonial Society in May 1896, which included a favorable report from Meinecke, "Zur Deportationsfrage," 9. *Ordentliche Hauptversammlung der Deutsche Kolonial-Gesellschaft* (1896); articles from *Die Kreuzzeitung* are in BA R30.01 no. 6103, and BA, Reichslandbund Pressearchiv, no. 1523.

33. E. A. Fabarius, "Deportation von Verbrechern nach den deutschen Kolonien?," in *Allgemeine Missions-Zeitschrift: Monatsheft für geschichtliche und theoretische Missionskunde* 23–24 (1896): 518, and the editor's note, 504. Also, D. Merensky, "Die Deportation als Strafmittel," *Jahrbuch für Kriminalpolitik*, 2 (1898): 26–35; Merensky was superintendent of a mission in southwest Africa. His opposition is discussed in Heinrich Seyfarth, "Über die Deportation von Verbrechern nach Deutsch-Sudwestafrika," *Blätter für Gefängniskunde. Organ des Vereins der deutschen Strafanstaltsbeamten* 34 (1900): 18–19.

34. Frank, *Freiheitsstrafe*; Reuss, "Ist die Deportation vom christlichen Standpunkt aus zu rechtfertigen?" *Die Christliche Welt* 11. Jhrg, nos. 25–26 (June 1897).

35. Seyfarth, "Über die Deportation," 1–2, 8; Frank, *Freiheitsstrafe*, 1. Frank credited Mittelstädt with "pulling the criminal policy movement out of its old tracks."

36. Bruck, for example, subtitled his 1896 work on deportation "a contribution to solving the social question." Mittelstädt had explicitly stated that penal deportation must be separated from any colonial or social-rehabilitative purpose.

37. Conrad Bornhak in *Berliner Börsenzeitung*, 31 August to 2 September 1898.

38. Bruck, *Noch Einmal*, 4.

39. Bruck, *Die Gegner*, 12–13.

40. Heinrich Seyfarth, "Über die Deportation von Verbrechern nach Deutsch-Südwestafrika," *Blätter für Gefängniskunde* 34 (1900): 181.

41. Frank, *Freiheitsstrafe*, 11. Frank's essay was originally given as an address at the meetings of the prison society for the province of Sachsen-Anhalt.

42. BA, Reichslandbund Pressearchiv. no. 1523, "Die Konkurrenz der Gefängnisarbeit," *Staatsbürger Zeitung*, nos. 2/3 und 2/5 (1899). This was an old dispute by the labor movements in a range of European countries. Revealingly, Marx and Engels were among the few critics of the unions' opposition to prison labor. They argued that the unions were buying into the "myth" of free labor and ultimately deprived the underclass of a vital opportunity for self-betterment. Dario Melossi and Massimo Pavarini, *The Prison and the Factory: Origins of the Penitentiary System* (London:

Macmillan, 1981); Georg Rusche and Otto Kirchheimer, *Punishment and Social Structure* (New York: Russell andy Russell, 1939).

43. Bruck, *Gegner*, 12–14, 20.

44. Frank, *Freiheitsstrafe*, 11. The German term I am translating as "ex-offender" was *Vorbestrafte*, meaning literally one who has been punished. This underscores the fact that public mistrust focused not simply upon the fact that the individual had committed an offense, but that he or she had been through the humiliation (and perhaps the destructive effects) of punishment.

45. Bruck, *Gegner*, 56.

46. Ibid., 110.

47. Seyfarth, "Über die Deportation," 12–13; this was an especially prominent theme in the wave of literature appearing in the wake of Hans Leuß's popular prison memoir, *Aus dem Zuchthause. Verbrecher und Strafrechtspflege* (Berlin: Raede, 1903).

48. Bruck, *Gegner*, 53.

49. Ibid., 53–54. For the IKV, recidivism was the "only criterion that could be operationalized for the identification of mentally deficient offenders." Peter Becker, *Verderbnis und Entartung. Eine Geschichte der Kriminologie des 19. Jahrhunderts als Diskurs und Praxis* (Göttingen: Vandenhoeck und Ruprecht, 2002), 278.

50. Frank, *Freiheitsstrafe*, 19–22.

51. German colonialists were intensely disssappointed at the tepid support for colonial development in general among government and business leaders during the late 1880s and early 1890s. In that sense, all colonial holdings were perceived as "neglected" lands. Woodruff Smith, *The German Colonial Empire* (Chapel Hill: University of North Carolina Press, 1978), 55–56.

52. Richard Julius Hindorf, *Denkschrift über die Entwickelung der deutschen Schutzgebiete*, 1894–1895. Hindorf later authored a series of works on agriculture in Sub-Saharan Africa.

53. Kurt von Francois, *Grenzboten*, no. 41 (1897); Theodor Rehbok, *Deutsch-Südwestafrika* (Berlin: Reimer, 1898).

54. Hindorf, *Denkschrift*, quoted in Bruck, *Die Gegner*, 17. In subsequent years, serious arguments were made for building sanatoria for tuberculosis in German Southwest Africa. Wolfgang Eckart, *Medizin und Kolonialimperialismus: Deutschland 1884–1945* (Paderborn/München/Vien: Schöningh, 1997).

55. Smith, *German Colonial Empire*, 55.

56. Leutwein to Seyfarth, 27 September 1897, reprinted in Heinrich Seyfarth, "Über die Deportation von Verbrechern nach Deutsch-Sudwestafrika," *Blätter für Gefängniskunde* 34 (1900). Leutwein later reversed himself on the question of deportation to German Southwest Africa.

57. BA R30.01 no. 6101. *Kreuz-Zeitung*, 28 May 1898.

58. Peters to Seyfarth, 4 September 1898. Reprinted in Seyfarth, "Über die Deportation," 15–16.

59. Karl Alexander Wettstein, *Die Strafverschickung in deutsche kolonien* (Zurich: Zurcher, 1907), 8.

60. Bruck, *Gegner*, 27.

61. Ibid., 15.

62. Seyfarth, "Über die Deportation," 15–16.

63. BA R30.01 no. 6101. Deportationsverband. Petition to Reichstag, 21 January 1908.

64. Seyfarth, "Über die Deportation," 14.

65. Heinrich Seyfarth, *Hinter eisernen Gittern. Ein Blick in die Verbrecherwelt. Zuchthausstudien* (Leipzig: Verlag von Friedrich Richter, 1898); Detloff Klatt, "Zum 70. Geburtstag unseres Generallsekretärs und Herausgebers der Monatsblätter Dr. jur. h.d. Dr. Phil H. Seyfarth," *MDRG* 8, nos. 5/6 (1933): 163–67.

66. An early description of the project is at ADW CA 554, vol. 3. See Heinrich Seyfarth, "Die Tätigkeit des deutschen Hilfsvereins für entlassene Gefangene. Vortrag gehalten auf der Generalversammlung des Verbandes der Deutschen Schutzvereine in Halle, 22 September 1904." Seyfarth originally presented his plan at the meeting of the Rhenish-Westphalian Prison Society in 1902.

67. ADW, CA 554, vol. 3, Heinrich Seyfarth, "Über die Arbeitsbeschaffung für zur Entlassung kommende Gefangene in fremden Länder" (MS, undated).

68. Former inmates hoping to go to Brazil, for example, were automatically sent to the colony. ADW. no. 554, vol. 3, Seyfarth, "Die Tätigkeit," 14; *2. Jahresbericht des Deutschen Hilfsvereins für entlassene Gefangene zu Hamburg*, 4.

69. ADW CA 554, vol. 3, Heinrich Seyfarth, "Die Not der Entlassene und ein Versuch si zu lindern. Vortrag über die Ziele und die Tätigkeit des deutschen Hilfsvereins für entlassene Gefangene gehalten im January 1906 im Frankfurt a.M.," 5–7.

70. *Jahresbericht des Deutschen Hilfsvereins für entlassene Gefangene zu Hamburg* 1–6 (1904–1909).

71. Seyfarth referred to his project as "Die 'Sozialmachung' des Rechtsbrechers." ADW CA 554, Seyfarth, "Die Not der Entlassene," 6.

72. The most celebrated German prison memoir and "firsthand report" on the "outcasts" was by Hans Leuß, a former newspaper editor convicted of perjury. Leuß, *Zuchthause.*

73. ADW CA 554, vol. 3, Seyfarth, "Die Not der Entlassene," 4.

74. A major fear, in fact, was that other countries would follow the example of the United States in forbidding the immigration of former felons.

75. *3. Jahresbericht des Deutschen Hilfsvereins*, 8.

76. ADW CA 554, Seyfarth, "Die Tätigkeit," 11.

77. *1. Jahresbericht des Deutschen Hilfsvereins*; *2. Jahresbericht des Deutschen Hilfsvereins*, 3–4.

78. Seyfarth was incensed when daily newspapers around the turn of the century began publishing "completely superfluous reports" on prison inmates scheduled for release under administrative pardons. AdW no. 554, Seyfarth, "Die Not," 12.

79. *3. Jahresbericht des Deutschen Hilfsvereins*, 15–17.

80. Max Treu, *Der Bankrott des modernen Strafvollzuges und seine Reform. Ein offener Brief an das Reichsjustizamt* (Stuttgart: R. Lutz, 1904); Leuß, *Zuchthause.* According to law professor Joseph Heimberger, this work unleashed a "flood" of publications condemning the penitentiary. J. Heimberger, *Zur Reform des Strafvollzugs* (Leipzig: A. Deichert, 1905), 22–23.

81. Leuß, *Zuchthause*, 14–49.

82. Leuß describes himself as moving in a "leftward" direction, including an evolution from elitist to populist anti-Semitism. Ultimately, he declares, he arrived at a viewpoint similar to Zionism—an intriguing, if somewhat bizarre, observation from one who would later support deportation as a progressive measure. Leuß, *Zuchthause*, 1–9.

83. Ibid., 187.

84. In addition to his letter to the Justice Minister, Treu published "Die Deportation, Die Gesellschaft und das Verbrechen," in *Zeitschrift für Sozialwissenschaft* (1905) and *Strafjustiz, Strafvollzug und Deportation* (Leipzig: F. Dietrich, 1905).

85. Treu, *Bankrott*, 8.

86. Ibid., 99.

87. A similar point is argued at length by Heimberger, *Zur Reform*, 22ff.

88. Joseph Heimberger was another leader of the movement. Graf Pfeil had been one of the most radical and forceful advocates of German colonial expansion into East Africa in the 1880s. He wrote a number of books on the geography of Africa and lived for some time in the English-controlled region of Kaplande. Bruck, *Gesetzliche Einführung*, 43; Bade, *Friedrich Fabri*, 256, 288, 291. He seems to have had no direct knowledge of the South Seas.

89. BA R30.01 no. 6101. Petition. Deutscher Kolonialbund An den Reichstag, 21 January 1906. The precedent for creating reservations for the native population had been set in Southwest Africa, where the Hereros were forcibly resettled as early as 1897. Smith, *German Colonial Empire*, 63.

90. Its various petitions are in BA R30.01 no. 6101. See also *Stenographische Berichte über die Verhandlungen des Reichstages* (Berlin, 104. Sitzung. 18 February 1908), 3234, 3237, 3266, 3283, 3287, 3289, 3294, 3361.

91. BA R30.01 no. 6101, Chairman, Deutscher Kolonial-Bund to Reich-Chancellor von Bülow, 13 February 1905.

92. Petition, Deutscher Kolonialbund An den Reichstag, 21 January 1906. Gradnauer's book skewered every governmental institution in Imperial Germany and depicted punishment as a tool of bourgeois domination. G. Gradnauer, *Das Elend des Strafvollzuges* (Berlin: s.n., 1905) The author was the Minister of Justice in Saxony during the Weimar Republic.

93. Petition, Deutscher Kolonialbund An den Reichstag, 21 January 1906.

94. BA R30.01 no. 6101, Chairman of Deutscher Kolonial-Bund, to Reich Chancellor Grafen von Bülow, 13 February 1905; and Petition, Deutscher Kolonialbund to the Reichstag, 21 January 1906.

95. Conrad, "Eingeborenenpolitik."

96. Johann Hinrich Wichern, "Rede auf dem Wittenberg Kirchentag," in *Samtliche Werke* (Hamburg: Luther, 1973).

97. Matthias Benad, ed., *Bethels Mission: Bethel in Spannungsfeld von Erweckungs-frömmigkeit und öffentlicher Fürsorge* (Bielefeld: Luther-Verlag, 2001); Martin Gerhardt, *Johann Hinrich Wichern. Ein Lebensbild* (Hamburg: Agenter des Rauben Hauses, 1927–31), vol. 1, 261.

98. Cesare Lombroso, *Crime: Its Causes and Remedies* (Boston: Little, Brown, 1911).

99. Leuß, *Zuchthause*, vii.

100. BA R30.01 no. 6101, Auswärtiges Amt, Kolonial Abteilung to Reichsjustizamt, 19 September 1905; Bericht. Gouverneur Neu-Guinea. 19 June 1905. RJA State Secretary Nieberding summarized his findings for the Reichstag. *Nord Allgemeine Zeitung*, 20 February 1898.

101. *Kreuzzeitung*, 17 April 1897.

102. Fabarius, "Deportation"; D. Merensky, "Die Deportation als Strafmittel," in *Jahrbücher für Kriminalpolitik* 2 (1898). R. Braune, "Die Deportation der Gefangenen," *Blätter für Gefängniskunde* 30 (1896): 9–10.

103. Quoted in BA, Reichslandbund Pressarchive, no. 1523.

104. "Die Besiedelung der Kolonien," *Staats-Zeitung* (no. 7/a, 1899).

105. BA R30.01 no. 6101, Höffel, Alldeutscher Verband to Sekr. Nieberding, Reichsjustizamt, 6 October 1908. The report indicates there was support for Liebert's comment.

106. Ann Laura Stoler, "Sexual Affronts and Racial Frontiers: European Identities and the Cultural Politics of Exclusion in Colonial Southeast Asia," *Tensions of Empire*, eds. Frederick Cooper and Ann Laura Stoler (Berkeley: University of California Press, 1997).

107. *Nothenblatt Stuttgart*, 21 January 1898.

108. The concern with escapees also figures prominently in Josef von Bülow's and E. A. Fabarius's critiques of Bruck's proposal. See Bruck, *Gesetzliche Einführung*, 48–50, and Fabarius, "Deportation," 519–20. The latter expressed concern that former prisoners, once settled on the land, would be "only too often inclined to hide their less fortunate comrades."

109. *Tageszeitung*, 24 June 1897.

110. Ibid.; *Tageszeitung*, 22 July 1897.

111. *Tageszeitung*, 24 June 1897.

112. Cited in Bruck, *Gesetzliche Einführung*, 41.

113. Lora Wildenthal, "She Is the Victor: Bourgeois Women, Nationalist Identities, and the Ideal of the Independent Woman Farmer in German Southwest Africa," in *Society, Culture and the State in Germany 1870–1930*, ed. Geoff Eley (Ann Arbor: University of Michigan Press, 1996), 372.

114. The most important figure to become disillusioned with the deportation ideal in the wake of the uprising was Theodor Leutwein, the governor of German Southwest Africa from 1894 to 1905.

115. Fabarius, "Deportation," 520.

116. BA R30.01 no. 6101, Abschrift. Kaiserlichen Generalkonsulat in Kapstadt. gez. Reimer to Reichskanzler Bülow. 10 February 1908; Reimer to Bülow, 11 April 1908. There is special irony in this editorial given the Germans' negative image of the Boers. See Hannah Arendt, *The Origins of Totalitarianism* (New York: Harcourt Brace Jovanovich, 1973), 191–207.

117. BA R30.01 no. 6101, Auswärtiges Amt. Kolonial Abteilung to Reichsjustizamt, 19 September 1905.

118. BA R30.01 no. 6101, Reichsjustizamt to Staatssekretär des Auswärtigen Amts, 4 January 1909. The German Foreign Office solicited information from France, Italy, England, and Spain, though the information provided was hardly more detailed than what had been published in numerous scholarly studies.

119. Robert Heindl, *Meine Reise nach den Strafkolonien* (Berlin-Wien: Ullstein, 1913).

120. BA R30.01 no. 6101. Auswärtiges Amt to Reichsjustizamt, 13 August 1909. Heindl's earlier reports on his travels were published in the press. BA R30.01 no. 6103. Robert Heindl, "Briefe aus einer Verbrecherinsel," *Der Rheinisch-Westphallischen Zeitung*, 8–10 August 1910; and "Der Misserfolg der Deportation," *Der Tag*, 27 June 1911.

121. Heindl, *Reise*, 23. By way of contrast, the handsome, grinning, energetic young author is pictured (presumably in the tropics) in the uniform of a proper European professional, including dark coat with tails, dark striped pants, collar and tie.

122. Ibid., 3–6.

123. Heindl offers a similar description of an Indian penal colony, along with two harrowing photos. One entitled "the murderer as shaver" shows an Indian shaving a white man, the razor poised at his jugular. The next photo shows a South Asian man posed with two small girls. The caption reads "the murderer as nanny" (ibid., 368).

124. Heindl's repeated use of theatrical metaphors in describing these scenes calls to mind Foucault's famous contrast between "spectacles" of punishment under the old regime and the techniques of "discipline" used in modern France. Foucault, *Discipline and Punish*, 3–7.

125. Heindl, *Reise*, 53–58.

126. BA R30.01 no. 6103. Dr. Mueller, "Die Deportation der Verbrecher," *Berliner Tageblatt*, 12. November 1912, and "Die Verschickung von Sträflingen," *Berliner Boursen-Courier*, 1 March 1913.

127. Franz Kafka, "In the Penal Colony," in *The Penal Colony: Short Stories and Short Pieces* (New York: Schocken Books, 1948), 191–230. There is no proof that Kafka based the story on Heindl's work, but the parallels seem too numerous to be accidental. Kafka had been a student of Heindl's mentor, the criminologist Hans Gross. Walter Müller-Seidel, *Die Deportation des Menschen: Kafkas Erzählung in der Strafkolonie im europäischen Kontext* (Stuttgart: Metzler, 1986).

128. Joseph Heimberger, "Deportation," in *Handwörterbuch der Kriminologie* (Berlin: de Gruyter, 1933).

129. Hyan, *Verbrechen und Strafe*, 26. Hyan was well known as a journalist and activist against capital punishment.

130. The Prussian Justice Ministry later hired Hyan to investigate Prussian prisons. Hyan, "Strafkolonisation," *Berliner Tageblatt*, 5 April 1921.

131. Hyan, "Strafkolonisation."

132. Seyfarth remained proud of his earlier efforts. The failure of the deportation movement, in his view, was strictly a matter of the limits and the defeat of German imperialism. Seyfarth, *Probleme des Strafwesens* (Berlin: Heymanns, 1928).

Chapter 4

1. Winfried Löschburg, *Ohne Glanz und Gloria: Die Geschichte des Hauptmanns von Köpenick* (Berlin: Ullstein, 1998); Benjamin Carter Hett, "The 'Captain from Köpenick' and the Transformation of German Criminal Justice, 1891–1914," *Central European History* 1–43 (2003); LAB. rep. 30, no. 1091. Personalakten des Königlichen Polizei-Präsidiums Berlin. Wilhelm Voigt.

2. Maximilian Harden, "Köpenick," *Die Zukunft*, reprinted in *Denkwürdigkeiten des Hauptmanns von Köpenick: Der 'Räuber-Hauptmann' in der internationalen. Karikatur und Satire* (Berlin: Verlag der Lustigen Blätter, 1906), 50; see also comments by Prussian Minister of the Interior Bethmann-Hollweg in *Stenographische Bericht. Preussisches Abgeordnetenhaus*. 20. Legislaturperiode, III. Session 19 February 1907. On Lindbergh, Modris Ecksteins, *The Rites of Spring* (New York: Anchor Books, 1989), 242–52.

3. Peter Fritzsche, *Reading Berlin 1900* (Cambridge, Mass.: Harvard University Press, 1996).

4. Ibid., 159–69. On the broader context of crime reporting, Eric A. Johnson, *Urbanization and Crime: Germany 1871–1914* (Cambridge: Cambridge University Press, 1995).

5. *Berliner Lokalanzeiger*, 19 and 26 October 1906.

6. "Der Köpenicker Kassenräuber ergriffen," *Berliner Lokalanzeiger*, 26 October 1906.

7. Ibid.

8. "Russian Ruse in Prussia," *New York Times*, 17 October 1906.

9. The *Times* later underscored its view of "teutonic" absurdities by publishing a news article on the aftermath of the event—without any explanation—written entirely in mock-German grammar. "Koepenickers Defiant Are. Mayor, by Cruel Fraud Deceived, to Unresign is Urged," *New York Times*, 21 October 1906.

10. "Le Fetichisme en Allemagne," *Le Petit Parisien*, 19 October 1906.

11. *National Zeitung*, 3 December 1906; *Vorwärts*, 18–19 October 1906.

12. LAB. Personalakten. Voigt; Naumann, "Der Hauptmann von Köpenick," *Die Hilfe* 12, no. 44 (4 November 1906).

13. Bernhard Diebold, *Frankfurter Zeitung*, 8 March 1931, reprinted in Carl Zuck-

mayer, *Der Hauptmann von Köpenick*, ed. Hartmut Scheible (Stuttgart: Reclam, 1977), 30–35.

14. GStA 84a. no. 3740, "*Große Polizei-Ausstellung*"; Oskar Dressler, ed., *Die Große Polizei-Ausstellung Berlin in Wort und Bild* (Vienna: Internat. öffentliche Sicherheit, 1927).

15. Carl Zuckmayer, *Die Deutschen Drama* (Stockholm: Bermann-Fischer-Verlag, 1947); Wilhelm Schäfer, *Der Hauptmann von Köpenick* (München: Georg Müller, 1930). Richard Oswald produced another version of the film for Hollywood in 1945, entitled "I Was a Criminal." After World War II, two different versions of the film were produced in West and East Germany, both premiering in 1956, and both based more or less upon the Zuckmayer script.

16. An exception is Hett, "Captain from Köpenick."

17. Löschburg, *Ohne Glanz*, 9, 49.

18. Anthony Greenville, "Authoritarianism Subverting Democracy: The Politics of Carl Zuckmayer's Der Hauptmann von Köpenick," *Modern Language Review* 91 (October 1996): 637. See also John R. McKenzie, *Social Comedy in Austria and Germany 1890–1933* (Bern and New York: Lang, 1992), 148–67.

19. Greenville, "Authoritarianism," 640.

20. *Stenographische Bericht. Preussisches Abgeordnetenhaus.* 20. Legislaturperiode, III. Session 19 February 1907.

21. *Germania*, 31 October 1906; *Berliner Lokalanzeiger*, 26–27 October 1906; On Scherl, Fritzsche, *Reading Berlin*, 72–77.

22. "He'd gladly have been a property owner. Marriage. Late Good Fortune. Frau Riemer. [Voigt's girlfriend]. Penitentiary again. Hope in his old age: shoe business. Nice plan. It bothered the police. Out! Banished. Pushed about, west, east. The legal system passes the test delightfully." "Der Held," *Der Tag* (Berlin) reprinted in *Denkwürdigkeiten*, 38.

23. The attitude of the press is noted in numerous exasperated statements by Prussian officials. Dr. Schlichting, "Die Ausweisung von Inländern durch die preußische Polizei," *Die Polizei*, 2 February 1907; *Stenographische Berichte über die Verhandlungen des Preussischen Hauses der Abgeordneten*, 20. Legislaturperiode, III. Session 1907, vol. 1, 990–92; Germania, 31 October 1906; "Opfern des Polizeiaufsicht" *Posener Zeitung*, 30 December 1906.

24. *Vossische Zeitung*, 1 December 1906. A transcript of the trial was quickly published in book form with drawings of Voigt speaking forcefully at his trial, sitting with "the family of his employer" with one child on his knee and another gazing at him adoringly, and (on the cover) shaking hands with the judge, who is looking up at him admiringly. *Der Hauptmann von Cöpenick vor Gericht. Aktenmässig dargestellt mit zahlreichen Abbildungen* (Berlin: Verlagshaus für Volksliteratur und Kunst, 1906).

25. Ibid., 30–31; Walter Bahn, *Meine Klienten. Beiträge zur modernen Inquisition* (Berlin: Seeman Nachf., 1908), vol. 42 of *Großstadt Dokumente*, ed. Hans Ostwald, 92ff.

26. Benjamin Carter Hett, *Death in the Tiergarten: Murder and Criminal Justice in the Kaiser's Berlin* (Cambridge, Mass.: Harvard University Press, 2004), 185.

27. This was certainly the perception of the Prussian legislature and the Prussian Minister of the Interior. *Stenographische Berichte über die Verhandlungen des Preussischen Hauses der Abgeordneten*, 20. Legislaturperiode, III. Session 1907, vol. 1, 990–92. Excerpted in GStA, Merseburg rep. 169, "Fürsorge für entlassene Gefangene Allgemein." The boulevard press, again, led the way in reconstructing his image. *Welt Am Montag*, 1–6 December 1906.

28. Karl Schwindt, "Erinnerungen an den Hauptmann von Köpenick," *Der Montag*, 20 September 1926. Lawyer Walter Bahn calls Voigt a "martyr" and reprints a lugubrious letter from Voigt to his sister, noting Voigt's "detached resignation." Bahn, *Klienten*, 88.

29. Löschburg, *Ohne Glanz*, 208–13.

30. Hett, *Death*, 189–90.

31. *Abendblatt*, 18 August 1908.

32. Löschburg, *Ohne Glanz*, 218–20.

33. *Berliner Tageblatt*, 2 October 1908; *Berliner Lokalanzeiger*, 15 January 1909.

34. LAB. Abschrift. Sign. illegible, 24 August 1908; and Personalakten. Der Regierungs-Präsident to Polizei Präsident, Breslau, 7 October 1908; also, Löschburg, *Ohne Glanz*, 210–36.

35. Löschburg, *Ohne Glanz*, 239–40; Berliner *Allgemeine Zeitung*, 19 June 1909.

36. Hans Hyan, *Aus der Tiefe des Lebens: Verbrechergeschichten* (Berlin und Leipzig: Hillger, 1906). On Hyan's activism against the death penalty, see Richard J. Evans, *Rituals of Retribution: Capital Punishment in Germany 1600–1987* (New York: Oxford University Press, 1996), 472–77.

37. On Zola's mix of biological determinism and progressive ideology, see Daniel Pick, *Faces of Degeneration* (Cambridge: Cambridge University Press, 1989), 74–96.

38. Wilhelm Voigt, *Wie ich Hauptmann von Köpenick wurde* (Berlin: Jul. Emil Gaul, 1909); Löschburg claims that Hyan ghost-wrote Voigt's entire memoir.

39. Voigt, *Hauptmann*, 5–7.

40. Ibid., 13–14.

41. Ibid., 16–71.

42. Ibid., 67. In general the tone of Voigt's memoir is unremittingly earnest, pious, and patriotic.

43. Hyan, *Der Hauptmann von Köpenick. Eine schaurig-traurige Geschichte vom beschränkten Untertanverstand* (Berlin, 1907); Hyan, "Vorwort," in Voigt, *Hauptmann*; Walter Bahn, *Meine Klienten*.

44. In the previous five years, the police banished from Berlin an average of 435 persons per year. This number presumably does not include persons who were prohibited from settling in Berlin under the exceptions clause of the 1867 Freedom of Mobility law, which allowed states to keep out any ex-felon who was banned by another state, as well as persons convicted in the past twelve months of recidivist

begging or vagrancy. "Über die Ausweisung bestrafter Personen," *Berliner Lokalanzeiger*, 12 February 1907; Schlichting, "Ausweisung von Inländer."

45. Robert von Hippel, "Der Hauptmann von Köpenick und die Aufenthaltsbeschränkungen bestrafter Personen," *Deutsche Juristenzeitung* 11, no. 23 (1906): 1303–04. Portions of Hippel's short article were read aloud at Voigt's trial and apparently influenced the presiding judge. Hett, *Death*, 185.

46. Both of the photos were presumably inauthentic, with Voigt's head pasted on to another man's body. *Denkwürdigkeiten*, 33.

47. Gustav Westphal, *Hauptmann von Köpenick: Tragikömödie in 4 Handlungen und einem Soldaten-Intermezzo* (Danzig: G. Macholz, 1906).

48. "Opfern des Polizeiaufsicht" *Posener Zeitung*, 30 December 1906.

49. "Über die Ausweisung"; Stenographische Berichte, Verhandlungen des Reichstags, 12 Legislaturperiode, 1. Session, vol. 228. 20 April 1907; Stenographische Berichte über die Verhandlungen des Preussischen Hauses der Abgeordneten, 20. Legislaturperiode, 3. Session. 19 February 1907.

50. "Today . . . no one feels so non-chalant and free, as when he is under the supervision of the butt police." "Unter polizeilicher Aufsicht," *Der Floh* (Vienna), reprinted in *Denkwürdigkeiten*, 32.

51. Ibid., 51, 81.

52. Bezirksamt Treptow-Köpenick, Heimatmuseum Köpenick, "Sympathie-Postkarte für Wilhelm Voigt dem Hauptmann von Köpenick."

53. One hundred marks was the equivalent of a month and three-quarter's wages for an average industrial worker. "Geschäftsbericht über das Vereinsjahr 1906 erstattet von dem Schriftführer Pastor Haarmann," *23. JGGSA* (1907): 59–60.

54. LAB no. 30, Bericht des Strafanstaltsdirektors. 22 December 1905.

55. Lindenau, "Polizeiaufsicht und Polizeiausweisung," *23. JGGSA* (1907); *Stenographische Berichte über die Verhandlungen des Preussischen Hauses der Abgeordneten*, 20. Legislaturperiode, 3. Session 1907, vol. 1, 990–92.

56. Brandenbürgisches Hauptstaatsarchiv. Pr. Br. rep. 2A. Regierung Potsdam I. Pol. no. 3356. Bülow letter to Prussian governors.

57. GStA rep. 84a no. 7935, "Polizeiaufsicht"; the 13 June 1895 decree authorized administrative pardons for criminal offenders sentenced to no more than six months in prison. The novelty of this decree was that an agreement to undergo welfare supervision could be considered grounds for the suspension of punishment. Ernst Rosenfeld, *Zwei Hundert Jahre Fürsorge der Preußischen Staatsregierung für die entlassene Gefangenen* (Berlin: J. Guttentag, 1905), 46–48.

58. Gustav Aschaffenburg, "Zur Psychologie des Hochstaplers," *März. Halbmonatschrift für deutsche Kultur*, I (1907). Edited by Hermann Hesse, Ludwig Thoma, and Albert Langen, *März* had a particular interest in crime, punishment, and culture.

59. Ibid., 309; Robert von Hippel, "Der Hauptmann von Köpenick und die Aufenthaltsbeschränkungen bestrafter Personen," *DJZ* 11, no. 23 (1906).

60. *Berliner Lokalanzeiger*, 18 October 1906.

61. Voigt, *Hauptmann*, 126–30.

62. ADW CA 554, vol. 3, "Fürsorge für Entlassene," Letter, Dr. Stahl to [illegible], 1 July 1907.

63. AdW CA 554, vol. 3, Auszug aus der Korrespondenz für Innere Mission, 14 March 1909; ADW CA 554, Pastor Dross to Pastor Kunze, 16 July 1907.

64. BA R30.01 no. 5683. Vorstand des Vereins für Berliner Stadtmission an den Central Auschuß, Innere Mission. 3 July 1912. See also chapter 2 above.

65. BA R30.01 no. 6109. Der Erste Staatsanwalt (Halle) an den Justizminister (Reich), 18 February 1910. "Betrifft Strafvollstreckung gegen den Bergmann Ewald Ulze in Bergerhausen." See also *Berliner Tageblatt*, 2 February 1910.

66. Franz von Liszt, "Bedingte Verurteilung und Bedingte Begnadigung," *Vergleichende Darstellung des Deutschen und Ausländischen Strafrechts*, ed. Karl Birkmeyer, Reinhard Frank, Robert Hippel, Wilhelm Kahl, Franz von Liszt, and Fritz van Calker (Berlin: Verlag von Otto Liebmann, 1908); BA R30.01 no. 6109. Liszt's speech to the Reichstag, 89th Session, 13 January 1909.

67. James Q. Whitman, *Harsh Justice: Criminal Punishment and the Widening Gap between America and Europe* (Oxford: Oxford University Press, 2003), 132–36.

68. GStA 84a no. 7935, *Volkszeitung*, 13 May 1908; *Die Post*, 23 May 1908; "Polizei Aufsicht," *Hannoversche Courrier*, 28 July 1911; *Berliner Börsencourrier*, 28 December 1911.

69. *Statistisches Jahrbuch des deutschen Reiches* (Berlin: Schmidt, 1930), 69.

70. D.A., "Arbeit als Erziehung der Unsozialen," *Berliner Lokal-Anzeiger*, 14 January 1912.

71. Ibid. See also Karl Wiesenthal, "Aus den preußischen Staatsgefängnissen," *Berliner Volkszeitung*, 22 March 1912.

Chapter 5

1. Alfred Bozi, *Die Sozialen Rechtseinrichtungen in Bielefeld* (Stuttgart: Deutsche Gesselschaft für Soziales Recht, 1917), 5. On war and the science of human energy, see Anson Rabinbach, *The Human Motor: Energy, Fatigue and the Origins of Modernity* (Berkeley: University of California Press, 1990), 259–64.

2. On the atmosphere of repression during the war, see Gerald Feldman, *Army, Industry, and Labor in Germany, 1914–1918* (Princeton: Princeton University Press, 1966), 31–32; and Albrecht Mendelssohn-Bartholdy, *The War and German Society: The Testament of a Liberal* (New Haven: Yale University Press, 1937), 107–13.

3. Ludwig Preller, *Sozialpolitik in der Weimarer Republik* (Kronberg: Athenäum/Droste, 1978). Preller's book was originally published in 1949. One can see the essential thrust of Preller's argument already in interwar analyses of welfare by Weimar scholars. See Mendelssohn-Bartholdy, *War and German Society*.

4. Preller, *Sozialpolitik*, 83–85.

5. Ibid., 85.

6. Feldman, *Army*, 73–96, 203–35; Ursula Ratz, *Zwischen Arbeitsgemeinschaft und Koalition: burgerliche Sozialreformer und Gewerkschaften im Ersten Weltkrieg* (Munchen: K. G. Saur, 1994), 37–127, 207–306. See also Ratz, "Sozialdemokratische Arbeiterbewegung, bürgerliche Sozialreformer und Militärbehörden im Ersten Weltkrieg. Die Berichte des Bureaus für Sozialpolitik," *Militärgeschichtliche Mitteilungen* 37 (1985).

7. Gerald Feldman, *The Great Disorder: Politics, Economics, and Society in the German Inflation, 1914–1924* (New York: Oxford University Press, 1993), 68–73.

8. Jürgen Kocka, *Facing Total War: German Society 1914–1918* (Cambridge: Cambridge University Press, 1984), 42–44.

9. Ibid., 132–40, 155.

10. Christoph Sachße and Florian Tennstedt, *Geschichte Der Armenfürsorge in Deutschland. Band 2. Fürsorge Und Wohlfahrtspflege 1871 Bis 1929* (Stuttgart: Kohlhammer, 1988), 46. See also Sachße, Christoph, *Mütterlichkeit als Beruf. Sozialarbeit, Sozialreform und Frauenbewegung 1871–1929* (Frankfurt am Main: Suhrkamp, 1986), 162–73.

11. Paul Weindling, "The Medical Profession, Social Hygiene and the Birth Rate in Germany 1914–1918," in *Upheaval of War: Family, Work and Welfare in Europe, 1914–1918*, ed. Richard Wall and Jay Winter (Cambridge: Cambridge University Press, 1988). On the mobilization of psychiatry, see Paul Lerner, "Rationalizing the Therapeutic Arsenal: German Neuropsychiatry in World War I," in *Medicine and Modernity: Public Health and Medical Care in Nineteenth and Twentieth Century Germany*, ed. Manfred Berg and Geoffrey Cocks (New York: Cambridge University Press, 1997). On the broader influence of medical models, see Alfons Labisch and Reinhard Spree, eds., *Medizinische Deutungsmacht im sozialen Wandel des 19. und 20. Jahrhunderts* (Bonn: Psychiatrie-Verlag, 1989).

12. Paul Weindling, *Health, Race and German Politics between National Unification and Nazism, 1870–1945* (Cambridge: Cambridge University Press, 1989), 281–90. See also Young-Sun Hong, "World War I and the German Welfare State: Gender, Religion and the Paradoxes of Modernity," in *Society, Culture, and the State in Germany, 1870–1933*, ed. Geoff Eley (Ann Arbor: University of Michigan Press, 1996), 350–53.

13. Weindling, "Medical Profession."

14. Weindling, *Health*, 281.

15. Elisabeth Domansky, "Militarization and Reproduction in World War I Germany," in Eley, *Society, Culture*, 435. Feldman likewise asserts that the war was "the momentary realization of the dream that society could maintain itself in a state of political and social paralysis." *Army*, 30.

16. Sachße, *Mütterlichkeit*, 170–72. Sachße's analysis of social reform during the war complements Evans's argument about the abandonment of liberalism in the women's movement after 1908. The doctrine of separate spheres, Evans argues, which was enshrined in the program of the leading bourgeois women's organization in 1919, "registered the abandonment by the feminist movement of any attempt to carve out

new roles for the German woman outside her traditional sphere of the home and its extension into public life via social welfare activities." Richard J. Evans, "Liberalism and Society: The Feminist Movement and Social Change," in *Rethinking German History: Nineteenth Century Germany and the Origins of the Third Reich* (London: Allen and Unwin, 1987).

17. Sachße's insistent generalizations about "the" women's movement seem strange given his own evidence for the diversity of organizational forms and tasks fulfilled by local women's organizations during the war. *Mütterlichkeit*, 165–69.

18. Sachße and Tennstedt, *Geschichte*, 38; on the impact of the war, 46–56.

19. Sachße, *Mütterlichkeit*, 168.

20. Weindling, *Health*, 297. An identical argument is made by Detlev Peukert, "The Genesis of the Final Solution from the Spirit of Science," *Nazism and German Society, 1933–1945*, ed. David Crew (London: Routledge, 1994), 284–85.

21. Young-Sun Hong, *Welfare, Modernity and the Weimar State, 1919–1933* (Princeton: Princeton University Press, 1998), 147. For an argument that stresses the importance of "humanitarian" concerns in German social reform up until the Great Depression, see Peter Stachura, *The Weimar Republic and the Younger Proletariat: An Economic and Social Analysis* (New York: St. Martin's Press, 1989).

22. David Crew, "The Ambiguities of Modernity: Welfare and the German State from Wilhelm to Hitler," in Eley, *Society, Culture*.

23. Feldman, *Army*, 64.

24. Guest workers from enemy countries were in many cases forced to remain in Germany and continue working under police surveillance and special regulations. As the demand for industrial labor increased, such compulsory labor was employed in factories as well. Lothar Elsner, "Ausländerbeschäftigung und Zwangsarbeitspolitik in Deutschland während des Ersten Weltkrieges," *Auswanderer—Wanderarbeiter— Gastarbeiter: Bevölkerung, Arbeitsmarkt und Wanderung in Deutschland seit der Mitte des 19. Jahrhunderts*, ed. Klaus Bade (Ostfildern: Scripta-Mercaturae-Verl, 1984), 527– 34. Ulrich Herbert, *A History of Foreign Labor in Germany, 1880–1980* (Ann Arbor: University of Michigan Press, 1990), 90, 93–119.

25. HBAB, 2/12–16, Bodelschwingh to Oberlandesgerichtspräsident Geheimen Rat Dr. Holtgreven, 11 September 1915; HBAB, 2/12–16, "Die Tagung der Wanderfürsorgeverbände am 14. Oktober 1915 in Berlin." Another pastor later quoted Avé-Lallement's observations on the Thirty Years' War: "The unbounded, horrible practice of war was a training ground out of which complete masters of crime were produced": Theodor Just, "Wie wehren wir der drohenden Zunahme der Straffälligkeit als einer Folgeerscheinung des Krieges?," in *33. JGGSA* (1917): 40–41. For the larger context of social fears in reference to demobilization, see Richard Bessel, *Germany after the First World War* (New York: Oxford University Press, 1993).

26. HBAB, 2/12–16, "Tagung," 32.

27. The Siege Law divided Prussia into twenty-four districts, each ruled by an Army corps, or "General Commando," under the leadership of a Deputy Commanding

General. The law gave the Commandos primary responsibility for "public safety," which, according to Feldman, was a term vague enough to include any element of the "political, economic, cultural and social life of the country." Feldman, *Army*, 31.

28. HBAB, 2/12–16, "Tagung," 28.

29. HBAB, 2/63–68, VII. Armeekorps. Stellvertr. Generalkommando, 11 November 1915.

30. HBAB, 2/12–16, "Tagung," 29.

31. Ibid., 27–29. One of the dissenters was Hermann Luppe, the liberal Mayor of Frankfurt am Main, who argued that the army's intervention would not provide a sound basis for future policies and represented an overblown effort for the sake of netting a few people.

32. Ewald Frie, *Wohlfahrtsstaat und Provinz. Fürsorgepolitik des Provinzialverbandes Westafalen und des Landes Sachsen 1880–1930* (Paderborn: Schoeningh, 1993), 90.

33. *Der Wanderer*, no. 34. (1917).

34. HBAB, 2/12–16, "Tagung."

35. Founded in the same year as the DEF, the Frauenhülfe was committed to strict adherence to Paul's command of silence (*Schweigegebot*) for women. In Zoellner's words, the organization sought to "awaken the eye and the ability of woman for the duties of Christian love . . . but without using these duties for the achievement of rights." Quoted in Ursula Baumann, *Protestantismus und Frauenemanzipation in Deutschland 1850 bis 1920* (Frankfurt am Main: Campus Verlag, 1992), 148. On Zoellner's role in Church politics, see Erich Foerster, "Die Stellung der Evangelischen Kirche," *Geistige und sittliche Wirkungen des Krieges in Deutschland*, vol. 1, ed. Otto Baumgarten et al. (Stuttgart: Deutsche Verlagsanstalt, 1927), 126–27. Foerster calls him the "smartest and most able" of the Lutheran leaders.

36. HBAB, 2/12–16, "Tagung," 26–27.

37. HBAB, 2/63–68, "VII. Armeekorps."

38. HBAB, 2/12–16, "Tagung," 29.

39. Erich Foerster writes that "the entire people streamed to the Church, recognizing in her its spiritual home, demanding its services. Even in the most unreligious communities . . . in the industrial suburbs of Berlin . . . the religious houses filled up and there was manifested a tremendous press toward the building of a religious community." Foerster, "Stellung," 120.

40. Ibid., 126, 129–31; Marion Kaplan, *The Making of the Jewish Middle Class: Women, Family, and Identity in Imperial Germany* (New York: Oxford University Press, 1991), 219–27.

41. Wolfgang Ayass, *Das Arbeitshaus Breitenau. Bettler, Landstreicher, Prostituierte, Zuhalter und Fursorgeempfanger in der Korrektions und Landarmenanstalt Breitenau* (Kassel: Gesamthochschule Kassel, 1992), 241.

42. Hage, "Geschäftsbericht über das Vereinsjahr 1915," 32. *JGGSA* (1916): 9–10; *Bericht über die Wirksamkeit des Vereins zur Besserung der Strafgefangenen* 88 (1916).

43. HBAB, "Tagung," 41–43.

44. *11. Jahresbericht des Deutschen Hilfsvereins für entlassene Gefangene* (Hamburg: H. O. Persiehl, 1915); Hage, "Geschäftsbericht über das Vereinsjahr 1915," 8; Hage, "Geschäftsbericht über das Jahr 1916," *33. JGGSA* (1917): 7–8. A scholarly assessment of this phenomenon had to wait a decade or more, at which point a number of studies were published. See especially Moritz Liepmann, *Krieg und Kriminalität in Deutschland* (Stuttgart: Deutsche Verlags-Anstalt, 1930).

45. Just, "Wie wehren," 42.

46. "Im Verein zur Besserung der Strafgefangenen," *Der Reichsbote*, 11 September 1917.

47. Franz Exner, *Krieg und Kriminalität* (Leipzig: Wiegandt, 1926), 14.

48. Again this was confirmed, and much discussed, by later criminological studies. Ibid., 8; Liepmann, *Krieg*, 156–59; Sebastian von Koppenfels, *Die Kriminalität der Frau im Kriege* (Leipzig: Wiegandt, 1926).

49. SB NB no. 38, "Bericht des Katholischen Fürsorgevereins für Mädchen, Frauen und Kinder EG zu Münster und des Katholischen Fürsorgeheims GmbH zu Münster über das Geschäftsjahr 1918."

50. Wilhelm Müller, ed., *Wie Deutschlands Jugend den Weltkrieg Erlebt* (Dresden: Mitteldeutsche Verlagsanstalt, 1918).

51. Bundesarchiv, R30.01, no. 6109, speech by Wolfgang Heine, Reichstag, 164, 13 May 1918.

52. A "Vergehen" was any crime for which the punishment was more than three weeks but less than one year in jail. It was not unusual, however, for the term "*Kriegsvergehen*" to be used in reference to what were technically felonies (*Verbrechen*). SB NB no. 38, Bozi to Schiffer, 24 April 1918.

53. Alfred Blaschko, "Die Prostitution in Kriegszeiten," *Deutsche Strafrechtszeitung* 1, nos. 8–9 (1914). Just, "Wie wehren," 47–50; Anna Pappritz, "Der Kampf gegen die öffentliche Unsittlichkeit," in *Recht, Verwaltung, und Politik im neuen Deutschland*, ed. Alfred Bozi and Hugo Heinemann (Stuttgart: Enke, 1916). Whether any real increase took place in the numbers of prostitutes was later disputed. Writing in 1926, one scholar cites unspecified "information" from Anna Papritz as evidence that prostitution did not increase. Koppenfels, *Kriminalität*, 30.

54. Lutz Sauerteig, "Militär, Medizin und Moral: Sexualität im Ersten Weltkrieg," in *Die Medizin und der Ersten Weltkrieg*, ed. Wolfgang Eckart and Christoph Gradmann (Pfaffenweiler: Centauras, 1996), 205, 216–18. The brothels were first introduced in early 1915. Magnus Hirschfeld, *The Sexual History of the World War* (New York: Panurge Press, 1934), 141–55. The Frauenhülfe leaders sent discrete letters to the Reich government, protesting such brothels. Ursula Baumann, *Protestantismus und Frauenemanzipation in Deutschland 1850 bis 1920* (Frankfurt: Campus, 1992).

55. Just, "Wie wehren," 48.

56. Nancy Reagin, *A German Women's Movement: Class and Gender in Hanover, 1880–1933* (Chapel Hill: University of North Carolina Press, 1995), 198. Domansky asserts that "it became legally admissible to report women who had several male

visitors in a month's time to the police as suspected prostitutes. [If] such denunciations occurred repeatedly, women could be forced to register as prostitutes." Domansky, "Militarization," 450. In principle such a state of affairs already existed prior to 1914.

57. Pappritz, "Der Kampf."

58. Prison societies in the Prussian province of Sachsen-Anhalt found themselves increasingly overwhelmed by women and girls released from prison. Hage, "Geschäftsbericht 1915," 32. *JGGSA* (1916): 10–11.

59. Just, "Wie wehren," 48.

60. HBAB, 2/12–16, Gefängnishülfsverein Bielefeld to Minden Regierungspräsident, 27 July 1915.

61. "Verhandlungen der 32. Jahresversammlung am 20. Juni 1916 in Halle a.S.," 32. *JGGSA* (1916): 18, 24. Moral reformers campaigned against female factory work in the prewar era. Kathleen Canning, "Social Policy, Body Politics: Recasting the Social Question in Germany, 1875–1900," *Gender and Class in Modern Europe*, ed. Laura Frader and Sonya Rose (Ithaca: Cornell University Press, 1996).

62. Westfälische Frauenhülfe to the General-Kommando in Münster, 11 April 1916. Landeskirchliches Archiv Bielefeld, 13, 1 no. 20 Fasc. 8. Reprinted in Kaiser, *Frauen*, 86–87.

63. Christoph Beck, *Die Frau und die Kriegsgefangenen. Die deutsche Frau und die fremden Kriegsgefangenen* (Nürnberg: Döllinger und Co., 1919).

64. Liepmann, *Krieg*, 79.

65. 33. *JGGSA* (1917): 20.

66. Wilhelm Müller, "Jugendliche Wanderbettler, Landstreicher und Großstadtbummler," in *Wie Deutschlands Jugend den Weltkrieg Erlebt* (Dresden: Mitteldeutsche Verlagsanstalt, 1918).

67. Bundesarchiv, R 30.01, no. 6109. "Aktennotiz Zimmerle," 22 June 1917; Reichstag. 164. Sitzung, 13 May 1918, S. 5119.

68. 32. *JGGSA* (1916): 11.

69. Hans Hentig, *Mein Krieg* (Berlin: A. Kuhn, 1919), 6–7; Artur Hellwig, *Der Krieg und die Kriminalität der Jugendlichen* (Halle: Buchhandlung des Waisenhauses, 1916).

70. Julia Dünner, "Die Verschiebung der sozialen Schichten durch den Krieg," in *Die christliche Frau* (1919): 175. Prison clergy and other welfare advisers frequently characterized offenders as narcissistic and possessing unrealistic expectations about work and their place in society.

71. Liepmann, *Krieg*, 107.

72. Julia Dünner, *Handwörterbuch der Wohlfahrtspflege* (Berlin: Heymann, 1929), 252.

73. BA, R30.01 6109. Reichstag 164. Sitzung, 13 May 1918.

74. Just, "Wie wehren."

75. On the army's role in prewar criminal policy, see chapter 4 above.

76. Karl Krohne, *Lehrbuch der Gefängniskunde* (Stuttgart: Enke, 1889), 241–42.

77. On the importance of military service to social integration in Prussia, see Michael Geyer, *Deutsche Rüstungspolitik 1860–1980* (Frankfurt: Suhrkamp, 1984). On militarism and the liberal ideal of citizenship more generally, see Carole Pateman, *The Sexual Contract* (Cambridge: Polity Press, 1988).

78. Krohne, *Lehrbuch*, 241.

79. Franz von Liszt, "Kriminalpolitische Aufgaben," *Strafrechtliche Aufsätze und Vorträge* (Berlin: Guttentag, 1905), 403–4.

80. Rudolf Franz, "Der Segen des Krieges für die Strafgefangenen," *Blätter für Gefängniskunde* 49 (1915): 223.

81. Friedrich Freund, "Strafvollzug und Krieg," *Blätter für Gefängniskunde* 49 (1915): 168.

82. Schwandner, "Heeresdienst und Strafvollzug mit besonderer Berücksichtigung der Zuchthausstrafe," *Blätter für Gefängniskunde* 49 (1915).

83. Hans Gross, "'Antisoziale' Elemente," *Archiv für Kriminologie, Kriminalanthropologie und Kriminalstatistik* 64, no. 1, 2 (1915). The preoccupation with the "burden" of an unproductive, outcast populations led to massive reductions in living standards for prison and asylum inmates. Hans Hyan, *Berliner Gefängnisse* (Berlin: Puttkammer und Mühlbrecht, 1920). Also J. Werthauer, *Strafunrecht* (Hamburg: Pulvermacher, 1918), and Hugo Heinemann, *Reform des Strafrechts* (Berlin: Verlag fuer Sozialwissenschaft, 1919). Michael Burleigh asserts that over 70,000 inmates died of "hunger, disease, or neglect" in German asylums during the war. Michael Burleigh, *Death and Deliverance: 'Euthanasia' in Germany 1900–1945* (Cambridge: Cambridge University Press, 1994), 11.

84. *Jahresberichte des Deutschen Hilfsvereins für entlassene Gefangene* 10–11 (1914–1915); ADW CA 554, vol. 3, "Fürsorge für Entlassene."

85. A number of the individuals who weighed in on the soldiering question were veterans of the deportation debates. Most prominent among them was Friedrich Freund, the professor of law who had written the Rhenish-Westphalian Prison Society's report in favor of deportation. See chapter 3 above.

86. Heinrich Seyfarth, "Strafvollzug und Kriegsdienst," *Blätter für Gefängniskunde* 49 (1915): 186–87.

87. Seyfarth, "Strafvollzug," 185, 194–95; Seyfarth's activities during the war are described in Richard Voß, *Aus einem phantastischem Leben. Errinerungen.* (Stuttgart: Engelhorn, 1920), 417–19.

88. Jahresbericht, Berliner Verein für Gefangenenfürsorge (1915); Hans Ellger, "Feldpostbriefe früherer Gefangener," *Deutsche Strafrechts-Zeitung* 2 (1915). Detloff Klatt, *Die Unbekannte Armee* (Berlin-Zehlendorf: E. Kammer, 1915); Hage, "Geschäftsbericht über das Jahre 1915," 8.

89. BA, Reichslandbund Pressearchiv, no. 142; Detloff Klatt, "Der Krieg im Gefängnis," *Leipziger Tagesblatt* (date illegible).

90. Klatt, "Der Krieg"; book reviews and reports on lectures at BA, Reichslandbund Pressearchiv, no. 142.

91. Detloff Klatt, *Das Los der Vorbestraften* (Berlin: Verlag von Alfred Metzner, 1926), 22–23.

92. Gross, "Antisoziale"; Kurt Boas, "Kriminalistische Studien," *Archiv für Kriminologie* 64, no. 1, 2 (1915); Freund, "Strafvollzug"; Anon., "Der Einfluß des Krieges auf die Strafanstalten, Waldheim i.S.," *Blätter für Gefängniskunde* 4 (1915).

93. Gross, "Antisoziale," 52–53.

94. "Jahresbericht des Zweigvereins Aschersleben für das Jahr 1916" and "Jahresbericht des Gefängnisvereins zu Halle für das Jahr 1916"; in *33. JGGSA*, 20–21; GStA 84a, no. 50908, Der Oberstaatsanwalt (Coeln) an Preussische Justiz Minister, 22 November 1919. By contrast, the associations had difficulty during the war in finding jobs for educated former prisoners, many of whom remained in halfway houses for long periods of time. Some reformers blamed women for taking the white-collar jobs vacated by men at the front. *32. JGGSA* (1916).

95. "Arbeitsplan der Gefängnis-Gesellschaft" and Hage, "Geschäftsbericht über das Jahr 1916," *33. JGGSA*, 15–18, 10.

96. Freund, "Strafvollzug," 167–68; BA, R30.01, no. 6109. *Stenographische Berichte über die Verhandlungen des Reichstages*, 164, Sitzung, Speech by Wolfgang Heine, 13 May 1918.

97. There were almost 260,000 prison sentences in Prussia in 1912 against 205,000 in 1918. Erwin Bumke, "Die Freiheitsstrafe als Problem der Gesetzgebung," in *Handbuch Deutsches Gefängniswesen* (Berlin: F. Vahlen, 1928), 17; "Der bedingte Strafaufschub in Preussen," *Statistisches Jahrbuch für den preussischen Staat* (Berlin: Landesamt, 1917/1920).

98. "Beurlaubung der Strafgefangenen," GStA rep. 84, no. 7863; "Aufschub der Strafverfahren gegen Krieger," in *Deutsche Strafrechts-Zeitung* 1 (1914); "Neue Gnadenerweise für Kriegsteilnehmer," in *DSZ* 2 (1915); Klatt, "Der Krieg"; Ellger, "Feldpostbriefe," in *Jahresbericht. Berliner Verein für Gefangenenfürsorge* (1917).

99. "Die Niederschlagung von Strafverfahren gegen Kriegsteilnehmer," *Deutsche Strafrechts-Zeitung* 3 (1916). The percentage of offenders sentenced to the penitentiary dropped from 3.5 percent in the years 1904–1913 to 1.9 percent during the first three years of the war. Franz Exner, "Zur Praxis der Strafzumessung," in *MKS* 17 (1926): 371. James Q. Whitman, *Harsh Justice: Criminal Punishment and the Widening Divide between America and Europe* (New York: Oxford University Press, 2003), 135.

100. Hentig, *Mein Krieg*; See also Exner, *Krieg*, 12–13.

101. BA, Reichslandbund Pressearchiv, no. 142. "Der Zuchthausfreibrief," *Rostocker Tageszeitung*, 13 October 1916; Hans Rückert, "Eine Gute Zeit für Zuchthäusler," *Leipziger Staatszeitung*, November 1916.

102. Robert Heindl, in *Leipziger Staatszeitung*; Patrick Wagner, *Volksgemeinschaft ohne Verbrecher. Konzeptionen und Praxis der Kriminalpolizei in der Zeit der Weimarer Republik und des Nationalsozialismus* (Hamburg: Christians, 1996), 19.

103. Robert Heindl, in *Archiv für Kriminalanthropologie* 1916; BA, Reichslandbund Pressearchiv no. 142. Ruckert, "Eine Gute Zeit."

104. BA, R30.01, no. 6109. Heine speech in Reichstag, 13 May 1918.

105. BA, R30.01, no. 6109. Müller. Anfrage an dem Reichsjustizamte. 29 January 1917.

Chapter 6

1. Ursula Nienhaus, "Einsatz für die 'Sittlichkeit': Die Anfänge der weiblichen Polizei im Wilhelminischen Kaiserreich und in der Weimarer Republik," in *'Sicherheit' und 'Wohlfahrt': Polizei, Gesellschaft und Herrschaft im 19. und 20. Jahrhundert*, ed. Alf Lüdtke (Frankfurt: Suhrkamp, 1992).

2. On the police perspective, Peter Becker, "Randgruppen im Blickfeld der Polizei. Ein Versuch über die Perspektivität des 'praktischen Blicks,'" *Archiv für Sozialgeschichte* 32 (1992).

3. Friedrich Thimme and Carl Legien, eds., *Die Arbeiterschaft im neuen Deutschland* (Leipzig: Verlag S. Hirzel, 1915); Alfred Bozi and Hugo Heinemann, eds., *Recht, Verwaltung, und Politik im neuen Deutschland* (Stuttgart: Ferdinand Enke, 1916). On the rhetoric of "provincialism" within municipal modernism, see Jennifer Jenkins, *Provincial Modernity: Local Culture and Liberal Politics* (Ithaca: Cornell University Press, 2004).

4. Bozi's unpublished manuscript on the history of legal reform is revealing. His discussions of criminal law reform barely mention Franz von Liszt, the International Penal Union, or the influence of criminology upon legal discourse. Instead he focuses on how theories and practices in civil law after the 1890s helped judges break free of confining juridical norms and seize greater leeway in decision making. Central to this discussion is the work of Ernst Kantorowicz and the "Free Law School." SB NB no. 2, "Reformbewegung und Ideengeschichte" (MS, undated). For thoughts on the relationship between the free law movement and criminal law reform, see Benjamin Hett, *Death in the Tiergarten: Murder and Criminal Justice in the Kaiser's Berlin* (Cambridge, Mass.: Harvard University Press, 2004), 19–21.

5. Alfred Bozi, "Die Angriffe gegen den Richterstand," *Die Gegenwart* 18 (April 1896). Quotes are from the republished version, *Angriffe gegen den Richterstand* (Breslau: W. Koebner, 1896).

6. Bozi, *Angriffe*, 22. This is, more or less, the policy in contemporary Germany.

7. Ibid., 21.

8. Population figures are from Gerhard Adelmann, "Die Stadt Bielefeld als Zentrum fabrikindustrieller Gründungen nach 1850," *Die Stadt in europäischen Geschichte*, ed. Werner Besch (Bonn: Röhrscheid, 1972), 894. On the Bozi firm, see Otto Sartorius, *Hundert Jahre Spinnerei Vorwärts* (Bielefeld: Küster, 1950).

9. The company went public in 1854, with the Bozi family retaining four of nine spots on the board. Karl was eventually pushed out as director, but other family members, Alfred in particular, maintained a strong relationship with the firm. Sartorius, *Hundert Jahre*, 22–23, 66.

10. Karl Ditt, "Technologischer Wandel und Strukturveränderung der Fabrikarbeiterschaft in Bielefeld, 1860–1914," in *Arbeiter im Industrialisierungsprozeß: Herkunft, Lage und Verhalten*, ed. Werner Conze (Stuttgart: Klett-Cotta, 1979).

11. Reinhard Vogelsang, *Geschichte der Stadt Bielefeld. Bd. 2 von der Mitte des 19. Jahrhunderts bis zum Ende des Ersten Weltkriegs* (Bielefeld: Gieselmann, 1988), 111. Delius was an important figure in the Inner Mission, having earlier brought Wichern to Bielefeld in order to set up a pastorship for the employees of his textile factory. Martin Gerhardt, *Johann Hinrich Wichern, ein Lebensbild* (Hamburg: Agentur des Rauhen Hauses, 1927–1931), 429.

12. In 1885 the city spent a week under a veritable state of siege because of labor unrest. Karl Ditt, *Industrialisierung, Arbeiterschaft und Arbeiterbewegung in Bielefeld* (Dortmund: Gesellschaft für Westfälische Wirtschaftsgeschichte, 1982), 233–39. As recently as 1898, after a political assassination in Geneva (!), the police rounded up the town's working-class leadership on suspicion of "anarchist sympathies." Carl Severing, *Mein Lebensweg, Bd. 1. Vom Schlosser zum Minister* (Cologne: Greven Verlag, 1950), 74–75. The perceptions of a reduction in violent protest may have been illusory, but, if so, these were widely held illusions. For criticism of historical studies that take this teleological narrative at face value, see Geoff Eley, "Labor History, Social History, *Alltagsgeschichte*: Experience, Culture, and the Politics of the Everyday—a New Direction for German Social History?," *Journal of Modern History* 61 (1989): 305ff.

13. On the crisis of Honoratiorenpolitik, see Geoff Eley, *Reshaping the German Right* (New Haven: Yale University Press, 1980). On the relationship between the decline of bourgeois control, the rise of administrative professionals and the development of "proto-corporatist" bodies in the municipalities, see George Steinmetz, *Regulating the Social: The Welfare State and Local Politics in Imperial Germany* (Princeton: Princeton University Press, 1993), 189–203.

14. Vogelsang, *Geschichte der Stadt Bielefeld*, 111.

15. Bozi's professional career had reached a kind of dead-end around this time. In 1908, he had been turned down for a position as Director of the Provincial Court (Landesgericht). Due to a legal conflict with the prosecutor, he was awarded the position of City Court judge in Bielefeld only under the condition that he never assume the position of supervising judge. Staatsarchiv Detmold-Lippe, Landessgericht, Personalakten "Alfred Bozi."

16. Two other Rathenaus were members of the society. There was also a member of the illustrious Siemens family. SB NB no. 19, "Verein Recht und Wirtschaft."

17. SB NB no. 19, Newsarticle. *Plutus*. Berlin, 10 June 1911.

18. SB NB no. 19, Aufruf. "Um das Recht der Gegenwart!"

19. SB NB no. 19, Rathenau to Bozi, 12 January 1915.

20. On Duisburg's sycophantic relationship with the military leadership, see Gerald Feldman, *Army, Industry, and Labor in Germany, 1914–1918* (Princeton: Princeton University Press, 1966), 53–54, 160–61.

21. SB NB no. 19, "Meinen austritt aus Recht und Wirtschaft, 29 September 1915 von R. Deinhardt, OLG Jena"; and "Aufruf. Verein. Recht und Wirtschaft," 2 June 1916.

22. SB NB no. 37, various letters. Onnasch had been director of the Hofnungsthal Asylum near Berlin, administered by Bethel. Ursula Baumann, *Protestantismus und Frauenemanzipation in Deutschland 1850 bis 1920* (Frankfurt am Main: Campus Verlag, 1992), 109, 148–49.

23. The board included Margarethe Bennewiz, Anna Schultz, and Else Lüders, as well as the SPD deputy Max Quarck. Gertrud Bäumer and Karl Severing later joined the editorial staff of its publications with the Friedrich Enke Verlag. SB NB no. 6, Aufruf. Deutsche Gesellschaft für Soziales Recht.

24. Ursula Ratz, " 'Die Arbeiterschaft im neuen Deutschland.' Eine bürgerlich-sozialdemokratische Arbeitsgemeinschaft aus dem Jahre 1915," *Internationale wissenschaftliche Korrespondenz zur Geschichte der deutschen Arbeiterbewegung* (1971): 14.

25. Bozi and Heinemann, *Recht*. In his later correspondence with Severing, Bozi declared that he had edited the book "nach aussen mit Heinemann, im Innenverhältnis aber mit Ihnen." Archiv der sozialen Demokratie. Friedrich Ebert Stiftung, Bozi to Severing, 28 November 1933. Heinemann was a radical critic of criminal justice, but a "right-wing" Social Democrat on political matters. Heinemann, *Neue Fesseln für das Proletariat durch die Strafgesetzgebung* (Berlin: Singer, 1912), and *Zur Reform der Strafprozessordnung* (Stuttgart: Dietz, 1909). For more on Heinemann's politics, see Ratz, "Arbeiterschaft," 5, 13–14.

26. Ratz, *Zwischen Arbeitsgemeinschaft*, and Ratz, "Sozialdemokratische Arbeiterbewegung, bürgerliche Sozialreformer und Militärbehörden im Ersten Weltkrieg. Die Berichte des Bureaus für Sozialpolitik," *Militärgeschichtliche Mitteilungen* 37 (1985): 17.

27. ". . . da die vornehmsten Erkenntnisquellen für das Soziale neben den realen Vorgängen selber nur die Lebensanschauungen aller Volksschichten sind." SN NB no. 23, Bozi to Jellinek, 12 July 1919.

28. SB NB no. 23, Bozi to Frau Anna Schütz, 6 November 1918.

29. Peter Fritzsche notes how "myths" around the crowds of July and August 1914 helped to "define a new political community." Peter Fritzsche, *Germans into Nazis* (Cambridge, Mass.: Harvard University Press, 1998), 18–19. Modris Eksteins claims that "most Germans regarded the armed conflict they were entering in spiritual terms": Modris Eksteins, *Rites of Spring: The Great War and the Birth of the Modern Age* (New York: Anchor Books, 1989), 90–94.

30. Bozi, "Lebenserrinerungen," 148. Bozi was frustrated when grand corporatist goals like industrial mediation overshadowed "practical" incremental reforms on the local level. SB NB no. 29, Enke to Bozi, 22 May 1916.

31. SB NB no. 6, Programm der Gesellschaft für Rechtssoziologie. (Draft) undated.

32. Bozi to Reichsjustizminister, 3 October 1919, Bundesarchiv, Außenstelle Hoppegarten, Reichsjustizministerium, "Strafrechtsreform."

33. Bozi, "Lebenserrinerungen," 144.

34. SB NB no. 6, Programm der Gesellschaft für Rechtssoziologie. (Draft) Undated. Of course, many Germans (and French and British) intellectuals welcomed the war with similar paeans to an expected great awakening. Ute Frevert, *Women in German History: From Bourgeois Emancipation to Sexual Liberation* (Oxford: Berg, 1989), 151–52; see also Wolfgang Mommsen, ed., *Kultur und Krieg: Die Rolle der Intellektuellen, Künstler und Schriftsteller im Ersten Weltkrieg* (Munich: Oldenbourg, 1995); Eksteins, *Rites*, 90–94.

35. HBAB, 2/12–16, Bozi to Bodelschwingh, 19 August 1915; NB no. 38, Bozi to Schiffer, 24 April 1918.

36. The institution had its roots in the labor courts (*Gewerbegerichte*), which existed in many German cities and were first established in Bielefeld in 1912. The labor courts dealt with the arbitration of wage and termination disputes and were required to have an equal representation of workers and employers as judges, along with a "neutral" city official as chair. George Steinmetz, "Workers and the Welfare State in Imperial Germany," *International Labor and Working Class history* 40 (1991): 28. According to Bozi, the labor courts in Bielefeld were rarely used.

37. SB NB no. 39, Bozi to Harnisch, 6 August 1920. Saxony at that point was under Social Democratic control and was a leading site for experiments in criminal justice.

38. The League was known especially for its vigorous support of women workers. Christina Klausman, *Politik und Kultur der Frauenbewegung im Kaiserreich. Das Beispiel Frankfurt a.M.* (Frankfurt: Campus, 1997), 73–87.

39. SB NB no. 23, Bozi to Anna Schütz, 6 November 1918.

40. SB NB no. 23, Bozi to Jellinek, 12 July 1919. On motherliness as social practice, see Christoph Sachße, *Mütterlichkeit als Beruf. Sozialarbeit, Sozialreform und Frauenbewegung 1871–1929* (Frankfurt am Main: Suhrkamp, 1986). Mary Louise Roberts notes that "in postwar discourse of all kinds, motherhood served as a panacea for an impressive host of . . . anxieties." Roberts, *Civilization without Sexes: Reconstructing Gender in Postwar France, 1917–1927* (Chicago: University of Chicago Press, 1994), 91.

41. Renäte Schade, "Frauen Helfen Frauen. Camilla Jellinek und die Rechtsschutzstelle für Frauen in Heidelberg," *Feministische Studien* (1989): 135–44. On Bennewitz, see *Mitteilungen des Rechtsschutzverbandes. Organ der dem Verband angeschlossenen Rechtsschutzvereine und Rechtsschutzsstellen* 14, no. 96. (June 1919). Bozi also sought the participation of sociologist Marianne Weber. SB NB no. 23, Bozi to Weber, 5 December 1918.

42. Thieme was a leader of the morality movement in Frankfurt. SB NB no. 23, Bozi to Frau Camilla Jellinek, 6 January 1919. Onnasch was a disciple of Adolph Stoecker active in Berlin social welfare. Baumann, *Protestantismus*.

43. SB NB no. 23, Bozi to Leyen, 11 July 1919.

44. On the split between the Evangelical women's movement (DEF) and the liberal feminists (BDF), see Barbara Greven-Aschoff, *Die bürgerliche Frauenbewegung in Deutschland 1894–1933* (Göttingen: Vendenhoeck und Ruprecht, 1981), and Reagin,

German Women's Movement, 200. Reagin notes that "on the local level, the meaning of the DEF's break [with the BDF] was . . . largely psychological or symbolic."

45. SB NB no. 23, Rundschreiben. Arbeitsausschus. An die Justizbehörde, April 1918.

46. Michael Willrich, *City of Courts: Socializing Justice in Progressive Era Chicago* (Cambridge: Cambridge University Press, 2003), 123.

47. SB NB no. 23, Bozi to Frau Schirmer, 3 September 1921.

48. On the relationship between local and national patriotism, see Celia Appelgate, *A Nation of Provincials: The German Idea of Heimat* (Berkeley: University of California, 1990).

49. Friedrich von Bodelschwingh, *Saat und Segen in der Arbeit von Bethel: ein Ruckblick auf die Zeit seit dem Tode des Anstaltsvaters* (Bethel bei Bielefeld: Verlagshandlung der Anstalt Bethel, 1932).

50. Friedrich von Bodelschwingh, *Friedrich Von Bodelschwingh. Ein Blick in Sein Leben* (Bielefeld: Pfennigverein, 1924).

51. A skilled metal worker, Severing became union secretary in Bielefeld in 1901. He quit in 1912 to become editor of the Bielefeld-based *Volkswacht*. His prewar political experience included serving as a Reichstag member from 1907 to 1911. After 1918, Severing was a leader in the Social Democratic Party in Prussia, serving on two occasions as Prussian Interior Minister. After 1945, he was again, briefly, a parliamentary deputy for Bielefeld.

52. Ditt, *Industrialisierung*, 241–42. According to Ditt, the workers embraced collective bargaining in Bielefeld earlier than most regions of the country. On suspicions toward wage negotiation among the union rank and file, see Michael Schneider, *A Brief History of the German Trade Unions* (Bonn: Dietz, 1991), 101–3.

53. Severing, *Lebensweg*, 74.

54. Ibid., 178–79. In all likelihood Severing and others exaggerated or overestimated his authority among Bielfeld workers. Nevertheless, his influence at critical moments was clear, and the perception of Severing as a great moderating (and pacifying) force was important.

55. SB NB no. 38, Severing to Schiffer, 27 April 1918. SB NB no. 3, Bozi. "Deutschland's Erneuerung," 1933; "Lebenserrinerungen," 1937.

56. SB NB, Manuskript. "Lebenserrinerungen," 1937, 145–46; Severing, *Lebensweg*, 217–18.

57. SB NB no. 49, Alfred Bozi, "Lebenserrinerungen" (MS, 1937). Count von Baudissin was a prominent theologian and the former rector of Berlin University.

58. Sixteen people on a total list of 211 listed their address as "Bethel." Other participants presumably could have worked in Bethel while living in Bielefeld proper. SB NB no. 77, Membership/Participation Chart (untitled, starting date not indicated).

59. Archiv der sozialen Demokratie, Friedrich Ebert Stiftung (FES). Nachlaß Severing (NS) no. 37. Bozi to Severing, 28 November 1933.

60. SB NB no. 77, Membership Chart. See also Severing, *Lebensweg*, 218.

61. Steinmetz, *Regulating the Social*, 202–13; Ratz, *Zwischen Arbeitsgemeinschaft*, 207ff.

62. SB NB no. 49, Alfred Bozi, "Lebenserrinerungen" (MS, 1937).

63. HBAB, 2/12–16. "Besprechung mit Bozi, Pastor Hesselmann, Lehrer Bitter und Kaufmann Barlag, und Fraülein Hermelbrecht," 17 March 1915.

64. HBAB, 2/12–16, Bodelschwingh to Chairman of the Association for Catholic Worker Colonies, 5 June 1915.

65. HBAB, 2/12–16, "Die Tagung der Wanderfürsorgeverbände am 14. Oktober 1915 in Berlin," 34–37. Friedrich von Bodelschwingh, "Grosse Kinder," *Bethel* 3, no. 1 (1911). Georg Steigerthal, "Die Bekämpfung asozialer Elemente durch die Nachhaftsstrafe," 41. *JGGSA* (1925); Otto Mönkemöller, "Die Bewahrung Asozialer," *MKS* 15 (1924).

66. HBAB, 2/12–16, "Tagung," 37.

67. HBAB, 2/12–16, Bodelschwingh to Pastor Just, 17 June 1915.

68. SB NB no. 38, Bozi to Schiffer, 24 April 1918; Georg Bamberger, *Geldstrafe statt Gefängnis* (Stuttgart: Schriften der deutschen Gesellschaft für soziales Recht, 1917).

69. HBAB, 2/12–16, Bozi to Bodelschwingh, 19 August 1915.

70. SB NB no. 39, Vorsitende des Kreisausschusses des Landkreis Bielefeld to Herrn Amtsmänner, 20 July 1920.

71. SB NB no. 37, Berufsvormund des Amtes Schildesche-Jöllenbeck to Bozi, 15 December 1915.

72. HBAB, 2/12–16, Bielefeld Gefängnis-Hülfsverein to dem Herrn Präsidenten der Königlichen Regierung Minden, 19 March 1915. Bozi later declared that he had originally considered using the morality association itself as the principal partner in this project. SB NB no. 38, Bozi to Frau Dr. Quarck, 22 October 1918.

73. In fact, so far as I can ascertain, the police and the military authorities were absent from the Discussion Association meetings more generally. By contrast, the conservative Protestant welfare associations in Münster, where the Seventh District Commando was headquartered, seem to have had close contact with the authorities. HBAB, 2/12–16, "Tagung." The relationship between the civil government in Minden and the military Commando in Münster is unclear. The District Officers (*Regierungspräsident*) historically possessed extraordinary direct and personal power. See Herbert Jacob, *German Administration since Bismarck: Central Authority versus Local Autonomy* (New Haven: Yale University Press, 1963), 14–15.

74. See various correspondence in HBAB, 2/12–16, and SB NB no. 38.

75. HBAB, 2/12–16, "Besprechung." This proposal was similar to the institution of probation, which was introduced in the United States and England in the decade before World War I, a primary difference being the continued emphasis upon private supervision in Germany. The striking differences in the cultural and social implications of the institutions are discussed below. David Garland, *Punishment and Welfare: A History of Penal Strategies* (Aldershot: Gower, 1985), 19–22; David J. Rothman, *Conscience and Convenience: The Asylum and its Alternatives in Progressive America* (Boston: Little, Brown, 1980), 82–116.

76. HBAB, 2/12–16, Bielefeld Gefängnis-Hülfsverein to dem Herrn Präsidenten der Königlichen Regierung Minden, 19 March 1915.

77. Even after the implementation of the system, however, there was uncertainty about how the minimum duration of welfare supervision would be determined. In the end, it was to be set at a maximum duration corresponding to the maximum period for police custody described in the Imperial Penal Code. The minimum duration was then set by the judge, in consultation with the prison society. SB NB no. 37, Bodelschwingh to Bozi, 22 April 1915.

78. HBAB, 2/12–16, Bodelschwingh to Hilgemann (Hausvater Wilhelmsdorf), 30 April 1915.

79. SB NB no. 37, Regierungspräsident von Borries (Minden) to Bodelschwingh, 9 April 1915.

80. SB NB no. 37, Der Landeshauptmann der Provinz Westfallen to Bozi, 4 November 1915.

81. SB NB no. 37, Bodelschwingh to Bozi, 15 May 1915. Karl Finkelnburg, *Die Bestraften in Deutschland* (Berlin: J. Guttentag, 1912).

82. HBAB, 2/12–16, Bozi to Bodelschwingh, 15 April 1915.

83. GStA 77 tit. 1104 no. 18 Adh.III, Prussian Minister of Justice to the chief state's attorneys. 23 December 1916. The minister's intepretation of the law was challenged by other. GStA 1104, 18adh3, Oberpräs Hannover to Min des Innern, 11 February 1917.

84. HBAB, 2/12–16, Gefängnishülfsverein Bielefeld to Minden Regierungspräsident, 27 July 1915; Bozi to Bodelschwingh, 19 August 1915.

85. HBAB, 2/12–16, Bozi to Bodelschwingh, 17 May 1915.

86. SB NB no. 37, Bodelschwingh to Bozi, 29 December 1916. Bethel did, however, sponsor one relatively small worker colony for women in Erkner near Berlin.

87. See chapter 5 above.

88. HBAB, 2/12–16, Gefängnishülfsverein Bielefeld to Minden Regierungspräsident, 27 July 1915.

89. Alfred Bozi, *Die Sozialen Rechtseinrichtungen in Bielefeld* (Stuttgart: Deutsche Gesselschaft für Soziales Recht, 1917), 15.

90. HBAB, 2/12–16, Gefängnishülfsverein Bielefeld to Minden Regierungspräsident, 27 July 1915; Bozi, *Soziale Rechtseinrichtungen*, 14.

91. ADW CA GF/St no. 325, Licentiat Bohn, "Die Frage und Lage der Ländlichen Arbeiterinnen-Kolonien," *Berliner Wohlfahrtsblatt*, 7 July 1929.

92. SB NB no. 37, Bodelschwingh to Bozi, 16 June 1917. The Prussian Ministry of the Interior endorsed the proposal in the summer of 1918, based on the understanding that the Rhineland-Westphalian Prison Society would build both a Catholic and a Protestant worker colony to serve women in these provinces. HBAB, 2/12–16, Minister des Innern. Entwurf, 15 July 1918. Meanwhile, a small colony for women was created in 1917 at Wengern on the Ruhr, under the directorship of Wilhelm Zoellner and the Westfälisches Frauenhülfsverein. Bozi spoke at the Frauenhülfeverein in the spring of 1916 and provoked controversy, but also a great deal of passionate support

from among the rank and file. SB NB no. 37, Frau Rollertz to Bozi, 25 April 1916 and 7 May 1916.

93. The duties are described in various documents. Eventually, Hermelbrecht's job description called upon her to participate in court cases involving women or children in *any* capacity: whether as defendants, victims, or witnesses. SB NB no. 23, Bozi to Schütz, Bozi to van den Leyen. 1918.

94. HBAB, 2/12–16, Bozi to Bodelschwingh, 19 August 1915.

95. SB MV 416, "Dienstanweisung für die Polizeiassistentin in Bielefeld," 11 July 1917.

96. HBAB, 2/12–16, Gefängnishülfsverein to Minden Regierungspräsident, 27 July 1915.

97. SB MV 416, Frau Hermelbrecht an das Wohlfahrtsamt Osnabruck, 23 January 1916 (?).

98. SB NB no. 39, Abschrift. Frau Kirschner. 1919.

99. Anna Pappritz, "Der Kampf gegen die öffentliche Unsittlichkeit," in *Recht, Verwaltung, und Politik im neuen Deutschland*, ed. Alfred Bozi and Hugo Heinemann (Stuttgart: Enke, 1916), 317. Pappritz founded the Berlin branch of the International Abolitionist Federation in 1899 and was a widely published author on prostitution, venereal disease, and women's rights. See especially Anna Pappritz, *Die Wirtschaftlichen Ursachen der Prostitution* (Berlin: Walter, 1903). Bozi seemed mildly obsessed with her, complaining constantly—and for years thereafter—of her political radicalism and intellectual intolerance during the war years. SB NB no. 38, Bozi to Frau Quarck, 22 October 1918; and no. 23, Bozi to Ruth van den Leyen, 11 July 1919.

100. Pappritz, "Der Kampf," 318.

101. Ibid., 317. On the mixing of medical and moral concepts of degeneration in general, see Edward Ross Dickinson, *The Politics of German Child Welfare from the Empire to the Federal Republic* (Cambridge, Mass.: Harvard University Press, 1996), 62–68. The central concept of "waywardness" (*Verwahrlösung*) in youth welfare seems to illustrate this phenomenon, though Dickinson initially describes the term as excluding social considerations in favor of purely individual-moral considerations (11–12). For a more nuanced discussion, see Derek Linton, *"Who Has the Youth, Has the Future": The Campaign to Save Young Workers in Imperial Germany* (Cambridge: Cambridge University Press, 1991), 48–56. Historians of fin-de-siècle degeneration theory, especially in France, have frequently noted how social, moral, and medical thinking were intertwined. See especially Robert Nye, *Crime, Madness, and Politics in Modern France: The Medical Concept of National Decline* (Princeton: Princeton University Press, 1984); Ruth Harris, *Murders and Madness: Medicine, Law and Society in the Fin de Siecle* (Oxford: Oxford University Press, 1990); Daniel Pick, *Faces of Degeneration: A European Disorder, c.1848–c.1918* (Cambridge: Cambridge University Press, 1989).

102. Even the Westfälisches Frauenhülfsverein, in spite of its virulent anti-feminism and its pro-military posture, played an important role in this process. In addition to

founding the first women's worker colony in Westphalia, the Hülfsverein wrote the military authorities and the Kaiser, discretely protesting the army brothels.

103. SB MV 416, Clara Hermelbrecht, "Frauenfürsorge bei der Stadtverwaltung Bielefeld," offprint from *Zeitschrift für die Bekampfung der Geschlechtskrankheiten* (issue and date uncertain, probably 1915).

104. Ibid.

105. SB NB no. 8, "Merkblatt: Worauf es bei einer Schutzaufsicht ankommt?" (undated, probably 1919).

106. SB MV 416, Hermelbrecht, "Frauenfürsorge bei der Stadtverwaltung," 59.

107. See chapter 1 above.

108. HBAB, 2/12–16, Entwurf. F. 705. Minister of the Interior von Loebell to Regierungspräsidenten and Polizeipräsidenten, 23 November 1916.

109. The proposed revisions to the Imperial Penal Code from before the war would have excluded recidivist offenders from the chance of a pardon. Kohlrausch, untitled report, in *Mitteilungen der IKV* (1928): 11–21.

110. GStA 77 tit. 1104 no. 18, Adh.III, Drechsler, "Referat auf der Sitzung der ausserordentlichen Landesdirektorenkonferenz," 28 June 1917.

111. "Verhandlungen der 33. Jahresversammlung am 19. Juni 1917 in Halle a.S.," in *33. JGGSA* (1917): 32–35. Based in Halle, the Sachsen-Anhalt Prison Society was the third oldest among such organizations and was generally considered the most modern and progressive. Its yearbooks often included essays by prominent academics from the Modern School and it was, for a long time, under the chairmanship of D. Hering, a professor of law in Halle. Hage took over the organization in October 1915, after years as a prison pastor in Gardelegen.

112. Ibid., 32–33.

113. Ibid., 34. Just, the head of the Rhenish-Westphalian Prison Society, was a featured speaker and guest participant the Sachsen-Anhalt Society meeting in 1917.

114. Finger opposed Liszt's 1904 proposed law on diminished responsibility and served as editor of the classical-liberal standard-bearer, *Gerichtssaal*. Richard Wetzell, *Inventing the Criminal: A History of German Criminology 1880–1945* (Chapel Hill: University of North Carolina Press, 2000), 93–94.

115. "Verhandlungen," 34.

116. SB NB no. 38, Polizeirat Dr. [?] (illegible) to Bozi, 25 July 1918.

117. GStA 84a no. 50904, "Hessen-Nassau Gefängnis Gesellschaft."

118. SB NB no. 37, Pastor Klein to Bozi, 29 September 1917. The letter from the Oberlandesgerichtsdirektor is quoted there in full.

119. SB NB no. 38, Winnel (Zentral-arbeiter Sekretariat), Berlin to Bozi, 23 April 1918.

120. Ernst Rosenfeld, *Die Geschichte des Berliner Vereins zur Besserung der Strafgefangenen, 1827–1900; Ein Beitrag zur Geschichte des preussischen Gefängniswesens und des Fürsorgewesens für Entlassene Gefangene* (Berlin: O. Liebmann, 1901).

121. SB NB no. 38, Rosenfeld to Bozi, 8 June 1918.

122. GStA 77 tit. 1104 no. 18 Adh.III, Fritz von Bodelschwing, "Die Bisherherigen Überweisungen in die Arbeiterkolonien auf Grund des Ministerialerlasses vom 26. 11. 1916," 2 May 1918.

123. SB NB no. 38, Minister of the Interior to Bozi, 3 July 1918.

124. HBAB, 2/12–16. Entwurf. Minister des Innern. F. 705, 15 July 1918.

125. Hans Ostwald, *Sittengeschichte der Inflation: ein Kulturdokument aus den Jahren des Marktsturzes* (Berlin: Neufeld und Henius, 1931); Richard Bessel, *Germany after the First World War* (New York: Oxford University Press, 1993), 234–35.

126. Jürgen Kocka, *Facing Total War: German Society 1914–1918* (Cambridge, Mass.: Harvard University Press, 1984); Ulrich Kluge, *Soldatenräte und Revolution: Studien zur Militärpolitik in Deutschland 1918–19* (Göttingen: Vandenhoeck und Ruprecht, 1975); and Ulrich Kluge, *Die Deutsche Revolution 1918/1919. Staat, Politik und Gesellschaft zwischen Weltkrieg und Kapp-Putsch* (Frankfurt: Suhrkamp, 1985).

127. SB NB no. 23, Bozi to Frau Anna Schutz (Frankfurt), 6 November 1918.

128. On populism as a political force, see Geoff Eley, *Reshaping the German Right* (Ann Arbor: University of Michigan Press, 1994), and Peter Fritzsche, *Germans into Nazis* (Cambridge, Mass.: Harvard University Press, 1998). The latter explicitly links the mobilizations of 1914, 1918, and 1933.

Chapter 7

1. Wolfgang Mittermaier, "Grundgedanken der Gerichtshilfe," *Die Justiz* 6, no. 1 (October 1930): 7.

2. *Mitteilungen der IKV* 4 (1930): 68. Gustav Radbruch, *Gesamtausgabe* (Heidelberg: CF Mueller, 1987–2005).

3. Mittermaier, "Grundgedanken," 8; *Mitteilungen der IKV* 4 (1930): 36–37; Gustav Radbruch, "Sozialismus und Strafrechtsreform," *Sozialistische Monatshefte* 33 (1927): 526. Radbruch was Reich Minister of Justice for a short time in the Weimar Republic and was, like Mittermaier, a close and loyal student of Franz von Liszt.

4. Richard Messerer, "Soziale Gerichtshilfe," *Münchener Zeitung*, 29 April 1930.

5. Walter Böhmert, in *Mitteilungen der IKV* 3 (1929).

6. Hentig's essays from 1919 are collected in *Die Entartung der Revolution* (Leipzig: Koehler, 1920). Hentig rose to prominence in criminological circles before the war as the author of a eugenic-oriented study of criminal behavior, *Strafrecht und Auslese. Eine Anwendung des Kausalgesetzes auf den rechtbrechenden Menschen* (Berlin: Verlag von Julius Springer, 1914). He became the co-editor of Aschaffenburg's *Monatschrift* in 1921 and a professor in Kiel in 1929.

7. ADW CA 554, vol. 3. Theodor Just, "Gefangenen und Entlassenenpflege" (MS); Hans von Hentig, *Aufsätze zur Revolution* (Berlin: Springer, 1919), 2; see also Hans von Hentig, *Mein Krieg* (Berlin: A. Kuhn, 1919).

8. GStA 84a no. 8195, Albert Hellwig, "Verbrechensbekämpfung und Ausbildungs-reform" (the title of the newspaper is illegible), 23 September 1919; Hentig, *Aufsätze*, 2,

6. Theories of revolution and criminality were commonly associated with fin-de-siècle French thinkers like Taine and Le Bon. See Susanna Barrows, *Distorting Mirrors: Visions of the Crowd in Late Nineteenth Century France* (New Haven: Yale University Press, 1981).

9. Albert Hellwig, "Verbrechensbekämpfung." Hellwig, a former student of von Liszt, was a judge in Frankfurt and a well-known progressive. He later served as an official in the Prussian Ministry of Justice and later still as chief justice for the Province of Brandenburg.

10. Hentig, *Aufsätze*, 10.

11. "Das Schaufenster im Dienst der kriminalpolizei. Der Raubmord im Hotel Adlon," and "Raubüberfall in der Prenzlaueralle," *Berliner Morgenpost*, 22 March 1919. "Die Bekämpfung des Berliner Verbrechertums. Maßnahmen des Polizeipräsidenten Ernst," *Berliner Morgenpost*, 23 March 1919. *Berliner Morgenpost*, 27 March 1919; "Überfall einer vierköpfigen Räuberbande," *Berliner Morgenpost*, 28 March 1919.

12. Richard Bessel, *Germany after the First World War* (New York: Oxford University Press, 1993), 223, 228, 235.

13. Thomas Wehrling, "Berlin Is Becoming a Whore," in *The Weimar Republic Sourcebook*, ed. Anton Kaes, Martin Jay, and Edward Dimendberg (Berkeley: University of California Press, 1994).

14. Otto Lindekam, "Verbrecherpraktikum," *Die Polizei*, 30 January 1919; Ernst Engelbrecht and Leo Heller, *Verbrecher* (Berlin: Hermann Paetel, 1924); Ernst Gennat, "Berlin um Mitternacht," *Die Woche*, 5 April 1925.

15. Cornelie Usborne notes that the panic over venereal disease seemed to have no relationship to reality. Usborne, *The Politics of the Body in Weimar Germany* (London: Macmillan, 1992), 83.

16. SB NB no. 38, Bozi to Max Quarck, 1 March 1919.

17. "Allgemeine Verfügung über Milderungen im Strafvollzuge," vom 19 December 1918, quoted in Alfred Behrle, *Die Stellung der deutschen Sozialisten zum Strafvollzug von 1870 bis zur Gegenwart* (Leipzig and Berlin: de Gruyter, 1931), 25–27; Nikolaus Wachsmann, "Between Reform and Repression: Prisons in Weimar Germany," *Historical Journal* 45 no. 2 (2002): 413–14.

18. BA R30.01 no. 6109. Vorlage der Staatsregierung. Gesetz über Massregeln zur Verhütung des Rückfalls.

19. ADW CA GF/St no. 1329/5. "Die Stellung der Innere Mission zur Strafrechts- und Strafvollzugsreform" (1927 or 1928, n.d.); Fritz Hartung, "Der Stand der Rehabilitationsfrage in Deutschland," in *Festschrift Edmund Mezger: zum 70. Geburtstag 15. 10. 1953*, ed. Karl Engisch (München: C. H. Beck, 1954), 503–4.

20. Robert Kuhn, *Die Vertrauenskrise der Justiz (1926–1928). Der Kampf um die 'Republikanisierung' der Rechtspflege in der Weimarer Republik* (Köln: Bundesanzeiger, 1983).

21. The most famous exposé on political bias in the judiciary was Emil Julius Gumbel, *Vier Jahre politischer Mord* (Berlin: Verlag der neuen Gesellschaft, 1922);

Heinrich and Elisabeth Hannover, *Politische Justiz 1918–1933* (Frankfurt: Fischer, 1966). Most of these cases in fact came from the conservative state of Bavaria. Hitler's trial after the Beer Hall Putsch was one prominent example.

22. Alfred Bozi, *Die Angriffe Gegen die Richterstand* (Breslau: W. Koebner, 1896); Gustav Aschaffenburg, *Das Verbrechen und seine Bekämpfung* (Heidelberg: Winter, 1903), 3–5; Bozi, *Soziale Rechtseinrichtungen in Bielefeld* (Stuttgart: Ferdinand Enke, 1917), 32.

23. Quoted in Kuhn, *Vertrauenskrise*, 44.

24. Franz Schuster and Dieter Osterroth, *Chronik der deutschen Sozialdemokratie. 2. Vom Beginn der Weimarer Republik bis zum Ende des Zweiten Weltkrieges* (Bonn: FES Library, 2001), 18 September 1921.

25. GStA 84a no. 8511, Am Zehnhoff to Minister of Finance, 30 June 1922.

26. "Die Vertrauenskrise der deutschen Justiz," *DJZ* 23, no. 31 (December 1926): 1665–66; Kuhn, *Vertrauenskrise*, 46–58.

27. Bertolt Brecht, *Die Dreigroschenoper* (Frankfurt: Suhrkamp, 1982), 71. Playwrights and novelists contributed to the negative image of judges and prosecutors. See Jakob Wassermann, *Der Fall Maurizius* (Munich: dtv, 1988), and Ricarda Huch, *Der Fall Deruga* (Cologne: Insel Verlag, 1992).

28. BA R30.01 no. 6109. Vorlage der Staatsregierung. Gesetz über Massregeln zur Verhütung des Rückfalls. National Versammlung.

29. Young-Sun Hong, *Welfare, Modernity and the Weimar State, 1919–1933* (Princeton: Princeton University Press, 1998), 44–70.

30. Werner Gentz, "Der Fürsorgeanspruch des entlassenen Gefangenen," in *MDRG* 1, no. 3 (March 1926); and "Gefangenenfürsorge als wirtschaftliches Problem," in *MDRG* 1, no. 4 (June/July 1926).

31. Behrle, *Stellung*, 28–31.

32. "Das Görlitzer Programm" (1921) in *Die ungeliebte Republik: Dokumentation zur Innen- und Außenpolitik Weimars, 1918–1933*, ed. Wolfgang Michalka (Munich: dtv, 1980); Behrle, *Stellung*, 57; De Niem, "Einheitsfront der Juristen. Ein Neujahrswunsch zum Januar 1922," *Deutsche Richterzeitung* 14, no. 1 (1 January 1922).

33. De Niem, "Einheitsfront der Juristen"; Karl von Lilenthal, "Laienbeteiligung in Strafprozess," *Deutsche Richterzeitung* 14., no. 3 (1 March 1922): 80–82. Aschaffenburg also felt the calls for laification went too far, contradicting the need for greater expertise in the courtroom. Gustav Aschaffenburg, "In letzter Stunde!" *MKS* 13 (1922).

34. Max Alsberg, "Vorwort," in *Berliner Gefängnisse* by Hans Hyan (Berlin: Puttkammer, 1920), 11–12.

35. Hans Hyan, *Verbrechen und Strafe im Neuen Deutschland. Flugschriften der Revolution. no. 4.* (Berlin: Verlag für Sozialwissenschaft, 1919), 23. See also Sebastian Haffner, "Auch sie können morgen Richter sein!" *Koralle. Wochenschrift für Unterhaltung, Wissen, Lebensfreude*, 10 November 1938.

36. " 'Augen Auf!'—2000 Mark Belohnung," *Berliner Morgenpost*, 13 November

1919. See also Peter Fritzsche, *Reading Berlin 1900* (Cambridge, Mass.: Harvard University Press, 1996), 83–86. Even the sober-minded *Vossische Zeitung* published articles intended to train the public in recognizing criminals. See "Bienstmädchen Einbrüche. Vorsicht bei Neveinstellungen," *Vossische Zeitung*, 24 February 1920.

37. Eberhard Schmidt, *Einführung in die Geschichte der Deutschen Strafrechtspflege* (Göttingen: Vandenhoeck und Ruprecht, 1947); Christian Müller, *Verbrechensbekämpfung im Anstaltsstaat. Psychiatrie, Kriminologie und Strafrechtsform in Deutschland. 1871–1933* (Göttingen: Vandenhoeck und Ruprecht, 2004), 184–89.

38. SB NB no. 39, Bozi to [illegible], 20 February 1920; Bozi to Dr. Emilie Altenloh, 26 February 1920.

39. SB NB no. 23, Bozi to Heine, 28 December 1918.

40. SB NB no. 38, Bozi to Rosenfeld, 22 January 1919.

41. SB NB no. 38, Bozi to Hage, 15 January 1919.

42. See chapter 5 above.

43. SB NB no. 38, Bozi to Schiffer, 18 April 1918.

44. See chapter 5. Heine was also a contributor to Bozi's volume on policy in the "new Germany."

45. BA R30.01 no. 6109; SB NB no. 38, Bozi to Schiffer, 18 April 1918. It was named after its originator, Eugen Schiffer, a law scholar and deputy who later served briefly as Reich Minister of Justice during the Weimar Republic.

46. SB NB no. 38, Bozi to Schiffer, 18 April 1918.

47. Hage, "Übergangsstation," 48.

48. SB NB no. 38, Seyfarth to Bozi, 4 August 1919.

49. An analysis of membership lists suggests that in most prison associations, prior to 1919, the few women members were usually wealthy philanthropists or aristocrats. Hamburg's Hilfsverein was an exception. *7. Jahresbericht des Deutschen Hilfsvereins für entlassene Gefangene für das Jahr 1910*, 56–57.

50. SB NB no. 23, Bozi to Professor Mittermaier, 5 November 1918.

51. SB NB no. 23, Heine to Bozi, 15 May 1919; Bozi to Camilla Jellinek, 19 May 1919; no. 38 Bozi to Professor Schmittmannn (Köln) 27 May 1919; no. 23, "Einschulungskurse für Frauen im Recht," June 1919. The courses were such a success that they soon enrolled women welfare personnel from other cities, including Kiel, Hanover, and Osnabruck. GStA 84a no. 8511, Tätigkeitsbericht. Verein für Soziale Gerichtshilfe. 1922.

52. In vintage form, Bozi told both factions that he agreed with them. SB NB no. 23, Bozi to van den Leyen, 11 July 1919 and Bozi to Jellinek, 12 July 1919.

53. SB NB no. 37, Alfred Bozi, *Lebenserrinerungen*, unpublished manuscript (1937).

54. GStA 84a no. 8511, Bericht betr. Soziale Gerichthilfe (1921); Bozi to Prussian Minister of Justice, 2 March 1922; and Tätigkeitsbericht Bielefeld Verein. 1923.

55. M. Kleeberg, "Die praktische Ausgestaltung der sozialen Gerichtshilfe," *Soziale Gerichtshilfe. Sonderheft der Nachrichtendienstes des Evangelischen Hauptwohlfahrtsamts Berlin* (1928): 33.

56. Fritz Grau and Karl Schäfer, *Das Preussiische Gnadenrecht* (Berlin: Georg Stilke, 1931), 79–83.

57. Fritz Hartung, *Jurist unter Vier Reichen* (Cologne: Heymanns, 1971), 34–40.

58. Hartung went on to become an important progressive advocate of welfare in criminal justice. *Frankfurter Zeitung*, 30 May 1925.

59. BA R30.01 no. 6109, "Staatsministerium. Erlaß von 2 August 1920" and "Allgemeine Verfügung vom 19. Oktober 1920 über die Strafvollstreckung durch die Gerichte"; Hartung, *Jurist*, 38–39.

60. GStA 84a no. 8511, Am Zehnhoff to Minister of Finance, Jun. 30, 1922. BL 12a no 1338, Abschrift. Preußische Justizminister, 3 October 1924. In 1924, 20,000 marks were made available for private associations to create Gerichtshilfe agencies.

61. *MDRG* 1, no. 9 (1926): 31, 35.

62. GStA 84a no. 8511, "Halle Gerichtshilfe."

63. BA R30.01 no. 5683. Abschrift. Reichsjustizminister, 4 October 1923.

64. *Jahresbericht. Verein zur Besserung der Strafgefangene* (1922); on public perceptions of the entitlement state, see Jochen-Christoph Kaiser, "Die Wohlfahrtspflege im Sozialstaat 1890–1945—Problemfelder und Forschungsperspektiven," in *Wohlfahrtsverbände im Wohlfahrtsstaat* ed. Christoph Sachße (Kassel: Universität-Gesamthochschule Kassel, Fachbereich Sozialwesen, 1994).

65. ADW CA 554, no. 1308, Elli Proebsting (Westfällischer Provinzialverband für Inneren Mission) to Evangelische Konferenz Für Straffälligenpflege, 12 April 1932. Pfarrer Oehlert to Evangelische Konferenz für Straffälligenpflege, 24 December 1932.

66. This complex of institutions was a product of aggressive institution-building and fundraising before and during the war years. See Wilhelm Hage, "Die Übergangsstation im Dienste der Fürsorge an den entlassenen Gefangenen," in *32. JGGSA* (1916): 41–52.

67. BL rep. 12A. Neuruppin. "Erklärung" von M. Neumann. 15 July 1925; and Bericht über die Tagung der Gerichtshilfe für Erwachsene in Halle, May 1925. See also E. Bozi, *Gerichtshilfe*, 22–26.

68. Magdalene Deimling-Triebel, *Die Eingliederung von Rechtsbrechern in Wirtschaft und Gesellschaft als Aufgabe der Gerichtshilfe* (Durlach: J. Widmann, 1932), 127.

69. SB NB no. 39, Survey by Lübeck Gerichts-Vorsitzender, September 1920; BL 12a no. 1338. "Vortrag"; Charlotte Meyer, "Entwicklung und Probleme der Berliner sozialen Gerichtshilfe," *Berliner Wolhfahrtsblatt* 5, no. 24; GStA 84a no. 8511, Vortrag, Oberlandesgerichtspräsident Köln, 30 April 1923. E. Bozi, *Gerichtshilfe*, 11.

70. Eventually, Gerichtshilfe work in Berlin would constitute over 50 percent of the female police assistants' activities. Patrick Wagner, *Volksgemeinschaft ohne Verbrecher. Konzeptionen und Praxis der Kriminalpolitzi in der Zeit der Weimarer Republik und des Nationalsozialismus* (Hamburg: Christians, 1996), 107–9.

71. BL, no. 1338. Vortrag von Herrn Obermagistratsrat Knaut, gehalten am 17. Juni 1926.

72. GStA 84a no. 8516, Kammergerichtspraesident Berlin to Prussian Minister of Justice, 3 June 1927; no. 8514. Bericht Düsseldorf, 1930.

73. E. Bozi, *Gerichtshilfe*, 19.

74. GStA 84a no. 8511, "Leitsätze. Bielefeld Verein."

75. GStA 84a no. 8511, Bozi, "Leitsätze" (undated, 1922 or 1923).

76. BL 12 a no. 1338. Abschrift. Preußische Minister für Volkswohlfahrt. 26 January 1923. BA, R30.01, no. 5683, Bericht. Besprechung vom 24 February 1925.

77. GStA 84a no. 8512, "Allgemeine Verfügung des Preuß. Justizministers vom 8. März 1926 über die Strafzumessung"; Walter Böhmert, "Die rechtlichen Grundlagen der Sozialen Gerichtshilfe im Rahmen des bestehenden und neuen Strafrechts," in *Soziale Gerichtshilfe. Sonderheft des Nachrichtendienstes des Evangelischen Hauptwohlfahrtsamts Berlin* (1928), 26–27.

78. GStA 84a no. 1308, "*Soziale Gerichtshilfe*."

79. BL 12a, no. 1338. Verein für Gefangenen- und Entlassenenfürsorge und Gerichtshilfe für Erwachsene in Neuruppin to Landesgerichtspräs, 7 January 1927 and 21 February 1927.

80. BL 12a no. 1338. Der Oberstaatsanwalt to Landgerichtspräsident, 13 May 1925; Landesgerichtspräsident Dr. Hellwig to Oberstaatsanwalt, 23 July 1925.

81. BA R30.01 no. 5683, Reich Minister of Justice to Reich Minister of the Interior, 16 February 1926; Reich Minister of the Interior to Reich Minister of Justice, 12 June 1926; Reich Minister of Justice to Reich Minister of Finance, aus Haushalt 2/1 (1927); Abschrift zu Reichsjustizminister no. VW. aus den Akten Haushalt 2/1 (1927).

82. Gustav Aschaffenburg, "Neue Folge," in *Mitteilungen der IKV* 2 (1928); SB NB no. 39, Bozi to Harnisch, 6 August 1920.

83. BL rep. 12a no. 1338. Neuruppin and Potsdam; GStA 84a no. 8512, Bericht Oberlandesgerichtspräsident Düsseldorf, 25 May 1926.

84. ADW CA GF/St no. 1308, "Aktenmäßige Behandlung der Gerichtshilfe Auskünfte," 26 April 1928.

85. These included the indictment (Vorverhandlung) and the formal presentation of charges (Anklageerhebung). BL 12a no. 1388. Bozi to Landgerichtspräsidenten and Oberstaatsanwalten. "Die Richtlinien in denen die Bestrebungen der Arbeitsgemeinschaft sich zweckmäßig zu bewegen haben" (n.d.).

86. ADW CA GF/St no. 1308, Elli Proebsting (Westfällischer Provinzialverband für Inneren Mission) to Evangelische Konferenz Für Straffälligenpflege, 12 April 1932. Pfarrer Oehlert to Evangelische Konferenz für Straffälligenpflege, 24 December 1932. Also ADW CA GF/St no. 1308, "Aktenmäßige Behandlung der Gerichtshilfe Auskünfte," 26 April 1928; GStA 84a, no. 8511, Bericht. Halle, 22 March 1923.

87. Helene von Koerber, *Meine Erlebnisse unter Strafgefangenen* (Stuttgart: Haedecke, 1928); Detloff Klatt, *Das Los der Vorbestraften* (Berlin: Alfred Metzner, 1926); Elizabeth Schucht, *Gezeichnete. Meine Erlebnisse unter Gefangenen und Strafentlassenen* (Hamburg: Agentur des Rauhen Hauses, 1930).

88. Gustav Wolf, *Gerichtshilfe* (Rastatt: Rastatter Zeitung GmbH, 1931), 13.

89. Gustav Radbruch, "Strafrechtsreform und Strafprozessreform" in *Gesamtaus-*

gabe vol. 7, ed. Arthur Kaufmann (Heidelberg: CF Müller, 1998), 304–6 (originally published in *Juristichen Rundschau*, 1928).

90. GStA 84a no. 8513. Alsberg to Prussian Minister of Justice, 14 November 1928.

91. BL 12a no. 1338. Landgerichtspräsident Neuruppin an den Amtsgerichte Neuruppin, and Kammergerichtspräsident und Generalstaatsanwalt bei dem Kammergericht an Präsident und Oberstaatsanwalt bei dem Landgericht in Neuruppin, 29 October 1926. See also Otto Krebs, *Straffälligenfürsorge* (Berlin: Hauptausschuß für Arbeiterwohlfahrt, 1930); Karl Finkelnburg, *Berliner Tageblatt*, 27 October 1928; Magdalene Deimling-Triebel, *Die Eingliederung von Rechtsbrechern in Wirtschaft und Gesellschaft als Aufgabe der Gerichtshilfe* (Durlach: J. Widmann, 1932); Hugo Pfefferkorn, *Die Gerichtshilfe* (Berlin: Heymann, 1930).

92. Gröschner, "Die Frankfurter Gerichtshilfe," *MDRG* 2, nos. 11–12 (November/December 1927); *Mitteilungen der IKV* 4 (1930): 33–34; BA R30.01, no. 5726. Bericht an Preuss. Justiz Ministerium, 1929; ADW CA GF/St no. 1308, Fritze, "Abschrift," 19 October 1926.

93. Werner Gentz, "Die Gerichtshilfe. Wohlfahrt im Strafrecht," *Vossische Zeitung*, 23 May 1929. Emphasis in the original.

94. Gustav Radbruch, "Sozialismus und Strafrechtsreform," *Sozialistische Monatshefte* (1927); also remarks by Muthesius in *Mitteilungen der IKV* 4 (1930): 27.

95. Mittermaier, "Grundgedanken"; *Mitteilungen der IKV* (1930); Krebs, *Straffälligenfürsorge*, 11–12.

96. BL 12a Neuruppin. Abschrift. Die Polizeidirektion, Kriminal-Abteilung. Dr. Pott. Oberregierungsrat an die Justizkommission des Senats, 14 March 1927; ADW CA GF/St no. 1308, Arbeitsgemeinschaft Deutscher Gerichtshilfestellen, June 1928.

97. Exner, "Zur Praxis der Strafzumessung," 372. For a discussion of Exner's impact on German criminology, see Richard Wetzell, *Inventing the Criminal: A History of German Criminology 1880–1945* (Chapel Hill: University of North Carolina Press, 2000), 107–24.

98. Robert Heindl, *Der Berufsverbrecher. Ein Beitrag zur Strafrechtsreform* (Berlin: Verlag Rolf Heise, 1926). On Heindl's influence, see *Mitteilungen der IKV* 3 (1928): 38.

99. Monika Frommel, *Präventionsmodelle in der deutschen Strafzwecksdiskussion: Beziehungen zwischen Rechtsphilosophie, Dogmatik, Rechtspolitik und Erfahrungswissenschaften* (Berlin: Duncker und Humboldt, 1987), 19; Adeline Rintelen, *Die Polizeiaufsicht und ihre Ersatzmittel im Entwurf 1928* (Würzburg: Buchdruckerei Bavaria, 1929).

100. Theodor Noetzel, "Bewährungsfrist," in *Handwörterbuch der Kriminologie*, ed. Alexander Elster and Heinrich Lingemann (Berlin and Leipzig: de Gruyter, 1933), 160; Grau, *Preussische Gnadenrecht*, 80.

101. Gustav Aschaffenburg, "Neue Folge," *Mitteilungen der IKV* 2 (1928): 100–101. See also Gustav Radbruch, "Die geistesgeschichtliche Lage der Strafrechtsreform," in *Gesamtausgabe*, vol. 7, 327. The modernists' aim was not ultimately to punish less, but to punish better.

102. "Diskussion," *Mitteilungen der Kriminalbiologischen Gesellschaft*, no. 2 (1928): 49.

103. Lothar Frede, "Richtlinien für die Ausübung von Schutzaufsicht über Volljährige," *MDRG* 4, nos. 10–11 (1929). Opposition came both from leftists who feared state coercion and conservatives defending the role of the charities.

104. Other continental countries also resisted a state role in such supervision. Civil liberties concerns seem to have loomed larger in countries like France and Belgium. Max Grünhut, *Penal Reform: A Comparative Study* (Montclair, N.J.: Patterson Smith, 1972), 297–309.

105. BA R30.01, no. 5686. Muntau (Reichszusammenschluss) to Reichsjustiminister, 2 December 1930; *Statistik über die Gefangenenanstalten der Justizverwaltung in Preußen* (Berlin: Strafgefängnis Berlin-Tegel, 1929).

106. HBAB, 2/12–16, Pastor Just to Bodelschwingh, 28 June 1915.

107. SB NB no. 37, Bodelschwingh to Bozi, 26 June 1915. Bodelschwingh expressed his objections at no. 37, Bodelschwingh to Bozi, 16 June 1917. HBAB, 2/12–16, Pastor Klein to Bodelschwingh, 16 June 1919.

108. ADW CA GF/St no. 325. Fiesel to Hauptkomitee des Vereins für Arbeiterkolonien Hannover, 5 November 1924; Der Landesdirektor Provinz Brandenburg to Central Committee for Inner Mission, 3 November 1924; Pastor Braune to Central Committee, 3 November 1924 (an exception to this was in the state of Baden, where the Ankenbuk colony was leased to the government starting in 1921); and Landesverein für Arbeiterkolonien in Baden to Central Committee, Berlin, 12 January 1925.

109. See preceding note.

110. Reports from Gerichtshilfe offices in GStA 84a no. 8511, Hamm, 3 January 1924; Kiel, 18 December 1923; Düsseldorf, not dated; Crefeld, not dated.

111. Georg Rusche and Otto Kirchheimer, *Punishment and Social Structure* (New York: Columbia University Press, 1939), 158–59; see also David Garland, *Punishment and Modern Society* (Chicago: University of Chicago Press, 1990), 83–110.

112. Fritz Kleist, "Die Welt Ohne Zuchthaus," *Die Justiz. Monatschrift für Erneuerung des Deutschen Rechtswesen. Zugleich Organ des Republikanischen Richterbundes* 6, no. 1 (1930): 49–57.

113. *Tätigkeitsbericht der Berliner Gefangenenfürsorge für die Zeit vom 1. Jan 1928 bis 31 Mar 1929.* See also Hans Hein, "Gefangenen-Fürsorge am Ende. Berliner Gefangenen-Fürsorge erklärt sich selbst bankrott," *Welt am Abend*, 24 September 1932.

114. In practice, judges authorized police supervision in continuously decreasing numbers over a forty-year period. There were 8,238 cases in 1882 and only 791 in 1928. *Statistiches Jahrbuch des deutschen Reiches* (Berlin: Schmidt, 1930), 69.

115. Theodor Noetzel, "Gerichtshilfe," *MDRG* 1, no. 9 (September 1926): 33. Numerous other authors refer to the same "saying" while seeking to discredit the growing use of the pardon. Whether it was really an underworld saying was disputed. Fritz Kleist, "Bewährungssystem und "Amnestie," *Die Justiz* 5, no. 6 (March 1930).

116. Biesenthal, "Der Zusammenbruch des Strafvollzuges," *Archiv für Kriminalanthropologie* (1926): 139–40; Albert Hellwig, "Kriminalbiologie und Strafzumessung," in *Mitteilungen der Kriminalbiologische Gesellschaft* 2 (1928): 92–99; Franz

Exner, *Studien über die Strafzumessungspraxis der deutschen Gerichte* (Leipzig: Wiegandt, 1931).

117. GStA 84a no. 3994, untitled document, with questions and themes submitted in advance for conference with the press, 22 September 1928.

118. "Tagung des Deutschen Reichsverbandes für Gerichtshilfe, usw., in Düsseldorf am 16. und 17. Juni 1926," *MDRG* 1, nos. 8–9 (1926).

119. Theodor Noetzel, "Gerichtshilfe," *MDRG* 1, no. 1 (January 1926).

120. Noetzel, "Über den derzeitigen Stand der Gerichtshilfefrage," *MDRG* 3, no. 6 (June 1928): 114.

121. *DJZ* 31, no. 19 (1926).

122. ADW CA GF/St no. 1308, report by H. Bäcker, November 1932.

123. Seyfarth, "Aufgaben und Ziele des Deutschen Reichsverbandes für Gerichtshilfe, Gefangenen- und Entlassenenfürsorge," in *MDRG* 1, no. 1 (January 1926). Seyfarth's official title was "General Secretary." The presidency was held by Johannes Muntau, the head of the penal office in Celle.

124. ADW CA GF/St no. 1308, Bäcker to Ulrich. Bäcker noted that Catholic penal reformers in Caritas were quicker to support the judges' standpoint; ADW CA GF/St no. 1308, Bäcker, "Bericht."

125. Ibid., Bericht des Leiters der Magdeburger Gerichtshilfe, Müller (1928); and Hermeline Bäcker, Bericht, "Über die evangelische Mitarbeit in der Sozialen Gerichtshilfe." (1931); and Bäcker to Ulrich, 19 June 1931.

126. Young-Sun Hong notes a similar tension within welfare debates more generally. Hong, *Welfare, Modernity*, 69ff.

127. BA R30.01 no. 5683. Entschliessung des 26. Deutschen Caritastages 1925.

128. ADW CA GF/St 1308d. Kommission zur Vorbereitung des Entwurfs zur Regelung der Sozialen Gerichtshilfe am 14.11.32 im Sitzungszimmer des Untersuchungsgefängnis.

129. Heinrich Seyfarth, "Der Humanitätsgedanke im Strafvollsung," *MDRG* 6, nos. 9–10 (1931) and "Durchhalten!" *MDRG* 7, nos. 9–10 (1932).

130. ADW CA GF/St no. 1308, Bericht. Tagung. "Rechtspflege und Fürsorge," 18 October 1927; BL 12a no. 1338, Bozi, "Richtlinien." Bozi played only an intermittent part in the reform movement after 1926 because of poor health, especially eye disease; SB NB, Bozi, "Lebenserrinerungen" (ms.).

131. Bozi, "Die Soziale Gerichtshilfe als Rechtseinrichtung," *MKS*, no. 11. (1928). SB NB, Bozi, "Deutschlands Erneuerung," (unpublished ms.) 1938.

132. "Konferenz sozialdemokratischer Juristen. Beratung über Sozialen Gerichtshilfe," *Vorwärts*, 28 May 1929. Albert Hellwig, "*Soziale Gerichtshilfe* und Strafrechtsreform," *Königsburg. Hartungsche Zeitung*, 2 June 1929.

133. Werner Gentz, "Die Gerichtshilfe. Wohlfahrt im Strafrecht," *Vossische Zeitung*, 23 May 1929. Emphasis in the original.

134. Walter Böhmert, *Mitteilungen der IKV* 4 (1930).

135. Werner Peifer, *Berlin Börsen Courier*, 18 July 1929.

Chapter 8

1. Siegfried Rosenfeld, "Justiz und Republik," *Die Justiz* 6, no. 9 (June 1931).

2. Hsi-Huey Liang, *The Berlin Police Force in the Weimar Republic* (Berkeley: University of California Press, 1970); Carl Severing, *Mein Lebensweg. 2. Im Auf und Ab der Republik* (Cologne: Greven Verlag, 1950).

3. GStA 77, no. 788, "Die Grosse Polizei-Ausstellung"; Ernst van den Bergh, "Protokoll" and Carl Severing, "Eröffnungsrede," in *Die Große Polizei-Ausstellung Berlin in Wort und Bild*, ed. Oskar Dressler (Vienna: Internat. Öffentl. Sicherheit, 1927); Ernst van den Bergh, *Polizei und Volk* (Berlin: Gersbach, 1926), 6–15, 106.

4. GStA 77, no. 788, "Die Grosse Polizei-Ausstellung."

5. Egon Erwin Kisch, "Die Polizei und ihre Beute," in *Razzia auf der Spree* (1926; Berlin: Aufbau Verlag, 1986), 92. Historians have shared Kisch's skepticism about whether the police was genuinely transformed at all. Richard Bessel, "Militarisierung und Modernisierung: Polizeiliches Handeln in der Weimarer Republik," in *'Sicherheit' und 'Wohlfahrt': Polizei, Gesellschaft und Herrschaft im 19. und 20. Jahrhundert*, ed. Alf Lüdtke (Frankfurt: Suhrkamp, 1992), 323–43.

6. ADW CA, Propaganda Dienst 162. "Grosse Polizei-Ausstellung." Eleven books were published in a special series edited by Prussian police official Wilhelm Abegg. See *Die Polizei in Einzeldarstellungen*, ed. W. Abegg (Berlin: Gersbach, 1926).

7. GStA 77, no. 788, "GPA," Bericht des Ausstellungskommisars; Siegfried Kracauer, *From Caligari to Hitler: A Psychological History of the German Film* (Princeton: Princeton University Press, 1947), 122.

8. "Polizei als Berater, Erziener und Freund. Eine Konferenz in Polizei-Präsidium," *Vorwärts*, 8 December 1926; Magnus Heimannsberg, "Die Polizei als Erziener des Volkes!" *Germania*, 5 January 1927.

9. Winfried Löschburg, *Ohne Glanz und Gloria: Die Geschichte des Hauptmanns von Köpenick* (Berlin: Der Morgen, 1996), 244–53; *Deutsche Allgemeine Zeitung*, 25 September 1926.

10. See especially the review by Bernhard Diebold, *Frankfurter Zeitung*, 8 March 1931, reprinted in *Der Hauptmann von Köpenick*, ed. Hartmut Scheible (Stuttgart: Reclam, 1977), 30–35. The film and the play were disrupted by Nazi protests in Berlin. "Carl Zuckmayer zur Entstehungsgeschichte" in *Der Hauptmann*, 26–28.

11. Löschburg, *Ohne Glanz*, 253–57.

12. Erich Kaltosen, "Filme aus dem Gebiete der Straffälligenfürsorge," in *Literatur Rundschau für Mitarbeiter in der Straffälligenfürsorge* (April/May 1930). Other films about ex-offenders included *Die Ausgestoßenen. Heimkehr des Herzens* (1927); *Die Verrufenen. Der fünfte Stand* (1927); *Die—da unten.* (1928); and *Menschen unter Menschen* (1929). Journalist Rolf Nürnberg wrote in 1928 that attacks on the justice system constituted the latest "successful genre in danger of being . . . overburdened." *12-Uhr Blatt*, *Berlin*, 15 October 1928.

13. Max Alsberg, *Konflikt: Schauspiel in 7 Bildern* (Berlin: Bong, 1933); Karl Finkelnburg, *Amnestie!* (Berlin: Volksbühnen, 1929); Erich Wulffen, *Die Geschlossene Kette*

(Berlin: Sieben Stäbe, 1929); Karl Credé-Hoerder, *Justizkrise. Schauspiel in vier Akten und Dialogen* (Berlin: Dietz, 1930). One scholar counts forty dramas during the Weimar Republic that critically engaged with justice. Stephanie Birrell, "Das Zeitstuck in den zwanziger Jahren" (Ph.D. diss., University of Johannesburg, 2005), 109.

14. The would-be screenwriter Pastor Fritz Namenhauer was also the author of three novels. He sought funding for his film from the Reichsverband. Coböken-Film Gmbh to Muntau, 18 March 1927 (screenplay attached), Seyfarth to Muntau, 22 March 1927, BA R30.01 no. 5684.

15. The work was banned in the Nazi era, but has been periodically revived in German theaters down to the present. Karl Maria Finkelnburg, *Amnestie: Schauspiel in drei Akten* (Berlin: Volksbühnen-Verlags- u. Vertriebs-G.m.b.H., 1930).

16. Karl Maria Finkelnburg, "Amnestie," and Siegfried Rosenfeld, "Finkelnburgs Schauspiel 'Amnestie,'" *Die Justiz* 5 no. 6 (March 1930): 345–47, 353.

17. Thomas Mann, "Amnestie," *Die Justiz* 5, no. 6 (March 1930): 337–40. Bronnen was a strong supporter of conservative causes and, in spite of his Jewish father, increasingly sympathetic to the Nazis. Arnolt Bronnen, "Die Zerstörung des Rechts," *Berliner Lokalanzeiger*, January 1930.

18. BA R3001 no. 5683. Karl Finkelnburg, "Wie das Tor der Hoffnung Wurde. Eine Festrede," in *2. Jahresbericht. Hedwig Wangel Hilfe*. The institution also gained token support from the Reichsverband. "Tor der Hoffnung," *MDRG* 2, no. 1 (1927).

19. BA R3001 no. 5684. Wangel to Severing, 7 November 1929; "Das Tor der Hoffnung. Einweihung des Hedwig Wangel-Heims in Wilhelmshöhe," *Berliner Börsen-Courier*, 16 October 1926; BA R30.01 no. 5684. Wangel to Severing, 7 November 1929.

20. "Die Mutter der Entgleisten. Ein Besuch bei Hedwig Wangel," *Deutsche Allgemeine Zeitung*, 27 October 1926.

21. Karl Maria Finkelnburg, *Die Bestraften in Deutschland* (Berlin: J. Guttentag, 1912).

22. Fritz Kleist, "Bewährungssystem und 'Amnestie,'" *Die Justiz* 5, no. 6 (March 1930): 353–59; Nikolaus Wachsmann, *Hitler's Prisons: Legal Terror in Nazi Germany* (New Haven: Yale University Press, 2004), 43–44.

23. BA R3001 no. 5684. Among the guests were the wives of Reichspräsidenten Ebert, Karl Severing, and Otto Braun.

24. BA R30.01 no. 5683. Jahresbericht der Hedwig Wangel-Hilfe E.V., 21–31 March, 1928.

25. Ibid.

26. BA R30.01 no. 5685. Prussian State Commissioner for the Regulation of Welfare to Hedwig Wangel, 15 January 1931.

27. ADW CA GF/St no. 325. Director Fiesel (Kästorf) to Hauptkommittee des Vereins für Arbeiterkolonien Hannover, 5 November 1924.

28. ADW CA GF/St no. 326. Evang Wohlfahrtsamt Berlin. "Streit um Hedwig Wangel." Undated, and no. 326. Ref. Gefährdetenfürsorge to Verein für Innere Mission Frankfurt. 4 March 1927.

29. ADW CA GF/St no. 326. Pastor Engelmann, "Der Hedwig Wangel Film 'Menschen zweiter Güte.'" 18 November 1930.

30. ADW CA GF/St no. 326. Evangelische Pfarramt der Strafanstalt Rheinbach to Geschäftsstele des "Sonntagsgruss," Essen, 28 October 1930.

31. ADW CA GF/St no. 326. Fr. Dr. Sprengel an Pfarrer W. Thieme, 22 August 1926, and Sprengel, "Hedwig Wangel," MS n.d.

32. Seyfarth's appropriation of Liszt as one in a long line of otherwise religious-based reformers was an interesting sign of the stakes in this argument. Heinrich Seyfarth, "Der Humanitätsgedanke im Strafvollzug," *MDRG* 6, no. 10 (1931): 68.

33. Gierke quit the Conservative Party after she felt discriminated against for being the daughter of Jewish converts to Protestantism. Rafael Scheck, *Mothers of the Nation: Right-Wing Women in Weimar Germany* (Oxford: Berg, 2004), 27.

34. BA R3001 no. 5685. Multiple news clippings, 6 October 1929 to 18 December 1930.

35. *Geschlecht in Fesseln: Die Sexualnot der Strafgefangenen*; Essem-Film GmbH; Premier: 24 October 1928, Berlin (Tauentzien-Palast); Dir: Wilhelm Dieterle; Screenplay: Herbert Juttke, Geor C. Klaren; based on the work by Franz Höllering und Material von Karl Plättner.

36. Blasius, Dirk. *Bürgerliche Gesellschaft und Kriminalität. Zur Sozialgeschichte Preußens im Vormärz* (Göttingen: Vandenhoeck und Ruprecht, 1976).

37. Lenka von Koerber, *Meine Erlebnisse unter Strafgefangenen* (Stuttgart: Haedecke, 1928) and *Menschen im Zuchthaus* (Frankfurt: Societätsverlag, 1930). The idea that "normal" sexual relations were necessary to adult mental and physical health was widespread, especially among the Weimar left. Atina Grossmann, *Reforming Sex: The German Movement for Birth Control and Abortion Reform, 1920–1950* (New York: Oxford University Press, 1995), 20–31.

38. The patronage was important to getting the film passed the censor. *Illustrierte Film-Kurier*, Berlin 1928; *12-Uhr Blatt*, 15 October 1928.

39. Artur Landsberger, *Die Unterwelt von Berlin* (Berlin: Paul Steegemann, 1929), with an afterword by Max Alsberg, 113–14. An excerpt from this book, in which the author critiques welfare for released prisoners, was published as "Die Unterwelt Spricht" *Berliner Boursen-Courier*, 3 February 1929; Hirschfeld and Abraham, "Begleitwort," in Plättner, *Eros im Zuchthaus* (Berlin: Mopr-Verl, 1929), 5–10; Ernst Toller, "Bericht. Kongress für Sexualreform," *Frankfurter Zeitung*, 30 September 1930. Also Georg Fuchs, *Wir Zuchthäusler. Errinerungen des Zellengefangenen nr. 2911.* (München: Langen, 1931).

40. GStA rep. 84a, no. 58322.

41. Werner Gentz, "Das Sexualproblem im Strafvollzug," *ZStW* 32 (1930): 406–24.

42. BA R15.01 Staatsminister des Innern an die Filmoberprüfstelle, 9 November 1929.

43. Rudolf Michel, "Zur Psychologie und Psychopathologie der Strafhaft," *MKS* 15 (1924); Seyfarth, "Humanitätsgedanke," 70–73..

44. Sächsisches Hauptstaatsarchiv. Justiz Min. no. 409. Seyfarth to Minister der Justiz, 5 April 1933.

45. GStA 84a no. 8202, *Berliner Tageblatt*, 27 October 1928.

46. Werner Gentz, "Die Gerichtshilfe. Wohlfahrt im Strafrecht," *Vossische Zeitung*, 23 May 1929.

47. *Vorwärts* 25 November 1927; see also Gustav Radbruch, "Sozialismus und Strafrechtsreform," *Sozialistische Monatshefte* 33 (1927): 524.

48. Adolf Baumbach, "Der Bankerott der Strafjustiz," *DJZ* (January 1928).

49. August Finger, "Kritische Bemerkungen zur Lehre vom Tatbestand und der Rechtswidrigkeit," *Gerichtssaal* 96 (1928); Alexander Graf zu Dohna, "Der Stand des Streits um die Strafrechtsreform," *DJZ* (January 1928).

50. Heinrich Berl, *Was ist der fünfte Stand? Variationen zu einem Thema* (Karlsruhe: Kairos Verlag, 1931).

51. BA R30.01 no. 5685. Hans Pitak to State Secretary Meissner, 20 August 1930; Prussian Minister of Justice to Reich Minister of Justice, 6 September 1930; Archiv für Wohlfahrtspflege to Paula von Harnack, 29 August 1930.

52. Karl Fees, *Die Krisis im Recht* (Karlsruhe: Kairos Verlag, 1931). The inmates' associations, or "Ringvereine," were probably not criminal organizations on the order of the American underworld, but neither were they the sport clubs and benevolent societies they claimed to be. Their notoriety dates from a much-publicized trial in 1929. LAB 358.01, no. 2220. Reservemordkommision. Bericht. 29 January 1929. On the Congress of Vagabonds, see Kunstlerhaus Bethanien, ed., *Wohnsitz, Nirgendwo: Vom Leben und vom Überleben auf der Strasse* (Berlin: Frölich und Kaufmann, 1982).

53. Manfred Krohn, *Die Deutsche Justiz im Urteil der Nationalsozialisten 1920–1933* (Frankfurt: Lang, 1991).

54. Heinrich Berl, *Die Männerbewegung. Ein antifeministisches Manifest* (Karlsruhe: Kairos Verlag, 1931). See *Deutsche Richterzeitung. Organ des deutschen Richterbundes* (1920–1933); *Mitteilungen des Gross-Berliner Juristenbundes* (1928–1930). Ultimately, fewer than forty women succeeded in becoming judges before the Nazi seizure of power. All were subsequently fired by the new regime.

55. Ellen Scheuner, "Fachliteratur," *MDRG* 6, nos. 5–6 (1931).

56. Georg Dahm, "Der Richter im modernen Strafrecht," *48. JGGSA* (1932); Georg Dahm and Friedrich Schaffstein, *Liberales Oder Autoritäres Strafrecht?* (Hamburg: Hanseatische Verlagsanstalt, 1933); Herman Schmidt, "Bankerott des Strafvollzuges? Die kriminalität der Vorbestraften," *MDRG* 6, nos. 1–2 (1931).

57. BA R30.01 no. 5686, Seyfarth to Reichsjustizminister Gürtner 22 March 1933, Seyfarth to Reichspropagandaminister Goebbels, 7 July 1933; Alfred Bozi, "Zur Neuorientierung des Rechts," *Deutsches Recht* (1933).

58. BA R30.01 no. 5685. Tätigkeitsberichte. Berliner Gefangenen-Fürsorge. (1930–1932); and Hans Hein, "Gefangenen-Fürsorge am Ende. Berliner Gefangenen-Fürsorge erklärt sich selbst bankrott," *Welt am Abend*, 24 September 1932; and Hans Klein, "Schwerer Weg in die Freiheit. Die Amnestierten in der Fursorgesstellen," *Berlin Tageblatt*, 24 December 1932; and Bericht. Frankfurt Gefangenen-Fürsorge (1930).

59. Noetzel, "Die Gerichtshilfe an der Jahreswende 1928/29," *MDRG* 4, nos. 1–2 (1929); and "Die Gerichtshilfe im Jahre 1930," *MDRG* 6, nos. 1–2 (1931).

60. GStA 84a no. 8517, Abschrift. Der Landesgerichtspräsident Aachen. 23 September 1930; ADW CA GF/St 1308C, "Fragebogen" (1927); BL, no. 1338. "Formular"; GStA 84a no. 8514, Bericht vom Landesgerichtspräsident Halle, 12 August 1930.

61. Richard J. Evans, *Rituals of Retribution: Capital Punishment in Germany 1600–1987* (New York: Oxford University Press, 1996), 526–36; Paul Weindling, *Health, Race and German Politics between National Unification and Nazism 1870–1945* (Cambridge: Cambridge University Press, 1989), 441–80.

62. Young-Sun Hong, *Welfare, Modernity and the Weimar State, 1919–1933* (Princeton: Princeton University Press, 1998), 42–43. Wetzell, *Inventing the Criminal*, 137–43, 246–54. Evans, *Rituals*, 528–29.

63. GStA 84a, no. 8514, Bericht vom Landesgerichtspräsident, Halle, 12. August 1930. "Es ist bereits zum Ausdruck gebracht und selbstverständlich, dass die KB Forschungstelle sich bei ihrer Ermitelungen der Gerichtshilfe bedienen muss." Also, Hermann Schmidt, "Die preussishce Justizverwaltung beim Jahreswechsel 1928/1929," *Juristische Wochenschrift* 1 (1929).

64. Rudolf Sieverts, "Gedanken über Methoden, Ergebnisse und kriminal politische Folgen der kriminal-biologischen Untersuchungen im bayrischen strafvollzug," *MKS* 23 (1932): 589–92.

65. Nikolaus Wachsmann, "Between Reform and Repression: Prisons in Weimar Germany," *Historical Journal* 45, no. 2 (2002); Christian Müller, *Verbrechensbekämpfung im Anstaltsstaat. Psychiatrie, Kriminologie und Strafrechtsform in Deutschland. 1871–1933* (Göttingen: Vandenhoeck und Ruprecht, 2004), 233–66.

66. Wachsmann, "Between Reform and Repression," 416; Müller, *Verbrechensbekämpfung* 234–40.

67. Theodor Viernstein, "Die Kriminalbiologischen Untersuchungen an Strafhauszugängen in den bayerischen Strafanstalten in ihrer Auswirkung auf Stufenstrafvollzug, Strafrechtspraxis vor Gericht und auf die Wissenschaft," *45. JGGSA* (1929), and Viernstein, "Die Kriminalbiologische Forschung in Bayern," *MDRG* 6, nos. 8–9 (1931).

68. Wetzell, *Inventing the Criminal*, 128–37.

69. Müller, *Verbrechensbekämpfung*, 235. See also Oliver Liang, "The Biology of Morality: Criminal Biology in Bavaria," in *Criminals and Their Scientists: The History of Criminology in International Perspective*, ed. Peter Becker and Richard Wetzell (Cambridge: Cambridge University Press, 2006), 425–46.

70. Alfred Behrle, *Die Stellung der deutschen Sozialisten zum Strafvollzug von 1870 bis zur Gegenwart* (Leipzig/Berlin: de Gruyter, 1931); Michael Schwartz, "Protestantismus und Weimarer Eugenik," in *Sozialer Protestantismus und Sozialstaat. Diakonie u Wohlfahrtspflege in Deutschland 1890 bis 1938*, ed. Jochen Kaiser und Martin Greschat (Stuttgart: Kohlhammer, 1996).

71. Sächsisches Hauptsstaatsarchiv, Justizministerium, no. 1587. Fetscher to Sächsische Ministerium der Justiz, 12 March 1925.

72. Sächsisches Hauptsstaatsarchiv, Justizministerium, no. 1587. Dr. Fetscher to Bezirksfürsorgeverbände, 7 December 1927. See also Rainer Fetscher, "Kriminalbiologie und Fürsorge," 45. *JGGSA* (1929).

73. A major influence on Fetscher's project was Ernst Kretschmer, the founder of characterology, whose work *Character and Bodily Build* presented the best-known typologies for "relating physical to mental qualities." Weindling, *Health*, 385.

74. Sächsisches Hauptsstaatsarchiv, Justizministerium, no. 1587, Fragebogen.

75. "Kriminalbiologischer Dienst?" *Volksstimme*, 11 February 1926.

76. BA R30.01 no. 5688. Seyfarth to Reichsjustizminister, 22 September 1926. Werner Gentz, "Der Ausbau des Strafvollzuges in Stufen in Preussen," *MDRG* 5, nos. 1–2 (1930); Theodor Viernstein, "Die Kriminalbiologische Forschung," *MDRG* 6, nos. 11–12 (1931); Viernstein, "Gedanken über die Durchführung einer Strafentlassenen Fürsorge in Bayern," *MDRG* 7, nos. 1–2 (1932); Viernstein, "Stufenstrafvollzug, Entlassenfürsorge, Sicherungsverwahrung," *MDRG* 7, nos. 9–10 and 11–12 (1932); Rainer Fetscher, "Arbeitslosigkeit und Kriminalität," *MDRG* 7, nos. 11–12 (1932).

77. Heinrich Seyfarth, "Die erbbiologische Forschung in ihrer Bedeutung für Strafvollzug und Entlassenenfürsorge," *MDRG* 1, nos. 10–11 (1926): 23. In subsequent issues, there were both frequent articles on criminal biology and articles that more seamlessly integrated racial-hygienic themes.

78. "Kriminalbiologische Tagung in Dresden," *Leipziger Volkszeitung*, 8 October 1928.

79. Schmidt, "Bankerott des Strafvollzuges?" 19–22.

Conclusion

1. Archive der sozialen Demokratie, Friedrich Ebert Stiftung. Nachlass Severing 51, Bozi to Severing, 28 November 1933.

2. It is possible that Bozi's letter was intended to protect Severing from further attacks, but the basic sentiments here are mirrored in his unpublished manuscripts from this era. SB NB no. 2, "Maschinenschriftliches Skript zur Entstehungs- und Entwicklungsgeschicte der Justizreform seit 1890" (not dated, probably 1937); SB NB no. 3, "Deutschlands Erneuerung," unpublished manuscript, 1933.

3. Wolfgang Ayass, *'Asoziale' Im Nationalsozialismus*. (Stuttgart: Klett-Cota, 1995); Robert Gellately, *Backing Hitler: Consent and Coercion in Nazi Germany* (New York: Oxford University Press, 2001), 90–96.

4. BL 12 A. Landgericht Berlin. "Richtlinien für den Vollzug der Untersuchungshaft im Berlin-Moabit 1933." On the prisons, see Dienst und Vollzugsordnung für die Gefangenenanstalten der Preussischen Justizverwaltung (1 August 1933); and Nikolaus Wachsmann, *Hitler's Prisons: Legal Terror in Nazi Germany* (New Haven: Yale University Press, 2004).

5. ADW CA GF/St no. 1308–5. Hermine Baecker, memo regarding agreement of 14 July 1933; Rudolf Sieverts, "Die Gerichtshilfe in Kunftigen Strafrechts. Vortrag Gehalten anläßlich der Tagung für Soziale Gerichtshilfe in Berlin im November 1952" (unpublished MS, 1952).

6. Heinrich Seyfarth, "Wie können Kriminalität und Rückfall wirksam bekämpft werden?" *MDRG* (1933). Seyfarth was an especially prolific correspondent with Nazi officials. Sächsisches Hauptstaatsarchiv, Justizministerium, no. 409. Seyfarth to Minister of Justice (Saxony), 5 April 1933; BA R30.01 no. 5686, Seyfarth to Reich Minister of Justice Gürtner, 22 March 1933, and Seyfarth to Reich Minister of Propaganda Goebbels, 7 July 1933.

7. Seyfarth, "Wie können."

8. Paul Braune, "Die Wandererfürsorge im Dritten Reich. Hauptreferat auf der gemeinsamen Tagung der Wandererfürosrgeverbände im Oktober 1933 in Goslar," *Der Wanderer* 50 (1933).

9. W. Schwerdtfeger, "Gedanken über die Sicherungsverwahrung," *MDRG* 10 (1934–1935).

10. James Q. Whitman, *Harsh Justice: Criminal Punishment and the Widening Gap between America and Europe* (New York: Oxford University Press, 2003), 149.

11. Verfügung des Reichsministers der Justiz vom 7 October 1937, cited in Roland Freisler, *Leitfaden für die Helfer der Ermittlungshilfe* (Berlin: Decker, 1938); Sieverts, "Gerichtshilfe."

12. Fritz Hartung, "Gerichtshilfe Einst, Ermittlungshilfe Heute." *MDRG* 13, no. 10 (1937); Rudolf Sieverts, "Zur Frage Gerichtlichen Ermittlungshilfe." *MKS* 28, no. 10 (1937).

13. Wolf Gruner, *Der Geschlossene Arbeitseinsatz Deutscher Juden. Zur Zwangsarbeit als Element der Verfolgung 1938–1943.* (Berlin: Metropol, 1997); Gellately, *Backing Hitler*, 256–58; Gisela Diewald-Kerkmann, *Politische Denunziation im NS-Regime oder die kleine Macht der 'Volksgenossen'* (Bonn: Dietz, 1995); Reinhard Mann, *Protest und Kontrolle im Dritten Reich: Nationalsozialistische Herrschaft im Alltage einer rheinischen Grosstadt* (Frankfurt am Main: Campus, 1987); and Klaus Marxen, *Das Volk und sein Gerichtshof: eine Studie zum nationalsozialistischen Volksgerichtshof* (Frankfurt am Main: Klostermann, 1994).

14. The conference was organized by the Federal government. Arndt Meyer-Reil, *Strafaussetzung zur Bewährung. Reformdiskussion und Gesetzgebung Seit dem Ausgang des 19. Jahrhunderts.* (Berlin: LIT Verlag, 2006), 205–9.

15. Sieverts, "Die Gerichtshilfe."

16. Marxen, *Das Volk*; Ingo Müller, *Hitler's Justice: The Courts of the Third Reich* (Cambridge, Mass.: Harvard University Press, 1991).

17. Alfred Weber and Alexander Mitscherlich proposed that judges play a central role in all aspects of social and economic regulation. Katharina Hausmann, *'Die Chance, Bürger zu werden.' Deutsche Politik unter amerikanischer Besatzung: 'Die Heidelberger Aktionsgruppe' 1946–1947.* (Heidelberg: Verlag Regionalkultur, 2006);

Edward Dickinson offers intriguing suggestions about the Nazis' role in destroying traditional islands of corporatist power: Edward Ross Dickinson, *The Politics of German Child Welfare from the Empire to the Federal Republic* (Cambridge, Mass.: Harvard University Press, 1996).

18. *Datenreport 2002/2004* (Bonn: Bundeszentrale für politische Bildung, 2004); Marc Mauer, "Comparative International Rates of Incarceration: An Examination of Causes and Trends," presented to the U.S. Commission on Civil Rights, 20 June 2003. <http://www.soros.org/initiatives/justice/articles_publications/publications/intl_incarceration_20030620/intl_rates.pdf>

19. Jonathan Simon, *Poor Discipline: Parole and the Social Control of the Underclass, 1890–1990* (Chicago: University of Chicago Press, 1994), and *Governing through Crime: How the War on Crime Transformed American Democracy and Created a Culture of Fear* (Oxford: Oxford University Press, 2007); Whitman, *Harsh Justice*, 69–95; Hans J. Schneider, *Kriminalpolitik an der Schwelle zum 21. Jahrhundert* (Berlin: de Gruyter, 1998).

20. Whitman, *Harsh Justice*, 55–56.

SELECTED BIBLIOGRAPHY

Archives

Archiv des Diakonischen Werkes der Evangelischen Kirche, Berlin
Brandenbürgisches Landeshauptstaatsarchiv, Potsdam
Bundesarchiv, Berlin
Geheimes Staatsarchiv Preussischer Kulturbesitz, Berlin-Dahlem
Hauptarchiv von Bodelschwinghsche Anstalt Bethel
Landesarchiv Berlin
Sächsisches Hauptsstaatsarchiv, Dresden
Stadtsarchiv Bielefeld

Primary Works

Aschaffenburg, Gustav. *Gefängnis oder Irrenanstalt?* Dresden: Vortrag gehalten in der Gehe-Stiftung, 1908.

——. *Das Verbrechen und seine Bekämpfung.* Heidelberg: Winter, 1906.

Auer, Fritz. *Zur Psychologie der Gefangenschaft, Untersuchungshaft, Gefägnis- und Zuchthausstrafe. Geschildert von Entlassenen. Ein Beitrag zur Reform der Voruntersuchung und des Strafvollzugs.* München: C. H. Beck, 1905.

Avé-Lallemant, Friedrich Christian Benedikt. *Das Deutsche Gaunerthum in seiner social-politischen, literarischen und linguistischen Ausbildung zu seinem heutigen Bestande.* Leipzig: Brockhaus, 1858–1862.

Behrle, Alfred. *Die Stellung der deutschen Sozialisten zum Strafvollzug von 1870 bis zur Gegenwart.* Leipzig and Berlin: de Gruyter, 1931.

van den Bergh, Ernst. *Polizei Und Volk. Polizei in Einzeldarstellungen.* Berlin: Gersbach, 1926.

von Bodelschwingh, Friedrich. *Ausgewählte Schriften. Veröffentlichungen Aus Den Jahren 1872 Bis 1910.* Bethel: Verlagshandlung der Anstalt Bethel, 1964.

——. *Friedrich von Bodelschwingh. Ein Blick in sein Leben.* Bielefeld: Pfennigverein, 1924.

von Bodelschwingh, Friedrich (the younger). "Grosse Kinder." *Bethel* 3, no. 1 (1911): 19–24.

Bozi, Alfred. *Die Angriffe Gegen die Richterstand.* Breslau: W. Koebner, 1896.

——. "Der Kommende Richter." *Westdeutsche Wirtschaft* 6, no. 1/3 (1929).

——. *Die Sozialen Rechtseinrichtungen in Bielefeld.* Stuttgart: Deutsche Gesselschaft für Soziales Recht, 1917.

——. "Soziales Recht." *Die Christliche Welt. Wochenschrift Der Gegenwartschristentum* 34, no. 41 (1920).

——. *Die Weltanschauung der Jurisprudenz.* Hannover: 1907.

——. "Zur Neuorientierung des Rechts." *Deutsches Recht* (1933).

Bozi, Alfred, and Hugo Heinemann, eds. *Recht, Verwaltung, Und Politik Im Neuen Deutschland.* Stuttgart: Ferdinand Enke, 1916.

Bozi, Else. *Gerichtshilfe für Erwachsene.* Stuttgart: Ferdinand Enke, 1925.

Braune, R. "Die Deportation der Gefangenen." *Blätter für Gefängniskunde* 30 (1896): 3–29.

Bruck, Felix Friedrich. *Fort mit den Zuchthäusern!* Breslau: Köbner, 1894.

——. *Die Gegner der Deportation.* Breslau: Marcus, 1901.

——. *Die gesetzliche Einführung der Deportation im Deutschen Reich.* Breslau: Marcus, 1897.

——. *Neu-Deutschland und seine Pioniere. Ein Beitrag zur Lösung der sozialen Frage.* Breslau: Köbner, 1896.

——. *Noch einmal die Deportation und Deutsch-Südwestafrika.* Breslau: Marcus, 1906.

Bumke, Erwin, ed. *Deutsches Gefängniswesen. Ein Handbuch.* Berlin: Vahlen, 1928.

Deimling-Triebel, Magdalene. *Die Eingliederung von Rechtsbrechern in Wirtschaft und Gesellschaft als Aufgabe der Gerichtshilfe.* Durlach: Widmann, 1932.

Denkwürdigkeiten des Hauptmann von Köpenicks. Berlin: Lustigen Blätter, 1906.

Dressler, Oskar, ed. *Die Große Polizei-Ausstellung Berlin im Wort Und Bild.* Vienna: Internat. Öffentl. Sicherheit, 1927.

Elster, Alexander, and Heinrich Lingemann, eds. *Handwörterbuch Der Kriminologie.* Berlin and Leipzig: de Gruyter, 1933.

Erdlenbruch, Kurt. "Die Wirtschaftliche Und Soziale Bedeutung der Deutschen Arbeiterkolonien." Giessen, 1928.

Exner, Franz. *Krieg und Kriminalität. Vortrag, Gehalten anlässlich der Universitäts Gründungsfeier am 3. Juli 1926 in Leipzig.* Leipzig: E. Wiegandt, 1926.

——. *Studien über die Strafzumessungspraxis der deutschen Gerichte.* Leipzig: Wiegandt, 1931.

——. "Zur Praxis der Strafzumessung." *Monatsschrift für Kriminalpsychologie Und Strafrechtsreform*, no. 17 (1926): 365–74.

Exner, Franz, J. Lange, and S. Sieverts. "Aschaffenburg zum 70. Geburtstag." *Monatsschrift für Kriminalpsychologie und Strafrechtsreform* 27 (1936).

Fabarius, E. A. "Deportation von Verbrechern nach den deutschen Kolonien?" *Allgemeine Missions-Zeitschrift: Monatsheft für Geschichtliche und Theoretische Missionskunde* 23–24 (1896).

Feuerbach, Paul Johann Anselm. *Aktenmäßige Darstellung merwürdiger Verbrechen.* 3rd ed. Frankfurt: G. F. Heper, 1849.

——. *Lehrbuch des gemeinen in Deutschland gültigen Rechts.* Giessen: G. F. Heyes, 1801.

Finkelnburg, Karl Maria. *Amnestie: Schauspiel in drei Akten*. Berlin: Volksbühnen-Verlags- und Vertriebs-G.m.b.H. 1929.

———. *Die Bestraften in Deutschland*. Berlin: J. Guttentag, 1912.

Fleischmann, Otto. *Deutsches Vagabunden und Verbrechertum in Neunzehnten Jahrhundert*. Barmen: Hugo Klein, 1887.

Flynt, Josiah. *Tramping with Tramps. Studies and Sketches of Vagabond Life*. New York: The Century Co., 1900.

Freund, Friedrich. "Strafvollzug und Krieg." *Blätter für Gefängniskunde* 49 (1915): 167–71.

Fuchs, Adolf. *Die Gefangenen-Schutzthätigkeit und Verbrechens-Prophylaxe*. Berlin: Carl Heymanns Verlag, 1898.

Gentz, Werner. "Aufgaben und Aufbau der Gerichtshilfe." *Zeitschrift für die Gesamte Strafrechtswissenschaft* (1929): 235–47.

———. "Der Ausbau des Strafvollzuges in Stufen in Preussen." *Monatsblätter Des Deutschen Reichsverbandes für Gerichtshilfe, Gefangenen- und Entlassenenfürsorge* 5 (1930).

———. "Der Fürsorgeanspruch des entlassenen Gefangenen." *Monatsblätter des Deutschen Reichsverbandes Für Gerichtshilfe, Gefangenen- und Entlassenenfürsorge* 1, no. 3 (1926): 3–9.

———. "Gefangenenfürsorge als Volksaufgabe." *45. Jahresversammlung der Gefängnisgesellschaft für die Provinz Sachsen und das Herzogthum Anhalt* (4 June 1929).

———. "Gefangenenfürsorge als wirtschaftliches Problem." *Monatsblätter des Deutschen Reichsverbandes für Gerichtshilfe, Gefangenen- und Entlassenenfürsorge* 1, no. 4 (1926): 7–15.

———. "Das Sexualproblem im Strafvollzug." *Zeitschrift für die Gesamte Strafrechtswissenschaft* 32 (1930): 406–24.

Geutz, Adolf. *Sträfling 788. Ein Kapitel Berufsleiden*. Berlin: Magazin Verlag, 1904.

Göhre, Paul. *Three Months in a Workshop: A Practical Study*. New York: Arno Press, 1972.

Gradnauer, Georg. *Das Elend des Strafvollzuges*. Dresden: Vorwaerts, 1905.

Grau, Fritz, and Karl Schäfer. *Das Preussische Gnadenrecht*. Berlin: Georg Stilke, 1931.

Gross, Hans. " 'Antisoziale' Elemente." *Archiv für Kriminologie, Kriminalanthropologie Und Kriminalstatistik* 64, no. 1, 2 (1915): 51–53.

Hartung, Fritz. *Jurist unter vier Reichen*. Cologne: Heymanns, 1971.

Heim, Hugo. *Die jüngsten und die ältesten Verbrecher nebst Lebensbeschreibung eines Zuchthaussträflings nach dessen eigenen Aufzeichnungen. Ein Beitrag zur Lösung der sozialen Frage*. Berlin: Verlag von Wiegandt & Grieben, 1897.

Heimberger, Joseph. *Zur Reform des Strafvollzugs*. Leipzig: Böhme, 1905.

Heindl, Robert. *Der Berufsverbrecher. Ein Beitrag zur Strafrechtsreform*. Berlin: Verlag Rolf Heise, 1926.

———. *Meine Reise nach den Strafkolonien*. Berlin: Ullstein, 1912.

Hellwig, Albert. *Die Bedingte Aussetzung der Strafvollstreckung in Preussen*. Berlin: Mueller, 1921.

——. "Kriminalbiologie und Strafzumessung." *Mitteilungen der Kriminalbiologischen Gesellschaft* (1928).

——. "Richter und Rechtspflege." *Monatsschrift für Kriminalpsychologie und Strafrechtsreform* (1922).

——. "Soziale Gerichtshilfe und Strafrechtsreform." *Koenigsburg Hartungsche Ztg.* (1929).

——. *Die Unbedingte Aussetzung der Strafvollstreckung in Preußen und im Reich*. Berlin: 1921.

von Hentig, Hans. *Aufsätze zur Revolution*. Berlin: Springer, 1919.

——. *Die Entartung der Revolution*. Leipzig: Koehler, 1920.

——. *Mein Krieg*. Berlin: A. Kuhn, 1919.

——. *Strafrecht und Auslese. Eine Anwendung des Kausalgesetzes auf den rechtbrechenden Menschen*. Berlin: Verlag von Julius Springer, 1914.

Hippel, Robert von. *Die Strafrechtliche Bekämpfung von Bettel, Landstreicherei und Arbeitsscheu*. Berlin: Verlag von Otto Liebmann, 1895.

——. *Zur Vagabundenfrage*. Berlin: Verlag von Otto Liebmann, 1902.

von Holtzendorff, Franz, and Heinrich Jagemann, eds. *Handbuch Des Gefängniswesens*. Hamburg: Richter, 1888.

Hyan, Hans. *Berliner Gefängnisse*. Berlin: Puttkammer & Mühlbrecht, 1920.

——. *Verbrechen und Strafe im neuen Deutschland. Flugschriften der Revolution. Nr. 4*. Berlin: Verlag für Sozialwissenschaft, 1919.

Just, Theodor. *Aus dreissigjähriger Rettungsarbeit an den Gefangenen und Entlassenen*. Düsseldorf: Westdeutschen Sittlichkeitsverlag, 1930.

——. "Das Fursorgeproblem und die Rheinisch-Westfalische Gefangnis-Gesellschaft." *Monatsblätter des Deutschen Reichsverbandes für Gerichtshilfe, Gefangenen- und Entlassenenfürsorge* (1929): 67–74.

Just, Theodor, and Gustav von Rohden. *Hundert Jahre Geschichte der Rheinisch-Westfälische Gefängnis-Gesellschaft 1826–1926*. Düsseldorf: Geschäftsstelle der Rheinisch-Westfälischen Gefängnis-Gesellschaft, 1926.

Klatt, Detloff. *Das Los der Vorbestraften*. Berlin: Verlag von Alfred Metzner, 1926.

von Koerber, Helene. *Meine Erlebnisse unter Strafgefangenen*. Stuttgart: Haedecke, 1928.

Koppenfels, Sebastian von. *Die Kriminalität der Frau im Kriege*. Leipzig: Ernst Wiegandt, 1926.

Krebs, Otto. *Straffälligenfürsorge*. Berlin: Hauptausschuß für Arbeiterwohlfahrt, 1930.

Krohne, Karl. "Die gegenwärtige Stand der Gefängniswissenschaft." *Zeitschrift Für Die Gesamte Strafrechtswissenschaft* 1 (1881).

Krohne, Karl. *Lehrbuch der Gefängniskunde*. Stuttgart: Enke, 1889.

Kunstlerhaus Bethanien, ed. *Wohnsitz, Nirgendwo: Vom Leben und vom Überleben auf der Strasse*. Berlin: Frölich & Kaufmann, 1982.

Leuß, Hans. *Aus dem Zuchthause. Verbrecher und Strafrechtspflege*. Berlin: J. Rade,
  1903.

Liepmann, Moritz. *Krieg und Kriminalität in Deutschland*. Stuttgart: Deutsche
  Verlags-Anstalt, 1930.

von Liszt, Franz. "Die Aufgaben der Gefängnis Gesellschaft." *10. Jahrbuch Der
  Gefängnis-Gesellschaft für die Provinz Sachsen und Anhalt*. 1895.

——. "Bedingte Verurteilung und Bedingte Begnadigung." In *Vergleichende
  Darstellung des Deutschen und Ausländischen Strafrechts*, ed. Karl Frank, Reinhard
  Hippel, Robert Kahl, Franz von Liszt, Fritz van Calker, and Karl Birkmeyer.
  Berlin: Verlag von Otto Liebmann, 1908.

——. "Die IKV. Ihre Aufgaben und ihre Arbeiten." *11. Jahrbuch der Gefängnis-
  Gesellschaft für die Provinz Sachsen und Anhalt*. 1893.

——. *Lehrbuch des Deutschen Strafrechts*. Berlin: J. Guttentag, 1905.

——. *Strafrechtliche Aufsätze und Vorträge*. Berlin: Guttentag, 1905.

Mann, Thomas. " 'Amnestie.' " *Die Justiz. Monatschrift für Erneuerung des Deutschen
  Rechtswesen. Zugleich Organ des Republikanischen Richterbundes* 5, no. 6 (1930).

Mittelstädt, Otto. *Vor der Fluth: Sechs Briefe zur Politik der deutschen Gegenwart*.
  Leipzig: Hirzel, 1897.

——. *Gegen die Freiheitsstrafen. Ein Beitrag zur Kritik des heutigen Strafensystems*.
  Leipzig: S. Hirzel, 1879.

Mittermaier, Wolfgang. "Grundgedanken der Gerichtshilfe." *Die Justiz* 6, no. 1
  (1930): 3–10.

——. "Grundsätzliches über das Verhältnis von Strafe und Fürsorge." *Monatsblätter
  des Deutschen Reichsverbandes für Gerichtshilfe, Gefangenen- und Entlassenenfürsorge*. 1929.

——. "Kann die Deportation im deutschen Strafstystem Aufnahme finden?"
  Zeitschrift für die Gesamte Strafrechtswissenschaft 19 (1899).

Mönkemöller, Otto. "Die Bewahrung Asozialer." *MKS* 15, no. 8–12 (1924).

——. *Korrektionsanstalt und Landarmenhaus; ein soziologischer Beitrag zur Kri-
  minalitat und Psychopathologie des Weibes*. Leipzig: 1908.

Ostwald, Hans. *Bekämpfung der Landstreicherei*. Stuttgart: 1903.

——. "Das Leben der Wanderarmen." *Archiv für Kriminalanthropologie* 13 (1905).

Pappritz, Anna. *Einführung in das Studium der Prostitutionsfrage*. Berlin: 1910.

——. "Der Kampf gegen die öffentliche Unsittlichkeit." In *Recht, Verwaltung, und
  Politik im neuen Deutschland*, ed. Alfred Bozi. Stuttgart: Enke, 1916.

Peabody, Francis Greenwood. "The German Labor-Colonies for Tramps." *The
  Forum* (1892): 751–61.

Pfefferkorn, Hugo. *Die Gerichtshilfe*. Berlin: Heymann, 1930.

Preussische Justizministerium (Hrsg.). *Strafvollzug in Preussen*. Mannheim:
  J. Bensheimer, 1928.

Radbruch, Gustav. *Gesamtausgabe*. Heidelberg: CF Mueller, 1987–2005.

——. "Sozialismus und Strafrechtsreform." *Sozialistische Monatshefte* (1927): 522–26.

Rosenfeld, Ernst. *Die Geschichte des Berliner Vereins zur Besserung der*

Strafgefangenen, 1827–1900; Ein Beitrag zur Geschichte des preussischen Gefangniswesens und des Fürsorgewesens für Entlassene Gefangene. Berlin: O. Liebmann, 1901.

——. "Zur Deportationsfrage." *78. Jahresbericht. Rheinisch-Westfälichen Gefängnis-Gesellschaft über das Vereinsjahr 1904/1905.* 1905.

——. *Zweihundert Jahre Fürsorge der Preußischen Staatsegierung für die entlassene Gefangenen.* Berlin: J. Guttentag, 1905.

Rosenfeld, Siegfried. " 'Der Bankerott der Strafjustiz.' " *Die Justiz* 3, no. 3 (1927).

——. "Finkelnburgs Schauspiel 'Amnestie.' " *Die Justiz. Monatschrift F. Erneuerung D. Deutschen Rechtswesen. Zugleich Organ Des Republikanischen Richterbundes* 5, no. 6 (1930).

Scheuner, Ellen. *Die Gefährdetenfürsorge.* Berlin: C. Heymann, 1930.

Schmölder, Robert. "Die alte und die neue Kriminalistenschule und der Strafvollzug." *Preußische Jahrbücher* (1904): 489–.

Schwandner. "Heeresdienst und Strafvollzug mit besonderer Berücksichtigung der Zuchthausstrafe." *Blätter für Gefängniskunde* 49 (1915): 198–200.

Severing, Carl. *Mein Lebensweg,* Vol. 1. *Vom Schlosser zum Minister,* 2. *Im auf und ab der Republik.* Cologne: Greven Verlag, 1950.

Seyfarth, Heinrich. "Aufgaben und Ziele des Deutschen Reichsverbandes für Gerichtshilfe, Gefangenen- und Entlassenenfürsorge." *Monatsblätter des Deutschen Reichsverbandes für Gerichtshilfe, Gefangenen- und Entlassenenfürsorge* 1, no. 1 (1926).

——. *Aus der Welt der Gefangenen.* Leipzig: 1913.

——. "Durchhalten!" *Monatsblätter des Deutschen Reichsverbandes für Gerichtshilfe, Gefangenen- und Entlassenenfürsorge* 7, no. 9–10 (1932).

——. "Erbbiologie und Rassenhygiene." *Monatsblätter Des Deutschen Reichsverbandes Für Gerichtshilfe, Gefangenen- Und Entlassenenfürsorge* 8/9 (1927).

——. "Die erbbiologische Forschung in ihrer Bedeutung für Strafvollzug und Entlassenenfürsorge." *Monatsblätter des Deutschen Reichsverbandes für Gerichtshilfe, Gefangenen- und Entlassenenfürsorge* 1, no. Heft 10/11 (1926): 20–23.

——. "Grundsätzliches zur Fürsorge für entlassenen Gefangene." *Monatsblätter des Deutschen Reichsverbandes für Gerichtshilfe, Gefangenen- und Entlassenenfürsorge* (1933).

——. *Hinter eisernen Gittern. Ein Blick in die Verbrecherwelt. Zuchthausstudien.* Leipzig: Verlag von Fridrich Richter, 1898.

——. "Der Humanitätsgedanke im Strafvollzug." *Monatsblätter des Deutschen Reichsverbandes für Gerichtshilfe, Gefangenen- und Entlassenenfürsorge* 6, no. 9/10 (1931).

——. *Die Not der Entlassenen und ein Versuch sie zu lindern. Vortrag.* Hamburg: 1908.

——. *Praktisches Christentum.* Leipzig: 1901.

——. *Probleme des Strafwesens.* Berlin: Carl Heymanns Verlag, 1928.

——. "Strafvollzug und Kriegsdienst." *Blätter für Gefängniskunde* 49 (1915).

——. "Über die Deportation von Verbrechern nach Deutsch-Sudwestafrika." *Blätter für Gefängniskunde. Organ des Vereins der Deutschen Strafanstaltsbeamten* 34 (1900).

Sieverts, Rudolf. "Gedanken über Methoden, Ergebnisse und kriminalpolitische Folgen der kriminal-biologischen Untersuchungen im bayrischen Strafvollzug," *Monatsschrift für Kriminalpsychologie und Strafrechtsreform* 23 (1932): 588–601.

——. "Die Gerichtshilfe in Kunftigen Strafrechts. Vortrag Gehalten Anläßlich der Tagung für Soziale Gerichtshilfe in Berlin im November 1952." Herausgegeben von Senator für Sozialwesen. Berlin, 1952.

Sommer, Margaret. *Die Fürsorge im Strafrecht.* Berlin: C. Heymann, 1925.

Statistisches Jahrbuch für den Preussischen Staat. Berlin: Landesamt, 1905–1933.

Statistisches Reichsamt. *Statistisches Jahrbuch für das Deutsche Reich.* Berlin: Schmidt, 1880–1937.

Steigerthal, Georg. "Die Bekämpfung asozialer Elemente durch die Nachhafts-strafe." *Jahrbuch der Gefängnis Gesellschaft für die Provinz Sachsen Und Anhalt* 41 (1925).

——. *Zwangsfürsorgische Maßnahmen gegenüber erwachsenen Personen.* Berlin: Carl Heymanns Verlag, 1926.

Viernstein, Theodor. "Gedanken über die Durchführung einer Strafentlassenenfür-sorge in Bayern." *Monatsblätter des Deutschen Reichsverbandes für Gerichtshilfe, Gefangenen- und Entlassenenfürsorge* (1931–1933).

——. "Die Kriminalbiologische Forschung in Bayern." *Monatsblätter des Deutschen Reichsverbandes für Gerichtshilfe, Gefangenen- und Entlassenenfürsorge* 6, no. 8/9 (1931): 118–32.

——. "Die Kriminalbiologischen Untersuchungen an Strafhauszugängen in den bay-erischen Strafanstalten in ihrer Auswirkung auf Stufenstrafvollzug, Strafrechts-praxis vor Gericht und auf die Wissenschaft." *45. Jahresversammlung der Gefängnisgesellschaft für die Provinz Sachsen und das Herzogthum Anhalt* (1929).

——. "Stufenstrafvollzug, Entlassenenfürsorge, Sicherungsverwahrung." *Monatsblät-ter des Deutschen Reichsverbandes für Gerichtshilfe, Gefangenen- und Entlassenen-fürsorge* 7, no. 9–12 (1932).

Die Versorgung asozialer Personen. Gekürzter Bericht über die Tagung der Vorbere-tenden Kommission zur Prüfung der Frage der Versorgung asozialer Personen am 7. und 8. Juli 1922 in Bielefeld. Frankfurt: Deutscher Verein für öffentliche und pri-vate Fürsorge, 1922.

Voigt, Wilhelm. *Wie ich Hauptmann von Köpenick wurde.* Berlin: Jul. Emil Gaul, 1909.

Wichern, Johann Hinrich. *Gesammelte Schriften.* Hamburg: Agentur des Rauhen Hauses, 1901–1908.

——. *Sämtliche Werke.* Ed. Peter Meinhold. Berlin: Lutherisches Verlagshaus, 1958–1988.

Wolff, Gustav. *Gerichtshilfe.* Rastatt: Rastatter Zeitung GmbH, 1931.

Secondary Works

Ayass, Wolfgang. *Das Arbeitshaus Breitenau. Bettler, Landstreicher, Prostituierte, Zuhalter und Fursorgeempfanger in der Korrektions und Landarmenanstalt Breitenau.* Kassel: Gesamthochschule Kassel, 1992.

Bade, Klaus J. *Friedrich Fabri und der Imperialismus in der Bismarckzeit. Revolution— Depression—Expansion.* Freiburg: Atlantis, 1975.

———. "From Emigration to Immigration: The German Experience in the Nineteenth and Twentieth Centuries." *Central European History* 28, no. 4 (1996): 507–36.

———. "Labour, Migration and the State: Germany from the Late 19th Century to the Onset of the Great Depression." In *Population, Labour and Migration in 19th and 20th Century Germany*, ed. Klaus J. Bade, 59–86. New York: Berg Press, 1987.

———. "Zwischen Mission und Kolonialbewegung, Kolonialwirtschaft und Kolonialpolitik in der Bismarckzeit: der Fall Friedrich Fabri." In *Imperialismus und Kolonialmission. Kaiserliches Deutschland und koloniales Imperium*, ed. Klaus J. Bade, 103–42. Wiesbaden: Steiner, 1984.

Baumann, Ursula. *Protestantismus und Frauenemanzipation in Deutschland 1850 bis 1920.* Frankfurt am Main: Campus Verlag, 1992.

Becker, Peter. "Randgruppen im Blickfeld der Polizei. Ein Versuch über die Perspektivität des 'praktischen Blicks.'" *Archiv für Sozialgeschichte* 32 (1992): 283–304.

———. *Verderbnis und Entartung. Eine Geschichte der Kriminologie des 19. Jahrhunderts als Diskurs und Praxis.* Goettingen: Vandenhoeck & Ruprecht, 2002.

———. "Vom Haltlosen zur Bestie. Das polizeiliche Bild des Verbrechers im 19. Jahrhundert." In *Sicherheit und Wohlfahrt. Polizei, Gesellschaft und Herrschaft im 19. und 20. Jahrhundert*, ed. Alf Lüdtke, 97–132. Frankfurt am Main: Suhrkamp, 1992.

———. "Weak Bodies? Prostitutes and the Role of Gender in the Criminological Writings of Detectives and Magistrates in 19th Century Germany." *Crime, History & Societies* 3 (1999): 45–69.

Becker, Peter, and Richard Wetzell, eds. *Criminals and Their Scientists: The History of Criminology in International Perspective.* New York: Cambridge University Press, 2006.

Berger, Thomas. *Die konstante Repression. Zur Geschichte des Strafvollzugs in Preussen nach 1850.* Frankfurt am Main: Verlag Roter Stern, 1974.

Bessel, Richard. *Germany after the First World War.* New York: Oxford University Press, 1993.

———. "Militarisierung und Modernisierung: Polizeiliches Handeln in der Weimarer Republik." In *'Sicherheit' und 'Wohlfahrt:' Polizei, Gesellschaft und Herrschaft im 19. und 20. Jahrhundert*, ed. Alf Lüdtke, 323–43. Frankfurt am Main: Suhrkamp, 1992.

Beyer, Heinz. *Arbeit steht auf uns'rer Fahne. Sozialer Protestantismus und bürgerlicher Antisozialismus im Wuppertal 1880–1914.* Köln: Einhorn, 1985.

Blackbourn, David. *The Long Nineteenth Century: A History of Germany 1780–1918.* New York: Oxford University Press, 1998.

Blackbourn, David, and Geoff Eley. *The Peculiarities of German History: Bourgeois Society and Politics in Nineteenth-Century Germany*. New York: Oxford University Press, 1984.

Blasius, Dirk. *Kriminalität Und Alltag. Zur Konfliktgeschichte Des Alltagslebens im 19. Jahrhundert*. Göttingen: Vandenhoeck und Ruprecht, 1978.

——. "Kriminologie und Geschichtswissenschaft: Bilanz und Perspektiven interdisziplinärer Forschung." *Geschichte Und Gesellschaft* 14 (1988).

——. *Der verwaltete Wahnsinn. Eine Sozialgeschichte des Irrenhauses*. Frankfurt am Main: Fischer, 1980.

Brakelmann, G. *Kirche und Sozialismus im 19. Jahrhundert. Die Analyse des Sozialismus und Kommunismus bei Johann Hinrich Wichern und bei Rudolf Todt*. Witten: Luther Verlag, 1966.

vom Bruch, Rüdiger, ed. *Weder Kommunismus noch Kapitalismus: Bürgerliche Sozialreform in Deutschland vom Vormärz bis zur Ära Adenauer*. München: C. H. Beck, 1985.

——. "1890—Gründungsjahr des Evangelisch-Sozialen Kongresses." In *Protestantische Wirthschaftsethik und Reform des Kapitalismus. 100 Jahre Evangelisch-Sozialer Kongress*, ed. Klaus Heienbrok and Hartmut Przybylski, 11–18. Bochum: Sozialwissenschaftliches Institut der Evangelischen Kirche in Deutschland, 1991.

Campbell, Joan. *Joy in Work, German Work*. Princeton: Princeton University Press, 1989.

Canning, Kathleen. "Gender and the Culture of Work: Ideology and Identity in the World behind the Mill Gate, 1890–1914." In *Elections, Mass Politics, and Social Change in Modern Germany: New Perspectives*, ed. James Retallack and Larry Eugene Jones, 175–99. New York: Cambridge University Press, 1992.

——. *Languages of Labor and Gender: Female Factory Work in Germany, 1850–1914*. Ithaca: Cornell University Press, 1996.

——. "Social Policy, Body Politics: Recasting the Social Question in Germany, 1875–1900." In *Gender and Class in Modern Europe*, ed. Laura Frader and Sonya Rose, 211–37. Ithaca: Cornell University Press, 1996.

Castel, Robert. "From Dangerousness to Risk." In *The Foucault Effect: Studies in Governmentality*, ed. Graham Burchell, Colin Gordon, and Peter Miller, 281–198. Chicago: University of Chicago Press, 1991.

Conrad, Sebastian. " 'Eingeborenenpolitik' in Kolonie und Metropole. 'Erziehung zur Arbeit' in Ostafrika und Ostwestfalen." In *Das Kaiserreich transnational. Deutschland in der Welt 1871–1914*, ed. Sebastian Conrad and Jürgen Osterhammel, 107–28. Göttingen: Vandenhoeck & Ruprecht, 2004.

Corbin, Alain. *Women for Hire: Prostitution and Sexuality in France after 1850*. Cambridge, Mass.: Harvard University Press, 1990.

Crew, David. "German Socialism, the State and Family Policy 1918–1933." *Continuity and Change* 1/2 (1986): 235–63.

——. *Town in the Ruhr: A Social History of Bochum, 1860–1914*. New York: Columbia University Press, 1979.

Daniel, Ute. *Arbeiterfrauen in der Kriegsgesellschaft*. Göttingen: Vandenhoeck & Ruprecht, 1989.

Davis, John A. *Conflict and Control: Law and Order in Nineteenth Century Italy*. London: Macmillan, 1988.

Dickinson, Edward Ross. "The Men's Christian Morality Movement in Germany, 1880–1914: Some Reflections on Politics, Sex, and Sexual Politics." *Journal of Modern History 75*, no. 1 (2003).

———. *The Politics of German Child Welfare from the Empire to the Federal Republic*. Cambridge, Mass.: Harvard University Press, 1996.

Ditt, Karl. *Industrialiserung, Arbeiterschaft und Arbeiterbewegung in Bielefeld*. Dortmund: Gesellschaft für Westfälische Wirtschaftsgeschichte, 1982.

Domansky, Elisabeth. "Militarization and Reproduction in World War I Germany." In *Society and Culture and the State in Germany, 1870–1933*, ed. Geoff Eley, 427–63. Ann Arbor: University of Michigan Press, 1997.

Donzelot, Jacques. *L'invention du Social. Essai sur le Déclin des Passions Politiques*. Paris: Éditions du Seuil, 1994.

———. *The Policing of Families*. Baltimore: Johns Hopkins University Press, 1997.

Dörner, Christine. *Erziehung durch Strafe. Die Geschichte des Jugendstrafvollzugs*. München: Juventa, 1991.

Dülmen, Richard van, ed. *Verbrechen, Strafen und Soziale Kontrolle*. Frankfurt: Fischer-Taschenbuch-Verlag, 1990.

Ein Jahrhundert Arbeiterkolonien: "Arbeit Statt Almosen"—Hilfe für Obdachlose Wanderarme 1884–1984. Freiburg: Zentralverband Deutscher Arbeiterkolonien, 1984.

Eley, Geoff. *From Unification to Nazism: Reinterpreting the German Past*. London: George Allen and Unwin, 1986.

———. "German History and the Contradictions of Modernity: The Bourgeoisie, the State and the Mastery of Reform." In *Society and Culture and the State in Germany, 1870–1933*, ed. Geoff Eley, 67–103. Ann Arbor: University of Michigan Press, 1997.

———. "Labor History, Social History, *Alltagsgeschichte*: Experience, Culture, and the Politics of the Everyday—A New Direction for German Social History?" *Journal of Modern History 61* (1989): 297–343.

———. *Reshaping the German Right: Radical Nationalism and Political Change after Bismarck*. Ann Arbor: University of Michigan Press, 1991.

———, ed. *Society, Culture and the State in Germany 1870–1930*. Ann Arbor: University of Michigan Press, 1996.

Engstrom, Eric J. "Review of Christian Müller, Verbrechensbekampfung im Anstaltsstaat: Psychiatrie, Kriminologie und Strafrechtsreform im Deutschland, 1871–1933." H-German, H-Net Reviews (July 2006).

Evans, Richard J. *Death in Hamburg: Society and Politics in the Cholera Years 1830–1910*. London: Penguin, 1987.

———, ed. *The German Underworld: Essays in the Social History of Crime in Germany From the Sixteenth Century to the Present*. London: Routledge, 1988.

——. "In Search of German Social Darwinism." In *Rereading German History 1800–1996: From Unification to Reunification*. New York: Routledge, 1997.

——. "Prostitution, State and Society in Imperial Germany." *Past and Present* 70 (1976).

——. *Rethinking German History: Nineteenth Century Germany and the Origins of the Third Reich*. London: Allen and Unwin, 1987.

——. *Rituals of Retribution: Capital Punishment in Germany 1600–1987*. New York: Oxford University Press, 1996.

——. *Tales From the German Underworld: Crime and Punishment in the Nineteenth Century*. New Haven: Yale University Press, 1998.

Ewald, Francois. *L'Etat Providence*. Paris: Grasset, 1986.

Feldman, Gerald. *Army, Industry, and Labor in Germany, 1914–1918*. Princeton: Princeton University Press, 1966.

——. "Economic and Social Problems of the German Demobilization, 1918–1919." *Journal of Modern History* 47 (1975): 1–47.

——, ed. *The Experience of Inflation: International and Comparative Studies*. New York: de Gruyter, 1984.

Foucault, Michel. "About the Concept of the 'Dangerous Individual' in 19th Century Legal Psychiatry." *International Journal of Law and Psychiatry* 1 (1978): 1–18.

——. *Discipline and Punish: The Birth of the Prison*. New York: Pantheon, 1977.

——. *The History of Sexuality, Vol. I: An Introduction*. New York: Pantheon, 1978.

——. *Madness and Civilization*. New York: Vintage Books, 1988.

——. *Power/Knowledge: Selected Interviews and Other Writings 1972–1977*. New York: Pantheon, 1980.

Frevert, Ute. *Krankheit als politisches Problem, 1770–1880: Soziale Unterschichten in Preussen zwischen medizinischer Polizei und staatlicher Sozialversicherung*. Göttingen: Vandenhoek, 1984.

——. "Professional Medicine and the Working Classes in Imperial Germany." *Journal of Contemporary History* 20 (1985): 637–58.

——. *Women in German History: From Bourgeois Emancipation to Sexual Liberation*. Oxford: Berg, 1989.

Friedlander, Henry. *The Origins of Nazi Genocide: From Euthanasia to the Final Solution*. Chapel Hill: University of North Carolina Press, 1995.

Fritzsche, Peter. *Germans into Nazis*. Cambridge, Mass.: Harvard University Press, 1998.

——. *Reading Berlin 1900*. Cambridge, Mass.: Harvard University Press, 1996.

——. "Vagabond in the Fugitive City: Hans Ostwald, Imperial Berlin and the *Großstadt-Dokumente*." *Journal of Contemporary History* 29 (1994).

Frommel, Monika. "C. J. A. Mittermaiers Konzeption einer praktischen Strafrechtswissenschaft." In *Carl Joseph Anton Mittermaier*, ed. Wilfried Küper. Heidelberg: Decker und Müller, 1988.

——. *Präventionsmodelle in der deutschen Strafzwecksdiskussion: Beziehungen*

zwischen Rechtsphilosophie, Dogmatik, Rechtspolitik und Erfahrungswissenschaften.
Berlin: Duncker und Humboldt, 1987.

Funk, Albrecht. *Polizei und Rechtsstaat: Die Entwicklung des staatlichen Gewalt-monopols in Preussen 1848–1918.* Frankfurt am Main: Campus, 1986.

Gall, Lothar. *Bürgertum in Deutschland.* Berlin: Siedler, 1989.

Gall, Lothar, and Dieter Langewiesche. *Liberalismus und Region: zur Geschichte des deutschen Liberalismus im 19. Jahrhundert.* München: Oldenbourg, 1995.

Garland, David. *Punishment and Welfare: A History of Penal Strategies.* Aldershot: Gower, 1985.

Gerhardt, Martin. *Johann Hinrich Wichern, ein Lebensbild.* Hamburg: Agentur des Rauhen Hauses, 1927–1931.

Geyer-Kordesch, Johanna, and Annette Kuhn, eds. *Frauenkörper, Medizin, Sexuali-tät.* Düsseldorf: Shwann, 1986.

Gründer, Horst. "Deutsche Missionsgesellschaften auf dem Wege zur Kolonialmis-sion." In *Imperialismus und Kolonialmission. Kaiserliches Deutschland und koloniales Imperium,* ed. Klaus J. Bade, 68–102. Wiesbaden: Steiner, 1984.

Hartewig, Karin. " 'Eine sogenannte Neutralität der Beamten gibt es nicht.' Sozialer Protest, bürgerliche Gesellschaft und Polizei im Ruhrgebiet (1918–1924)." In *'Sicherheit' und 'Wohlfahrt': Polizei, Gesellschaft und Herrschaft im 19. und 20. Jahrhundert,* ed. Alf Lüdtke. Frankfurt am Main: Suhrkamp, 1992.

Harvey, Elizabeth. *Youth and the Welfare State in Weimar Germany.* Oxford: Claren-don Press, 1993.

Hausen, Karin, ed. *Frauen Suchen ihre Geschichte. Historische Studien zum 19. und 20. Jahrhundert.* München: C. H. Beck, 1983.

Hett, Benjamin Carter. *Death in the Tiergarten: Murder and Criminal Justice in the Kaiser's Berlin.* Cambridge, Mass.: Harvard University Press, 2004.

Hitzer, Bettina. *Im Netz der Liebe. Die protestantische Kirche und ihre Zuwanderer in der Metropole Berlin (1849–1914).* Köln: Böhlau Verlag, 2006.

Hohendahl, Peter Uwe. *Building a National Culture: The Case of Germany 1830–1870.* Ithaca: Cornell University Press, 1989.

Hong, Young-Sun. *Welfare, Modernity and the Weimar State, 1919–1933.* Princeton: Princeton University Press, 1998.

——. "World War I and the German Welfare State: Gender, Religion and the Para-doxes of Modernity." In *Society, Culture, and the State in Germany, 1870–1933,* ed. Geoff Eley. Ann Arbor: University of Michigan Press, 1996.

Horn, David G. *Social Bodies: Science, Reproduction, and Italian Modernity.* Prince-ton: Princeton University Press, 1994.

Hübinger, Gangolf. *Kulturprotestantismus und Politik. Zum Verhältnis von Liber-alismus und Protestantismus im wilhelminischen Deutschland.* Tübingen: J. C. B. Mohr, 1993.

Hull, Isabel V. *Sexuality, State, and Civil Society in Germany, 1700–1815.* Ithaca: Cor-nell University Press, 1996.

Ignatieff, Michael. *A Just Measure of Pain: The Penitentiary in the Industrial Revolution, 1750–1850.* London: Macmillan, 1978.

Jackson, James H. Jr. "*Alltagsgeschichte*, Social Science History, and the Study of Migration in Nineteenth-Century Germany." *Central European History* 23, no. 2–3 (1990): 242–64.

Jessen, Ralph. *Polizei im Industrierevier: Modernisierung und Herrschaftspraxis im westfällischen Ruhrgebiet 1848–1914.* Göttingen: Vandenhoeck & Ruprecht, 1991.

Johnson, Eric A. *Urbanization and Crime: Germany 1871–1914.* Cambridge: Cambridge University Press, 1995.

Kaiser, Jochen-Christoph. "Freie Wohlfahrtsverbände im Kaiserreich und in der Weimarer Republik: Ein Überblick." *Westfälische Forschungen* 43 (1993).

Karrenberg, Friedrich. "Geschichte der sozialen Ideen im Deutschen Protestantismus." In *Geschichte der sozialen Ideen in Deutschland*, ed. Helga Grebing, 561–645. München: Olzog, 1969.

Kluge, Ulrich. *Die Deutsche Revolution 1918/1919. Staat, Politik und Gesellschaft zwischen Weltkrieg und Kapp-Putsch.* Frankfurt am Main: Suhrkamp, 1985.

———. *Soldatenräte und Revolution: Studien zur Militärpolitik in Deutschland 1918–19.* Göttingen: Vandenhoeck & Ruprecht, 1975.

Kocka, Jürgen. *Facing Total War: German Society 1914–1918.* Cambridge, Mass.: Harvard University Press, 1984.

Köllmann, Wolfgang. *Bevölkerung in der industriellen Revolution.* Göttingen: Vandenhoek & Ruprecht, 1974.

Kouri, E. J. *Der Deutsche Protestantismus und die soziale Frage 1870–1919. Zur Sozialpolitik im Bildungsbürgertum.* Berlin: de Gruyter, 1984.

Kracauer, Siegfried. *From Caligari to Hitler: A Psychological History of the German Film.* Princeton: Princeton University Press, 1947.

Küther, Carsten. *Räuber und Gauner in Deutschland. Das organisierte Bandewesen im 18. und 19. Jahrhundert.* Göttingen: Vandenhoeck und Ruprecht, 1976.

Labisch, Alfons. *Homo Hygienicus; Gesundheit und Medizin in Der Neuzeit.* Frankfurt am Main: Campus, 1992.

Lamott, Franziska. "Die Kriminologie und das Andere. Versuch über die Geschichte der Ausgrenzungen." *Kriminologisches Journal* 3 (1988): 168–90.

Langewiesche, Dieter. *Liberalismus in Deutschland.* Frankfurt am Main: Suhrkamp, 1988.

Langewiesche, Dieter, and Friedrich Lenger. "Internal Migration: Persistence and Mobility." In *Population, Labour and Migration in 19th and 20th Century Germany*, ed. Klaus J. Bade, 87–100. New York: Berg Press, 1987.

Lees, Andrew. *Cities, Sin, and Social Reform in Imperial Germany.* Ann Arbor: University of Michigan Press, 2002.

Leps, Marie-Christine. *Apprehending the Criminal: The Production of Deviance in Nineteenth Century Discourse.* Durham, N.C.: Duke University Press, 1992.

Lessmann, Peter. *Die Preussische Schutzpolizei in der Weimarer Republik. Streifendienst und Strassenkampf.* Düsseldorf: Droste, 1989.

Liang, Hsi-Huey. *The Berlin Police Force in the Weimar Republic.* Berkeley: University of California Press, 1970.

Linton, Derek. *"Who has the Youth, has the Future": The Campaign to Save Young Workers in Imperial Germany.* Cambridge: Cambridge University Press, 1991.

Lüdtke, Alf. *Police and State in Prussia, 1815–1850.* Cambridge: Cambridge University Press, 1989.

——, ed. *'Sicherheit' und 'Wohlfahrt': Polizei, Gesellschaft und Herrschaft im 19. und 20. Jahrhundert.* Frankfurt am Main: Suhrkamp, 1992.

Löschburg, Winfried. *Ohne Glanz und Gloria: Die Geschichte des Hauptmanns von Köpenick.* Berlin: Ullstein, 1998.

Machtan, Lothar, and Rene Ott. "'Batzebier!' Überlegungen zur sozialen Protestbewegung in den Jahren nach der Reichsgründung am Beispiel der süddeutschen Bierkrawalle vom Frühjahr 1873." In *Sozialer Protest: Studien zu traditioneller und kollektiver Gewalt in Deutschland vom Vormärz bis zur Riechsgründung,* ed. Heinrich Volkmann and Jürgen Bergmann. Opladen: Westdeutscher Verlag, 1984.

Meyer-Renschhausen, Elisabeth. "Antimodernistischer Protest als Motor der sozialen Rationalisierung? Soziale und alternative Bewegungen im späten 19. und frühen 20. Jahrhundert." In *Rationale Beziehungen? Geschlechterverhältnisse im Rationalisierungsprozeß,* ed. Dagmar Reese, Eve Rosenhaft, Carola Sachse, and Till Siegel, 142–69. Frankfurt am Main: Suhrkamp, 1993.

——. "Die Weibliche Ehre. Ein Kapitel aus dem Kampf von Frauen gegen Polizei und Ärzte." In *Frauenkörper, Medizin, Sexualität,* ed. Johanna Geyer-Kordesch and Annette Kuhn, 80–97. Düsseldorf: Shwann, 1986.

——. *Weibliche Kultur und Sozialarbeit: Eine Geschichte der Frauenbewegung am Beispiel Bremens 1810–1924.* Köln: Boehlau, 1989.

Mommsen, Wolfgang. *Max Weber and German Politics 1890–1920.* Chicago: University of Chicago Press, 1984.

Müller, Christian. *Verbrechensbekämpfung im Anstaltsstaat. Psychiatrie, Kriminologie und Strafrechtsform in Deutschland. 1871–1933.* Göttingen: Vandenhoeck & Ruprecht, 2004.

Müller-Seidel, Walter. *Die Deportation des Menschen: Kafkas Erzählung In der Strafkolonie im europäischen Kontext.* Stuttgart: Metzler, 1986.

Nienhaus, Ursula. "Einsatz für die 'Sittlichkeit': Die Anfänge der weiblichen Polizei im Wilhelminischen Kaiserreich und in der Weimarer Republik." In *'Sicherheit' und 'Wohlfahrt:' Polizei, Gesellschaft und Herrschaft im 19. und 20. Jahrhundert,* ed. Alf Lüdtke, 243–66. Frankfurt am Main: Suhrkamp, 1992.

Nipperdey, Thomas. *Deutsche Geschichte 1866–1918,* Vol. 1. *Arbeitswelt und Bürgergeist.* München: C. H. Beck, 1991.

——. *Germany from Napolean to Bismarck.* München: C. H. Beck, 1996.

——. *Religion im Umbruch. Deutschland 1870–1918.* München: C. H. Beck, 1988.

———. "Religion und Gesellschaft: Deutschland um 1900." *Historische Zeitschrift* 246 (1988): 591–615.

Nitschke, August, and Rüdiger vom Bruch, eds. *Jahrhundertwende: Der Aufbruch in Die Moderne, 1880–1930*. Reinbek bei Hamburg: Rowohlt, 1990.

Nye, Robert. *Crime, Madness, and Politics in Modern France: The Medical Concept of National Decline*. Princeton: Princeton University Press, 1984.

Oberwittler, Dietrich. *Von der Strafe zur Erziehung? Jugendkriminalpolitik in England und Deutschland, 1850–1920*. Frankfurt am Main: Campus, 2000.

Orlow, Dietrich. *Weimar Prussia 1918–1925: The Unlikely Rock of Democracy*. Pittsburgh: University of Pittsburgh Press, 1986.

Pasquino, Pasquale. "Criminology: The Birth of a Special Knowledge." In *The Foucault Effect*, ed. Graham Burchell and Colin Gordon. Chicago: University of Chicago Press, 1991.

Peukert, Detlev. "The Genesis of the Final Solution from the Spirit of Science." In *Nazism and German Society, 1933–1945*, ed. David Crew, 274–99. London: Routledge, 1994.

———. *Grenzen der Sozialdisziplinierung. Aufstieg und Krise der deutschen Jugendfürsorge 1878–1932*. Köln: Bund-Verlag, 1986.

———. *Max Webers Diagnose der Moderne*. Gottingen: Vandenhoeck und Ruprecht, 1989.

Pick, Daniel. *Faces of Degeneration: A European Disorder, c. 1848–c.1918*. Cambridge: Cambridge University Press, 1989.

Pierre, Michel. *Le Dernier Exil: Histoire des Bagnes et des Forcats*. Paris: Gallimard, 1989.

———. "La Transportation." In *Histoire des Galères, Bagnes et Prisons*. ed. Jacques-Guy Petit, Nicole Castan, Claude Faugeron, Michel Pierre, and André Zysberg. Toulouse: Bibliothèque historique Privat, 1991.

Prelinger, Catherine. *Charity, Challenge, and Change: Religious Dimensions of the Mid-Nineteenth Century Women's Movement in Germany*. New York: Greenwood Press, 1987.

Preller, Ludwig. *Sozialpolitik in der Weimarer Republik*. Kronberg: Athenäum/Droste, 1978.

Proctor, Robert. *Racial Hygiene: Medicine under the Nazis*. Cambridge, Mass.: Harvard University Press, 1988.

Rabinbach, Anson. *The Human Motor: Energy, Fatigue and the Origins of Modernity*. Berkeley: University of California Press, 1990.

Radzinowicz, Leon. *A History of English Criminal Law and Its Administration from 1750*. London: Stevens, 1948–1986.

———. *In Search of Criminology*. Cambridge, Mass.: Harvard University Press, 1962.

Ratz, Ursula. " 'Die Arbeiterschaft im neuen Deutschland.' Eine bürgerlich-sozialdemokratische Arbeitsgemeinschaft aus dem Jahre 1915." *Internationale*

Wissenschaftliche Korrespondenz zur Geschichte der Deutschen Arbeiterbewegung (August 1971): 1–26.

——. "Sozialdemokratische Arbeiterbewegung, bürgerliche Sozialreformer und Militärbehörden im Ersten Weltkrieg. Die Berichte des Bureaus für Sozialpolitik." *Militärgeschichtliche Mitteilungen* 37 (1985): 9–33.

——. *Zwischen Arbeitsgemeinschaft und Koalition: Burgerliche Sozialreformer und Gewerkschaften im Ersten Weltkrieg.* München: K. G. Saur, 1994.

Reagin, Nancy. *A German Women's Movement: Class and Gender in Hanover, 1880–1933.* Chapel Hill: University of North Carolina Press, 1995.

Reinke, Herbert. "'. . . hat sich ein politischer und wirtschaftlicher Polizeistaat entwickelt.' Polizei und Großstadt im Rheinland vom Vorabend des Ersten Weltkrieges bis zum Begin der zwanziger Jahre." In *'Sicherheit' und 'Wohlfahrt:' Polizei, Gesellschaft und Herrschaft im 19. und 20. Jahrhundert,* ed. Alf Lüdtke, 219–42. Frankfurt am Main: 1992.

——. "Die 'Liaison' des Strafrechts mit der Statistik—zu den Anfängen kriminalstatistischer Zählungen im 18. und 19. Jahrhundert." *Zeitschrift für Neuere Rechtsgeschichte* 12 (1990): 169–79.

Reulecke, Jürgen. "Die Anfänge der organisierten Sozialreform in Deutschland." In *Weder Kommunismus noch Kapitalismus: Bürgerliche Sozialreform in Deutschland vom Vormärz bis zur Ära Adenauer,* ed. Rüdiger vom Bruch, 21ff. München: C. H. Beck, 1985.

——. "Männerbund versus the Family: Middle Class Youth Movements and the Family in Germany in the Period of the First World War." In *The Upheaval of War: Family, Work and Welfare in Europe, 1914–1918,* ed. Richard Wall and Jay Winter. Cambridge: Cambridge University Press, 1988.

Rouette, Susanne. "Mothers and Citizens—Gender and Social Policy in Germany after the First World War." *Central European History* 30, no. 1 (1997): 48–66.

Rusche, Georg, and Otto Kirchheimer. *Punishment and Social Structure.* New York: Columbia University Press, 1939.

Sachße, Christoph. *Mütterlichkeit als Beruf. Sozialarbeit, Sozialreform und Frauenbewegung 1871–1929.* Frankfurt am Main: Suhrkamp, 1986.

Sachße, Christoph, and Florian Tennstedt. *Geschichte der Armenfürsorge in Deutschland. Band 2. Fürsorge und Wohlfahrtspflege 1871 bis 1929.* Stuttgart: Kohlhammer, 1988.

Sauerteig, Lutz. "Militär, Medizin und Moral: Sexualität im Ersten Weltkrieg." In *Die Medizin und der Ersten Weltkrieg.* ed. Wolfgang Eckart and Christoph Gradmann. Pfaffenweiler: Centauras, 1996.

Scheffler, Jürgen. "Die Wandererfürsorge zwischen konfessioneller, kommunaler und staatlicher Wohlfahrtspflege." In *Sozialer Protestantismus und Sozialstaat. Diakonie und Wohlfahrtspflege in Deutschland 1890 bis 1938,* ed. Jochen-Christoph Kaiser. Stuttgart: Kohlhammer, 1996.

Schick, M. *Kulturprotestantismus und soziale Frage. Versuche zur Begündung der*

Sozialethik vornehmlich in der Zeit von der Gründung des Evangelisch-Sozialen Kongresses bis zum Ausbruch des. 1. Weltkrieges (1890–1914). Tübingen: Mohr, 1970.

Schmidt, Eberhard. *Einführung in die Geschichte der deutschen Strafrechtspflege.* Göttingen: Vandenhoeck und Ruprecht, 1947.

Schönert, Jörg. *Erzählte Kriminalität: Zur Typologie und Funktion von narrativen Darstellungen in Strafrechtspflege, Publizistik und Literatur zwischen 1770 und 1920.* Tübingen: Max Niemeyer Verlag, 1991.

Schulte, Regina. *Sperrbezirke: Tugendhaftigkeit und Prostitution in der bürgerlichen Welt.* Frankfurt am Main: Syndikat, 1979.

Schulz, Günther. "Bürgerliche Sozialreform in der Weimarer Republik." In *Weder Kommunismus noch Kapitalismus: Bürgerliche Sozialreform in Deutschland vom Vormärz bis zur Ära Adenauer,* ed. Rüdiger vom Bruch, 181–217. München: C. H. Beck, 1985.

Shanahan, W. O. *German Protestants Face the Social Question, vol. 1. The Conservative Phase, 1815–1871.* Notre Dame: University of Notre Dame Press, 1954.

Sheehan, James. *The Career of Lujo Brentano: A Study of Liberalism and Social Reform in Imperial Germany.* Chicago: University of Chicago Press, 1966.

Simon, Jonathan. *Governing through Crime: How the War on Crime Transformed American Democracy and Created a Culture of Fear.* Oxford: Oxford University Press, 2007.

———. *Poor Discipline: Parole and the Social Control of the Underclass, 1890–1990.* Chicago: University of Chicago Press, 1994.

Smith, Woodruff. *The German Colonial Empire.* Chapel Hill: University of North Carolina Press, 1978.

———. *The Ideological Origins of Nazi Imperialism.* New York: Oxford University Press, 1986.

Steinmetz, George. "The Myth of an Autonomous State: Industrialists, Junkers and Social Policy in Imperial German." In *Society, Culture, and the State in Germany, 1870–1933,* ed. Geoff Eley, 257–318. Ann Arbor: University of Michigan Press, 1996.

———. *Regulating the Social: The Welfare State and Local Politics in Imperial Germany.* Princeton: Princeton University Press, 1993.

———. "Workers and the Welfare State in Imperial Germany." *International Labor and Working Class History* 40 (1991).

Stoehr, Irene. "Fraueneinfluss oder Geschlechterversöhnung? Zur Sexualitätsdebatte in der deutschen Frauenbewegung um 1900." In *Frauenkörper, Medizin, Sexualität,* ed. Johanna Geyer-Kordesch and Annette Kuhn. Düsseldorf: Shwann, 1986.

———. "Organisierte Mütterlichkeit: Zur Politik der deutschen Frauenbewegung um 1900." In *Frauen suchen ihre Geschichte: Historische Studien zum 19. und 20. Jahrhundert,* ed. Karin Hausen. München: C. H. Beck, 1982.

Stoler, Ann Laura. *Race and the Education of Desire: Foucault's History of Sexuality and the Colonial Order of Things.* Durham, N.C.: Duke University Press, 1995.

———. "Sexual Affronts and Racial Frontiers: European Identities and the Cultural

Politics of Exclusion in Colonial Southeast Asia." In *Tensions of Empire*, ed. Frederick Cooper and Ann Laura Stoler. Berkeley: University of California Press, 1997.

Strathmann von Soosten, Ellen. "Themen und Diskussionen des Evangelisch-Sozialen Kongresses." In *Protestantische Wirthschaftsethik und Reform des Kapitalismus. 100 Jahre Evangelisch-Sozialer Kongress*, ed. Klaus Heienbrok and Hartmut Przybylski, 24–30. Bochum: Sozialwissenschaftliches Institut der Evangelischen Kirche in Deutschland, 1991.

Tenfelde, Klaus. "Großstadtjugend in Deutschland vor 1914. Eine historisch-demographische Annäherung." *Vierteljahreschrift für Sozial- und Wirtschaftsgeschichte* 69, no. 2 (1982): 182–218.

Usborne, Cornelie. *The Politics of the Body in Weimar Germany*. Ann Arbor: University of Michigan Press, 1992.

Wachsmann, Nikolaus. "Between Reform and Repression: Prisons in Weimar Germany." *Historical Journal* 45, no. 2 (2002): 411ff.

——. *Hitler's Prisons: Legal Terror in Nazi Germany*. New Haven: Yale University Press, 2004.

Walkowitz, Judith. *City of Dreadful Delight: Narratives of Sexual Danger in Late Victorian London*. Chicago: University of Chicago Press, 1992.

——. *Prostitution and Victorian Society: Women, Class, and the State*. Cambridge: Cambridge University Press, 1980.

Walser, Karin. "Prostitutionsverdacht und Geschlechterforschung: Das Beispiel der Dienstmädchen um 1900." *Geschichte und Gesellschaft* 11 (1985): 99–111.

Ward, W. R. *Theology, Sociology and Politics: The German Protestant Social Conscience 1890–1933*. Berne: Peter Lang, 1979.

Wehler, Hans-Ulrich. *The German Empire 1871–1918*. New York: Berg Publishers, 1985.

Weindling, Paul. *Health, Race and German Politics between National Unification and Nazism 1870–1945*. Cambridge: Cambridge University Press, 1989.

——. "The Medical Profession, Social Hygiene and the Birth Rate in Germany 1914–1918." In *Upheaval of War: Family, Work and Welfare in Europe, 1914–1918*, ed. Richard Wall and Jay Winter, 417–37. Cambridge: Cambridge University Press, 1988.

——. "The Modernization of Charity in Nineteenth Century France and Germany." In *Medicine and Charity before the Welfare State*, ed. Colin Jones and Jonathan Barry, 190–206. London: Routledge, 1991.

Weingart, Peter. "The Rationalization of Sexual Behavior: The Institutionalization of Eugenic Thought in Germany." *Journal of the History of Biology* 20, no. 2 (1987).

Wetzell, Richard. "Criminal Law Reform in Imperial Germany." Ph.D. diss., Stanford University, 1991.

——. *Inventing the Criminal: A History of German Criminology 1880–1945*. Chapel Hill: University of North Carolina, 2000.

——. "The Medicalization of Criminal Law Reform in Imperial Germany." In *Insti-*

tutions of Confinement: Hospitals, Asylums, and Prisons in Western Europe and North America, 1500–1950, ed. Norbert Finzsch and Robert Jütte, 275–83. Cambridge: Cambridge University Press, 1996.

Whitman, James Q. Harsh Justice: Criminal Punishment and the Widening Gap between America and Europe. Oxford University Press, 2003.

Willing, Matthias. Das Bewahrungsgesetz. Eine rechtshistorische Studie zur Geschichte der deutschen Fürsorge. Tübingen: Mohr Siebeck, 2003.

Willrich, Michael. City of Courts: Socializing Justice in Progressive Era Chicago. Cambridge: Cambridge University Press, 2003.

Wollasch, Andreas. Der Katholische Fürsorgeverein für Mädchen, Frauen und Kinder (1899–1945). Ein Beitrag zur Geschichte der Jugend- und Gefährdetenfürsorge in Deutschland. Freiburg: Lambertus, 1991.

INDEX

during wartime, 132–39, 164; reform of procedure for, 138–39, 173–
77, 181–82, 220, 225; criticism of, 190–
94, 216–17, 292 (n. 15); in Third Reich,
227, 229; in Federal Republic of Germany, 230. *See also* Conditional
sentencing.

Penal code: proposed reform of, 36, 42,
71–73, 133–35, 172, 193, 221, 230

Penal colonies, 33

—proposals for: in Southwest Africa,
78–87; on Admiral Islands, 92–95;
opposition to, 96–101

Philanthropy: royal, 42, 54,

Police: supervision of released offenders,
26–28, 29–30, 112–13, 118; and Great
International Police Exhibition of
1926, 202–3. *See also* Women: as
police assistants

Populism, 144–47, 150–51, 163–64, 171–
72

Prison: solitary confinement in, 25–26;
overseers, 26; critique of, 34–36, 71,
79–83, 91–92; and psychosis, 71, 211;
sexuality in, 211–16; progressive system in, 220–21, 225. *See also*
Rehabilitation

Prison associations, 30–31, 42–45, 65–
68, 115–17, 178–80; depression-era crisis of, 218–19

Prison societies: Rhenish-Westphalian
Prison Society, 30, 81, 129, 130, 160,
183, 209; Berlin Association for the
Improvement of Prisoners, 30, 118,
179, 218; Prison Society of Saxony and
Anhalt, 56, 72, 173, 174, 179

Probation. *See* Conditional sentencing;
Soziale Gerichtshilfe

Prostitution, 54–57, 155–59. *See also*
"Endangered" women and girls

Protective supervision: as alternative to
police supervision, 45, 61, 63–68, 113–

14, 117–18; as alternative to workhouse, 57–59, 152–62

Protestant charities. *See* Inner Mission

Prussian Ministry of the Interior, 20, 42,
66, 109, 113–14, 118, 159–62, 202–3

Prussian Ministry of Justice, 87, 161, 173,
177–78

Psychiatry, 2, 5, 69–71

Radbruch, Gustav, 166, 170, 172, 186, 187

Rawiczer System, 19–20, 26, 168

Rehabilitation: as purpose of punishment, 23–25, 32–33; critiques of, 35

Retribution, 19, 35, 60, 132, 189

Revolution of 1918, 123, 162, 167–68, 173

Schütz, Anna, 147

Severing, Carl, 144–45, 148–50, 163, 175,
202–3, 227, 280 (nn. 51, 54)

Sex in Chains (film), 211–14

Seyfarth, Heinrich, 36, 87, 232; as leader
of German Help-Association in Hamburg, 44–45; as advocate of deportation, 86, 87–93, 102; wartime activism,
133–34, 136; as advocate of Bielefeld
System and *Gerichtshilfe*, 175, 196; as
critic of progressive reformers, 209,
214; as supporter of Nazi policy, 218,
228; as proponent of criminal biology,
220, 222, 224

Shame sanctions (*Ehrenstrafe*), 20–21,
27–28, 132–37

Social Democrats (SPD), 34, 53, 78, 93,
128, 144–45, 149–50, 170, 171, 172, 187–
89, 198–99, 202–4

Society for Social Law (GSR), 144–48;
Committee for the Promotion of
Women's Participation in Justice, 147–
48, 175

Soziale Gerichtshilfe: origins of, 173–77;
state support for, 177–78, 181–83; varieties of, 178–81; and controversies

Lightning Source UK Ltd.
Milton Keynes UK
UKOW02f1057150416

272307UK00003B/365/P